Encyclopedia of Gangs

Encyclopedia of Gangs

Edited by LOUIS KONTOS and
DAVID C. BROTHERTON

GREENWOOD PRESS
Westport, Connecticut • London

Library of Congress Cataloging-in-Publication Data

Encyclopedia of gangs / edited by Louis Kontos and David C. Brotherton.
       p.   cm.
   Includes bibliographical references and index.
   ISBN 978-0-313-33402-3 (alk. paper)
   1. Gangs—United States—Encyclopedias.   2. Gangs—Encyclopedias.   I. Kontos, Louis.
II. Brotherton, David.
   HV6439.U5E53   2008
   364.1'0660973—dc22   2007029804

British Library Cataloguing in Publication Data is available.

Library of Congress Catalog Card Number: 2007029804
ISBN: 978-0-313-33402-3

First published in 2008

Greenwood Press, 88 Post Road West, Westport, CT 06881
An imprint of Greenwood Publishing Group, Inc.
www.greenwood.com

Printed in the United States of America

∞™

The paper used in this book complies with the
Permanent Paper Standard issued by the National
Information Standards Organization (Z39.48-1984).

10 9 8 7 6 5 4 3 2 1

Contents

Preface

Much has changed in "gangland" since the publication of the first empirical study on the topic, Thrasher's *The Gang*. In this study, "gang boys" are primarily children of immigrants living in industrial slums. Their participation in gangs is deemed a "natural" response to the problems and contradictions of their world; a mode of adaptation that includes rituals, symbolism, folklore, and concepts that provide a basis for solidarity and sense of collective purpose. The influence of Thrasher's account on theoretical and empirical work on gangs is strong in the 1930s and 1940s. A more deterministic (neo-positivist) logic can be found in the 1950s, which Hardman (1967) aptly characterizes as "the decade of theorizing." In two of the most influential works of this decade—Cohen (1955) and Miller (1958)—gang culture is theorized along a single dimension: norms and values. Cohen sees gangs as a mode of rebellion rather than adaptation. The typical gang, in this account, develops in opposition to mainstream (middle-class) values and institutional sources of judgment. Its subculture is deemed merely epiphenomenal—something gang members invent with the intent to shock outsiders, assert distaste, and reclaim dignity. Miller, by contrast, sees gangs as a collection of working-class youth whose habits and values are incongruent with the institutional logic of middle-class society. Incongruence leads to trouble, for instance, when young men are overly masculine and thereby confrontational, or when they cheat or steal because they are not accustomed to "delayed gratification." In this scenario, gang subculture is simply an extension of working-class culture without appropriate context, thereby pathological. Did gangland change all that much in an anti-social direction between the 1920s and 1950s? Yes and no.

Clearly there is a problem with generalizations about "gangs," since the people who study them display widely disparate motivating interests and theoretical assumptions, which are, at least in part, ideological in nature; and since ideological and theoretical tendencies in the literature on gangs have shifted widely over short periods of time, and from one "school" to the next. This manner of shift has been so dramatic over the last eighty years as to make real comparisons among any past and present gangs difficult. The most dramatic shift occurred in the 1960s, where "gang culture" virtually disappeared from the range of concerns of researchers, and where gang research effectively merged with other forms, for example poverty research. The most influential merger can be found in the work of Cloward and Ohlin (1960), which is ostensibly about the relation between "gang subculture" and structures of opportunity in "urban areas." This work tells us much about urban areas but little about the form or content of any "type" of gang subculture—only that different types of subculture prioritize and justify different modes of deviance, which the authors call "areas of specialization"—including violence and criminal enterprise. Contemporary gang research draws freely from these and other sources as a corpus of knowledge about gangs. There is no longer any dominant theoretical paradigm regarding gang subculture or any other aspect of gangland—although the bulk of criminologists seem to agree that violence and drugs endemically flow out of gang subcultures (cf. Bursik and Grasmick, 1996).

Gangland in Our Times

Gangland is now more complex than its earlier manifestations, in part because American society is more complex. The problems and contradictions that now confront gang members are typically more severe, even where immigration is not a factor. Unlike the gangs that appear in Thrasher's account, gang members today struggle to find a place in "adult society." The transition is not always accomplished. Moreover, "gangland" is now dominated by what Vigil (1993) calls "established" gangs; gangs that have been around for decades, outliving several generations of membership. Such gangs are not merely larger than the local neighborhood variety, but also increasingly economically and politically isolated—thereby more self-referential. At the same time, the nature of the relation between "gangs" and "the community" is more fluid and varies from case to case—several illustrations are provided in entries. Their subculture typically includes handbooks, manifestos, and other kinds of documents through which it is formalized and, by the same token, requires more substantial learning and commitment from members than what could be said of Thrasher's "gang boys." Even the symbolism associated with established gangs has become more complex; which is to say, more elaborate, intricate, and detailed, and therefore more obscure, unintelligible, and frightening to outsiders (Conquergood, 1993).

Against this backdrop it is not surprising that there is a growing public fascination with gangs. The popular culture not only reflects this fascination but also exploits it, that is, by presenting us with scary images and implausible scenarios, and by reinforcing stereotypes and creating new ones. The political culture does much the same—reflect and exploit. Public, political discourse on the topic is often shrill. Calm voices, even the attitude of benign neglect, have been drowned out by demands for ever more drastic solutions to the "gang problem." Over the last two decades, this demand has been translated by "liberal" and "conservative" political establishments alike into unqualified support for a growing criminal justice system and a more expansive and coercive system of social control; resulting in harsher criminal penalties, longer prison sentences, and greater disenfranchisement of gang youth. Scant evidence exists that such policies have "worked"—though, of course, it can always be argued that the "gang problem" would now be even worse in their absence. Inversely, it is an uncontroversial fact among researchers that the growth of the prison system has facilitated the growth and spread of gangs and gang culture (cf. Hagedorn, 1988).

The bulk of gang research does not support either the current "public opinion" or the current direction of public policy toward gangs—any more than it supports the romanticized image of gangs that was commonplace in American popular culture until the 1960s. Yet there is great disagreement among researchers as to the nature and extent of the "gang problem." This disagreement is not only the outcome of disparate research findings, but seems to permeate and prefigure the process of research. For instance, "liberal" researchers tend to prefer qualitative methods, which is to say, unstructured surveys or some form of participant observation with one or several gangs over a period time (Bookin-Weiner and Horowitz, 1983). Such research gives "voice" to gang members and draws focus to mundane aspects of group life as well as the day-to-day struggle for survival and against perceived injustices. Readers of such work witness many sides of gangs. But ethnography does not provide much of a basis for generalization or statements about "gangs in general"—something, it seems, which is increasingly expected of all gang research. The problem of over-generalization appears in a different form in research that uses quantitative methods—particularly structured surveys. Relevant questions with regard to such research include whether its respondents constitute a representative sample and whether their responses can be taken at face value. The largest "gang surveys," for instance, have drawn exclusively on officially processes and labeled gang members, such as prison inmates. Generalizability, in this case, comes with the cost of obfuscation of qualitative differences among "gangs," which are transformed into a mere aggregate.

The public demand for accurate and in-depth information about the "gang problem" remains unsatisfied thereby, in part, because gang research is fragmented, most of it highly specialized and inaccessible to the general reader and, in part, because gangland is changing rapidly and dramatically—more rapidly than the pace of researcher. To make matters more difficult, the world is becoming smaller. "American-style" gangs seem to be developing in other countries, such as El Salvador (largely as a result of U.S. deportation policies—the 1996 Immigrant Reform and Responsibility Act effectively reversed most immigration policy since the 1960s), and American gangland now includes a much broader variety of immigrant gangs than what existed even a decade ago—when the topic received some initial attention in the mainstream news media. The topic now receives more than enough media attention; in the process, obscuring the fact that gang membership is nowadays mostly a second- and third-generation phenomenon—thus providing a false reference as fodder for the current backlash against immigrants. Thus we have come full circle. The same kind of nativist reaction, with perhaps more overtly racist stereotypes, existed in the 1920s alongside romanticized images of gangs; but without the "get tough" policies and programs now in place to support them.

Globalization and Gangs

The American gang has always been understood by American and European researchers as a unique phenomenon—though with substantial disagreement as to what makes it unique and how it is possible to generalize in the first place. Assumed differences include "structure," in that gangs outside the United States have been traditionally understood by researchers as less organized, not rigidly hierarchical, and not formally or explicitly committed to any set of rules or regulations. In contrast to the American gang, other countries supposedly only have (adult) criminal organizations, youth subcultures, and delinquent groups of one type or another (current research from places like Brazil, Colombia, or South Africa—see entries—does not bear out these assumed differences). To be sure, all comparisons yield artifacts together with facts. For instance, the study of English delinquent groups and subcultures has traditionally involved a mixture of crime theories with political economy and other modes of theorizing that establish correspondence between this field of study and several others beyond sociology and criminology. In the U.S., the central gang theories remain essentially unchanged since the 1960s—notwithstanding the fact that there is now greater theoretical debate among researchers (though there are exceptions, including debates around theories of space, performance, social movements, and culture, see Hughes, 2004; Hagedorn, 1991; Conquergood, 1993; Brotherton and Barrios, 2004; Ferrel, 1993). Such theories, moreover, are neither original nor unique; but instead, they are derivations of established theories of individual "deviance" extended to the group.

Assumed differences between American and other gangs are problematic also as a result of two current developments. First, "American" style gangs are appearing in other countries—in fact, the same groups (or "gang subcultures") are appearing. Increased flows of immigration (and deportation) have made the idea of uniqueness problematic. Gang subculture is not only spreading within and beyond the United States, it seems to grow and change in the process (one could expect nothing different in a world in which so many people live transnational lives.) The elimination of barriers to communication, for example through the Internet, has facilitated this process. Second, "foreign" gangs are appearing in the United States. In most cases, this appearance follows the dynamics of gang formation among earlier waves of immigration. In other cases, the new immigrants appear to bring with them elements of gang subculture, political connections, and links with organized crime. Finally, a whole new set of gangs has appeared in countries that were thought not to have a "gang problem," or at least which had not until recently received much public attention or research interest.

The encyclopedia we have assembled provides the reader with a detailed overview of the great variety of gangs in American society and elsewhere. It also provides an overview of public policies and programs that seek to ameliorate the gang problem. Note that words in bold print indicate topics about which separate entries can be found in the encyclopedia. Cross-referencing through bold print is limited to the first time such words/topics appear in any entry—in order to avoid clutter.

References/Suggested Readings: Bookin-Weiner, Hedy, and Ruth Horowitz. 1983. The End of the Youth Gang; Fad or Fact? *Criminology*, 21 (4), 585–602; Brotherton, David C., and Luis Barrios. 2004. *The Almighty Latin King and Queen Nation: Street Politics and the Transformation of a New York Gang*. New York: Columbia University Press; Bursik, Robert J., and Grasmick, Harold G. 1996. The Collection of Data for Gang Research. In Malcolm W. Klein, Cheryl L. Maxson, and Jody Miller (eds.), *The Modern Gang Reader*. Los Angeles: Roxbury; Cloward, R.A., and Ohlin, L.E. 1960. *Delinquency and Opportunity: A Theory of Delinquent Gangs*. Glencoe, IL: Free Press; Cohen, Albert K. 1955. *Delinquent Boys: The Culture of the Gang*. Glencoe, IL: Free Press; Conquergood, Dwight. 1993. Homeboys and Hoods: Gang Communication and Cultural Space. In Larry Frey (ed.), *Group Communication in Context: Studies of Natural Groups*. Hillsdale, NJ: Lawrence Erlbaum; Diego Vigil, James. 1993. The Established Gang. In Scott Cummings and Daniel J. Monti (eds.), *Gangs: The Origins and Impact of Contemporary Youth Gangs in the United States*. . Albany: State University of New York Press; Ferrell, J. 1993. *Crimes of Style*. Boston: Northeastern University Press; Hagedorn, J.M. 1991. Gangs, Neighborhoods and Public Policy. *Social Problems*, 38 (4), 529–542; Hagedorn, John. 1988. *People and Folks*. Chicago: Lake View Press; Hardman, Dale G. 1967. Historical Perspectives of Gang Research. *Journal of Research in Crime and Delinquency*, 4 (1), 5–27; Hughes, Lorraine. 2004. Studying Gangs: Alternative Methods and Conclusions. *Journal of Contemporary Criminal Justice*, 21 (2), 98–119; Miller, Walter, B. 1958. Lower Class Culture as a Generating Milieu of Gang Delinquency. *Journal of Social Issues*, 14, 5–19.

Acknowledgments

We thank our editor at Greenwood Press, Sarah Colwell, for guidance and patience. We also thank Angela Navarro and Rachel Bogin for proofreading and formatting the manuscript.

Introduction

This is the first encyclopedia of gangs in the United States. It appears at a time when the study of gangs has become popular in the nation's higher educational institutions, as well as a staple news item in mainstream media outlets. Twenty years ago the subject of gangs was a rare specialization in sociology and criminology. Only a few empirically based books on the topic exist from that period. Sociological and criminological explanations of gangs were limited to a few variants of Merton's paradigm of "strain," Chicago School notions of social disorganization, and the odd application of social bonding to underscore the claims of social control advocates. However, the epistemological assumptions upon which so many truth claims about gangs in the past were based have lately come under significant scrutiny—in part as a response to the growing complexity of gangland. The spread of gangs from urban to suburban areas of the United States and beyond has ensured that the subject is consistently developing, being revised, and producing all kinds of questions for which we do not yet have answers. Thus the range of contributions that you will find in this volume and the different approaches taken by the authors is reflective of both the qualitative and quantitative changes in gang studies.

Thus we are left with a variety of approaches to the study of gangs, a growing array of gang theories, and a panoply of gang types which to the outsider may seem confusing and perhaps overwhelming. Are gangs inherently violent? Do they always have criminal intentions? Should they be treated as criminal organizations? Are they distinguishable along race and ethnic lines? What is the nature of the relationship between prison gangs and street gangs? Does gang membership tend, still, to be a male affair? Such questions are being consistently asked not only by students fresh to the study but also by researchers who have spent much of their careers trying to grasp the complexity of the subject. The encyclopedia provides a glimpse of the gang field; we believe enough to get you oriented, to stimulate your curiosity, and to provide you with guidance for continued investigation.

So what do we have in store for you? Let us just mention four areas that are well represented in this volume to get you started: gang theory, gang practices, gang types, and gang expansion.

Gang Theory

The gang theories discussed in this volume cover a wide range of literature. The history and variations in subcultural thought, the contributions of the Chicago School, particularly those of gang researcher pioneer Frederic Thrasher, the importance of labeling theory, and the arrival of social constructionist approaches to the topic. Such approaches draw attention to ways in which the topic is framed—ideologically—in the media accounts, scholarship, and public and political discourse; as well as ways in which various claims and accounts regarding the "gang problem" are adopted in the formation of public policies and programs of social control. Most theoretical explanations now engage the concept of post-industrial society, particularly with regard to the transformation of modes of segregation and exploitation that occurs with the disappearance of industrial slums; and with regard to the growth of consumerism and transformation of identity from producer to consumer that entails for the ordinary member of society, including the gang member. Other, more recent theoretical approaches may be construed as interpretivist rather than explanatory, in that they seek to understand the gang on its own terms—for instance, to understand why some prefer the label "street organization" to that of "gang." Such approaches also draw attention to the relation between the histories of particular gangs and social history, and, where ethnography is involved, to the way gang members recollect or understand the history of their own group. For instance, several entries trace the popularity of groups like the Bloods and the Crips to the suppression and failure of the social movements of the 1960s. Some groups, particularly the Almighty Latin King and Queen Nation and Gangster Disciples are shown to have documented their own history and the reasons for various changes in organizational philosophy and other forms and instances of historical transformation. Such literature as the Latin King Bible might strike the reader as merely a propaganda exercise, as it does some researchers and theorists, but arguably when read along with other accounts of the group, or as a component of qualitative or quantitative research, the result is a fuller understanding; one that makes it possible to see the gang as an agent of change rather than merely a product of situations or social forces.

Clearly, therefore, many active researchers agree that thinking about theory is a critical component of learning about gangs. Nonetheless, they are far from agreed on what theory we should use and why. This seeming paradox in gang studies is important for students to grasp, for it speaks to the need to constantly be aware of the many overt and covert assumptions contained in gang analyses which affect findings, data collection, and the methods of inquiry themselves. For example, adherents of "strain" theory tend to see gang deviance and all other forms as related to internalized but unattainable goals—the American Dream—which translate directly into a source of judgment regarding the worth of individuals and groups. To be sure, as adherents routinely point out, "strain" is more severe when local cultures and traditions of working-class society break down, such that differential class symbols of success disappear and all that remains is a generalized standard—where only money, status, and power prove success. Adherents of social bonding theory, by contrast, have a particular view of the human condition, warning that we should be much less tolerant of rule-breaking behavior, particularly among youth, and the need for stronger social controls to constrain the inner proclivities toward deviance that all of us are said to possess. Adherents of the labeling perspective are more concerned about the mechanisms by which social institutions categorize and socially construct the "outsiders" among us, including gang members. For advocates of this approach we need to pay much more attention to the audience, the host of state and non-state agencies that discover deviance and then build regimes of thought, disciplines, and virtual industries to reign in the aberrant subject(s). For the newer, more critical approaches outlined above, there is little faith in social engineering of any kind, thereby of the possibility of an informed public policy ameliorating the "gang problem." They seek instead, among other things, to engage the grievances of gang members, while identifying the ideology and politics of public policies that so routinely fail as if by design. If the failure of a broad range of policies is predictable, in other words, if the gang problem has indeed grown in scope and severity, it might be worth considering what other kinds of things anti-gang policies accomplish.

In the period in which this text is published, an epoch which many call post- and/or late modernity, the weight attached to regimes of thought about gangs is significant: it has increasingly influenced policies that deeply affect basic societal institutions such as schools, work, the family, government, the correctional system, as well as of course the media and entertainment industry. Just think about what theories of social order lie behind the myriad statutes passed by local legislatures calling for gang members to be detained if they congregate in groups of more than three, or motivate prosecutors who invoke anti-Mafia laws (e.g., The Racketeer Influenced and Corrupt Organizations Act, RICO) and/or anti-terrorist laws to dismantle relatively typical street gangs, or campaigns to "clean up" the popular music industry. In other words, while theory is an important aspect of the way we think about gangs, for instance, what they are and how they have come to be, it also plays a critical role in developing the slew of measures adopted to lessen their purported negative impact on society.

These points made about theory are simply to get you, the reader, to think about your own conceptual framework for understanding gang issues and to compare and contrast concepts and theories when trying to come to a deeper understanding of the topic at hand. It is also important to bear in mind that theories can be read and interpreted differently by different readers and entire cultures. A good example of the way theoretical concepts and ideas can be differently read and applied is the case of gang subcultural theory so heavily influenced by the work of Robert Merton and then by Albert Cohen, Richard Cloward and Lloyd Ohlin, David Matza, and Walter Miller. The theoretical contributions of these researchers traveled to Britain in the 1960s and 1970s, playing a big part in the establishment of what has become known as the Birmingham School under the leadership of Stuart Hall (among others). However, the British school of thought was very much a neo-Marxist intervention in the social sciences, quite different from the pragmatic tradition that dominated the U.S. academy. Thus, adherents of this school in Britain saw the subcultures proliferating among youth as more than an outgrowth of society's internal "strains" more than a product of labeling, but rather as a profound reflection of capitalism's insoluble structural and cultural contradictions.

Unfortunately, the circuit of ideas tended to stop there as far as criminology was concerned, and the insights of the Birmingham School were strangely never taken up by their U.S. criminological counterparts, including those engaged in gang studies. Nonetheless, theories and analyses from this school did cross the Atlantic to play an important role in other U.S. social scientific fields. For example, in education, particularly in studies of social reproduction in schools, the work of Paul Willis has been extremely influential; in cultural studies, which took a great deal from Stuart Hall,

Tony Jefferson, Angela McRobbie, and Dick Hebdige; not to mention more generally in sociology, which drew on not only the work of all of those mentioned above but also those of a generation just prior who were associated with another neo-Marxist turn known as New Criminology such as Stan Cohen, Ian Walton, and Jock Young (see **moral panics**).

Gang Practices

This volume contains many entries that detail the various practices of gangs. The violence, the drugs, the cafeteria-type crimes, the politics, the language, the symbols, and the music are all mentioned in various contributions. A big question that needs to be asked is: are gang members that different from the rest of us? What makes their practices so worthy of study? This question has been approached by a variety of researchers. For some, like Yablonsky, it is only particular aspects and types of gangs that we need to be concerned about—namely, gangs that attract opportunistic youth and/or whose leadership is sociopathic. Others would argue that group identity is important to understand, if only to understand how gangs reproduce themselves from generation to generation (see, e.g., **gang identity as performance**). Most would agree that the gang needs to be studied as a particular form of collective or group behavior and that its practices are both particular to itself and to groups and individuals outside of the subculture.

When we think about gang violence, it is important to be precise about the terms. Are we discussing the violence carried out by gang members as part of a group-related endeavor or is it simply a violent action executed by a gang member as an individual? In the words of two prominent gang researchers (Block and Block, 1993) trying to disentangle the difference between "expressive" and "instrumental" gang violence in Chicago, "In an expressive violent confrontation, the primary goal is violence or injury itself, and other motives are secondary. In contrast, the primary purpose of an act of instrumental violence is not to hurt, injure, or kill, but to acquire money or property." Other researchers argue that gang violence is primarily an adaptational strategy brought about by the needs of the marketplace for what other means are there to ensure drug market domains and settle disputes other than through force? Consequently any discussion of gang violence has to begin with the complexity of the issue and consistently relate it to the context in which it arises, rather than settle for the syllogism that gangs equal violence equals crime, which is the tendency of both criminal justice reasoning and media representations in the present period.

This same caveat can be issued for many of the other practices that are associated with gangs. For example, the involvement of gangs in the drug trade for many in the general public would appear to be a given. We are constantly reading about crack and heroin gangs and about busts of gang members who are involved in this aspect of the informal economy, therefore the relationship would seem to be obvious. But on further inspection of the research, it is far from obvious and there are many researchers who are insistent that street gangs are not well equipped to be thriving drug entrepreneurs (e.g., Klein, 1995), while others in this volume talk about major conflicts within gangs over the role of the drugs trade, and still others assert a strong relationship between the two. All this might appear confusing for the reader, but it is again crucial to bear in mind that the phenomenon of gangs takes many different forms across time even, though there are some researchers who prefer to emphasize the more universal nature of gangs throughout industrial and post-industrial society (Sanchez Jankowski, 1991).

Perhaps, to highlight this point, one of the most important new endeavors of gangs in recent years has been their involvement in the rap industry. It is difficult to think of gang involvement in this form of cultural production prior to the 1970s except for in the most irregular of cases. However, with the development and spread of this form of music and the availability of relatively cheap modes of music recording and production, there has clearly developed a significant relationship between gangs and the rap music industry and its different offshoots. Consequently, both producers and subjects of the music gangs have become involved in a complex circuitry of symbols and informational flows that obviously change how they seem themselves and how others see them. This is not the place to belabor this point, but it should be well understood that many gang practices have changed over time and that their involvement in a new set of aesthetic and cultural dynamics has powerful repercussions for the study of gangs not only in their local settings but in their broader, global contexts.

Gang Types

We have seen an extraordinary number of gang types. In this volume authors have made various contributions on the history of the Mafia (e.g., Godfathers, Black Hand, Jewish gangs, Korean gangs, Vietnamese gangs), the development of the well-known gangs, such as Latin Kings, Ñetas, Bloods, Crips, and Gangster Disciples, the role of female gangs, and the emergence of white-only gangs such as the skinheads and biker gangs. This proliferation of gang types, of course, depends on how loosely to some extent we come to define the gang; and there is a long, complex discussion between researchers that has been underway on this subject for some time. Nonetheless, for the general reader and the curious student it is enough to conclude that gangs come in a range of organizational forms, are tending to appear in a wide variety of communities, including rural and suburban locales, and they are now, perhaps more than ever, a global phenomenon.

What does this mean for the study of gangs? For one thing, we can see how gangs differ by type across regions. Latino gangs in Los Angeles, for example, have quite different structures to those in New York City and Chicago. The difference between a skinhead gang and its requirement of a fairly defined racist ideology for many of its members is quite different from that of most other street gangs. In some gangs there are clear divisions between youth and adult members and they belong to separate sub-organizations of the group; for others the lines of demarcation are minimal. In some groups there is a strong presence of females whereas in others no females are allowed to join. Some groups appear to be a rainbow assortment of race and ethnic group, but in others there is a clear restriction on which ethnic or racial group may be allowed to enter. These are just some of the differences that are revealed in the following pages.

Gang Expansion

The time was ripe for a contribution of this kind to introduce a general audience, both the novice and the well-schooled, to the fullest range of gang-related subjects we could muster. From illustrations of theoretical debates and controversies, to detailed accounts of old and new gangs in the United States. In addition, a large portion of this encyclopedia is comprised of entries about gangs in countries outside the United States, including Germany, Brazil, France, Russia, Spain and Australia. The topics covered will enable readers to gain a basic idea of the range of specialized subjects that have some relationship to gangs and a list of references that can help them navigate their way through an increasingly complex and sometimes arcane field.

References/Suggested Readings: Block, Caroly, R., and Block, Richard. 1993. Street Crime in Chicago. *Researcher in Brief* (December), Office of Justice Programs, Washington, DC; Jankowski, M. 1991. *Islands in the Street: Gangs and American Urban Society*. Berkeley: University of California Press; Klein, Malcolm W. 1995. *The American Street Gang: Its Nature, Prevalence, and Control*. New York: Oxford University Press.

List of Entries

Guide to Related Topics

Crime

The Black Hand
Chinese Organized Crime and Gangs
Criminal Organizations
Criminal Career Paradigm
Criminal Subcultures and Gangs
Gangs and Drugs
Godfathers
Japanese Organized Crime and Gangs
Korean Organized Crime and Gangs
Little Brother Syndrome
Organized Crime
Terrorism and Gangs
Vietnamese Organized Crime and Gangs
Yablonsky and *The Violent Gang*

Criminal Justice

Gangs in Prison
Police Repression Tactics against U.S. Street
    Gangs
Restorative Justice and Gang Crime
Terrorism and Gangs
Williams, Stanley Tookie

Economics

Gangs and the Underground Economy
Gangs and Post-Industrialism
Gangs as Social and Economic
    Organizations

Ethnicity

The Black Hand
Chavos Banda in New York City
Chicano Gangs
Chinese Organized Crime and Gangs
Japanese Organized Crime and Gangs
Jewish Gangs and Gangsters
Korean Organized Crime and Gangs
Vietnamese Organized Crime and Gangs

Foreign Gangs

Australian Youth Gangs
French Gangs
German Gangs
Latin Gangs in Barcelona
Russian Gangs
South African Gangs

Spanish Gangs

Transnational Gangs

Gang Culture

Criminal Subcultures and Gangs

Differential Association Theory

Gang Clothing

Gang Graffiti

Gang Identity as Performance

Gang Symbols

Kingism: Luis Barrios

Latin King Bible

Rap Music

Subcultural Theory

Subculture of Gangs

Gender

Gang Females

The Latin Queens

Ideology

Kingism

Latin King Bible

Immigration

Chavos Banda in New York City

Chinese Organized Crime and Gangs

Jewish Gangs

Korean Organized Crime and Gangs

Mexican Gangs

Vietnamese Organized Crime and Gangs

Intervention

Gang Workers

Operation Ceasefire

PATHE (Positive Action Through Holistic
   Education)

Politics

The Almighty Latin King and Queen Nation
   (ALKQN)

The Asociación Ñeta

Kingism

Theory

Criminal Career Paradigm

Differential Association Theory

Subcultural Theories of Gangs

Thrasher, Frederic

Yablonsky and *The Violent Gang*

Research

Qualitative Analysis and Gangs

Research Methods

The Encyclopedia

A

THE ALMIGHTY LATIN KING AND QUEEN NATION (ALKQN). It is difficult to say exactly when the Latin Kings started. According to their **manifesto**, it was in the Illinois prison system during the late 1940s, originating as a prisoner self-help group for Latino inmates; whereas community leaders in Chicago recall that it began as a street group called the Latin Angels during the 1950s and later became the Latin Kings during the 1960s (Brotherton and Barrios, 2004). Another explanation for the group's origin is given by George Knox, Director of Chicago's National Gang Research Center, who says that prior to 1965 there was little evidence of the Latin Kings, but by 1966 the group was "up and going strong throughout the City of Chicago" (Knox, 2000). According to Knox (see also Klein, 1971), it was the focus of Chicago's youth **gang workers** that gave the Kings their identity. Thus, Knox argues that a detached gang worker program affiliated to the YMCA had the unintentional consequence of facilitating the organization. This occurred after the youth workers organized a "shout out" to gang members in a certain area of Chicago with the result that local gangs like the Spanish Kings, Junior Sinners, and the Jokers came together and somehow formed the Latin Kings.

Whatever the precise origins of the group, according to an oft-cited prison study by Jacobs (1977), the group known as the Chicago Latin Kings moved from the streets to the prisons during the 1960s and 1970s, becoming a "supergang"; a group that was "larger and more violent than their predecessors [whose] . . . location at the intersection of the civil rights movement, the youth movement, and a reconstructed relationship between the federal government and grassroots society suggests a divergence from the traditional street gang" (1977, p. 139).

In time, the Chicago Latin Kings developed an auxiliary wing called the **Latin Queens**, each with their own very similar manifestos and both owing allegiance to the Supreme Crown of the entire organization, Gustavo Colón (Lord Gino), also known as the "Sun King," who is currently serving a life sentence in federal prison. During the early to mid-1980s, the Latin Kings spread beyond Chicago to other cities of the Midwest, for example Milwaukee (see Hagedorn, 1988) where a combination of the structural deindustrialization of the United States and the anti–working-class and anti-minority political policies of the Reagan administration had left a whole strata of inner-city youth in conditions described by many social scientists as typical of the so-called underclass. It is also during this period that the group extended beyond its Midwest origins, often due to policies of mass incarceration of lower-class blacks and Latinos, to the East Coast and saw chapters in Connecticut founded by Felix Millet and Nelson (Pedro) Millan in the mid-1980s and in New York State founded by Luis Felipe (a.k.a. **King Blood**) in 1986 at the Collins Correctional Facility. At this critical juncture, the group on the East Coast became known as the Almighty Latin King and Queen Nation with separate manifestos (or bibles as group members usually refer to them) often written by the leaders of each succeeding chapter, all of them pledging their allegiance to the Motherland, i.e., Chicago. By the mid-1990s, the group could boast substantial prison and civil society memberships in chapters throughout the Northeast (e.g., New York City, New York State, Connecticut, Massachusetts, New Jersey, and Pennsylvania), along with Florida and California. According to law enforcement officials the group is said to be in thirty-four states. Additionally, members of the group can be found in Puerto Rico, the Dominican Republic, Mexico, and Ecuador in the Americas and currently much further afield in parts of Europe where there are now chapters in such countries as Spain, Italy, and Belgium—all nations where a growing segment of the working class is increasingly globalized and Latin American.

Originally, membership of the group was open only to those who had traces of "Latin" blood—although, according to Conquergood (1993), the Chicago group's membership often reflected its immediate surroundings. However, to join the group, a member must pass through various stages of initiation and show that they are trustworthy and committed to the group under all circumstances, including physical threats coming from rival groups. Once in the group, according to the Chicago manifesto, a member passes through three stages of consciousness: (1) the Primitive Stage, wherein the neophyte member is expected to be "immature" and to be involved in such activities as "gang-banging" and being a street "warrior" without the full consciousness of **Kingism**; (2) the Conservative or Mummy Stage, which is where a member tires of the street gang life but is still accepting of "life as it has been taught to him by the existing system that exploits all people of color—dehumanizes them and maintains them under the conditions and social yoke of slavery"; and (3) the New King Stage, where the member "recognizes the time for revolution is at hand. Revolution of the mind! The revolution of knowledge! A revolution that will bring freedom to the enslaved, to all Third World people as we together sing and praise with joy what time it is—it is Nation time!"

The aims of the group originally were to create a semi-secret society which would heighten the notion of Latino/a identity for its members and to increase the possibility of Latino solidarity in a society that was endemically racist. Over time, however, the group in Chicago developed like many other gangs into a local, territorially oriented organization that, in turn, became a major player in the umbrella organization of Chicago gangs said to have formed in prison during the 1980s, the People Nation. The People Nation includes other large gangs such as the Black P-Stone Nation, The Vicelords, and the El Rukns, and stands in opposition to the Folk Nation which includes gangs such as the black **Gangster Disciples**, the Spanish Cobras, and the Simon City Royals.

The overall organizational structure of the group in a particular region is hierarchical with the leadership typically comprised of the Inca (President), Cacique (Vice-President), Treasurer, Enforcer or Peacemaker, and Spiritual Adviser. Within this structure are the local tribes whose leadership ranks are known as "crowns" (usually five) with the leader known as the Supreme Crown or Suprema. These structures vary slightly according to different regions. The rank-and-file of the membership is known as "the body." There are also other sub-organizations of the group such as the females and youth, with the former known as Latin Queens and the latter (under eighteen years of age) known as the Pee Wees. Alongside these organizations are different regional councils that provide overall leadership to the city or to the state, and the local tribes, which are essentially branches that represent specific neighborhoods. Such local branches often adopt names that relate to the indigenous and colonized history of the group's members or to the group's primary signifiers or symbols. For example, in New York City there are branches called the Caribe, the Taino, and the Arawak tribes which all take their names from once large native populations inhabiting the Caribbean, particularly Puerto Rico and the Dominican Republic, that were mostly exterminated by the Spanish during the sixteenth century.

Another important organizational characteristic of the group is its meetings. These take place weekly at the branch level where members come to pay their dues, usually about $5, deal with the group's local business, hear about infractions by members, and enforce the discipline of the group. Before each of the group's meetings the ALKQN's prayer is recited and it is important to acknowledge the role that an eclectic religiosity/spirituality plays in the group's rites, rituals, and ideology (see paragraph below). In some groups the discipline can include physical punishment, the stripping of a member's rank, community service, or a fine. Once a month, when possible, the group organizes a "universal," which is a mass meeting of the membership and in its most political form can take on the appearance of a grassroots community forum.

The ideology of the group also varies, to some extent, according to region. In New York State, for example, during the late 1990s, under the leadership of Antonio Fernández (a.k.a. King Tone) the group took a particularly radical turn (see Brotherton and Barrios, 2004) with an ideology that drew on the group's original interpretation of nationalism and Third World radicalism (see above) and a melding of social justice and self-affirmation themes from Catholicism, Pentecostalism, and different New World syncretic religions such as Santería and Yorùbá mythology. During this period of the group's transformation it came to be defined as a "street organization"—i.e., a hybrid street collective that had characteristics of both a social movement and a gang. Other branches of the group, however, were less overtly political and engaged in much more traditional street criminal activity such as drug and weapon sales as well as inter-gang violence (Knox, 1997).

Symbolically, the group is represented by the colors black and gold which adorns a member's clothing and beads and by its five-point crown which is also often on a member's attire and tattoos, as well as present in the group's graffiti. These points also "represent" the five principal lessons embodied in the group's moral code, which can also vary. For example, in Chicago the core principles of the group are respect, loyalty, love, wisdom, and obedience, whereas in New York they are respect, honesty, unity, knowledge, and love. When members greet each other it is usually in the form of a three-point crown that is first banged hard against the heart area of the upper body accompanied by the exclamation "ADR" or "Amor de Rey" (King Love) for males and "Amor de Reina" (Queen Love) for females.

U.S. law enforcement almost without exception considers the group one of the most "dangerous" in the nation and labels it a criminal organization. (The hostility of the criminal justice system toward this group is reflected in the sentence given to Luis Felipe, New York's founder, for ordering the killings of his own gang members while in prison. The sentence, 250 years with the first 45 to be spent in solitary confinement at the nation's most secure prison, Florence in Colorado, was the most severe of any federal inmate since World War II.) In contrast, from a social scientific standpoint, the group may be understood as a subcultural formation developed among lower-class youth and adults under quite specific social, economic, and cultural conditions of marginality. The group is capable of great variability in both its practices and ideology, and while some members are engaged in criminal deviance others are pursuing quite traditional working-class and lower middle-class lives such as attending school and college, raising families, and working in legitimate employment.

References/Suggested Readings: Brotherton, David C., and Luis Barrios. 2004. *The Almighty Latin King and Queen Nation: Street Politics and the Transformation of a New York Gang.* New York: Columbia University Press; Conquergood, Dwight. 1993. Homeboys and Hoods: Gang Communication and Cultural Space. In Larry Frey (ed.), *Group Communication in Context: Studies of Natural Groups,* pp. 23–55. Hillsdale, NJ: Lawrence Erlbaum; Hagedorn, John. 1988. *People and Folks.* Chicago: Lake View Press; Jacobs, Jack B. 1977. *Statesville: The Penitentiary in Mass Society.* Chicago: University of Chicago Press; Klein, Malcolm. 1971. *Street Gangs and Street Workers.* Englewood Cliffs, NJ: Prentice Hall; Knox, George. 2000. *Gang Profile: The Latin Kings.* Chicago: National Gang Research Center.

DAVID C. BROTHERTON

THE ASOCIACIÓN ÑETA. The Asociación Ñeta is a self-described prisoners' rights organization that was founded by Carlos "La Sombra" (the shadow) Torres-Irriarte (although his birth name is Melendez) in 1979 while serving time in the correctional facility Oso Blanco, located at Rio Pedras in Puerto Rico. Torres-Irriarte started the group to heighten the solidarity of inmates, stop the rampant abuse by prison guards, and as a mutual protection against a predatory prison gang called G'27 ("group 27"), or the "Insects." On March 30, 1981, La Sombra was murdered on orders by the leader of the Insects, El Manota, who himself was murdered in revenge later that year on September 30. The term *Ñeta* has several possible origins. According to the Ñeta manifesto, it came from the traditions of native Tainos who, at the birth of a baby, would hold the child toward the sky and cry out "Ñeta" three times, a ritual that was supposed to signify "victory, unity and the future." However, another explanation is that the word comes from the vernacular term *puñeta* which La Sombra supposedly shouted out as he was being shot and stabbed by his assailants. And a final though unlikely explanation is that the word stands for Never Tolerate Abuse.

Whatever the word's origins, the ideology of the group is heavily infused with Puerto Rican nationalistic themes while many members see themselves as part of a grassroots organization of the colonized and the oppressed and as the militant continuator of the struggle for independence from the United States in the tradition of revolutionary nationalists such as Pedro Albizu Campos. There are five basic goals or principles that the group struggles to achieve which particularly pertain to the prison culture: share, peace, education, harmony, and respect. A sixth principle of the group that is often mentioned in their texts is the commitment to struggle.

The group remained in Puerto Rico primarily as a prisoners' organization throughout the 1980s, and gradually became the biggest organization of inmates throughout the system. Since inmates in Puerto Rico can vote in elections this gave the group a certain amount of power and leverage with both prison authorities and politicians. As the institutional influence of the organization grew it played a major role in deciding to which prison a convicted felon would be sent based on the inmate code that separated economic from predatory crimes. For example, someone convicted of rape or incest could not go to a Ñeta-dominated facility, whereas someone convicted of drug sales (an economic crime) would be allowed.

In time, the group migrated to the United States as members and their families emigrated or as inmates were transferred to federal prisons. By the early 1990s, the Ñetas had a substantial presence on the streets of New York City and other Northeastern urban areas and soon became seen as a major gang threat by law enforcement, the prison authorities, and the criminal justice system. During the mid-1990s, the group in New York was run by La Madrina (the Godmother) who was later convicted (and sentenced to life imprisonment) along with a group of followers for drug sales, murder, and other conspiracy-related charges. During this time the group split effectively between those who wanted to remain true to the group's origins as a prisoners' rights organization and as an upholder of Puerto Rican culture and independence and those who wanted to turn the group into another street gang with ties to the informal economy. Currently, the group has migrated beyond the United States and Puerto Rico and can be found in Ecuador, where it has set up a non-profit foundation, Spain, Italy, and the Dominican Republic with members drawn from a variety of Latin American countries.

The group is organized hierarchically with a junta or council that presides over a rank-and-file of predominantly male members (about 90 percent). The leadership is comprised of a president, vice-president, secretary, advisor, sergeant-at-arms, and a coordinator. The age of members ranges from approximately sixteen years old to men and women in their forties and fifties. It is notable that this is the only organization of prisoners that allows gay members into the group. Each month on the thirtieth, the group's members meet to solidify their ranks, organize events, exchange information, and pay tribute to the martyrdom of Carlos "La Sombra." On March 30 of every year the group holds a special event to commemorate the passing of their leader.

The rules of the group follow a set of twenty-five norms which again particularly reflect the prison culture in which they were formed. These include such rules as "do not steal from your fellow man," "don't spread gossip," and "respect your fellow man's sleep. Respect the rules of silence."

Symbolically, members identify with the colors red, white, and black but sometimes blue is substituted for black. These colors can be seen in their bead necklaces and in their clothing. Probationary members wear all white beads until they are considered loyal; thereafter they can wear black beads among the white, plus a red one. The Ñeta emblem is a heart pierced by two crossing Puerto Rican flags with a shackled right hand with the middle and index fingers crossed. Each part of the flag has a specific significance. For example, the two white stripes signify "liberty" and "the rights of every honest Puerto Rican" while the five points of the star signify: Cuba, the Dominican Republic, Jamaica, the Virgin Islands and Haiti. Members salute each other by holding the crossed fore and index fingers of their right hand over their heart. This hand signal has the meaning "N" in sign language and it also means togetherness and unity. The group's explanation for its hand sign appears on the previous page.

References/Suggested Readings: Kontos, L., D.C. Brotherton, and L. Barrios (eds.), *Gangs and Society: Alternative Perspectives.* New York: Columbia University Press.

DAVID C. BROTHERTON

AUSTRALIAN YOUTH GANGS. The first social scientific study of gangs was undertaken by **Thrasher** in 1920s Chicago. His work laid the basis for understanding how gangs operate: a gang is a form of social organization built up through defending a territory against others. Thrasher's early study emphasized the importance of conflict with outsiders as a generator of loyalty to the group: external competition generating solidarity and attachment to a local territory. His study also underlined the importance of the immigration experience; the gangs he studied in the 1920s largely consisting of people who had immigrated to the United States from Europe, but who encountered different barriers to integrating into American society—language difficulties, racism, and also the very structure of the city, which tended to segregate different ethnic groups in different areas being another. The key to the emergence of gangs was not poverty, but experiences of being "between two worlds"—on the one hand, the world of the parents and community, on the other the mainstream society that appeared both attractive, as well as excluding the children of immigrants. Thrasher's colleagues at the University of Chicago introduced other themes to understand the gang as a form of social process—in particular the theme of **social disorganization**, which was an attempt to understand the ways traditional forms of social organization were weakened as a result of the immigration experience (in particular loss of status of parents associated with unemployment or low-status employment, parents lack of facility with the language of their adopted country). The migration experience was a powerful force undermining traditional forms of authority and the resources that this authority was based upon (in particular control of economic resources).

The classical studies leave us with two core concepts to understand gangs. First, gangs are a form of social organization that emerge in "in between" or border experiences, where young people in particular find themselves between two worlds. Second, gangs are forms of spatial organization that construct order (hierarchy, loyalty, and identity) in social worlds of disorder. In contexts where immigrants feel they are subject to stigmatization and disrespect, gang structure will mobilize traditional forms of honor and respect, as a way of countering experiences of racism and stigmatization.

The key to this is defending a territory: competition with outsiders generates internal loyalty, solidarity, and identity, while also gaining for the group valued resources.

The logics at work in these classical gangs are evident in gangs that we encounter in contemporary Australia. Australia is a country of high immigration, with 24 percent of the population born overseas (compared with 11 percent in the United States), and gangs associated with the immigration experience are evident in large cities such as Sydney (pop. 4.25 million) or Melbourne (3.8 million), among recent immigrants from Vietnam, Pacific Islands, and Lebanon—all groups where the unemployment rates at least double that of the population as a whole. Significantly gangs are not present among immigrants from the United Kingdom or New Zealand, who socially and culturally are little different from the dominant Australian population. In that sense, gangs emerge among immigrant groups who encounter significant barriers to social integration: language difficulties, racism, and urban spatial segregation.

Despite the success of Australia's immigration program, signs of new tensions are also emerging. In December 2005 riots took place in Sydney's southern beach suburbs when informal codes segregating beaches were broken (previously one beach was largely controlled by "Anglo" Australians and another, less desirable one, was largely frequented by "ethnics" who reside in suburbs some distance away). Disorganized violence developed into a riot with some 5,000 Anglo-Australians attempting to "take back" the beach, which in turn prompted destruction of cars, smashing shop windows, and assaults by young people of Arab origin. Such violence points to what may be increasing social and ethnic polarization in Australia's largest city.

Where Australian gang experience is significant is in the development of gangs among Aboriginal people in rural towns and settlements, where Aboriginals find themselves living either in slums on the edges of towns or in former reserves that were often run by religious organizations. In many of these contexts traditional social structures and norms governing important aspects of day-to-day life (relations between genders and generations, rules regulating who can be spoken to and who must be avoided) have collapsed. In particular in northern Australia, towns of Aboriginal people have developed in areas that were once reserves or religious-run missions. The town of Wadeye in Australia's north is an example. Home to some 2,500 Aboriginal people, it is spatially divided between two competing gangs, each of which has named itself after heavy metal music bands, and each controlling half the town's territory. In June 2006 confrontations between the two rival gangs left some 200 people homeless, forced to flee the town as a result of destruction of some 20 houses as well as numerous cars. These gangs have a strong visual dimension: wearing military-style clothing, carrying knives, the importance of wounds (real or imagined), celebrating the violence associated with heavy metal music.

The development of such gangs is concentrated in townships that were former religious missions. In these areas the lives of indigenous people were totally controlled—from clothing, diet, living arrangements—and the practice of traditional ritual life was forbidden. This had the effect of disassociating people from their culture and traditions, in particular as a result of destroying the social role of elders, whose power is based on, and renewed through, the practice of ritual. In areas where Aboriginal populations were employed in the cattle industry, and where their traditional forms of social and culture remain stronger, gangs are much less prevalent. In the former mission towns, traditional social and cultural structures have been destroyed, while they also lack any economic infrastructure or industry. In the former mission town of Wadeye, for example, the scene of important gang violence in 2006, only 15 percent of the Aboriginal population is in employment.

In such cases Aboriginal young people are in a desperate "in between" situation: traditional culture and social structures have largely been destroyed, while they are excluded from the consumer culture they encounter daily through the media or when they visit larger cities. Here again we encounter the twin processes of social exclusion and social disorganization. The gang allows those involved to reconstruct a form of social world that offers access to valued goods and excitement, and allows them to participate in an imaginary global consumer culture through listening to music and celebrating the rage they find there. In these towns gangs remain almost the only form of autonomous social organization among Aboriginal people—they are critical to developing any lasting response to the forms of violence and social disorganization that are so prevalent among Australia's Aboriginal population today.

References/Suggested Readings: McDonald, K. 1999. *Struggles for Subjectivity: Identity, Action and Youth Experience.* Cambridge: Cambridge University Press; White, R. et al. 1999. *Ethnic Youth Gangs in Australia: Do They Exist?* Melbourne: Australian Multicultural Foundation.

KEVIN MCDONALD

B

THE BLACK HAND. The Black Hand is often confused with the American Mafia or Costa Nostra since both have their roots in Italy. However, the Black Hand is not an organized criminal enterprise made up of several families. Rather, the Black Hand was an extortion technique that gangs would use to extort money from wealthy Italians. Typically, letters would be mailed to Italians of affluence threatening that "bad things" would happen to them if money was not paid. The bottom of such letters would often have a black hand drawn to instill fear in the victim. Further letters would be sent to assure the victim that the extorter was serious. Some letters directed the victim to find a "friend" who could help them in their time of need. This friend would be someone that had recently entered their lives and would be more than willing to help their new friend with such dreadful business. S/he would function as an intermediary between the victim and the blackmailers (Lomardo, 2002). This new friend was actually a part of the blackmail scheme, encouraging and persuading the victim to pay.

If the money was not paid, more letters could be expected. If these additional letters still failed to convince the victim to pay, violence would often ensue. Victims were shot at, beaten, or even killed to show the seriousness of the threat. The killing of the victim showed the seriousness of the Black Hand's intentions and authenticated their threats. Victims of the Black Hand gangs tended to be immigrants that had started to show signs of affluence in their neighborhood. Although some more industrious gangs made threats to richer victims, such as Chicago's richest Italian, Andrew Cuneo, in the early 1900s, or John D. Rockefeller's son in-law Harold F. McCormick. Some estimates show that wealthy Chicagoans received up to twenty-five Black Hand letters a week (Lombardo, 2002).

Although the Black Hand was able to operate successfully for years in Italy, it also worked in America for the first two decades of the early 1900s. During this time period, Italian and Sicilian immigration grew significantly. When the Italians reached the shores of America they sought out persons of similar background, often forming small pockets of culture that was nearly entirely Italian and, more specifically, Sicilian. Little Italys sprang up in nearly every major city. Although these neighborhoods gave the residents feelings of security and familiarity, the neighborhoods also helped to promote the old traditions of their homeland. One of these traditions was a distrust for authority, making the victims of the Black Hand afraid to go to the police. Their cultural experiences also led them to believe that blackmail was simply a part of becoming successful. In addition to continuing the cultural traditions, the neighborhoods conveniently centralized all the potential victims. This allowed the blackmailers to rely on the terror caused by their actions. In the rare cases where the blackmailers were forced to kill a victim as a result of failure to pay, they were able to use the victim's death as an example of what could happen if future victims chose not to pay.

Since most of the extortion letters were sent via the United States Postal Service, the federal government began taking action against the extortionists. The extortionists did not give up their scheme easily, however. The judge in the first court case brought against a Black Hand extortionist received a Black Hand letter threatening him, the judge, lest the Black Hand member was set free (Lombardo, 2002). The federal government's willingness to try cases of Black Hand extortion, combined with the fact that Italian immigrants were gaining trust in American institutions, helped bring the Black Hand to an end by the early 1920s.

References/Suggested Readings: Lombardo, R. 2002. The Black Hand. *Journal of Contemporary Criminal Justice*, 18 (4), 394–409; Lyman, M., and Potter, G. 2004. *Organized Crime* (3rd ed.). Upper Saddle River, NJ: Prentice Hall.

DAVID HOHN

BLOODS. The Bloods are a street organization that emerged as a direct result of the conflict that the **Crips** initiated with other black youth sets in the eJarly 1970s. Los Angeles black gangs have a long tradition of creating set alliances to fight common enemies. In the late 1960s and the early 1970s, the Crips launched an aggressive campaign to absorb other gangs and bring the rest into submission. This aggressive strategy prompted a diverse group of "sets" to join and form the Bloods in order to confront the Crips.

The Slausons, Huns, Farmers, Gladiators, Businessmen, and Pueblos are the antecessors of the late 1960s gangs such as the Pirus, the Brims, and the Bishops who were more like groups of "hustlers." Hustlers were youth who tried to survive their precarious social and economic environment by getting together to make money by "running numbers," "pimping," selling drugs (marijuana, cocaine, acid, "whites," and "blues") and taking advantage of naive youth. These early groups of hustlers often fought white youth gangs but rarely used extreme violence to achieve their goals. Violence was limited to fistfights and the use of belts and knives. The hustlers wore slick and stylish zoot suits. "Stacy Adams shoes, slacks, straps and brim hats—Godfather style" (Adis X, 1999). Hustlers used clothing to identify their clique, for instance the Brims took their name from the use of brim hats.

As Crips began to attack hustler groups, cliques, and other youth groups, they set in motion a set of alliances that would transform the south central Los Angeles hustlers into bangers and result in the creation of the Bloods.

In 1971, the Pirus, a strong set from Compton, declared war to the West Side Crips. The war between the Pirus and the Crips started first with fistfights in the local high schools and Leuders Park. When the Crips and Pirus began using guns to settle conflict, the fighting became lethal, the human cost atrocious. In just three years, gang-banging (gang fights with fire arms) between the Pirus and the Crips gained national attention. By 1975, when *Time* magazine's reporter Joseph N. Boyce interviewed Lyle Joseph Thomas, a.k.a. Bartender, an original leader of the Pirus, police estimated that ten members had been killed. "[When] Bartender who was a Piru Original got killed by some of the West Side Crips, the split occurred. The Brims joined up with the Pirus, then the red bandanas came in to identify them" (Boyce, 1975). The term "blood" had been in the lexicon of Southern blacks for a long time. They used it to identify people who were blood-related family. Eventually the term began to be used by southern blacks to greet each other and the new Blood alliance adopted it. The Blood alliance also adopted the red flag that was originally used to identify the Brims. According to Minister Adis X (1999):

> I am a product of responding to [the Crip violence], so the Slausons didn't do nothing but come turn right into Pueblo Bishop Bloods, cus they hooked up with the Brims and the Brims then was identified with a red rag. So, then once the Pueblos accepted the flag as bein red and they was already usin the word "Blood", then they joined up, and then now there's a distinction between being a Pueblo Bishop Hustler and a Pueblo Bishop banger.

Structure

Like the Crips, the Bloods are a loose network of small gangs structured as a federation or independent gangs. Blood members, however, rarely use the term gang to identify groups. They are more likely to use the term "hood" to refer to any group that claims control over a certain neighborhood or geographical area. The hood can be divided into "sets" that maintain specific areas under their "control." Finally, the set itself may be divided into age-graded groups of Original Gangsters and Young Gangsters (OGs and YGs). The "sets" take their name from specific places such as a local park, local streets, or housing projects under their control. Some of the names may indicate the roots of the set. For instance, the Five Duce Pueblo Bishop Bloods name indicates that this set is an off-shoot of the early Pueblo and the Bishops hustler groups. The name of this set also tells us that the hood controls E 52 Street and that the territory they control is within the Pueblo del Rio Housing Projects (Esteva Martínez, 2003).

Blood sets implement shifting alliances with other Blood sets in order to join forces against the Crips. For instance, in one occasion the Stone Villains' and the Pueblos attempted to bring the East Side together by joining forces. This alliance became known as the Five Duce Main City Gangster (MCG). However, this alliance did not survive because of the historical rivalry between the Stone Villains and the Pueblos. In addition, some sets rejected the name because of the C in the acronym. Later generations also stopped using the acronym and replaced it by FDP—Five Duce Pueblos.

The Bloods lack a written constitution and formal norms, rules, and regulations. Members learn their code of conduct by interacting with one another; members teach the rules orally. Some of the basic rules include a code of silence regarding any issues that may affect the hood negatively, a code of brotherly love that discourages fighting among hood members, and code of respect toward everything within the confines of the community.

Although, there may be inter-set conflict among the Bloods, their conflicts have not evolved into long-term warfare. Blood members from one set are able to move to other Blood neighborhoods and join them. They may also adopt the set's identity or just hang out with the set members and retain their old set identity.

Subculture

The Bloods subculture developed through the process of "affirmation by negation" identified by Dwight Conquergood (1997, 1993, 1992). Affirmation by negation refers to the strategy used by some gangs to affirm their identity by negating the symbolism of their rivals. Bloods' antagonism with the Crips permeates every aspect of the Bloods subculture. Their regalia include wearing a red bandana in the right back pocket of their pants. Their clothes of choice include Calvin Klein, highlighting the CK to represent Crip Killer. Bloods "flare up" or "flame up" by wearing all red clothing. Whenever they wear blue they wear it in their pants to "diss" Crips. Bloods avoid speaking the word "cousin" because it represents Crips, and instead use "relative" to refer to blood cousins. They also avoid using the letter C and when necessary they reverse it, cross it out, replace it with a B, or add a K to show disrespect to the Crips. The Bloods also have a particular way of walking and dancing called Blood-walk.

The social reproduction of the Bloods first occurred through the process of structural assimilation. Sets from different areas voluntarily joined the Bloods as a form of protection. At this first stage, active recruitment was not pervasive; however, this changed during the drug epidemic of the 1980s when Bloods begin actively recruiting soldiers in local schools and parks. Bloods "jumped in" black youth from the local neighborhood—sometimes entire groups of friends were jumped in. The crack cocaine economy of the 1980s was also responsible for the friction between different Blood sets. However, because the Bloods have always been smaller in numbers, compared to their archenemies, the Crips, they cannot afford to maintain continuous warfare against other Blood sets.

Bloods have also reproduced structurally by setting up franchises. The Rolling 20s, for instance, are the parent organization for sets such as the Rolling 20s Avenues Bloods, the Rolling 20s Filipino Bloods, the Rolling 20s Blood Demon Soldiers. The Rolling 20s solidarity is essential to their survival given their rivalry with the Rolling 30s, one of the strongest Crip sets in South Central.

The transfer of Blood inmates or the incarceration of Blood members in other states of the union facilitates the structural reproduction of the Bloods outside the Los Angeles area. In 1993, for instance, O.G. Mack, a member of a Blood set in Los Angeles was sent to prison in Rikers Island where he established the United Blood Nation. Like their counterparts in Los Angeles, the Bloods in New York emerged as a form of protection against Latino gangs such as the **Almighty Latin King and Queen Nation** and the **Asociación Ñeta**.

Cultural dissemination has also helped the establishment of Blood gangs in suburban areas and in countries such as New Zealand and England. With the help of mainstream media and new technologies, youth around the world have been introduced to Bloods culture through videos such as *Colors* and *Menace II Society*.

In the early 1990s, street activists begin working to try to implement a truce and a gang peace treaty between the Bloods and the Crips. In 1992, after the L.A. Uprising sparked by the acquittal of the LAPD officers who beat up Rodney King, the Bloods and the Crips embraced the Gang Truce and begin peace talks. Although the

Gang Truce soon crumbled, many OG Bloods, such as London Carter and Blood-hound, became street activists and began an active campaign to politicize the Bloods. Their dream is to unite all Blood sets and Crip sets to become the vanguard of the new civil rights movements.

References/Suggested Readings: Adis, X., 1999. Personal interview. J.F. Esteva Martínez. Los Angeles; Boyce, J.N. 1975. Portrait of a Gang Leader. *Times Magazine*; Conquergood, D. 1997. Street Literacy. In J. Flood, S.B. Heath, and D. Lapp (eds.), *Handbook of Research on Teaching Literacy through the Communicative and Visual Arts.*, New York, Macmillan, 354–375; Conquergood, D. 1993. Homeboys and Hoods: Gang Communication and Cultural Space in Group Communication. In L. Frey (ed.), *Context: Studies of Natural Groups.* Hillsdale, NJ: Lawrence Erlbaum; Conquergood, D. 1992. On Reppin' and Rhetoric: Gang Representations. CUAPR Working Papers. Evanston, IL: Northwestern University, Center for Urban Affairs and Policy Research. 92; Esteva Martínez, J.F. 2003. Urban Street Activists: Gang and Community Efforts to Bring Justice to Los Angeles Neighborhoods. In L. Kontos, D.C. Brotherton, and L. Barrios (eds.), *Gangs and Society: Alternative Perspectives.* New York: Columbia University Press.

JUAN FRANCISCO ESTEVA MARTÍNEZ

BRAZILIAN GANGS. In Brazilian *favelas* and *barrios* the word "gang" is usually associated with the U.S. gangs depicted in the media. The terms typically employed to describe gangs in Brazil are *facção* (faction or armed group), *quadrilha* (gang or mob), *bonde* (literally trolley or tram, but on the streets a large and heavily armed group within a specific gang or faction), *o tráfico* (the traffic, as in drug trafficking), *o movimento* (the criminal movement), and the once common *o coletivo* (the group that shares common interests).

Rio de Janeiro and São Paulo are the two cities that attract most national and international attention in regards to poverty, gangs, and violence. These two important states, with their mega cities, contain roughly one third of Brazil's population (Instituto Brasileiro de Geografia e Estatísticas, IBGE). Rio de Janeiro and São Paulo, situated at the forefront and center of Brazilian culture, media, and research, are where Brazil's two largest gangs, the CV and the PCC, are located.

O Comando Vermelho (CV), The Red Command

Most specialist and experts on the subject agree on the major occurrences and points in regards to the rise of gangs in Rio de Janeiro, such as the fact that they first emerged at the Devil's Calderon in the late 1970s and early 1980s. On the smaller details, however, such as who founded the CV, what role did Rogério Lengruber play, when did the Terceiro Comando (TC) and Amigos dos Amigos (ADA) organize, and so on, there are numerous renditions. We take Amorim's and Dowdney's work to be the most factual.

The public first heard of the CV in April 1981 as the police infiltrated a large apartment complex where several gangsters where hiding. The most notorious of them was Zé do Bigode. The police arrived with 400 officers, catching the gangsters off guard. They quickly arrested or killed all their targets except for Zé do Bigode, who was able to fend off the police for over eleven hours until he, along with many police officers and gang members, was killed. This incident was significant for reasons beyond the sensational news stories it yielded. As the conflict began, Zé do Bigode challenged the authorities by shouting, "Come and get me, I have enough bullets for all of you. . . . Come on, try me, this is the Comando Vermelho you're messing with!" The media carried the story nationwide, and the country first learned of the Comando Vermelho. Later, William da Silva Lima, known as "the Professor" (*o Professor*), wrote a book covering the history of the CV in honor of his fallen comrade, titled *Four Hundred Against One: A History of the Comando Vermelho*. This same "Professor" is generally recognized as the founder of the Comando Vermelho.

Thus, of particular note is that contemporary Brazilian gangs, like many of their international counterparts, originated in prison; which the *Instituto Penal Cândido Mendes* nicknamed *O Caldeirão do Diabo* (the Devil's Calderon), is where the CV's story begins. The conditions at the Devil's Calderon, located on a small island three hours from Rio, were wretched; and by the mid-1990s the prison was clandestinely destroyed. However, the resistance inside the prison and of the gangs it produced survived in the form of the CV.

The Brazilian government and the power elites were not blameless in the CV's development, for the powerful and influential turned a blind eye toward the abject poverty and extreme socioeconomic inequalities that nurtured it. The high levels of inequity and social injustice in Brazil have inevitably led to rising crime rates during the second half of the twentieth century. The military dictatorship contributed to the situation by imprisoning anti-government groups together with indigent common criminals as stated in decree article 27 or the *Lei da Segurança Nacional*, LSN (National Security Law) passed in 1969. This mixing of revolutionaries and criminals was particularly common in the Devil's Calderon.

While the majority of the prison ran amuck, some common criminals and the recently introduced political prisoners were residing together in an area of the compound known as the Galeria LSN or the *fundão*. As time passed the common criminals and the political prisoners in the *fundão* began exchanging ideas and learning from each other. The *Galeria LSN* came to be known as *o coletivo* (the collective). Many of its inmates were leftist intellectuals and strongly influenced by the works of Régis Debray, Che Guevara, and Karl Marx. In 1979 the Galeria LSN was baptized as the Comando Vermelho (Red Command). The CV began therefore as a progressive organization with the mission of ensuring that prisoners are treated with human dignity and respect. The CV's official slogan was and still remains "Peace, Justice and Liberty."

The CV established strict rules and guidelines which members had to memorize and obey under threat of severe punishment. Respect was a central component of the new gang, and members had to follow laws of honor and collective behavior. Inevitably, the prison's older nonpolitical gangs (*falanges*) and the collective CV clashed. The CV grew rapidly, offering prisoners an escape from a life of fear and terror, in contrast to the falange. By 1979, the CV gained complete control of the Devil's Calderon. Prison officials misjudged the situation again in 1980 by transferring several members of the CV to other prisons in Rio de Janeiro state. This strategic error introduced the CV's organizational methods and collective ideology to all of Rio's prison inmates. "The Professor" and two other important CV leaders escaped from the Devil's Calderon in early 1980 with the intention of revolutionizing and organizing crime in Brazil; employing the same tactics that proved successful behind bars. Once in the favelas the CV's first source of income came primarily from bank robbery. The city streets were confronted with "steal from the rich give to the poor" ideology as the CV aimed to gain the support of favelas residents. The ultimate goal was to organize a popular army of the poor in order to eventually take over the city.

In its initial stage the CV retained much of its collective ideology with lists of people to whom they donated money including; family members of fallen comrades, the poorest of the poor, and others close to the gang. "The Professor" was re-arrested by early 1981 and the original CV leaders were either dead or behind bars. The new street leadership was faced with a serious internal power struggle. By 1982 a schism developed within the higher ranks of the CV, splitting members. Some joined the older and smaller North Side Gang; which eventually evolved into the Terceiro Comando, TC (Third Command)—the CV's main rival.

The CV made the precarious and enterprising transition into the world of drug trafficking in 1982; which was much more lucrative and less risky than armed bank robbery. Little by little they assumed control of Rio's growing drug trade from the small-scale traffickers who were established in the favelas. Those who refused to relinquish power were essentially declaring war, and as a result by the early 1980s Rio's homicide rate began a steady rise.

The period of new CV leadership was chaotic. Many members had forgotten or abandoned the original ideologies, however, Rogério Lengruber, known as Bagulhão, was an exception. Bagulhão's charismatic leadership skills and his respect for the masses have immortalized him as the most popular figure in the history of **organized crime** and gangs in Brazil. The initials CVRL (Comando Vermelho Rogério Lengruber) are found throughout Rio and Brazil. Although Bagulhão maintained much of the original CV ideology and despite his popularity, he could not control the expanding CV. The new, less ideological, leadership largely replaced the original bosses, and the CV began to function more like a business. The thirst for profit overtook "Peace, Justice and Liberty" as the faction's principal goal, although the slogan still exists. The CV occupied the majority of Rio's important and strategically located favelas, and in many cases provided residents with basic services and assistance in times of need; crucial services the State was not sustaining.

Paralleling the rise in Rio's organized crime and gang culture was the city's homicide rate. For example, in 1982 the homicide rate in Rio de Janeiro was the same as New York City's at 23 per 100,000 (*New York Times*, August 21, 1993). By 1989 the rate leaped to 78 per 100,000 (Ministério da Justiça). During this time of rapid change Rio's favelas began the civil war that rages today—where the majority of gang soldiers are untrained youths. During the 1980s the CV signed its first contract with Pablo Escobar's Medellín Cartel for the large-scale importation of cocaine. In the mid- to late 1980s the CV control of roughly 70 percent of Rio's favelas. Many academics began referring to the situation in terms of "parallel power" or a "parallel State."

The deaths of several influential early CV leaders during the late 1980s cultivated mistrust and territorial rivalry among its leaders, as old disputes proved once again irreconcilable for the newer more economically ambitious bosses. Competing gangs took advantage of the opportunity. The 1990s marked the era in which rival gangs strengthened. First and most importantly the TC emerged; although a small gang, it had been loosely established for years. The TC organized as a purely business-oriented gang with the slogan "Viver e Deixar Viver" (Live and Let Live). Soon afterward the Comando Vermelho Jovem, CVJ (Red Command Youth) and the Amigos dos Amigos, ADA (Friends of the Friends) developed from continuing CV disputes. (There are differences of opinion concerning the emergence of rival gangs. Some scholars argue that they were present from the initial stages and that they merely grew and organized during the 1990s as the CV weakened.) The 1990s was an important and transitional decade as inter-faction rivalry and fierce *tiroteios* (shoot-outs) became the norm in Rio's favelas. The four principal gangs, smaller neutral factions, and police were involved in daily skirmishes across Rio; as the once "Marvelous City" was converted into one of the world's most violent. (Rio's favelas are generally considered among the world's most violent communities that are not engaged in official wars or conflicts such as those found in Iraq or Colombia. The U.S. Department of State has issued a warning that U.S. citizens are to avoid favelas, of which by 2006 there were anywhere from 700 to 800 spread throughout all areas of the city.) Also by the 1990s the local level gang structure and organization that exists today was developed.

The twenty-first century brought several important changes to Rio's gang/faction culture. There is strong evidence suggesting that the CVJ has rejoined the CV. There is also general agreement that the TC has made an accord with the ADA. The inter-gang fighting continues in the new millennium, as the weapons continue to become more powerful and sophisticated. Grenades, grenade launchers, and war-grade machine guns are typical in Rio's favelas. Children are increasingly involved in the factions, something the original CV did not permit. The CV is still Rio's largest and most powerful faction, but they do not maintain the same level of dominance they enjoyed during the 1980s and early 1990s. Due to the CV's weakened grip in Rio's prisons and favelas authorities believe that the PCC, from São Paulo, emerged as Brazil's largest gang/faction. However, many experts and most law enforcement officers suggest that the CV and the PCC are aligned.

Primeiro Comando da Capital, PCC (Capital's First Command)

The Brazilian gang/faction that has garnered the most attention during 2006 is the PCC. This is a result of the immense media attention surrounding the prison and street riots that began in mid-May 2006. From May to July 2006 as many as 500 people were killed in attacks between the PCC and the authorities. São Paulo, similar to Rio de Janeiro, has become nervously accustomed to violence during the last few decades. In 1982 São Paulo had a homicide rate (20 per 100,000) lower than New York City's (23 per 100,000), however, and in contrast to New York City, the rate rose steadily during the 1980s and 1990s. By the late 1990s São Paulo state was surpassing 11,000 homicides per year, with the capital's homicide rate approximately 69 per 100,000. Most of the killings take place in the cities impoverished *periferia* (periphery). São Paulo's periphery is where most of the state prison inmates come from, and the PCC, like the CV, was born in an oppressive prison system.

The PCC was founded in 1993 but its story began the year before on October 2, 1992. On that day Brazil's bloodiest and most tragic prison riot occurred. It took place at the Casa da Detenção in the Carandiru Prison Complex, in São Paulo's north side. The poorly trained police reacted to the uprising with extreme force, killing 111 inmates. The event drew international attention; particularly as autopsies revealed that the majority of prisoners were shot from behind, execution style. Ten months later, on August 31, 1993, the PCC was founded, largely inspired by and with a similar ideology to the early CV. The PCC was so heavily influenced by the CV that in 2001 they adopted the Comando Vermelho's motto, "Peace, Justice, and Liberty." Today the PCC is by far the most powerful gang in São Paulo, and probably Brazil's largest.

Drug Trafficking and Favela Faction Organization

There are basically three levels involved in Rio's drug trafficking and gang hierarchy. On the first level are the non–faction affiliated *atacadistas* and *matutos*.

The atacadistas (wholesalers) are responsible for coordinating the importation of cocaine and weapons into Brazil from neighboring countries. The matutos (transporters) then collect the contrabands from the atacadistas and deliver them directly into the favelas. The atacadistas and matutos are usually not aligned with any particular gangs/factions. They are independent actors with strong international contacts. The identity of the atacadistas and matutos is largely unknown, but it is certain that they are rich and powerful; the favela gangs could not function without them. The matutos sell the drugs and arms to the faction *donos* (gang leaders).

The second level is comprised of the donos. The donos are the leaders of Rio's gangs/factions and they are responsible for matters that occur in the prisons and favelas, where they have absolute control. Donos are located both inside and outside the prison system, with the highest ranking donos usually behind bars giving orders to the donos in the city. The donos do not often live in favelas, however, they visit them regularly and know everything that goes on. There is not a single all-powerful leader of the CV, or for any other gang in Rio. There are important figures, but because of the uniqueness of each favela, and police precinct responsible for it, a sole boss is impractical. Instead there exists a loose network of leaders, some more influential than others.

The third level is the favela, where the gangs are found. This level is comprised of the *gerente geral, sub-gerentes, gerentes de boca, soldados, fiéis, vapores, olheiros/fogueteiros*, and *endoladores*. The gerente geral (general manager) supervises all daily operations in the favela, from organizing drug sales to managing soldiers, and reports directly to the dono. Some favelas, such as Rocinha in 2006, have more than one gerente geral. Below the gerente geral there are the sub-gerentes (assistant managers). There are three main types of sub-gerentes: the gerente de preto (marijuana manager), the gerente de branco (cocaine manager), and the gerente de soldados (manager of the soldiers). The gerente de boca (drug-point manager) is in charge of supervising the gangs drug sale points. The soldados (soldiers) are responsible for protecting the community and for invading rival favelas. They are well armed and always ready for combat. The *fiel* (personal security guard) is responsible for the protection of either the gerente geral or the sub-gerentes. The vapor (drug dealer) is stationed at a drug point and sells directly to clients. Olheiros/fogueteiros (lookouts), although low in the gang's hierarchy, are extremely important. They are strategically located throughout the favelas and keep constant watch, equipped with radios, binoculars, and fireworks. At the first sight of anything suspicious they alert the other gang members. The *endolador* is responsible for packaging the drugs sold in the favela. All of Rio's favelas and gangs are unique and the organizational structures may vary although the the description above is generally the way the drug trade funtions with similar structures in São Paulo.

The PCC's main source of income comes from drug trafficking, however, they are also heavily involved in numerous other forms of illegal profit, including bank robberies, car-jackings, and kidnapping for ransom. The situation in São Paulo's favelas and prisons as well as the PCC's organizational structure are also different. Unlike Rio's gangs/factions, the PCC has recognized leaders. In the beginning there were Geléia and Cesinha, and by the time of the 2006 riots Marcola was the head boss. São Paulo's factions are probably more organized than Rio's in the prisons, but not as much at the local or favela level.

In Rio's and São Paulo's favelas, graffiti indicates which gangs are in control. *Funk* (pronounced "funky") music is also a vital part of favela culture. It is inspired by hip-hop but infused with local rhythms. The favela gangs/factions produce their own illegal version of funk called *proibidão* (prohibited) in which they boast about their faction and curse rival factions and police. They also sponsor raucous *bailes funk* (funk dance-halls) and *pagodes* (local samba) which they use to sell their product. São Paulo's gangs are more influenced by classic hip-hop culture. Over two decades have passed since Brazil's gangs first emerged. Cities like Rio and São Paulo are now facing the threat of an entire generation that has been raised in gang dominated culture—as gang life has become the norm.

References/Suggested Readings: Amorin, Carlos. 2003. *CV PCC: A Irmandade do Crime.* Editora Record; Arias, Enrique Desmond. 2006. *The Myth of Personal Security: Criminal Gangs, Dispute Resolution, and Identity in Rio de Janeiro's Favelas.* Latin American Politics and Society; Dowdney, Luke. 2003. *Children of the Drug Trade. A Case Study of Children in Organized Armed Violence in Rio de Janeiro.* 7 Letras, Rio de Janeiro; Gay, Robert. 2005. *Testimonies of a Brazilian Drug Dealer's Woman.* Temple; Leeds, Elizabeth. 1996. *Cocaine and Parallel Polities in the Brazilian Urban Periphery: Constraints on Local-Level Democratization.* Vol. 31 (3), pp. 47–83.

ANDRÉ SALES BATISTA AND MARCOS DAVID BURGOS

C

CHAVOS BANDA IN NEW YORK CITY. Mexicans have a long history of immigration into urban centers in the Northeast. However, it was not until the beginning of the 1990s that Mexicans immigrated into New York City in massive numbers—by some estimates, as many 250,000 (Hermo, 1998). New York Mexican immigrants are mostly from the central states of the Mexican Republic, including Puebla, Morelos, Estado de Mexico, and Mexico City, as well as from the southern states of Oaxaca and Guerrero. Despite their indigenous background, many of these immigrants are "urbanized indigenous," in that they have undergone previous socialization in the marginalized urban environments in cities such as Puebla or Mexico City, or have been exposed to it through the continuous internal migration cycles of community members from the provinces to the city (Valenzuela Arce, 2000). Many of these urbanized indigenous youth are the sons and daughters of the thousands of indigenous migrants that moved to the marginalized areas of the Mexican metropolitan areas to work in the emerging manufacturing industries and maquiladoras. These immigrants have more indigenous features both physically and culturally than their predecessors and, more importantly, a large number of them are very young.

The massive immigration of urbanized youth to the city of New York has accelerated the emergence of Mexican gangs. Like the early twentieth-century Italian, Polish, and Irish immigrant gangs, Mexican gangs in New York City are the product of structural forces that have set in motion a massive population shift. They are moving into the dilapidated neighborhoods of Spanish Harlem's El Barrio and lower Manhattan in the city, Astoria and Roosevelt in Queens, Bushwick in Brooklyn, previously occupied by European immigrants, and they are competing with these groups for scarce community resources. There are, however, some important differences. Among them, tremendous advancements in communication and transportation technologies have cut the price of migration considerably and accelerated the rate of immigration. And the development of well-organized smuggling rings has facilitated and accelerated the unsupervised migration of Mexicans into the country (Massey, 1986).

These factors have combined to produce two very unique qualities of today's immigrant Mexican gangs in New York City: (1) many, if not most, of the gang members have been introduced or highly socialized into the gang culture in Mexican urban areas; (2) some of these gangs are made in Mexico. Although Mexican gangs in New York have adopted cultural traits from Mexican gangs in the Southwest, Northeast and the Mexico–U.S. border, these have stronger cultural and, in some cases structural, ties to groups in Mexico. In other words, some the emerging gangs in New York City are 100 percent Mexican.

Chavos banda or *bandas* are groups of marginalized Mexican youth bound together by shared cultural practices, similar social experience and, in some cases, come from the same *colonias* or barrios in Mexico City and other major cities and urban areas in southern and central Mexico. Chavos banda emerged as an attempt to emulate the 1970s, 1980s, and 1990s countercultures of British and American youth who were rebelling against mainstream capitalist values and the culture of consumerism that permeated all aspects of the modern life. Ironically, the commodification of these countercultural trends by cultural industries (i.e., magazines, radio and television, movies, and video industries) became the driving force for the dissemination of these countercultures around the world (Zolov, 1999). Mexican youth adapted these cultural trends to their social milieu; transforming, molding, and mixing them with indigenous Mexican subcultures, creating a form of cultural syncretism.

The immigration of chavos banda to major American cities such as New York, San Francisco, and Los Angeles, represents the delayed reflection of the cultural waves emitted by American cultural industries to the rest of the world. These cultural waves shaped (or had a big influence on) the ideas and behavior of youth around the world and now were coming back to the source. In other words, as Mexican youth immigrate in high numbers to the Big Apple (the house of the biggest mass media conglomeration that has been an important source of cultural diffusion in the last century), they are bringing with them their cultural practices and forms of organization. The cultural waves sent by mainstream media were coming back in the form of a delayed cultural echo (reverberation), through the Mexican youth who migrated to take advantage of the economic opportunities created by the economic restructuring and its unsatisfying need for cheap labor.

Mexican youth gangs are organized around particular music and dancing styles. Among the subgroups of chavos banda hanging out on the street of New York, the Charangueros are the most conspicuous. Charanguero youth wear baggy Ben Davis–like pants, white T-shirts or dressy shirts, and slick (black shiny) shoes. Although their regalia appear similar to that of the Cholos from California and the Southwest, the Charanguero style comes out of the Pachuco-style regalia adopted by those who enjoy the dance moves and rhythms of the *música tropical* or Caribbean rhythms such as mambo, salsa, *cumbia, bachata, guaracha,* and cha-cha-cha. The Charanguero and Cholo style derive from the regional interpretation of the zoot suit subculture embraced by inner-city black and Chicano youth during the World War II years (Esteva Martínez, forthcoming).

Another manifestation of chavos banda in New York includes the Rocker Style. These youth wear tight jeans with Converse or Vans tennis shoes, long spiked hair, and black T-shirts stamped with the logos of famous American and British rock groups such as the Rolling Stones, Status Quo, the Sex Pistols, or the Ramones. Rockers are divided into other subgroups which include Rocanroleros, Punketos, Metaleros, Darketos, Goticos, and Trans (Valenzuela Arce, 1999). (These subcultural movements are Mexican adaptations of the American and European youth movements.) The subculture of the Rokeros chavos banda originated in the late 1970s, 1980s, and 1990s in Mexico City and expanded to the major cities of the central Mexican states of Puebla, Morelos, Tlaxcala, Estado de Mexico, and Guerrero and now they were making their presence felt in different neighborhoods throughout New York. This trend is evidence of the diffusion of the urban Mexican culture into the adjacent provincial states of central Mexico.

Last, a small numbers of Mexican youth are also adopting the Cholo subcultural styles of Chicano youth form the Southwest and the Baggies sub-cultural style of the hip-hop movement of the Northeast. These youth, however, are fewer in numbers and more likely to be second- or third-generation Mexicans, and they are more likely to prefer American music such as oldies, hip-hop, and rap.

Economic, social, and political marginalization prevents Mexican youth from accessing mainstream clubs, renting saloons, etc., and forces them into the underground club scene. Consequently, Mexicans do their "tocadas" or parties in places such as restaurants, apartment building basements, and improvised clubs, where all kinds of illegal activity takes place. Organizers often sponsor well-known Mexican *sonideros* or DJs such as Carita JC, La Changa, and El Conga, who draw youth from the five New York City boroughs.

In Mexico, for the most part, these youth socialized with other youth from their own particular subculture and rarely would hang out together. In New York City, however, something remarkable has occurred; Mexican youth from different subcultures were not only hanging out with members of other subcultures but were forming alliances of mutual support and protection and they were consolidating themselves into large bandas or gangs. Furthermore, Mexican youth are also influenced by prison culture; following the tradition of the East Coast prison gang subculture, these gangs had attempted to organize themselves into two major federations or nations (La Gran Raza and La Gran Familia). New York Mexican gangs originated out of the conflict between the arriving Mexican immigrants and the established Puerto Rican, Dominican, and black communities. The Ramblers from 116th Street in Spanish Harlem is a gang that claims El Barrio as its neighborhood or turf. According to Chino (names changed to protect identity), founder of the 116 Street gang, who claims to be *el que rifa* (the one who controls, dominates or is superior) among the Ramblers, the Mexican gangs began to form as a response to the violence committed by Puerto Rican, Dominican, and black youth against Mexican workers. (Other terms used to refer to the person that controls or dominates the groups are *efectivo* and *mero mero*.) Puerto Rican, Dominican, and black youth mugged Mexican immigrants at night as they were coming back from work and, in occasions, they were badly beaten. Chino asserts, "They [Puerto Ricans, Dominicans, and black] used to get the *paisas* and turn them up-side-down, take all their money and things of value. Back then [1984–85], we weren't that many Mexicans and this area was mostly Puerto Ricans and blacks. It was their barrio, the Puerto Rican Barrio" (Esteva Martínez, 2000). (*Paisa* is a term used by Mexicans to identified members of the same town area, region, state, or country. Its use is similar to the Italian term *paesani*. However, Mexicans also use this term in two different ways depending in the context of the conversation. In the United States it is used to identify anyone coming from Mexico. In its diminutive form, *paisanito*, its refers to people without formal education or to members of Mexico's indigenous community.) Around this same period, Phillip Bourgois (1995) documented how Puerto Ricans street thugs in El Barrio viewed Mexicans immigrants. Bourgois's informants describe Mexicans as "easy prey" due to their illegal status and rampant drunkenness. For them, mugging Mexicans became "the new thing to do," the "little crime wave." These thugs often employed various forms of violence, including beatings, stabbings, and shootings, to achieve their goals (Bourgois, 1995). However, as many more Mexicans moved into the neighborhood, the Mexican gangs grew in numbers and became stronger and better organized, gaining much more influence on the street of Manhattan's Spanish Harlem. As they grew in numbers and power, Mexican youth gangs began to claim the barrio as their own. "Now, we are many and we control the streets. It is no longer the Puerto Rican Barrio, that's over. Now it's the Mexican Barrio, it's our barrio, The Ramblers' barrio. We control it, whether [Puerto Ricans and Blacks] like it or not" (Esteva Martínez, 2001). A member of the Tricksters from the West Side of Manhattan makes a similar claim. "We [The Tricksters] controlled the West Side. From 42nd Street all the way up to 152nd Street. Dominicans and Puerto Ricans had their time, but now we control it." Similarly, Mexican youth are claiming territories in the Roosevelt area of Queens, Coney Island, the Sunset district in Brooklyn, and other places where Mexican immigrant communities had settled. Ironically, by achieving a balance of power with, or establishing dominance over, other groups in certain geographical areas, and claiming that area as their own barrio, Mexican youth began to direct their violence against each other. During the years I conducted research (1998–2001), most of the violence experienced by Mexican youth was committed by other Mexican youth.

Mexican gangs were no longer fighting against Puerto Ricans, Dominicans, or blacks but were fighting among themselves. In the case of Mexican immigrants, intra-gang violence is the direct result of the lack of a clear and well-defined set of norms and regulations that could facilitate the negotiation of social spaces and the distribution of limited resources. The extreme social and institutional isolation pushes Mexicans into the underground world where illegality is the rule of the jungle.

References/Suggested Readings: Bourgois, P.I. 1995. *In Search of Respect: Selling Crack in El Barrio*. Cambridge: Cambridge University Press; Esteva Martínez, J.F. 2000. Interview with Chino. *Mexicans in New York*, 15; Esteva Martínez, J.F. 2001. Interview with Pepé Gavilán. *Mexicans in New York,* 32; Esteva Martínez, J. F. (forthcoming). Institutional Isomorphism: New and Established Latino Immigrant Gangs in New York City, A Comparative Case Study of Dominican, Puerto Rican and Mexican Youth Gangs; Hermo, J. 1998. Métodos e instrumentos de investigacion. In J.A. Padilla Herrera (ed.), *La Construcción de Lo Juvenil: Reunión Nacional de Investigadores Sobre Juventud 1996*. Mexico: Causa Jovenes, Centro de Investigacion y Estudios Sobre Juventud, 122–132; Massey, D.S. 1986. The Settlement Process among Mexican Migrants to the United States. *American Sociological Review*, 51 (5), 670–684; Valenzuela Arce, J.M. 1999. La Siesta del Alma: Los Góticos y la Simbología Dark. *Jovenes: Revista de Estudios Sobre la Juventud*. Mexico: Instituto Mexicano de la Juventud, Centro de Investigacion y Estudios Sobre Juventud, 24–61; Valenzuela Arce, J.M. 2000. *Decadencia y auge de las identidades: cultura nacional, identidad cultural y modernización*. Tijuana: Plaza y Valdés; Zolov, E. 1999. *Refried Elvis: The Rise of the Mexican Counterculture*. Berkeley: University of California Press.

JUAN FRANCISCO ESTEVA MARTÍNEZ

CHICANO GANGS. In the 1940s, Chicano gangs drew attention to themselves by wearing elaborate clothing and by speaking Spanish-American slang. The subculture was termed "zoot suit" and it would establish the Chicano gang in the United States;

becoming the impetus for the negative labeling and scrutiny that gangs would receive from the media and law enforcement (Moore, 1985). The turning point was a murder in 1942—the Sleepy Lagoon case. Seventeen members of Chicano gangs were convicted. During the investigation, police targeted anyone that sported the zoot suit style, and there were police raids and mass arrests. "While there is no doubt the Chicano gangs were aggressive, this was the first time gangs and youthful Mexican violence became part of the media stereotype" (Gonzalez, cited in Moore, 1985, p. 6). The media and law enforcement began to portray the gangs in racist ways, referring to them as "rat packs" and as "savage" beasts out for blood (Moore, 1985). The gang came to accept the label and so did the rest of the population. Chicano gangs subsequently adopted the *cholo* way of life, which meant constructing a gangster look: wearing khakis, white T-shirts, bearing many tattoos, doing graffiti, and living by street rules and culture.

In the 1960s, such gangs developed a reputation as a source of resistance to Anglo American authority and oppression. "Many community leaders saw the Chicano movement as an extension of their life-long struggle for the advancement of Mexicans and sympathized with the *pintos* (prison gang members) as a segment of the community needing reintegration into barrio life—not rejection or further stigmatization" (Moore, 1985, p. 8). Community acceptance of Chicano gangs began to disappear the 1980s, as their reputation changed yet again. The media blamed Chicano gangs for the violence occurring in many prisons throughout the country and for the distribution of heroin in the Mexican neighborhoods. Major changes in police practice led to widely publicized indictments of Chicano gang members for trafficking heroin. Gang programs established by communities and the police to guide and help gang youth were subsequently eliminated, and a more aggressive approach appeared in the form of sheriff's and police department anti-gang units. Today, Chicano "gangs, gang members and their families are more and more isolated, and increasingly are left to the attention of law enforcement" (Moore, 1985, p. 9).

Membership

Adolescents who strive to become members of a Chicano gang usually form *klikas* (cliques). "Chicano gangs are graded by age . . . every few years a new klika, or cohort, forms in the gang as young, would-be members find themselves rejected by older, existing members" (Moore, Vigil, and Garcia, 1983, p. 183). Each klika forms its own identity. Most members of each distinct klika are from a single barrio; however some are non-residents but still manage to join the gang. "Membership is not based merely on residence, but is seen by active members as permanent and lifelong" (Moore, Vigil, and Garcia, 1983, p. 185). Once a youth becomes a member, he shares "something that transcends feelings based on proximity" (Moore Vigil, and Garcia, 1983, p. 185). Membership opportunities are occasionally extended to non-resident members in three ways: through boundary expansion, conflict alliance and kinship.

Relatives of gang members are normally accepted into the gang even when they reside outside the particular barrio where it is located, since "kinship is most important to Chicanos" (Moore, Vigil, and Garcia, 1983, p. 186). Another way gangs locate possible members is through boundary expansion. Gangs become larger with every member they recruit, and their size entails expansion into new areas until they eventually "own" that barrio (Moore, Vigil, and Garcia, 1983). For instance, one well-known klika, the White Fence, "expanded rapidly to incorporate at least four small neighboring gangs. Expansion feeds on itself" (Moore, Vigil, and Garcia, 1983, p. 189). Recruitment also takes place within penal institutions. In jails and youth detention facilities, "a long established, prestigious gang (Chicano) usually has a few members in any given juvenile facility who depend on each other for emotional and material support, as well as backup in fights" (Moore, Vigil, and Garcia, 1983, p. 189). Those that want to join the gang can show their willingness to do so by backing the gang in a fight on the streets or in a barrio, not just in prison. Once alliance has been established through supporting a klika in a fight, the ally becomes a homeboy, who is considered by members as "carnal," or blood brother (Moore, Vigil, and Garcia, 1983). He then becomes a part of the gang family.

Social Bonds and Social Controls

As Vigil (1998) notes, "gang members reflect an early and continuing street socialization and enculturation experience, and especially because the alternatives of school, family, sports and so on have failed to provide consistent direction" (p. 426). Economics and familial relations have much to do with why some youth identify with gangs. "For many gang members raised in female-centered households, where adult male models were absent or transient, real (female-raised) and feared (weak) identities come into conflict with the ideal (male, strong) identity that the street gangs represent" (Vigil, 1988, p. 430). In joining a gang, members are able to reinforce their sense of toughness daily, through "violence against others in the form of rampant gang fighting and slayings, and against oneself through the careless use of drugs and alcohol, which stem from tradition and technology (availability of guns and mind altering substances)" (Vigil, 1988, p. 431). The most widely used drug by gang members is marijuana (Mackenzie, Hunt, and Laidler, 2005). Chicano gang members use marijuana at higher frequencies than any other illicit drugs and their licit drug of choice is cigarettes coupled with alcohol. Although there is disagreement among researchers as to the extent of participation of Chicano gangs in drug markets, it is agreed that their main income stream is the sale of drugs. "Business among gang members refers principally to drug sales. Within the social context of the gang, drug sales are viewed as a legitimate hustle and money making strategy. Hanging out in a group on the street corner provides opportunity, a place to conduct business, and a level of protection within the group. In addition to the money that drug selling can produce, drug sellers represent a lifestyle that younger gang members can look up to and aspire to" (Mackenzie, Hunt, and Laidler, 2005, p. 110). One former Chicano gang member, a member of White Fence, illustrates this point by stating, "from age 11 to 12 until the time I turned 19, I was hard core cholo, didn't care about school, didn't care about anything. All I thought about was making that money, representing my hood" (Reyes, 2006, p. 171). Money, respect, and a sense of belonging are important to Chicano gang members as they are limited in their capacities to succeed at leading conventional law-abiding lives. Drug dealing is a way for the gang to generate income as well as a way to establish power and respect on the streets.

Summary

Chicano gangs have existed for decades. Communities are often conflicted in how they perceive such gangs that routinely commit illegal acts while espousing cultural pride. Their members are mainly adolescents with limited opportunities. They turn to gangs for the emotional fulfillment, friendship, acceptance, and a sense of self-worth.

Growing up in areas that are unsafe and violent, Chicano youth are often drawn to the powers and benefits they are afforded through gang membership.

References/Suggested Readings: MacKenzie, K., Hunt, G., and Laidler, K. 2005. Youth Gangs and Drugs: The Case of Marijuana. *Journal of Ethnicity in Substance Abuse*, 4, 99–134; Moore, J. 1985. Isolation and Stigmatization in the Development of an Underclass: The Case of Chicano Gangs in East Los Angeles. *Social Problems*, 33, 1–12; Moore, J., Vigil, D., and Garcia, R. 1983. Residence and Territoriality in Chicano Gangs. *Social Problems*, 31, 182–194; Reyes, Reynaldo III. 2006. Cholo to Me: From Peripherality to Practicing Student Success for a Chicano Former Gang Member. *Urban Review*, 38, 165–185; Vigil, D. 1988. Group Processes and Street Identity: Adolescent Chicano Gang Members. *Ethos*, 16, 421–445.

KARIN MICHONSKI

CHINESE ORGANIZED CRIME AND GANGS. Chinese organized gang activities did not just suddenly appear on the American scene. As students and observers of gang operations we must review what brought about these criminal gang activities from within a fairly stable Chinese society. A culture that stresses a Confucian code, which projects concepts that if all persons fulfilled their duties toward themselves, their families, states, and the world a "Great Harmony" would prevail (Freedman, 1966).

When we discuss the evolution of the Chinese gangs, we must also view the impact that Triads have had on these groups. Triad (triangle of heaven, earth, and man) groups first appeared in China in the late seventeenth century. These groups were formed in an attempt to overthrow the Quig (Ch'ing) government that had been created by Manchu invaders (Morgan, 1960). It wasn't until 1912 that the Quig regime finally collapsed. Some Triad leaders and members attempted to place themselves in the newly created Republic of China government. A large portion of those not assimilated into the new government reestablished themselves within their Triad associations in order to maintain some type of authority within their own associations. The secretive Triad organizations, which were originally civic minded and devoted to religious camaraderie, were slowly but surely deteriorating into what is known as organized crime factions. This took place once the leadership of the Triads were consumed by self-serving individuals who were able to impose their own standards of conduct on the organization for personal stature and gain (Chin, 1990).

Triad societies involvement in criminal activities increased tenfold during the first half of the twentieth century as many Chinese citizens became uneasy with the various officials struggling to control the government. Several influential organizations recruited Triad members and sanctioned strong-arm methods and violent tactics to ensure that the average person in society followed the organizations rules. The Triads were then authorized by these associations to set up and control prostitution, gambling, and opium houses (Seagrave, 1985). As the Triads enforcer status for the powerful political associations increased, there was a decrease in their patriotic interests and a decline in the ability of their leaders to control illegal activities of the membership.

In 1949, the Red Army defeated Chiang Kai-Shek's Kuomintang Party, leading to a mass migration of Kuomintang supporters to Taiwan and Hong Kong. It wasn't long after the defeat of Chiang Kai-Shek's army that the Chinese Communist Party started harassing and executing Triad members, with the result that Triad groups were quickly reformed in Hong Kong, even infiltrating the ranks of the Hong Kong police department. In fact, an investigation into officers assigned to the Hong Kong

Table I   Triads (The Formation of Secret Societies in China); Belief: Hung—Heaven, Earth, and Man

Seventeenth Century	
36 Oaths—Goodness	Patriotic, Brotherhood, Security, Secrecy, "One for all and all for one"
36 Strategies—Badness	
Eighteenth Century	Formation of Overseas Triads
Nineteenth Century	Tongs formed in North American King Sor, Kung Kuam or Hui, Protection for Chinese workers and new immigrants to America. Tong values almost carbon copy of Triads.
Twentieth Century	Street gangs formed and used as enforcers by Triads and Tongs. No values, strictly part of criminal enterprise.

Police Department's Triad Society Division disclosed that most of its members also held active Triad membership.

Hong Kong Connection

Triad societies have been active in Hong Kong since the seventeenth century but the Hong Kong groups participation in criminal activities started a lot sooner. Hong Kong was transferred to British control in 1842 and three years later the Triads were involved in unlawful operations. This forced the British government in Hong Kong to enact an Ordinance for the Suppression of Triads (the Societies Ordinances), which banned citizens from becoming members of Triad groups or partaking in any Triad activities (Chin, 1990). These laws helped to control the actions of Triads by moving most of their operations out of public view until the early twentieth century when Triad groups started to reestablish themselves as organizations to provide protection for territories chosen by peddlers. Triads, once again, started to flourish in Hong Kong, but not without conflict. A major part of the problem revolved around confrontations over the territorial rights of the vendor-Triad members. In an effort to settle these conflicts the Triad organizations held a joint meeting to form one association to supervise the activities and settle the disputes. During this conference all of the attendees voted to use the word *Wo* (peace) prior to the symbolic name of each Triad (e.g., Wo Sun Ye On).

Ultimately, these Wo groups evolved into some of the most powerful and disreputable chapters of the Hong Kong Triads (Chin, 1990). The major factors behind the increased growth and success of the Hong Kong Triad groups were:

1. The ability of members to infiltrate, recruit, and then take control over labor unions.

2. Triad cooperation with the Japanese military government during World War II. The Triads embellished their control over illegal activities by supporting the Japanese officials, who in turn, destroyed cooperating Triad members' prior criminal histories and permitted the Triad informers and enforcers to control gambling, prostitution, and opium operations in Hong Kong.

3. Once the war ended, the Hong Kong Triads continued their rapid growth but with this increased growth came the loss of control over Triad membership, camaraderie,

Table 2 Designations of Leaders and Members of Triads

FBI	Chin	San Francisco PD	Job Description
Leader Elder Brother 489	Shan Chu 489	Shan Chu Leader 489	Group Leader Boss of Group Older Brother Slang Tai Lo
Deputy Incense Burner Vanguard Leader 438	Yee Lu Yuan Fu Shan Chu 438	Fu Shan Chu Deputy Leader Heung Chu Incense Master 438 Sin Fung Vanguard Sheung Fa Double Flower	Second Brother Slang Yee Lo High Priest Status Rank General Affairs Recruiter

Red Pole Enforcer
426
	Hung Kwan	Hung Kwan
		Fighter Official
			Enforcer
			Responsible for gang
			  protection implementing
			  punishment

White Paper Fan Advisor 415	Park Tse Sin 415	Park Tse Sin White Paper Fan 415	Planner and Advisor
Grass Sandal Messenger 432	Cho Hai Liaison 432	Cho Hair Grass Sandal 432	Messenger Liaison Spy Infiltrate Police other Groups
Members Worker 49	Sey Kow Jai 49	Ordinary Member 49	
Recruits 36			

righteousness, and secrecy. A segment of the Hong Kong Triads membership had already sacrificed their nationalism when they joined forces with the Japanese during World War II. After the war other members also relinquished all the other values of these secret societies by becoming involved in criminal activities. All of these factors plus the ending of membership registration led to the further criminalization of what were now fractious criminal organizations (Chin, 1990).

As the prior figures indicate, the structure of Triad societies may be slightly different, but most organizations are arranged in the same basic manner. Numbers play an important role and are used as signs of identification related to Triad history. When the number four (4) is used as the first number in a specific numerical figure it signifies the ancient Chinese belief that earth is surrounded by four great seas.

Tongs

Chinese immigrants started arriving in the United States shortly after the discovery of gold in California in the late 1840s. Most of the early Chinese settlers were from the southern coastal areas of China. These new arrivals on U.S. soil learned the meaning of discrimination very quickly and found themselves being considered as outcasts because of their ethnic backgrounds. It wasn't long before small China-towns started to build up at almost every gold rush location. Soon family and local associations were set up according to the province in China where the majority of the residents were born. Ultimately, these fraternal organizations were combined and designated as Tongs. The history of Chinese Tongs goes back to the mid-nineteenth century. Tongs—a term used to describe meeting halls—were originally formed to protect Chinese businesses and new immigrants against the alien and hostile American communities. As time passed some Tongs were formed to serve new members of Chinese communities to locate relatives or friends and to assist immigrants in locating a place to stay and live. The majority of Tongs are national organizations whose members are legitimate people involved in assisting community businesses, ethnic societies, and politics. A smaller percentage of Tong members use these organizations to benefit themselves and other members of organized crime groups (Chin, 1990). Although Tongs were conceived on the North American continent, there is little doubt that the Chinese Triads had a hand in creating these associations. The Federal Bureau of Investigation has gone as far as to state that a major portion of all of the crimes in Chinatowns throughout the United States can be traced back to higher ranking Tong officials. In fact, both the FBI San Francisco and New York offices have linked murder, extortion, gambling, drug trafficking, and prostitution to the local Chinatown Tongs. Research indicates that one Low Yet, a Triad member and a leader of the Taiping rebellion, was the founder of Tongs in San Francisco. Yet formed the Chee Kong Tong which had over 1,000 members in 1887. This Tong was modeled after a Triad Yet had been a member of in Hong Kong (FBI, 1996).

The administrative structure of Tongs is very similar to that of La Cosa Nostra.

The **Godfather** type of rank in the Mafia would also be a highly influential position in the Tongs but one that is shared by a group of members who are perceived as "the elders." The lower ranks of the Tong structure contains the largest proportion of members all of whom fall into the rank of soldier worker. As far as membership in the Tongs is concerned, there are no restrictions on the number or background of newly recruited members. This has led to the rapid growth of membership in the Tongs within a short period of time. Tongs have embraced the same basic type of socialization process as the Triads. Initiation rites are mandatory for all new members, as are the reciting of oaths of loyalty, nationalism, and brotherhood. Like the Triads, the Tongs maintain a highly covert operation that restricts the identification of the leadership. This leaves a majority of the membership without any knowledge of the daily activities within the Tong. One problem facing the Tongs is that the politics within the Tong are usually fragmented because of the number of various

Table 3   Administrative Structure of the Mafia and Tongs

Mafia	Tongs
Boss	Chairman
Underboss	Vice Chairman
Consigliere	English-speaking Secretary
Caporegime	Tong Treasure
Capo	Tong Social Secretary

Source: U.S. Department of Justice, 1988.

factions in each association. An elected Tong leader in many cases can be considered nothing more than a puppet who is controlled by many factions instead of a strong leader elected by the majority (Chin, 1990). The Tong associations (presently 100 in New York City), are also part of the Chinese Consolidated Benevolent Association which is highly influential within the political circles of Chinatowns throughout the United States (U.S. Department of Justice 1988). There are several major Tong associations in the United States. According to the FBI the top three Tongs are: On Leone, Hip Sinq, and Hop Sinq (1996).

West Coast Gangs

Chinese street gangs started developing in San Francisco during the 1950s. The Chinese gangs were formed and structured in the same manner as other ethnic youth gangs. A street gang known as the Beigs was one of the first street gangs formed by American-born Chinese. This gang's area of criminal expertise was burglary and its members could be easily identified by the "Beatle" type of outfits they wore (Loo, 1976).

The Wah Ching (Youth of China) was the first immigrant gang and was formed to prevent assaults on foreign born Chinese immigrants by American born Chinese (Chin, 1990). U.S. immigration laws were modified, leading to an increase in the number of immigrants arriving from mainland China. The Wah Ching took advantage of the changes in U.S. immigration laws to become a more powerful gang by recruiting many of the younger immigrants. The power of this gang was soon recognized by members of the Chinese community who hired gang members to run errands and provide strong-arm protection for gambling operations (Chin, 1990).

The Hop Sing Tong saw the advantages of being associated with a street gang, brought the Wah Ching under their control by creating a youth branch within the organization. A short time later, the Suey Sing Tong created a youth gang known as the Young Suey Sing or the Tom Tom Street gang. Conflict between the Wah Ching and the Young Suey Sing led to many street confrontations. One group, the Yau Lai (Yo Le) or Joe Fong Boys was formed in 1969 by discontented members of the Wah Ching gang. Many of these dissatisfied Wah Ching members left the gang because of restrictive controls placed on the gang members by the Hop Sing Tong (Chin, 1990).

During the early 1970s both the Wah Ching and the Joe Fong Boys started to expand their criminal activities by targeting people in the Asian community as victims of their crimes. As the membership of the Wah Ching and Joe Fong Boys multiplied there was also an increase in the number of violent conflicts between the two groups over territorial rights. This was especially evident between 1973 and 1977 when twenty-seven people were killed in gang related incidents. On one occasion five people were killed and eleven seriously injured (not one a gang member) during a vicious attack by members of the Joe Fong Boys (Chin, 1990). The San Francisco area probably has the largest amount of Chinese gang activity on the West Coast. The Hop Sing Boys, the Kit Jars, the Asian Invasion, and the Local Motion are some of the Chinese gangs that operate criminal enterprises in the Bay area. Wah Ching is considered the largest street gang in California with about 600 to 700 active members of which 200 can be considered tenacious. The Wah Ching gang formed an alliance with the Sun Yee On Triad in 1987 (FBI, 1996).

The Los Angeles branch of the Wah Ching was formed in 1965 by Wah Ching members from San Francisco. Wah Ching was formed in Los Angeles to stop the constant harassment of newly immigrated Chinese youths by **Mexican gangs**. Despite the formation of the Chinese gangs, conflicts did not cease and have continued right up until the present. One specific area outside of Los Angeles, Monterey Park, has seen its Chinese population double between the late 1970s and the early 1980s, partly by Taiwanese police arrests of covert individuals in the late 1970s and early 1980s, forcing many immigrants with **criminal** connections to seek asylum in the United States.

Many of the transgressors brought with them the experience to set up two new gangs, the Four Seas and the United Bamboo. The Four Seas gang originally appeared in Taiwan in 1955 only to dissipate within a few years. A short time later the Four Seas was resurrected under new leadership that fortified the gangs economic status by opening and controlling houses of prostitution and gambling casinos. Membership in the Four Seas increased as legal and illegal Taiwanese gang members reached the United States and was soon expanding its criminal enterprise to include legal as well as illegal ventures.

The United Bamboo was dispersed by the Taiwanese police in 1958 only to re-emerge in the 1960s as a dominant street gang. During the 1980s, United Bamboo expanded its operations into the entertainment business. The gang mentioned above also increased its membership and listed seventeen additional new branches for a combined total of twenty-five chapters. Although total membership in the United States is unknown, it is estimated that the United Bamboo in Taiwan has over 10,000 members (Chin, 1990).

The gang gained nation wide attention in 1984 when some of their leaders were involved in the murder of Henry Lui, a formidable Chinese writer. Lui wrote a biography that made derogatory statements about the then Taiwanese president and was preparing a manuscript related to the unethical practices of Taiwanese politicians. Media reports indicate that two United Bamboo leaders, Chen Chi-li and Swei Yi Fund, and the chief of Taiwan's Military Intelligence Bureau, Vice Admiral Wong Shi-Lin, met in 1984 and discussed punishing Lui for what they considered "Traitorous Acts." Originally, the Los Angeles United Bamboo was to take some action against Lui but was unable to carry out this mission. Vice Admiral Wong then had Chen and Swei trained to fulfill the contract on Lui. Upon Chen's arrival in the United States, he was joined by United Bamboo's West Coast enforcer Wu Tun. Another member from Taipei, Tung Kwei-Sen, soon joined Chen and Wu to partake in this conspiracy. A short time after Tung's arrival, Wu and Tung entered Lui's house and murdered him (Chin, 1990). Besides being involved in the most notorious murder of a Chinese American writer, the United Bamboo are also heavily involved in heroin importing, extortion, and gun running (Grennan, 1992).

East Coast Gangs

Prior to the immigration law changes in 1965, the only active Chinese street gang in New York City were the Continentals. This gang was formed in 1961 to protect Chinese students from attacks on them by other ethnic groups. The Continentals were made up of American-born Chinese youths who did not get involved in street crimes or were associated with any of the Chinatown Tongs (Chin, 1990).

Then in 1964, the On Leong Tong formed the On Leong Youth Club. It wasn't long before this group became known as the White Eagles gang. This gang was made up of foreign-born Chinese youths and they were deployed throughout Chinatown to prevent any type of discriminate activities by outsiders against Chinese businessmen and residents (Chin, 1990). Another gang known as Chung Yee appeared on the streets of Chinatown. Like its antecedent, On Leong, the membership of the Chung Yee was made up of new arrivals from mainland China. This gang operated in the same fashion as the On Leong, protecting the rights of Chinatown citizens and business-people. Chinese street gangs continued to increase and gangs like the Quen Ying, Liang Shan, the Flying Dragons, and the Black Eagles started appearing on the streets of Chinatown. The early history of these gangs indicates that they were all martial arts clubs used to prevent visitors from harassing local businessmen and residents (Chin, 1990).

The early 1970s saw an increase in the amount of violence being used by Chinese gangs. The two elements that caused an elevation of the amount of disorder by Chinese gangs were the increase in the availability of weapons and the conflict between the growing number of street gangs coupled with the "restlessness" of the new immigrant youths whose violent behavior threatened all of the residents of Chinatown.

During this period, the youth gangs started extorting money and food from local business establishments through the use of fear and strong-arm tactics and then extended their criminal activities, including by robbing local gambling dens. The Tongs, seeing their businesses being extorted and robbed, hired the gang members to perform private security as the Tong's enforcers and protectors. This led to some of the gangs becoming part of the Tong Family (White Eagles and On Leong Tong and Flying Dragons and Hip Sing Tong) (Chin, 1990).

The problem with the Chinese street gangs was that by 1974 some of the gangs were completely out of control. The White Eagles gang members, hired by the On Leong Tong to protect On Leong members and businesses, were openly robbing, extorting, and humiliating the Tong members on Chinatown streets. The On Leong Tong started to disassociate itself from the White Eagles by stopping all monetary payments and weapons to the gang and prompting the Ghost Shadows street gang to replace the White Eagles as the On Leong Tong's street gang.

After a short struggle the Ghost Shadows took charge of just about all of the most profitable locations in Chinatown while the White Eagles removed themselves from the On Leong's portion of Chinatown. A realignment of all the territories within Chinatown was completed a short time after the removal of the White Eagles and all the gangs seemingly content about territorial adjustments, went back to their criminal ventures. The hostilities between the gangs continued as did an increase in street violence (Chin, 1990).

The year 1976 turned out to be Chinatown's most violent year as internal and external gang hostilities increased sharply. Most of the gangs criminal activities expanded to include the use of coercion, which was so intimidating the majority of Chinatown's businessmen feared for their lives. During this time, there were several gunfights between the Flying Dragons and the Ghost Shadows, resulting in the killing of one Ghost Shadow and one innocent restaurant customer, and the wounding of one Flying Dragon and five innocent bystanders.

During the gang warfare between the territorial Chinatown gangs the presence of Wah Ching gang members in the Chinatown vicinity increased drastically. Local gang leaders reticent of the Wah Ching's propinquity set up a meeting of gang leaders to announce the termination of the gang warfare and that gang members would be seeking employment. The first indication after this announcement was that the gangs were working together to prevent a turf invasion by outside groups but purported gang unity and promises of peace was not to last long. Within a month a dispute over turf rights broke out between the Ghost Shadows and the Black Eagles gangs. It resulted in the wounding of Black Eagle Leader Paul Ma and four other

Black Eagle associates. A short time later a Ghost Shadow member was shot and killed and this was followed in a week by the killing of a Black Eagle gang members.

Prior to 1976 the majority of confrontations were between opposing gangs over the rights to certain areas in Chinatown. During 1976 problems within different gangs surfaced and struggles ensued over control and money causing increased internal conflict within several of the major New York City gangs. The intra-gang hostilities continued as did the gangs' ability to increase their turf holdings. This became apparent when the owners of a midtown Manhattan Chinese restaurant were murdered for refusing to pay extortion money to the Black Eagles gang. Another indication of how far out of control gang violence had become was the attempted murder of Man Bun Lee. Lee, the former president of the Chinatown Community Business Association, gained media attention by requesting that additional police enforcement units be assigned to remove the gangs from Chinatown. This resulted in Lee being stabbed five times. Lee survived this assault and his assailant was arrested and convicted of this crime. But both of these incidents sent a message to the Chinese community not to cross the gangs because they controlled the streets. Another factor related to Chinatown street gangs was the fact that it did not matter who or how many gang members were arrested and/or convicted by law enforcement authorities. This has been evident since the mid-1970s when the police started taking action against the Chinese gangs. No matter what the police have done the gangs have continued to participate in their chosen crime ventures without any serious interruptions from either federal or local law enforcement.

Since the early 1980s several new street gangs have appeared in the Chinatown area. The Fuk Ching, the White Tigers (which were a result of intra-gang warfare), the Tune On, the Green Dragons, and the Born to Kill are the names of some of the new gangs. The criminal activities of some of these gangs has expanded the gang operations to all five boroughs of New York City. In most cases these new gangs have attempted to avoid conflict with the original older ones. This has been done by not impinging on the older groups territories, instead, the new gangs have taken control of turf outside of Chinatown and, in some cases, outside of Manhattan. One thing that does seem apparent is that these new gangs are more violent than their predecessor.

References/Suggested Readings: Chin, K. 1990. *Chinese Subculture and Criminality: Non-traditional Groups in America.* Westport, CT: Greenwood Press; Federal Bureau of Investigation. 1996 (July). An Introduction to Organized Crime in the United States; Freedman, M. 1966. *Chinese Lineage and Society: Fuckien and Kwangtung.* New York: Humanities Press; Grennan, S. 1992 (Fall). Threatening Issue of Oriental Organized Crime. *IALEIA Journal*, 7 (1), 1–7; Morgan, W.P. 1964. *Triad Societies in Hong Kong.* Washington, DC: Government Printer; Seagrave, S. 1985. *The Song Dynasty.* New York: Harper and Row.

SEAN GRENNAN

THE CRIMINAL CAREER PARADIGM

What Is a Criminal Career?

In recent years, there has been a growing interest in the analysis of offending patterns across the life course, with increased investments in longitudinal studies of criminal and deviant behavior. Various paradigms have been developed to explain the changes occurring in the patterns of offending across time, namely the criminal career paradigm and the life-course approach.

The criminal career is defined as the "longitudinal sequence of offenses committed by an offender who has a detectable rate of offending during some period" (Blumstein, Cohen, and Farrington, 1988, p. 2). The term *career* is not to be taken in the sociological sense (Blumstein, Cohen, and Hsieh, 1982, p. 2):

> This characterization of an individual's criminal activity as a "career" is not meant to imply that offenders derive their livelihood exclusively or even predominantly from crime. The concept of a criminal career is intended only as a means of structuring the longitudinal sequence of criminal events associated with an individual in a systematic way.

The different dimensions of the criminal career are often referred to as *criminal career parameters*. These characteristics provide valuable information regarding the distribution of offending across the life course. Participation distinguishes individuals who are active in offending versus those who are not. Age of onset is defined as the age at the time of the first offense. Offending frequency is defined as the number of offenses committed by individuals who are active in crime. Individuals may exhibit patterns of acceleration (increase in offending frequency) or deceleration (reduction in offending frequency) across various stages of the criminal career. Escalation or de-escalation illustrate changes in the seriousness of offending (i.e., from serious to minor offenses, or vice versa). Issues of specialization and versatility investigate whether individuals tend to commit similar types of offenses across time, or whether they engage in a wide range of different activities. Career length or duration refers to the time between the first and last offenses. Although desistance is often defined as the cessation of all criminal activity, alternative definitions have been developed in the literature in recent years. For instance, Le Blanc and Loeber (1998) have developed an extended definition of desistance, characterizing it as a reduction in frequency, seriousness, and versatility of offending.

Hirschi and Gottfredson (1983; see also Gottfredson and Hirschi, 1990) believed that the predictors of the onset of delinquency are similar to those of persistence and desistance from crime, and that these parameters are all behavioral manifestations of one underlying construct (e.g., criminal propensity). Akers (1985) also argued that the variables explaining the onset of delinquency are similar to those explaining desistance from crime (e.g., delinquent peer associations). Conversely, Farrington et al. (1990) maintained that the causes and correlates of onset are likely to be different from those of desistance and persistence in crime, a concept that Uggen and Piliavin (1998) have referred to as *asymmetrical causation*.

From a theoretical viewpoint, the potential implications linked to the issue of asymmetrical causation are of substantial importance. If the predictors of onset are indeed different from those of desistance, then this would defy some of the basic principles of a "general theory of crime." From a policy viewpoint, if the causes and correlates of various criminal career dimensions are similar, then post-onset intervention efforts do not need to be adapted to each specific parameter (see Piquero, Farrington, and Blumstein, 2004). Furthermore, if the predictors of desistance are similar to those of onset, then this would suggest that it is possible to make accurate long-term predictions about criminal career outcomes.

Why Study Patterns of Offending across Various Periods of the Life Course?

The association between age and crime is one of the most established facts in the field of criminology. It is generally agreed that aggregate crime rates peak in late adolescence/early adulthood and gradually drop thereafter, but there is still very little consensus regarding the causes of this decline (Hirschi and Gottfredson, 1995; Maruna, 2001; Moffitt, 1993).

Adolescent samples of offenders may not be ideal for the study of persistent criminal offending, because most juvenile delinquents do not become adult offenders (Moffitt, 1993). In this respect, investigations of the causes and correlates of criminal career outcomes that are based on cross-sectional data (or data limited to the adolescent years) may offer a biased picture of the topic at hand. For these reasons, it is highly useful to follow up individuals longitudinally and to obtain valid data on offending in adulthood.

Short follow-up periods can result in misleading estimates of criminal career parameters. In a follow-up of adjudicated males up to age 25, Le Blanc and Fréchette (1989) found that the average age at last conviction was 19.9 years. When the follow-up extended to the early forties, the average age at last conviction was thirty-one years. In a comparative study of London and Stockholm males, Farrington and Wikström (1994) found that the mean age of termination up to age 25 was 22.4 years in both samples. Later results from the Cambridge Study in Delinquent Development (when respondents were followed up to their late forties) showed that the average age of desistance (age at last conviction) was 25.6 years. In short, when prospective longitudinal data is not available and observation periods are short, "desistance" is more likely to refer to a state of "temporary nonoffending" (Bushway et al., 2001).

Studies have shown that the causes of long-term involvement in offending can be traced back to early ages (Gottfredson and Hirschi, 1990; Le Blanc and Fréchette, 1989; Le Blanc and Loeber, 1990; Moffitt, 1993; Sampson and Laub, 1993). Such studies have emphasized the importance of early detection and intervention in order to prevent long-term criminal persistence. However, developmental crime prevention is not always among policy makers' priorities, and it is important to consider alternative prevention strategies. For instance, what type of preventive measures can be adopted after individuals have been initiated to crime? In a post-onset context, what should be the target-areas for intervention initiatives? Do these key areas differ from one type of offender to another, or from one period of the life course to another?

Once onset has occurred, it would be useful to invest efforts in limiting the length, intensity and seriousness of criminal careers. Identifying life-course transitions and cognitive factors that contribute to desistance from crime can provide useful information for post-onset interventions. For instance, it has been suggested that acquiring a better understanding of the cognitive processes that promote desistance from crime may be highly useful in the development of efficient cognitive-behavioral programs (Ward, Hudson, Johnston, and Marshall, 1997). Improved social and cognitive skills may result in the establishment of stronger social bonds and increased social integration.

An increasing number of researchers seem to agree that there is both stability and change in offending patterns across the life course (Ezell and Cohen, 2005; Farrington and West, 1995; Horney, Osgood, and Marshall, 1995; Moffitt, 1993; Sampson and Laub, 1993). The fact that offending trajectories in adulthood are not fully explained by childhood experiences highlights the importance of change, and the need for sustained post-onset intervention efforts to trigger and accelerate the desistance process.

Some authors have stressed that little attention has been given to within-individual change in offending patterns across the life course (Horney, Osgood, and Marshall,

1995; Le Blanc, and Loeber, 1998). In their discussion on within-individual change, Le Blanc and Loeber (1998, p. 116) stated that "an important feature of this approach is that individuals serve as their own controls." Unsurprisingly, between-individual comparisons tend to demonstrate that individuals with higher self and social control are less likely to be characterized by highly active criminal careers when compared to those with lower self and social control. One of the key features of criminal career and life course research is the ability to investigate internal and external factors explaining changes in criminal career patterns *within* individuals. In other words, using individuals as their own controls, do changing cognitive and social characteristics have an impact on the progress made toward the termination of criminal careers? This question is crucial to the development of efficient post-onset intervention initiatives. From a theoretical viewpoint, the emphasis on within-individual change speaks directly to debates on stability and change, namely the general theory hypothesis (Gottfredson and Hirschi, 1990).

In summary, life course and criminal career research offer an interesting outlook for the analysis and explanation of offending behavior. Although these approaches have their respective limitations (see Gottfredson and Hirschi, 1986), they show great promise for the investigation of issues relating to prevention, intervention, and public policy in criminology and criminal justice.

References/Suggested Readings: Akers, R. 1985. *Deviant Behavior: A Social Learning Approach* (3rd ed.). Belmont, CA: Wadsworth; Blumstein, A., Cohen, J., and Farrington, D.P. 1988. Criminal Career Research: Its Value for Criminology. *Criminology*, 26 (1), 1–36; Blumstein, A., Cohen, J., and Hsieh, P. 1982. *The Duration of Adult Criminal Careers: Final Report to National Institute of Justice*. Pittsburgh, PA: Carnegie-Mellon University; Bushway, S.D., Piquero, A.R., Broidy, L.M., Cauffman, E., and Mazerolle, P. 2001. An Empirical Framework for Studying Desistance as a Process. *Criminology*, 39 (2), 491–515; Ezell, M.E., and Cohen, L.E. 2005. *Desisting from Crime: Continuity and Change in Long-Term Crime Patterns of Serious Chronic Offenders*. Oxford: Oxford University Press; Farrington, D.P., Loeber, R., Elliott, D.S., Hawkins, J.D., Kandel, D.B., Klein, M.W., et al. 1990. Advancing Knowledge about the Onset of Delinquency and Crime. *Advances in Clinical and Child Psychology*, 13, 283–342; Farrington, D.P., & West, D.J. 1995. Effects of Marriage, Separation, and Children on Offending by Adults Males. In *Current Perspectives on Aging and the Life Cycle* , 4, 249–281; Farrington, D.P., and Wikström, P.-O.H. 1994. Criminal Careers in London and Stockholm: A Cross-National Comparative Study. In E.G.M. Weitekamp and H.-J. Kerner (eds.), *Cross-National Longitudinal Research on Human Development and Criminal Behavior* (pp. 65–89). Dordrecht, The Netherlands: Kluwer Academic Publishers; Gottfredson, M.R., and Hirschi, T. 1986. The True Value of Lambda Would Appear to be Zero: An Essay on Career Criminals, Criminal Careers, Selective Incapacitation, Cohort Studies, and Related Topics. *Criminology*, 24 (2), 213–234; Gottfredson, M.R., and Hirschi, T. 1990. *A General Theory of Crime*. Stanford, CA: Stanford University Press; Hirschi, T., and Gottfredson, M.R. 1983. Age and Explanation of Crime. *American Journal of Sociology*, 89, 552–584; Hirschi, T., and Gottfredson, M.R. 1995. Control Theory and the Life-Course Perspective. *Studies on Crime and Crime Prevention*, 4 (2), 131–142; Horney, J., Osgood, D.W., and Marshall, I.H. 1995. Criminal Careers in the Short-Term: Intra-Individual Variability in Crime and its Relation to Local Life Circumstances. *American Sociological Review*, 60, 655–673; Le Blanc, M., and Fréchette, M. 1989. *Male Criminal Activity from Childhood through Youth: Multilevel and Developmental Perspectives*. New York: Springer-Verlag; Le Blanc, M., and Loeber, R. 1998. Developmental Criminology Updated. *Crime and Justice*, 23, 115–198; Maruna, S. 2001. *Making Good: How Ex-Convicts Reform and Rebuild their Lives*. Washington, DC: American Psychological Association; Moffitt, T.E. 1993. "Life-Course Persistent" and "Adolescence-Limited" Antisocial Behavior: A Developmental Taxonomy.

Psychological Review, 100, 674–701; Piquero, A., Farrington, D.P., and Blumstein, A. 2003. The Criminal Career Paradigm. *Crime and Justice: A Review of Research,* 30, 359–506; Sampson, R.J., & Laub, J.H. 1993. *Crime in the Making: Pathways and Turning Points Through Life.* Cambridge, MA: Harvard University Press; Uggen, C., and Piliavin, I. 1998. Assymetrical Causation and Criminal Desistance. *Journal of Criminal Law and Criminology,* 88 (4), 1399–1422; Ward, T., Hudson, S.M., Johnston, L., and Marshall, W.L. 1997. Cognitive Distortions in Sex Offenders: An Integrative Review. *Clinical Psychology Review,* 17 (5), 479–507.

LILA KAZEMIAN

CRIMINAL ORGANIZATIONS. Criminal organizations include gangs, organized crime groups, business groups who engage in criminal activities for purposes of profit and intimidation of competition, and other self-identified groups engaged in crime on either a short-term or long-term basis. The so-called Russian Mafia exemplifies this latter conceptualization of a criminal organization whereby individuals join together for short-term criminal enterprises and disband afterward. Such organizations challenge the conventional definition of organized crime that emphasizes permanence and a rigid hierarchy. Smith suggests that all organizations operate on a behavioral continuum ranging from saintly to sinful and that at any time a legitimate organization can be a criminal organization in its daily operation. The case of Enron and its chief executives is a case study in such a conceptualization. Related to the idea of criminal organizations is the idea of a "continuing criminal enterprise" which is found in American criminal law. A continuing criminal enterprise is specifically an illegal drug trafficking organization. Similarly, the Racketeer Influenced and Corrupt Organizations Act (RICO) has been used to prosecute criminal organizations ranging from Mafia groups involved in labor unions to an unsuccessful attempt to prosecute anti-abortion protestors. The key component in RICO is that the criminal offense be a pattern or enterprise in violation of state or federal law. Isolated criminal acts would not qualify for RICO prosecution (Abadinsky, 2007). This broad conceptualization allows for the inclusion of seemingly legitimate organizations for purposes of prosecution.

References/Suggested Readings: Abadinsky, H. 2007. *Organized Crime.* New York: Thompson-Wadsworth; Smith, D.C. 1975. *The Mafia Mystique.* New York: Free Press.

ALBERT DICHIARA

CRIMINAL SUBCULTURES AND GANGS. That which is considered normal, appropriate, popular, and wrong throughout society varies considerably across different social groups. *Cultural conflict* is, along with cultural variation, a defining characteristic of a subculture. Accordingly, it is important to make the conceptual distinction between subculture and population segment. The subcultural values of a gang, for example, may intensify even though membership is reduced through police and other criminal justice system actions. In short, normative conflict is inherent in social structure and subcultures are a significant manifestation of this conflict.

Al Cohen's work is typically, within criminology and sociology, the beginning point for the discussion of subcultures and gangs in a theoretical context (Shoemaker, 1984; Reid, 1990; Lilly, Cullen, and Ball, 1989; Martin, Mutchnick, and Austin, 1990). Cohen focused on internal social conditions of subcultures, culminating in a strain theory dependent on social structural forces, as well as addressing the essence of subcultural ideas (Vold and Bernard, 1986). Cohen's repute as the founder of a distinct **subcultural theory** is based on his seminal work, *Delinquent Boys: The Culture of the Gang* (1955). In this revised version of his doctoral dissertation, Cohen develops a general theory of subcultures through a detailed annotation of delinquent gang formation and behavior through five categories: prevalence, origins, process, purpose, and problem (Martin et al., 1990). Prevalence refers to the uneven distribution of delinquency across class strata in society. Gang members from the bottom end of the socioeconomic scale shared difficulty conforming to the dominant society that largely rejects them, according to Cohen. The emergence of subcultures was an alternative for various persons to their mutual rejection, a collective response to a shared problem. Dismissal of societal standards and norms is a defining characteristic of a subculture and generates cultural conflict (Vetter and Silverman, 1980).

Due to social structural constraints largely beyond their control, lower-class youths experience a socialization process that devalues success in the classroom, deferred gratification, long-range planning, and the cultivation of etiquette mandatory for survival in the business and social arenas (Cohen, 1955). Cohen also observed that working-class juveniles generally did not participate in wholesome leisure activity, opting instead for activities typified by physical aggression, consequently stunting the development of intellectual and social skills valued in the mainstream culture. The overall learning experience of lower-class males leaves them ill prepared, says Cohen (1955, p. 129), to compete in a world gauged by a "middle-class measuring rod," a concept which captures the essence of cultural conflict. Deficiencies are most noticeable in the classroom, where working-class youth are frequently overshadowed and belittled by their middle-class counterparts. Turning to membership in a delinquent gang is but a normal adaptation to status frustration resulting from clashing cultures.

Whereas a correct chronological listing of subculture theories would move from Cohen (1955) to Walter B. Miller (1958), Richard Cloward and Lloyd Ohlin's subcultural theory of delinquency (1960) is naturally paired with Cohen, for it too has been classified a strain theory (Vold and Bernard, 1986). Like most criminological theory of this era, Ohlin and Cloward focused on delinquency and gangs (Williams and McShane, 1988). Not dissimilar from Cohen, their major work, *Delinquency and Opportunity: A Theory of Delinquent Gangs* (1960), is rooted in Merton's anomie and Sutherland's **differential association theories**.

Cloward and Ohlin further Cohen's hypothesis by offering a more detailed accounting of both subculture emergence and the nature of defiant out-groups via a typology of gangs. Typically considered "an opportunity theory" (Shoemaker, 1984; Bartol, 1980; Lilly et al., 1989), the basic assumptions of Cloward and Ohlin's theory are (1) limited and blocked economic aspirations generate frustration and negative self-esteem, and (2) these frustrations prompt youth to form gangs that vary in type. The ratio of conventional and criminal values to which a juvenile is consistently exposed accounts for the variation in gang types. Cloward and Ohlin's basic premise is that lower class teenagers realize they have minimal opportunity for future success by normative standards and thus resort to membership in one of three types of gangs, the "type" of gang actually representing similar, but distinct, delinquent subcultures.

Their typology of gangs is a hierarchy with the criminal gang at the top. Individuals reacting to frustration from failure may blame society rather than themselves. Part of this rationalization includes justifying successful illegal activity. Role models for lower-class youth are not the formally educated professionals that middle-class youth seek to emulate, but rather opportunistic hustlers and criminals in their immediate environment. This ecological influence (Shaw and McKay, 1942) suggests children learn that crime is an attractive option in economically depressed environments.

Cloward and Ohlin note that not all have the skills and composure to integrate into the criminal gang, which screens potential members for certain abilities and willingness to conform to a code of values necessary to the unit's success. Mandatory skills include self-control, demonstrated solidarity to the group, and desire to cultivate one's criminal ability (Bartol, 1980, pp. 98–99). The criminal gang revolves around stealing in a social context, the deviant act itself serving to positively reinforce the mutual co-dependence between the juvenile and the gang.

Because some strained youth are precluded from gangs that primarily steal, they congregate around violent behavior. This type of subgroup is called a "conflict gang" (Cloward and Ohlin, 1960) and is often the result of an absence of adult role models that are involved in utilitarian criminal behavior. Violent behavior, such as fighting, arson, and serious vandalism, are attributable to a sociological factor, absence of social control. A lack of interest by adults in the future success or failure of their sons and other young males in the neighborhood symbolizes rejection, the adaptation to which is "exploration of nonconformist alternatives" (Cloward and Ohlin, 1960, p. 86). While all three gang types emerge in lower socioeconomic neighborhoods, the particular form they assume is related to the degree of organization of both licit and illicit activity in an area.

Cloward and Ohlin also observed that some youth were neither violent nor successful in criminal endeavors and "retreat" into a third variety of gang characterized by drug use (Cloward and Ohlin, 1960, p. 183). Members of this kind of comparatively unorganized gang turn to drugs as an escape from status frustration. Although Cloward and Ohlin framed a theory that is more descriptive than Cohen's, it has been criticized for its unnaturalistic rigidity (Empey, 1982, p. 250; Lilly et al., 1989). Gang members do not realistically choose between theft, vandalism, or drug use through a conscious affiliation with gang types. Instead, any one of the gang types may engage in all or a combination of these behaviors. In sum, Cloward and Ohlin followed a strain tradition viewing society as a constraining mechanism that prompted lower-class juveniles to respond by forming gangs. The type of gang a frustrated youth joins, in this view, is dependent on the opportunity structure of a neighborhood and the mixture of criminal and law-abiding values held by adult role models.

Unlike the delinquency theories of Cohen and Cloward and Ohlin, Walter B. Miller envisioned a pure cultural theory explaining gang delinquency. His theory, presented in an article titled "Lower Class Culture as a Generating Milieu of Gang Delinquency" (1958), argued the existence of a distinct and observable lower-class culture. Whereas the middle class has values, the lower class has defining "focal concerns." They are trouble, toughness, smartness, excitement, fate, and autonomy. These concerns advocate the formation of street corner gangs, while undermining the positive reinforcement needed for the development of conventional values. Smartness, for example, warrants respect in the lower-class culture and refers to the ability to "con" someone in real-life situations. This skill contrasts with formal knowledge that is relatively inapplicable and often resented in poorer areas. The notion of fate discourages the work ethic and minimizes hope for self-improvement. Deviance is normal and to be expected in lower-class cultures because the focal concerns make conformity to criminal behavior as natural as acceptance of conventional mores for the middle class. Miller (1958, p. 167) observes that juveniles accepting a preponderance of these "cultural practices which comprise essential elements of the total life pattern of lower class culture automatically violate legal norms."

Miller's theory is an explanation of delinquency situated in depressed inner cities, wherein the majority of households are headed by females. Evaluation of the theory has centered around two significant criticisms. First, some of the focal concerns contended to be exclusive to the lower class are also observable in the middle class (Shoemaker, 1984). A second and more controversial issue concerns the use of race rather than class in assessing the relationship between delinquency, matriarchal households, and an exaggerated sense of masculinity associated with physical aggression (Berger and Simon, 1974; Moynihan, 1967). Unfortunately, a focus on blacks and the inseparable issue of atypical family structure moves discussion away from the veracity of a lower-class value system to differences in racial groups. It is surprising that critics neglect the possible benefits of a comparative analysis between urban and rural lower classes, which might highlight obvious differences and similarities. While it is probable that both groups share similar focal concerns due to alienation stemming from economic and social disadvantage, it is also likely that family structure among the rural poor is traditional (Duncan, 1992). Such a comparison may produce significant ramifications for Miller's theory that rests heavily on the absence of positive male role models.

The impact of the theories of Cohen, Cloward and Ohlin, and Miller were significant in two respects. First, they developed a general subcultural theory around what was perceived to be a timely issue. Second, the early studies as a whole focused on what was then a novel problem, the emergence of gangs. Gangs in the future were to be defined as delinquent and subcultures considered inherently deviant. Moreover, subculture became a major concept in sociology, a convenient comparative device for highlighting normative standards.

Subculture theories dominated criminological thought during the 1950s and 1960s. In stressing that deviant behavior was more or less normal for those within the subculture, several theorists built upon the initial efforts of Cohen (1955), Miller (1958), Cloward and Ohlin (1960), and Wolfgang and Ferracuti (1967). Systematic descriptions of the generating processes and patterns of delinquency, often in a gang context, became standard criminological practice (Bordua, 1961; Arnold, 1965; Kobrin, Puntil, and Peluso, 1967). Gangs, with their symbolic and collective features, epitomized a social problem of severe proportions: juvenile delinquency. Rebellious youth, associated with the emergence of the rock and roll era and aided by the appearance of automobiles into daily life, presented a new, visible threat to authority. Policing gangs was equated with addressing a larger issue and funding was available for social science attention to the problem. Major studies thus focused on the gang, built upon subcultural explanations of delinquency. In short, the rise of the subculture perspective was aided by the circumstances of social transition, a point that also explains, in part, its decline.

By the 1960s a number of interrelated social movements (including the civil rights crusade, anti–Vietnam War protest, and the counterculture) were under way. In varying degrees they expressed the same themes: distrust and defiance of authority which was perceived to be used by elite factions to create and maintain a social hierarchy, exploitation of crime and delinquency, and opposition to the oppressiveness of the criminal justice system. As bandwagon shifts to the political left transpired, **labeling theory** soon replaced subcultural explanations as the leading theory (Bookin-Weiner and Horowitz, 1983). The main thrust of labeling theory is that crime and delinquency are definitions and labels assigned to persons and events by operatives of the criminal justice system. Explaining crime and delinquency, from this perspective then, is explaining the way in which the labeling process works, and how it singles out certain people for labeling and not others. In its more extreme formulations, labeling theory was not concerned with the explanation of the behavior we call crime and delinquency because criminals and delinquents were not assumed to differ very much in their behavior from other people. Rather, the real difference is said to be the degree of vulnerability to the labeling activities of the criminal justice system.

During this period of interest in labeling, theoretically oriented research on the relationship between crime and culture languished but did not disappear. More moderate versions of labeling theory propelled some research (e.g., research on gang behavior and emphasis on the role of official processing and labeling in the development of that behavior), but the leading cause of crime and delinquency was considered the criminal justice system itself (Werthman, 1967; Armstrong and Wilson, 1973). Specifically, criminal and delinquent behavior was portrayed as a rational and justified response to social inequality and class oppression (Bookin, 1980).

Much of the contemporary literature of the period (1970s), not just on gangs but on social problems generally, was not only indifferent to subculture theory but was actively opposed to it. This literature included works such as Chambliss's *The Saints and the Roughnecks* (1973) that emphasized a conflict perspective which viewed the subculture theories as conservative. Social control was deemed reactionary because crime and delinquency were considered direct, reasonable, and even justifiable adaptations to injustice.

The rise of social control theory (e.g., Hirschi, 1969) did not seriously factor into the subculture perspective either, though seemingly well suited to do so (Bookin-Weiner and Horowitz, 1983; Vold and Bernard, 1986). The central elements of attachment to others, degrees of commitment to conventionality, daily routine, and belief in a moral order speak to why subcultures exist and have implications for criminal behavior therein. Ensuing research interests moved toward macro-level determinants of crime and further away from culture and group behavior. Consequently, subcultures were largely ignored until the mid-1980s when they were connected with gang-related drug and violence problems (Curry and Spergel, 1988).

While historical developments set into motion a chain of events that moved criminological theorizing away from the subculture, the theory was further marred by paradigmatic shifts in social science **research methods**. The rise of positivism delivered subculture theory a would-be deathblow. There was suddenly a disjuncture between the subculture approach and the new preferred theoretical-methodological symmetry: variable assignment, measurement, and analysis congruent with causality as established by levels of statistical correlation. Critics of subculture theory (e.g., Kistuse and Dietrick, 1959; Ball-Rokeach, 1973; Kornhauser, 1978) focused on the growing belief that acceptable science must subscribe to particular precepts that subculture explanations did not meet. The theory could not, via a variable analysis format, be adequately tested. Beyond the operationalization problems thwarting concept measurement, there was the more fundamental restraint of tautological reasoning. It was argued that there was unclear separation of cause and effect. Did the subculture, as an independent variable, generate crime, the dependent variable, or vice versa? For many, the inability to answer this question satisfactorily rendered the theory obsolete.

References/Suggested Readings: Arnold, W.R. 1965. The Concept of the Gang. *Sociological Quarterly,* 7, 59–75; Armstrong, G., and Wilson, M. 1973. City Politics and Deviance Amplification. In I. Taylor and L. Taylor (eds.), *Politics and Deviance.* New York: Penguin Books; Ball-Rokeach, S.J. 1973. Values and Violence: A Test of the Subculture of Violence Thesis. *American Sociological Review* 38, 736–749; Bartol, C.R. 1980. *Criminal Behavior: A Psychosocial Approach.* Englewood Cliffs, NJ: Prentice Hall; Berger, A.S., and Simon, W. 1974. Black Families and the Moynihan Report: A Research Evaluation. *Social Problems,* 22, 145–161; Bookin, H. 1980. "The Gangs That Didn't Go Straight." Presentation to the Society for the Study of Social Problems, New York; Bookin-Weiner, H., and Horowitz. 1983. The End of the Youth Gang: Fad or Fact? *Criminology,* 21, 585–602; Bordua, D.J. 1961. Delinquent Subcultures: Sociological Interpretations of Gang Delinquency. *Annals of the American Academy of Social Science,* 338, 119–136; Chambliss, W.J. 1973. The Saints and the Roughnecks. *Society,* 11 (1), 24–31; Cloward, R.A., and Ohlin, L.E. 1960. *Delinquency and Opportunity: A Theory of Delinquent Gangs.* Glencoe, IL: Free Press; Cohen, A. 1955. *Delinquent Boys.* Glencoe, IL: Free Press; Curry, D.G., and Spergel, I.A. 1988. Gang Homicide, Delinquency and Community. *Criminology,* 26 (3), 381–406; Duncan, C. 1992. *Rural Poverty in America.* New York: Auburn House; Empey, L. 1982. *American Delinquency: Its Meaning and Construction.* Homewood, IL: Dorsey; Hirschi, T. 1969. *Causes of Delinquency.* Berkeley: University of California Press; Kitsuse, J., and Dietrick, D.C. 1959. Delinquent Boys: A Critique. *American Sociological Review,* 24, 208–215; Kobrin, S., Puntil, J., and Peluso, E. 1967. Criteria of Status among Street Groups. *Journal of Research in Crime and Delinquency,* 4 (1), 98–118; Kornhouser, R.R. 1978. *Social Sources of Delinquency.* Chicago: University of Chicago Press; Lilly, R.J., Cullen, F.T., and Ball, R.A. 1989. *Criminological Theory: Context and Consequences.* Newbury Park, CA: Sage; Lynch, M.J., and Groves, W.B. 1986. *A Primer in Radical Criminology.* New York: Harrow and Heston; Martin, Randy, Mutchnick, R.J., and Austin, W.T. 1990. *Criminological Thought: Pioneers Past and Present.* New York: Macmillan; Miller, W.B. 1958. Lower Class Culture as a Generating Milieu of Gang Delinquency. *Journal of Social Issues,* 14, 5–19; Moynihan, D.P. 1967. *The Negro Family: The Case for National Action.* Washington, DC: U.S. Government Printing Office; Reid, S.T. 1990. *Crime and Criminology.* Fort Worth, TX: Holt, Rinehart, and Winston; Shaw, C.R., and McKay, H.D. 1942. *Juvenile Delinquency and Urban Areas.* Chicago: University of Chicago Press; Shoemaker, D.J. 1984. *Theories of Delinquency: An Examination of Explanations of Delinquent Behavior.* New York: Oxford University Press; Vetter, H.J., & Silverman, I.J. 1978. *The Nature of Crime.* Philadelphia: W.B. Saunders; Vold, G.B., and Bernard, T.J. 1986. *Theoretical Criminology* (3rd ed.). New York: Oxford University Press; Werthman, C. 1967. The Function of Social Definitions in the Development of Delinquent Careers. In P.G. Garabedian and D.C. Gibbons (eds.), *Becoming Delinquent: Young Offenders and the Correctional Process.* Chicago: Aldine; Williams, F.P. III, and McShane, M.D. 1988. *Criminological Theory.* Englewood Cliffs, NJ: Prentice Hall; Wolfgang, M. E., and Ferracuti F. 1967. *The Subculture of Violence: Towards an Integrated Theory in Criminology.* London: Tavistock.

J. MITCHELL MILLER

CRIPS. The Crips are a street organization founded in 1969 by Raymond Lee Washington in the south central area of Los Angeles, California. According to local folklore, the name comes from the combination of the word *crib* and the acronym R.I.P. (Rest In Peace) that denotes the intergenerational nature of the gang and membership from birth to death (Sloan, 2005). Other important Crip figures include **Stanley Tookie Williams,** founder of the West Side Crips, Michael Concepcion, and Jamel Barnes. The FBI and other law enforcement agencies describe the Crips as the largest, most violent, and most notorious gang in the history of the United States. The Crips began as an urban phenomenon, yet, there are reports that the gang has spread to most of the major cities in the United States and that Crips gangs are emerging in some suburban areas in the United States and in cities around the world.

Organizational Structure

Because of the lack of codified rules and regulations, the Crips structure is very flexible and malleable. The Crips gang has evolved from a small gang into a loose network of sets resembling a federation of independent units each one with similar but unique organizational structures. Crip sets create alliances with one another in order to fight rival gangs such as their archenemies the **Bloods** and other **Chicano** and Latino gangs. Ironically, the lack of a centralized governing structure that could implement rules and regulations among all Crips gangs foments inter-set warfare. One of the longest and most violent Crip-to-Crip rivalries is that between the 83 Eight Trays and the Rolling 60s. According to Kody Scott, a former member of the Eight Trays Crips, this war cost more human life to both of these sides than their war against any Blood or Chicano sets (Shakur, 1994).

The Crips gangs are territorial and claim specific geographical areas or 'hoods. The Crips actively recruit African American youngsters from their neighborhoods and schools under their control. They may "jump in" individuals or absorb entire groups of young crews or cliques. Similar to Chicano gangs, the Crips gangs have shown a form of intergenerational reproduction—that is, the sons and daughters of some Crips members have followed the steps of their parents or older brothers by joining the gang.

The social reproduction of the Crips occurs through the process of cultural dissemination and structural proliferation. Cultural dissemination refers to the adoption of Crips subcultural values by "wannabe" gang members. Youngsters adapt the Crip walk, regalia (blue bandana, blue-laced British Knights tennis shoes, blue army belt) and slang or Crip talk (i.e., using the word *Cuzz* to refer to each other) to represent their neighborhoods. Eventually, wannabes either stop imitating the gang culture, join adjacent sets, or start a set of their own. Movies such as *Colors, Menace II Society, C-Walk, Redemption, Boyz in the Hood,* and *Ricochet* have disseminated a stereotypical view of gangs into areas outside the city of Los Angeles and have contributed to the emerging of Crips gangs in other parts of the United States. Gangsa rap has also served as a vehicle to spread gang culture into mainstream society. Snoop Dogg is one of the most well-known Crip artists around the world. His music, manners, and way of dressing have deeply influenced modern youth culture. More recently, the Internet has provided a forum from which gang members can disseminate their message. In cyberspaces such as MySpace and YouTube, one can find hundreds of Web pages with information about the Crips gang cultural practices. Many youth in the United States and around the world have adapted some aspects of the Crip culture without even being aware of it.

Structural proliferation occurs when members of the gang expand their operation to adjacent neighborhoods by opening a gang franchise. The new franchise is usually comprised of members of the original set. The franchise may retain the name of the original set but add a distinctive identifier such as the name of a geographical location. For example, the Rollin 40s and Rollin 90s Crips gangs are thought to be franchises of the Rollin 60s Crips. Structural proliferation was one of the main practices during the 1980s when L.A. gangs moved into the drug dealing business. In order to expand their territory, Crips gangs often fought for control of apartment buildings and housing projects. Maintaining control of the newly acquired territory required the implementation of a new set or the establishment of a franchise that owned alliance to the original set. However, structural proliferation has not always occurred peacefully; when disgruntled members left the organization and established their own set, they often took an antagonistic position against their mother set.

A second form of structural proliferation occurs through a process of set splitting driven by intergenerational conflict. As younger members of the gang begin to socialize together, they create new age-graded set and develop a group identity independent of the original set; eventually, the new set secedes either peacefully or violently from the original set. In fact, the Crips started as a Young Gangster (YG) set from the Avenues Gang taking the name of Baby Avenues and eventually changing their name to Avenues Cribs and eventually to Crips.

The internal organizational structure may differ from set to set but, for the most part, the sets are organized horizontally. A horizontal structure allows the group members to make decisions independently while at the same time recognizing leadership roles within the group. This type of structure also allows for a more egalitarian relationship among members of a same age-graded level. Members rotate different roles according to needs and skills.

Origins

There are three main narratives explaining the origins of the Crips. The first narrative places the origins of this gang in the context of institutional racial violence encountered by southern blacks moving into the city of Los Angeles. A second narrative places the origin of the Crips within a political context and explains its emergence as a product of the political vacuum created by the undermining of political community based organizations such as the Black Panthers and the United Slaves. The third narrative simply describes the Crips as a group of hoodlums and drug dealers who came together to victimize their own communities. The existence of multiple narratives is perhaps a product of both the relatively long historical existence of the gang and of the loose nature of the Crips' structure.

Institutional Racial Violence

The Crips emerged in an era when blacks in Los Angeles experienced a heightened economic dislocation and social isolation that resulted in the emergence of the American black hyper-ghetto (Massey and Denton, 1993; Wacquant, 2001). In the 1950s and 1960s, when an increasing number of blacks moved to L.A. to occupy the booming manufacturing jobs, white residents received them with hostility and distrust. Whites often used violence to prevent them from moving into their neighborhoods and schools. As more black families moved to L.A., white families began to move out of these areas and blacks became concentrated in the South Central area of the city. In 1965, many manufacturing industries moved to Latin America in order to take advantage of cheap labor and cheap production cost offered by newly implemented Border Industrialization Program. During the 1970s as the border cities experienced an economic boom, U.S. inner cities such as South Central experienced a rapid and drastic economic decline. As work disappeared, many of these communities experienced the beginnings of social decay and extreme social isolation from mainstream America (Wilson, 1987; Davis, 1992; Esteva Martínez, 2003).

According to Mike Davis (1992), in the 1950s black youth created gangs such as the Businessman, Slausons, Gladiators, and Watts as a defensive mechanism against violence perpetrated by white youth gangs. However, by the late 1960s and early 1970s, as white residents began moving out of the inner city and into the suburbs, groups such as the Black Panthers, CORE, the Nation of Islam, and the United Slaves began recruiting gang members into their ranks. Black youth learned the ideology and organizing strategies used by community-based organizations and implemented them within their own sets.

Political Mobilization

Ex–Black Panther member Mumia Abu-Jamal traces the origins of the Crips to a community organization named Community Relations for an Independent People. This organization espoused the ideas of self-determination, black nationalism, and community activism characteristic of many black organizations from the 1960s. The main activities of the community space included cultural affirmation and group socialization (Abu-Jamal, 2005). However, police and government agencies truncated the early political roots of the Crips when they declared war against black political activists of this era. Black political leaders were either imprisoned or assassinated, leaving a social and political vacuum in these neighborhoods.

The Crips then developed in an era in which the black community experienced extreme social, political, and economic marginalization. Although there were several attempts to redirect them toward political and community oriented goals, the new generation of Crip members became lost in a vicious circle of endless violence for street supremacy. Crips began victimizing other black youth and forcing them to join.

The victimization of other black youth led to the emergence of the Bloods gang in the early 1970s. The crack epidemic as well as the ready availability of semi-automatic weapons exacerbated the cycle, destroying the lives of hundreds of youth and adults. It also laid the basis for the self-hatred that permeated the streets of South Central.

Throughout the history of the Crips, street activists have attempted to redirect the organization to their political roots. Black Panther member Michael Zinzun R.I.P. and Piru member Twilight Bay from the Coalition Against Police Abuse and the Community In Support of the Gang Truce have worked with gang members to resurrect their political roots. Today in Los Angeles, Crip Young Gangsters have began to recognize and celebrate these roots by redefining the word Crips as (1) Community Revolution In Progress, (2) Community Resources for an Independent People, (3) Community Reform In Progress, (4) Continuing Revolution In Progress, and (5) Clandestine Revolutionary International Party.

References/Suggested Readings: Abu-Jamal, M. 2005. Keepin' It Gangsta? Prison Radio, a Project of the Redwood Justice Fund; Davis, M. 1992. *City of Quartz: Excavating the Future in Los Angeles.* New York: Vintage Books; Esteva Martínez, J.F. 2003. Urban Street Activists: Gang and Community Efforts to Bring Justice to Los Angeles Neighborhoods. In L. Kontos, D.C. Brotherton, and L. Barrios (eds.), *Gangs and Society: Alternative Perspectives.* New York, Columbia University Press; Massey, D.S., and Denton, N.A. 1993. *American Apartheid: Segregation and the Making of the Underclass.* Cambridge, MA: Harvard University Press; Shakur, S. 1994. *Monster: The Autobiography of an L.A. Gang Member.* London: Pan; Sloan, C.B. 2005. *Bastards of the Party.* New York: HBO; Wacquant, L. 2001. Deadly Symbiosis. *Punishment and Society,* 3 (1), 95–134; Wilson, W.J. 1987. *The Truly Disadvantaged: The Inner City, the Underclass, and Public Policy.* Chicago: University of Chicago Press.

JUAN FRANCISCO ESTEVA MARTÍNEZ AND
MARCOS ANTONIO RAMOS

D

DIFFERENTIAL ASSOCIATION THEORY. Differential association is the most well known of a number of learning theories of crime. The point of differential association theory is to explain the processes by which individual learn to behavior in contradiction of the law. According to Edwin Sutherland (1947) the theory of differential association is based upon nine postulates:

1. Criminal behavior is learned.
2. Criminal behavior is learned in interaction with others persons in a process of communication.
3. The principal part of the learning of criminal behavior occurs within intimate personal groups.
4. When criminal behavior is learned, the learning includes techniques of committing the crime, which are sometimes very complicated, sometimes simple and the specific direction of motives, drives, rationalizations, and attitudes.
5. The specific direction of motives and drives is learned from definitions of the legal codes as favorable or unfavorable.
6. A person becomes delinquent because of an excess of definitions favorable to violation of law over definitions unfavorable to violation of the law.
7. Differential associations may vary in frequency, duration, priority, and intensity.
8. The process of learning criminal behavior by association with criminal and anti-criminal patterns involves all of the mechanisms that are involved in any other learning.
9. While criminal behavior is an expression of general needs and values, it is not explained by those general needs and values, since noncriminal behavior is an expression of the same needs and values.

Sutherland was aware of the importance of **social disorganization** in the structural context of crime, but was most interested in the processes of social learning that make the release of criminality more likely. He said that individuals vary in terms of the interactions they have with those who have definitions favorable to violation of the law, so not all those who have interaction with delinquent peers are likely to become criminal. The key factor is variation in the frequency, duration, priority, and intensity of contacts with criminal peers. Therefore, constant meaningful interaction with criminal peers over a long period of time and the importance placed on deviant values by the actor are the key to the release of criminality in differential association theory. Walter Miller's idea of "focal concerns," issues that dominate the thinking of lower-class youth who are trying to negotiate their way in society, and David Matza's idea of neutralizations, techniques learned by criminals to lessen guilt and rationalize crime, are related to the idea of differential association. Differential association theory has been criticized as being difficult to test empirically and fails to appreciate the importance of media in criminal behavior.

References/Suggested Readings: Matza, D. 1964. *Delinquency and Drift*. New York: Wiley; Miller, W. n.d. Lower Class Culture as a Generating Milieu of Gang Delinquency. *Journal of Social Issues,* 14, 5–19; Sutherland, E. 1947. *Principles of Criminology*. Philadelphia: Lippincott.

ALBERT DICHIARA

F

FOOTBALL HOOLIGANS. Supporter violence at football (soccer) matches can be traced back to the end of the nineteenth century, when groups of supporters began the practice of attacking rival supporters, players and referees (Dunning, Murphy, and Williams, 1988). Although football violence took place often throughout the twentieth century, it did not receive much attention until the 1970s, when it appeared more frequent and intense. In 1975 football violence reached a high point in Great Britain, and Manchester United and Chelsea both gained international reputations for violence (Van Limbergen and Walgraven, 1988). During this same period, football violence appeared to spread throughout Europe (Haley and Johnston, n.d.; Van der Vliet, 2003). Europa-Cup games, in which English teams participate, are the sites of the biggest trouble (Van der Vliet, 2003). Supporter violence escalated during the 1980s, with the Heysel stadium drama in Belgium (May 29, 1985), when English football hooligans rioted during a Europa-Cup final between Juventus and Liverpool, resulting in the deaths of 39 persons and 150 injured (Poutvaara and Priks, 2005; Van der Vliet, 2003). Consequently, English clubs were not allowed to compete in European competitions until 1990 (Liverpool not until 1991).

Football Hooliganism

There exist different theories about the origin of the word "hooligan." The most popular theory is that the term originated sometime in the nineteenth century from an Irish immigrant family in London called "Hooligan" that terrorized the "East End" (Williams and Wagg, 1991). The term was quickly associated with destructive criminal behavior and became associated with "football" decades later (Haley and Johnston, n.d.).

The term "football hooliganism" is now used to describe the disorderly behavior of supporters of professional football clubs and national teams, frequently evidenced before, during, and after football matches (Haley and Johnston, n.d.). The (criminal) acts of football hooligans can range from throwing stones at the police (Van der

Vliet, 2003), trashing public transportation and the (area surrounding the) stadium (Bogaerts, Spapens, and Bruinsma, 2003), to the killing of a fan from a rival club. This happened in the Netherlands in Beverwijk on March 23, 1997, when a group of 450 Feyenoord and Ajax supporters prearranged a meeting to fight. One supporter was stabbed and died (see Van der Vliet, 2003). Some hooliganism takes place between organized gangs ("firms") for whom the violence appears to be more important than the game itself; whereas other hooliganism breaks out spontaneously in connection with incidents in the match (Elsea, 2003). Yet, it rarely involves random violent acts of unorganized groups. Hooligans aim their attacks mostly at rival hooligan "gangs," although sometimes rival groups come together to form a "new," temporary, hooligan group, for example, when supporting the national team abroad to battle hooligans from other countries. Once back in their home country, though, this group splits up again into rival hooligan groups (Haley and Johnston, n.d.).

Due to effective measures taken by law enforcement and soccer authorities, the violence in and around the stadiums has decreased in recent years. However, this has caused a displacement of confrontations and, as a consequence, conflicts not only take place on football days, but on other days as well without the need of a rival group being present (Van der Vliet, 2003). The police, security guards, and displays of a rival club (for example the showing of a documentary of a rival club in a theater) can become catalysts for violent interactions (CIV, 2001).

The Hooligan Subculture

Football hooliganism can be considered a subculture (Van der Vliet, 2003), which can be witnessed not only at the stadium but also outside of it (De Vries, 1998). Whoever is part of the subculture is expected to help the others at all times. Supporters are ostensibly connected to each other through devotion to their club and to their need for sensation and excitement. This subculture may be considered a response to the boredom of daily life, a way of overcoming fears, providing brotherhood, and a "kick" (Van der Vliet, 2003). Hooligans alone share close friendship ties and both brotherhood and solidarity are considered important (Van der Torre and Spaaij, 2003). Within the subculture, certain norms, values, and rules exist (Van der Torre and Spaaij, 2003; Van der Vliet, 2003) and hard-core hooligans establish their own territory at stadiums and make sure that through intimidation and violence, whoever sits there abides by their norms (Van der Torre and Spaaij, 2003). The consumption of alcohol and drugs (mostly soft drugs, but also cocaine and ecstasy) before and during matches is a norm of the subculture (Van der Torre and Spaaij, 2003; Van der Vliet, 2003).

Another way to express the hooligan subculture is through *clothing*. The intention is to make a visual distinction between regular supporters and real hooligans (Van der Vliet, 2003). In the late 1970s and early 1980s, many U.K. hooligans started to wear expensive European designer clothing, like Abercrombie and Fitch, Burberry, Lacoste, and Stone Island. Their intention was to avoid attracting the attention of the police. This clothing style culture became known as "casual" and the ones wearing it as "the Casuals."

Football hooligans have their own brand of humor, which they display by making fun of the rival club and hooligans, especially with chants (Van der Torre and Spaaij, 2003). Football chants are repetitively sung by the crowd at matches. In Europe and Latin America, it is normal for supporters to shout at players, rivals, and referees. The lyrics of popular songs are changed so as to glorify a particular football team.

The songs are intended not only to encourage favored teams but also to insult rivals. The lyrics are usually vulgar and antagonistic. They generally contribute to the atmosphere and are an important part of the football culture.

Organization

Hooligans display many "gang characteristics" (Junger-Tas, 1985). "In terms of organized violence between hooligan 'gangs,' feelings of community, tribalism and sheer enjoyment of being involved in football disorder" are clearly present (www.liv.ac.uk/footballindustry/hooligan.html). Hooligan groups, however, display a much looser and more diffuse structure (Junger-Tas, 1985). The groups are dynamic, and structure and composition change regularly (Ferweda, Beke, and Van Wijk, 1998).

There exist, in fact, different kinds of hooligan groups: hard-core, opportunists, wannabes, firms, and ultras (Van der Vliet, 2003). The *hard core* is a little group of approximately ten people, mostly older males, with strong leadership. At most clubs there is not only one hard core but multiple ones (see Bogaerts, Spapens, & Bruinsma, 2003). This type has been active in the organization of riots. Opportunists and wannabes provide cover for the criminal activities of the hard core. There are many more *opportunists* than hard-core members. They are mostly males between the age of fifteen and twenty-five. They gain status through the association and appear willing to go to great lengths to achieve this. They are, indeed, mostly at the frontlines of conflicts. *Wannabe* groups have no discernible structure, and their adherents briefly seek sensation and excitement, and football is the place to find it. It's debatable whether they deserve the title of "hooligan." They seldom commit serious offenses, and most of their activities are limited to taunting the supporters of the rival club (Bogaerts et al., 2003). Football *firms* are organized gangs (mostly supporting a football club) that engage in fights with rival firms (firms supporting other clubs). To make it hard for the police to interrupt, fights usually take place on sites far away from the football grounds. Some football firms are occasionally linked with extreme right-wing political groups, especially in Southern and Eastern Europe. *Ultras* are similar to firms. These groups started in Italy, where Italian fans created a fanatical brand of football supporters, now a major force in the Italian game and other European countries as well.

Football Hooligans

Although football hooligans are a heterogeneous group, most, in fact, are males between the age of twelve and thirty, native, and lower class (Van der Vliet, 2003). Almost all of the hard-core hooligans have been detained multiple times for football violence, for violent , and for traffic offenses. A great number of the older ones have boring and frustrating jobs. Most hooligans have attained only a low level of education and sometimes one or both of their parents have been hooligans. Many members of the hard core grow up in a social environment (family, school, neighborhood) where aggression is already a part of daily life. They typically possess a lot of "street knowledge" and know how to "survive." But being a hooligan gives them added status, arguably more than they could achieve at school or in other domains (Van der Torre and Spaaij, 2003).

References/Suggested Readings: Bogaerts, S., Spapens, A.C. and Bruinsma, M.Y. 2003. *De bal of de man? Profielen van verdachten van voetbal gerelateerde geweldscriminaliteit.* Tilburg: IVA Tilburg; Centraal Informatiepunt Voetbalvandalisme (CIV). 2001. *Jaarverslag voetbalseizoen 2000/2001.* Utrecht; Dunning, E.G., Murphy, P.J., and Williams, J.M. 1988. *The Roots* *of Football Hooliganism: A Historical and Sociological Study.* London: Routledge; Elsea, M. 2003. Football Hooliganism. *Bulletin of the International Society for Research on Aggression,* 25 (2), 24–26; Ferwerda, H., Beke, B, and Wijk, A., Van. 1998. *Kwaliteit op en rondom het voetbalveld; naar een integrale aanpak van onveiligheidsproblemen.* Arnhem, Advies- en Onderzoeksgroep Beke; Haley, A.J. and Johnston, B.S. *Menaces to Management: A Developmental View of British Soccer Hooligans, 1961–1986.* Available online at www .thesportjournal.org/vol1no1/menaces.htm; Junger-Tas, J. 1985. De theorie van sociale controle of sociale binding. *Tijdschrift voor de criminologie,* 27, 242–265; Limbergen, K. Van, and Walgrave, L. 1988. *Sides, Fans en Hooligans; voetbalvandalisme: feiten, achtergronden en aanpak.* Leuven; Poutvaara, P., and Priks, M. 2005. *Hooligans.* Available online at www .diw.de/english; Torre, E.J. Van Der, and Spaaij, R.F.J. 2003. Hooligan-aanwas: patronen en preventie. *Tijdschrift voor de politie,* 64 (4), 29–33; Torre, E.J. Van Der, and Spaaij, R.F.J. 2003. Harde kern hooligans: verder dan geweld *Tijdschrift voor de politie,* 64 (7/8), 28–33; Vliet, L.L. van der. 2003. *De kick is niet te beschrijven: Een onderzoek naar de achtergronden en kenmerken van de nieuwe aanwas risicosupporters en hoe sociaalpreventief op deze groep kan worden ingespeeld.* Unpublished thesis; Vries, H.de. 1998. Verklaringen van voetbalvandalisme. *Tijdschrift voor de politie,* 60 (5), 19–24; Williams, J., and Wagg, S. 1991. *British Football and Social Change: Getting into Europe.* Leicester: Leicester University Press.

CHABELI MIRALLES SUEIRO

FRENCH GANGS. In France, "street subcultures" have a history that can be traced back to the 1960s with the "black jackets" (*blousons noirs*), and the hooligans of the 1970s (*loubards*). These groups had common features such as collective forms of sociability, language, and attitude; anti-social tendencies reflected in intra-group and inter-group conflicts (i.e., against rival groups called *bastons* and the police); acts of delinquency including vandalism and robbery; and general status offenses including truancy; the consumption of beer and drugs; listening to rock music; and riding motorcycles. Such characteristics of these subcultures were associated with male virility, which allowed the loubards, for example, to acquire sufficient symbolic capital to create a (dis)valued social identity. The culture milieu of these groups was a place where one learned virile behavior and prepared oneself for factory work. The membership in such groups was temporary and ended when the members started work, did their military service, or got married. The members' physical strength was transformed into the ability to labor and the culture of the street was replaced by the culture of the factory.

In the late 1980s, other organized groups of youths emerged, some of which were based on "ethnicity." These groups were vehicles for black males (such as the Vicious Sharks, *Requins Vicieux,* or the Black Dragons) to become involved in different delinquent activities, fights against other rival groups, and to become engaged in hiphop. Such groups, however, were an ephemeral phenomenon inspired by American gangs and were nothing compared to the latter, lacking their deep historical origins and level of organizational sophistication.

More recently, the Tribe KA (*Tribu KA*—K for Kemite the black people, and A for Aton the Egyptian god) was created in 2004 by Kémi Séba, a young man of twenty-five years of age, who is the *fara* (leader) of the group. He is French of Beninese descent and was a member of the Nation of Islam in Paris. Tribu KA is a militant group made up of young black males whose ideology is based on Kemitism and Afrocentrism, and whose membership is only open to blacks. This group claims the right to defend "every single black person" who is assaulted on the basis of his or her skin color.

They recently descended on neighborhoods where black people were attacked or injured to show their presence and to try to deter people from such assaults. They have been accused of anti-Semitism after they descended on a predominantly Jewish neighborhood in Paris to do battle with activists of two far right Zionist groups of defense, the *Ligue de Défense Juive* (the French branch of the American Jewish Defense League considered as a terrorist organization by Israel and the United States but not by France) and the *Bétar*. The Ministry of the Interior has asked the President to disband the Tribu KA for inciting racial hatred. They are under the surveillance of the antiterrorist section of the police who have closed its website and arrested its leader on June 4, 2006, and then released.

However, this type of group with a clearly defined political and religious ideology is marginal in the suburbs of France's main metropolises. The group or *bande* is more a social construction used to describe youths who form discernible groups and who are perceived as aggressive or menacing. In response, such groups often avoid congregating in public spaces in the housing projects (*cités*) and many of them leave these cités entirely. The "youths from these cités" therefore are very diverse. Some of them are first- or second-generation immigrant males whose families come from the former French colonies of North Africa and the sub-Sahara, while others are native French with some Italian or Portuguese roots. The females in the cités belong to the private sphere and are much less present than the males. Some youths of the cités are less involved in the activities of such groups due to their possession of more economic/cultural capital. Some youths of the cités hang around in the street during the whole day while others stay for only a few hours. Often, the familial cell of these youths is in competition with the street. For example, youths who are under strong parental supervision spend more time at home with their parents, brothers, and sisters. Others are freer to be more involved in the street life and occupy the public spaces that counterbalance their material and symbolic deprivation. Many youths oscillate between all these possibilities.

The gathering of youths into a bande (the word is not really used by the youths themselves who instead are more likely to say "my buddies" or "guys from my cité") is an example of symbolic capital to which youths are looking for social recognition or "respect." With the growing number of youths from the cités there are different types of activities that require a range of skills, from drug dealing/consumption, sports, to hip-hop culture. Usually, the bande is organized on the basis of those skills. For instance, in Marseilles, the "Dog Brothers" is a bande made up of about ten teenagers who play soccer in the playground of the neighborhood (Sauvadet, 2006).

Due to the decomposition of working-class territory and cultural traditions as a result of de-industrialization starting in the 1970s, youths in the *banlieue* informally gathered across "ethnic lines" mainly to deal with distress and tediousness (*galère*) through leisure activities and sports, but also through marginalized/delinquent activities. There are no traditional "leaders"—the so-called elder brothers (*les grands frères*)—but instead "charismatic" agents (in a Weberian sense), i.e., young males who are respected, feared, and sometimes admired after winning fame and a bit of social honor by exceptional achievement especially in sports or in delinquent activities (*caïd*, big boss). Such youth are the legitimate embodiment of physical and symbolic authority and become paternalistic figures with an important degree of social capital. Nevertheless, the virile character of these bandes has become more and more infused by the desire for wealth, like luxurious cars or fancy clothes which all become valued as signs of social accomplishment and acknowledgment.

In a context of economic and social deprivation and disqualification, individual and collective strategies have developed as substitutes for the formal labor market and as a way to survive. Since the 1980s, drug dealing has increased, especially the trafficking of cannabis. Such activities are seen often as forms of social redistribution—which the (Welfare) State has had difficulty in providing to the working class. However, there is not an informal economy as often developed in the American ghetto. The French banlieue (suburb) does not become an "Americanized" ghetto mainly because it is not race-based but rather ethnically mixed. Furthermore, there is a lower unemployment rate, less spatial segregation, and social and public services are still present. Consequently, youths who are part of a quasi-professional informal economy constitute a minority (Jazouli, 1992). Still, there does exist a "parallel economy" or a micro-economy (*bizness* or *gouillema*, the slang for *magouille*, graft) which is based on the trade of stolen goods that are said to "have fallen off the truck" (*tombés du camion*). In comparison, a city like Marseilles is the exception. For here we see a territory with a long tradition of drug trafficking and the presence and organization of a professional criminal milieu (e.g., "the French connection") which provides youths from the cité with an opportunity structure, allowing them to graduate from delinquent activities to **organized crime** if they show appropriate skills.

Often, the youths from relegated neighborhoods have disvalued college degrees, when they have one, and go through periods of unemployment, precarious employment, and vocational training. These are "youths in perpetuity," i.e., unable to have a stable job, to gain autonomy from their parents, and to create a family. They therefore engage themselves in the "culture of the street." As a mode of socialization, transgression allows their integration to the peer group. A "deviant" act is a rite of initiation for the perpetrator and reinforces the cohesion and the borders of the group, and the opposition with rival bands strengthens its identity. Usually, the violent competition between youths from one housing project and another can be related to informal economic competition linked to the control over the local cannabis market. The violence is not necessarily an expression of anomie, for it also generates social relationships and networks based on attack and defense, assault and retaliation. The fact that youths collectively defend the peer group can be explained, at least partially, by the need for protection against social insecurity and the hardships they experience in everyday life.

Territorial identity of this kind can extend beyond the group to a wider urban territory—usually the project (cité)—and often to the mythical representation of this territory, but rarely to ethnicity. The identification with the marginalized neighborhood is a way of reversing the social and spatial stigma imposed on those urban spaces. It provides a substitute for the social milieu that becomes a new matrix of integration. The youths form informal peer groups without a formal hierarchy but a symbolic one (that often is denied because of the masculine rejection of submission) that is not very stable and quite porous. The socio-spatial segregation brings about a stigmatization of the marginalized and their decomposed urban territories, and their collective responses aim at reversing the stigma. It is an ambivalent place of production and reproduction of physical and symbolic violence, but also of resistance against domination and marginalization.

In these groups, an antagonistic logic emerges which appears in the form of challenging looks, insults, fights, or even "riots"—which occurred periodically, usually the result of the death of a youth perceived, rightly or wrongly, as a police blunder or instance of brutality. Since the ethics of the youths are based on the logic(s) of honor, a lot of youths feel solidarity toward the victim and expect apologies and/or punishment for those responsible. But when no regret is expressed or the perpetrators are found not guilty or when insult is added to injury, some youths from the cités express their rage through reprisal against the police who are perceived as the rival. At first sight, to burn cars or public buildings seems to be irrational and even absurd to "outsiders," since the cars are always those of their neighbors or acquaintances. However, those practices are inscribed by a general warlike logic in which a large amount of collateral damage is deemed acceptable. The decomposition of the family, school failure, and absence from the job market provide the setting in which these youth look for a protective and compensating alternative in the "street culture" that values physical strength, toughness, and virile values.

References/Suggested Readings: Dubet, François. 1987. *La galère: jeunes en survie*; Paris: Fayard; Jazouli, Adil. 1992. *Les années banlieues*. Paris: Éditions du Seuil; Lepoutre, David. 1997. *Coeur de banlieue. Codes, rites et langages*. Paris: Odile Jacob; Mauger, Gérard. 2003. *Le monde des bandes et ses transformations. Une enquête ethnographique dans une cité HLM*. Rapport final de l'enquête financée par la DIV; Sauvadet, Thomas. 2006. Les jeunes *"de la cité"*: comment forment-ils un groupe? *Socio-logos*, 1.

AKIM OUALHACI

G

GANG AND NON-GANG GRAFFITI. Over the past quarter century the graffiti of illicit youth subcultures has emerged as a pervasive public phenomenon, increasingly marking alleys, back walls, subways, trains, and freeway overpasses throughout the United States and beyond. Because of this, political leaders, legal authorities, and many among the general public have come to closely associate graffiti with the individual and collective criminality of young people; in many ways, graffiti has emerged as perhaps the most potent public symbol of youthful delinquency and danger. In this context debates over graffiti, and attempts to address the graffiti "problem," often invoke broader concerns regarding youthful misbehavior and the unraveling of public order, and so regularly take on a tone of **moral panic** (Cohen, 2002). Fueling this moral panic, both in public debates over graffiti and in legal programs focusing on graffiti abatement, is the assumed linkage between graffiti and youth gang activity, and associated fears over graffiti's role as a facilitator of gang influence and infiltration. In reality, though, the role of graffiti in public life, and in the lives of young people, is far more complex than a simple equating of graffiti and youth gangs.

Throughout the United States, Canada, Europe, and elsewhere, the most prominent and publicly visible form of graffiti is in fact not youth gang graffiti, but *non-gang hip-hop graffiti*. Growing out of ethnic minority and immigrant neighborhoods of New York City during the 1970s, hip-hop graffiti emerged as a component of the larger, do-it-yourself hip-hop youth scene that also incorporated rap music, breakdancing, and other forms of cultural innovation. For many of its practitioners, hip-hop graffiti and other dimensions of the hip-hop subculture quickly became street-level alternatives to gang life and gang conflict; like **rap** music and breakdancing, hip-hop graffiti offered an alternative medium for contesting identity, acquiring status, and resolving conflict. Then as now, hip-hop graffiti "writers" and the "crews" to which they belong post their "tags" (subcultural nicknames) in places of public visibility, and design and execute elaborate public "pieces" (murals), in an attempt to confirm their abilities as artistic innovators and to gain subcultural "fame." In this way hip-hop graffiti operates as a highly stylized form of ongoing public interaction, with writers employing graffiti to offer aesthetic challenges to other writers, to inscribe artistic declarations and manifestos, and to comment on the merits of existing graffiti (Ferrell, 1996).

Yet hip-hop graffiti functions as more than interactive public inscription; it also provides for its young practitioners an experiential alternative to the tedium of school and work. As hip-hop graffiti writers regularly note, the practice of writing illegal graffiti offers, along with subcultural status, a seductive "adrenaline rush" of pleasure and excitement. As the writers also emphasize, this adrenaline rush is defined partly by the illicit and nocturnal nature of graffiti writing—but it is also driven by the immediate experience of accomplishing long-practiced subcultural artistry under conditions of physical and legal risk. In this way the often-described adrenaline rush of hip-hop graffiti writing operates as a matter of both individual experience and collective meaning, and so becomes all the more powerful in the construction of youthful identity.

Like the larger culture of hip-hop, the practice of hip-hop graffiti has over the past quarter century spread throughout the United States, Europe, and beyond, with well-established hip-hop graffiti undergrounds now common in major cities and smaller towns alike. The initial interactive dynamics that defined hip-hop graffiti have also continued to develop. Along with spray paint cans and ink markers, writers now utilize etching tools, pretagged stickers, and computer-generated images. They "tag the heavens"—that is, write tags in the highest and least accessible of locations, such as building rooftops and freeway overpasses—so as to gain public visibility and to demonstrate risky subcultural commitment. Building from the original practice of tagging and piecing urban areas widely enough to "go citywide," writers now "go nationwide" by tagging and piecing outbound freight trains, and "go worldwide" through hip-hop graffiti Web sites and magazines. Increasingly functioning as the folk artists of ethnic minority communities, hip-hop graffiti writers also paint signs and advertisements for local businesses, and execute commissioned "rest in piece" memorials for those lost to neighborhood street violence.

In these same neighborhoods and elsewhere, gang graffiti also functions as a medium for negotiating status and shaping identity—but does so as part of a dynamic much different than that of hip-hop graffiti. In a variety of ways, youth gangs utilize graffiti to define membership status, to issue symbolic warning or threat, and to demarcate gang property and gang space. Latino/Latina and Mexican American gang graffiti, for example, is often employed as a form of "barrio calligraphy" designed to symbolize and reinforce the convergence between gang and neighborhood. In this cultural context such gangs often inscribe barrio walls with their *placas*—stylized insignia that define gang and barrio boundaries, symbolize the collective public presence of the gang, and warn away potential intruders. While such gang graffiti in this way certainly signifies some sense of trouble or threat, it also references historical traditions of public communication and mural painting, and so signifies a sense of community solidarity and ethnic pride as well (Sanchez-Tranquilino, 1995).

For other Latino/Latina youth gangs, and for many African American gangs, gang graffiti can also function as a more direct demarcation of gang influence and power, and as a street-level advertisement of a gang's economic or territorial domination (Phillips, 1999). Here the widespread writing of a particular gang's graffiti throughout a neighborhood is often complemented by the symbolic degradation of rival gangs through coded threats or the "crossing out" of rival gang graffiti. Such symbolic provocations can, within particular neighborhood contexts, invite interpersonal aggression or spawn physical violence. Yet even here, the link between graffiti and gang violence remains ambiguous at best. Often the symbolic violence of gang graffiti displaces the need for physical confrontation; by demarcating urban space and setting cultural and territorial boundaries, gang graffiti can operate to regulate, if not fully obviate, physical conflict. In addition, gang graffiti often includes "roll calls" of murdered gang members, and so offers suggestions of commemoration as much as retaliation. Ironically, a somewhat less ambiguous link between gang graffiti and gang violence can be seen among those often and erroneously omitted from discussions of gangs and graffiti: **skinhead** and neo-Nazi youth. The graffiti of these gangs seems clearly designed to communicate terror and threat, and to accompany larger campaigns of interpersonal violence against gays and lesbians, immigrants, and others.

The pervasive public visibility of youthful graffiti over the past quarter century has spawned a variety of equally high-profile legal and political responses, almost all of them couched in terms of "anti-graffiti campaigns" or "wars on graffiti." Many of these campaigns have in turn been predicated on a "broken windows" model (Wilson and Kelling, 1982)—a model that argues for the policing of everyday crimes like graffiti writing so as to prevent the emergence of more serious criminality—and so have been intertwined with other high-profile political campaigns against "quality of life crimes" like loitering and begging. At a minimum, such campaigns have raised serious concerns about the legal targeting of minor criminality based on the politics of ethnic and social class bias. Beyond this, anti-graffiti campaigns have been beset in particular by their persistent inability (and unwillingness) to distinguish hip-hop graffiti from gang graffiti, and by their inattention to the localized dynamics of either.

In terms of both street policing and public pronouncements, anti-graffiti campaigns tend to conflate hip-hop graffiti and gang graffiti—or more to the point, to define all youthful graffiti as gang graffiti. While this ongoing error may of course simply result from ignorance, the regularity with which it occurs seems also to suggest racialized and essentialist assumptions about urban youth populations, and to suggest that anti-graffiti campaigns are designed as much to arouse politically profitable moral panic as to reduce the incidence of public graffiti. Relatedly, these campaigns, and the "broken windows" model that underwrites them, propose that youthful graffiti offers only a single public meaning: a sense of generalized threat and insecurity to those who see it. Yet as already seen, this model not only misses the radically different meanings of hip-hop graffiti and gang graffiti; it also fails to note the multiple, fluid meanings that are negotiated *within* each of these types of graffiti. Engaged in symbolic conversations largely interior to their own subcultures, both hip-hop graffiti writers and gang graffiti practitioners in reality hide in the light of public display.

A quarter century of highly politicized anti-graffiti campaigns has in some cases served to reduce the public presence of youthful graffiti, and has led to the arrest and conviction of numerous young graffiti writers. More significantly, these campaigns have altered the nature of graffiti writing itself. For many hip-hop graffiti writers, legal campaigns against graffiti have served to enhance the very experience of writing graffiti, with increased legal pressure and public notoriety accelerating the adrenaline rush they so readily embrace. Further, ongoing and aggressive anti-graffiti campaigns, and within them the consistent stigmatization of all graffiti practitioners as gang members, have pushed some hip-hop graffiti writers toward greater political militancy, and have shaped some quarters of the hip hop graffiti subculture into an anti-authoritarian counterculture.

Some final developments offer especially instructive ironies. First, the attempt to utilize highly visible campaigns to police a highly visible form of youthful misbehavior has of course served to make the misbehavior all the more visible, and so has served to recruit new graffiti practitioners and to spread contemporary forms of graffiti far beyond their origins. Under such conditions some young graffiti writers mature into criminal careers—but others mature into successful careers as independent artists, graffiti magazine publishers, and Web designers (Snyder, 2006). Global corporations and their advertising agencies see this proliferation of public graffiti as well, and notice ongoing anti-graffiti campaigns—and in response increasingly appropriate youthful graffiti into clothing lines, CD covers, and advertising schemes in an effort to cash in on its illicit credibility (Alvelos, 2004).

References/Suggested Readings: Alvelos, H. 2004. The Desert of Imagination in the City of Signs: Cultural Implications of Sponsored Transgression and Branded Graffiti. In J. Ferrell, K. Hayward, W. Morrison, and M. Presdee (eds.), *Cultural Criminology Unleashed*, pp. 181–191. London: Glasshouse; Cohen, S. 2002. *Folks Devils and Moral Panics* (3rd ed.). London: Routledge; Ferrell, J. 1996. *Crimes of Style: Urban Graffiti and the Politics of Criminality*. Boston: Northeastern University Press; Phillips, S.A. 1999. *Wallbangin': Graffiti and Gangs in L.A.* Chicago: University of Chicago Press; Sanchez-Tranquilino, M. 1995. Space, Power, and Youth Culture: Mexican American Graffiti and Chicano Murals in East Los Angeles, 1972–1978. In B.J. Bright and L. Bakewell (eds.), *Looking High and Low: Art and Cultural Identity*, pp. 55–88. Tucson: University of Arizona Press; Snyder, G.J. 2006. Graffiti Media and the Perpetuation of an Illegal Subculture. *Crime, Media, Culture,* 2 (1); Wilson, J.Q., and Kelling, J.L. 1982. Broken Windows: The Police and Neighborhood Safety. *Atlantic Monthly* (March), 29–38.

JEFF FERRELL

GANG CLOTHING. Gang members are often easy to identify by a tattoo or a complex hand gesture or sign. However it becomes difficult to identify gang membership simply by looking at clothing color and style, unless you are a gang member or well acquainted with gang symbols. The primary, personal accessories which identify gang affiliations are hats, handkerchiefs, shoelaces, colored belts with gang initials on the buckle, and jewelry.

Colors

The most noticeable gang member attire involves colors or symbols displayed in shoes/sneakers, shoelaces, hats and bandanas. For instance, **Bloods** wear red, **Crips** wear blue, **Latin Kings** wear gold/yellow and black, and Central wears green. Gangs represent themselves with colors to show that they have power and belong to an organized group. Some members wear gangster clothes to instill fear or anger in those not affiliated with gangs.

Certain gangs prefer a specific style and brand name of clothing, wearing it in a predefined manner. For example, members of People Nation roll up their left pant leg while Folk Nation members roll up their right. This also applies to the way they wear their jewelry, hats, and belt buckles. Another example can be seen in Los Angeles where Crips are known for wearing Dickies brand cotton work pants, selected athletic clothing, and British Knight (BK) sneakers; for them, the BK stands for Blood Killer (KnowGangs, 1997). **Vice Lords** gang members wear Louis Vitton (VL reversed) caps. Some gang members write their gang's name under the bill of their hat (Burke, 1991).

Gang members also use items normally associated with popular sport teams, their religion, nationality, and hairstyle to represent their gang (GangsOrUs, 2006). For example, the New York Yankees colors are black, blue, and white which represent the **Gangster Disciples** colors, and the Chicago Cubs use the letter C as their symbol which stands for the Spanish Cobras gang (GangsOrUs, 2006). Religious symbols such as the five-point star, a symbol of Islam (along with the crescent moon) are adopted by the People Nation. In the **Asociación Ñeta** gang, members often display the Puerto Rican flag stitched on their clothing and/or hats (KnowGangs, 1997).

Jewelry

In some cases, accessories such as beads and gold chains are used as symbols of gang affiliation. Black and gold/yellow membership beads are popular within the Latin Kings. Latin King members at the high end of the leadership structure are given symbolic stones to add to their beads to represent their crown position and title (Brotherton and Barrios, 2004). Members of the Ñetas identify themselves by red, white, and blue beads. If a Ñeta violates any of the gang's rules, he/she is put on probation; if he/she is not 100 percent accepted he/she might have to "wear all white beads until they are considered loyal" (KnowGangs, 1997). In general, on the West Coast, most gangs wear bandanas while the East Coast gangs wear color beaded necklaces (KnowGangs, 1997). Some members wear their symbol on a pendant hanging from their gold or silver chains. For example, some Latin Kings wear a five-pointed star or a crown and members of the Black Guerilla Family may be seen with a crossed rifle, a machete symbol, or the letters BGF.

Clothing as a Symbol of Gang Involvement

Sheley and Wright (cited in Bjerregaard, 2002) administered surveys to 1,663 men and women from 10 inner-city high schools in California, Illinois, Louisiana, and New Jersey. Results show that more organized gangs have "special clothing associated with their gang" (Bjerregaard, 2002, p. 44); however, they also found that less than 50 percent of the gang members indicated that clothing was a characteristic of their group (Bjerregaard, 2002).

Individuals are stereotyped as gang members by the way they dress. It is not true that gang members always wear their hats backward in particular ways, or wear baggy clothing, etc. Essentially, anyone can appear to be a gang member. According to Garot and Katz (2003), individuals wear baggy clothing because they feel more attractive to the females not because they are in a gang. Someone may simply enjoy the hip-hop, **rap** fashion and accidentally fall into what the public, readers, and researchers believe is the gang style. When individuals wear team jerseys, it is typically because they support and like that team not because they are in a gang. Moreover, gang members themselves often choose to hide their affiliation with their gang to deceive law enforcement, other gang members, schoolteachers, and family (Garot & Katz, 2003).

In summary, gang symbols help create a sign of belonging to a powerful organization where individuals can easily identify themselves with others. Personal accessories, hats, handkerchiefs, shoelaces, colored belts, and beaded necklaces are used to represent gang membership. When trying to determine if someone is part of a gang, one should evaluate the usage of colors in combination with other symbols such as hand signs and tattoos. It should also be understood that the color of clothing and the predefined manner of wearing it can be deceiving.

References/Suggested Readings: Bjerregaard, B. 2002. Self-Definitions of Gang Membership and Involvement in Delinquent Activities. *Youth and Society*, 34 (1), 31–54; Brotherton, D.C., and Barrios, L. 2004. *The Almighty Latin King and Queen Nation: Street Politics and the Transformation of a New York City Gang*. New York: Columbia University Press; Burke, J. 1991. Teenagers, Clothes, and Gang Violence. *Educational Leadership*, 49 (1), 11–13; Gangs OR Us, Robert Walker. 1999–2006. Gang Identification Expert. Retrieved October 8, 2006, from www.gangsorus.com/clothing.html; Garot, R., and Katz, J. 2003. Provocative Looks: Gang Appearance and Dress Codes in an Inner-City Alternative School. *Ethnography*, 4 (3), 421–454; Know Gangs, The nation's leading gang experts. 1997. Gang Profiles. Retrieved October 8, 2006, from www.knowgangs.com/gang_resources/profiles/surenos; Our Lady of Guadalupe. 2005. Parent/Student Handbook 2006–2007. Retrieved October 8, 2006, from www.guadalupe-school.com/handbook04-05.htm; Texas Youth Commission. 2006. Prevention Summary. Gang Related Clothing. Retrieved October 8, 2006, from www.tyc .state.tx.us/prevention/clothing.html.

JESSICA CASTANON

GANG FEMALES. Although girls' involvement in gangs is not a new phenomenon, beginning in the early 1990s it became, and currently remains, a popular subject of both media and scholarly interest. It is difficult to discern whether female gang membership has notably changed in the past twenty years, but media coverage—fueled by a rise in girls' arrest rates—has certainly captured the public's attention with stories of the new breed of hyper-aggressive gangster girls. Though girls account for 29 percent of all juvenile arrests, their arrest rate for violent crimes has been rising while boys' rates have been decreasing (Snyder, 2004). There is no conclusive evidence which suggests that girls' arrest increases are attributable to gang involvement, but it may be a contributing factor. A growing body of scholarly research on girls' gang involvement provides a more nuanced and balanced picture of these groups and their members than the sensational stories presented through media coverage of the topic.

Girls' gang membership has been documented since the 1800s, but much of the traditional literature on gangs either ignored females completely or made only passing reference to them. When early researchers did discuss female gang members, the focus was typically on their psychological dysfunctions and social maladjustment. Since most of the traditional gang studies were undertaken by male researchers who interviewed male gang members, the older literature represents male gang members' perceptions of female members, rather than firsthand accounts of girls' gang experiences. As such, these early accounts produced stereotypical images of gang girls. They were generally described as either "tomboys" or "sex objects" whose primary function was to serve male members as girlfriends; providers of sexual services; stashers of weapons and/or drugs; spies against rival gangs; and/or bait for luring rival male gang members to fighting locations.

These stereotypes prevailed until the late 1970s and early 1980s when researchers first began to directly examine female gangs. Although some of the functions outlined above were corroborated in these later accounts, girls' gang roles were revealed to be much more complex and meaningful than previous "gang studies" had documented. A new body of qualitative research emerged, which situated females' gang involvement in relation to the broader context of their lives—examining how their families, ethnicity/race and cultural heritage, gender, communities, and the urban economy influenced their gang membership.

In contrast to the earlier depictions of female gang members as completely subservient to male members, this newer body of research revealed that girls' gang activity was neither wholly dependent upon—nor focused solely around satisfying—gang males. The most in-depth account of female gang involvement to date comes from Anne Campbell's (1991) study of young women involved in New York City gangs in the early 1980s. Consistent with the other research from this time period, she noted that girls sought asylum in the gang to escape the current limitations of their poverty, and the problems and difficulties they expected to face in the future. The gang represented a temporary refuge from the harshness and drudgery of their lives. Campbell noted five problems that may drive young women to seek asylum in a gang: (1) a future of meaningless domestic labor with little possibility of educational or occupational escape, (2) subordination to the man in the house, (3) responsibility for children, (4) social isolation of the housewife, and (5) powerlessness of underclass membership. Although the gang would not provide a permanent escape from poverty and marginalization, it provided camaraderie and something to do during their adolescent years. Based on her research, Campbell acknowledged that the male gang still paved the way and opened doors for the female affiliates, but she also noted that once formed, the female gang developed its own individual solidarity and that sisterhood had values and ways to attain status that did not revolve around male members.

Campbell's work, along with the other research undertaken during this time period (1980s), demonstrated that previous stereotypes of gang girls inadequately explained their gang involvement. Female gangs were neither completely at the mercy of male gang members, nor completely free of their influence. Joan Moore's research on former Mexican American male and female gang members in Los Angeles barrios also revealed some autonomy for females within their cliques, but did not find sexism to be completely lacking. In comparing the male and female gang experience, Moore noted that female gang members were more likely to (a) come from extremely troubled home environments—families with alcoholic, drug-addicted, and/or criminally involved members, and (b) suffer more long-term harm or "social injury" from their gang membership.

In the past fifteen years there have been several qualitative studies and quantitative analyses examining the nature and extent of young women's participation in gangs and gang delinquency/crime. While some of the studies suggest possible increases in female gang membership and activity, others present portraits largely consistent with prior research. Overall, these findings confirm females' continued involvement in gangs but offer varying accounts of: the prevalence of their membership; their equality/autonomy or subordination to males; the ways in which race and ethnicity (and cultural norms related to these) affect girls' gang roles and delinquency; and the extent to which they participate in gang crime and violence. Studies indicate that the primary reasons that girls join gangs are (a) to feel a sense of belonging and family/sisterhood; (b) protection (from other gangs and/or individuals); and (c) to gain status or respect (in their neighborhood and/or among their peers).

Various cross-sectional and longitudinal survey data generally reveal females' gang membership and delinquency/crime to be greater than was previously recognized, but do not necessarily indicate increases in either (Deschenes and Esbensen, 1999; Esbensen and Huizinga, 1993; Fagan, 1990). It's difficult to assess shifts in girls' gang membership and/or gang-related crime given the lack of previous data collected on these issues. Self-report data from several single-city studies reveal relatively high involvement rates for girls. For example, Bjerregaard and Smith found that 22 percent of the adolescent girls they surveyed indicated gang membership, as compared to 18 percent of boys; some other studies indicate even higher rates of girls' membership. National estimates of female gangs—though riddled with accuracy problems—have not changed much in the past twenty-five years. According to these counts, females represent no more than 10 percent of all gang members nationwide. It is important to note, however, that many police departments and community agencies still do not acknowledge the presence and/or relevance of female gang involvement, despite its existence. Essentially, as a matter of policy in some jurisdictions, females cannot be classified as gang members (while other agencies may count a girl who is a girlfriend of a male gang member, but not actually a gang member herself) thereby further confounding prevalence statistics.

Recent qualitative studies of gangs (in Columbus, Milwaukee, San Francisco, Chicago, New York, Boston, and a few other cities) present interesting, and somewhat varied, pictures of the gender dynamics and norms within today's female gangs (Brotherton and Salazar-Atias, 2003; Hagedorn and Devitt, 1999; Joe and Chesney-Lind, 1999; Lauderback, Hansen, and Waldorf, 1992; Miller, 2001; Nurge, 2003; Taylor, 1993; Venkatesh, 1998). Such groups continue to come in a variety of forms, the most common being (a) auxiliary/affiliate groups, which are separate from—but generally linked to, and usually at least somewhat overseen by—the male gang; (b) co-ed groups, in which males and females share common membership, leadership, etc.; and (c) independent/autonomous, all-female groups. Although the first two, mixed-sex types of gangs appear to remain the most common, there has been some speculation (but minimal hard evidence) suggesting that autonomous female groups are on the rise.

Recent research on female gangs in Boston revealed wider variation in group structure and function that the traditional typology suggests; Nurge's research included the study of cliques, which were typically small groups of girls whose primary activities including fighting and socializing. Other research, by Miller, has examined the gender ratio within mixed-sex gangs and suggests that girls' behavior within their groups is influenced by the extent to which those groups are gender-balanced or skewed. Brotherton and Salazar-Atias studied Latino street organization membership in New York and observed young women to be struggling to gain power and influence in their traditionally male-dominated group, and that both male and female members have mixed feelings about embracing equality. Venkatesh's Chicago research on female gang members' drug sales and relationship with a local male gang presents another interesting example of the complexities of gender, power, and criminal opportunities within mixed sex gangs. These recent studies tap into, and uncover, different dimensions of girl gang membership, dynamics, and activity, but cumulatively, they reveal that female gang membership is much more varied and complex than the early stereotypes (of tomboy and sex object) suggested. Gang prevention, intervention, and suppression efforts are gradually recognizing—and attempting to respond to—girls' gang involvement, and gender-specific programming is receiving greater attention and funding than it had in the past.

References/Suggested Readings: Brotherton, D.C. and Salazar-Atias, C. 2003. Amor de Reina! The Pushes and Pulls of Group Membership among the Latin Queens. In L. Kontos, D. Brotherton, and L. Barrios (eds.), *Gangs and Society: Alternative Perspectives*. New York: Columbia University Press; Campbell, A. 1991. *The Girls in the Gang* (2nd ed.). Cambridge, MA: Basil Blackwell; Chesney-Lind, M., and J. Hagedorn, J. 1999. *Female Gangs in America: Essays on Girls, Gangs and Gender*. Chicago: Lakeview Press; Deschenes, E.P., and Esbensen, F. 1999. Violence among Girls: Does Gang Membership Make a Difference? In M. Chesney-Lind and J.M. Hagedorn (eds.), *Female Gangs in America*. Chicago: Lakeview Press; Esbensen, F., and Deschenes, E.P. 1998. A Multi-site Examination of Youth Gang Membership: Does Gender Matter? *Criminology*, 36, 799–827; Esbensen, F., and Huizinga, D. 1993. Gangs, Drugs and Delinquency in a Survey of Urban Youth. *Criminology*, 31, 565–589; Fagan, J. 1990. Social Processes of Delinquency and Drug Use among Urban Gangs. In C.R. Huff (ed.), *Gangs in America*. Newbury Park, CA: Sage; Hagedorn, J., and Devitt, M. 1999. Fighting Females: The Social Construction of the Female Gang. In M. Chesney-Lind and J. Hagedorn (eds.), *Female Gangs in America*. Chicago: Lakeview Press; Joe, K., and Chesney-Lind, M. 1995. "Just Every Mother's Angel": An Analysis of Gender and Ethnic Variations in Youth Gang Membership. *Gender and Society*, 9, 408–431; Lauderback, D., Hansen, J., and Waldorf, D. 1992. "Sisters Are Doin' It for Themselves": A Black Female Gang in San Francisco. *Gang Journal*, 1, 57–72; Miller, J. 2001. *One of the Guys: Girls, Gangs and Gender*. New York: Oxford University Press; Miller, J. 1998. Gender and Victimization Risk among Young Women in Gangs. *Journal of Research in Crime and Delinquency*, 35, 429–453; Moore, J. 1991. *Going Down to the Barrio: Homeboys and Homegirls in Change*. Philadelphia: Temple University Press; Moore, J., and J. Hagedorn. 2001. Female Gangs: A Focus on Research. *Juvenile Justice Bulletin*; Nurge, D.M. 2003. Liberating Yet Limiting: The Paradox of Female Gang Membership. In L. Kontos, D. Brotherton, and L. Barrios (eds.), *Gangs and Society: Alternative Perspectives*. New York: Columbia University Press; Taylor, C. 1993. *Girls, Gangs, Women and Drugs*. East Lansing: Michigan State University Press; Venkatesh, S. 1998. Gender and Outlaw Capitalism: A Historical Account of the Black Sisters United "Girl Gang." *Signs* (Spring).

DANA M. NURGE

GANG GRAFFITI: EAST COAST VS. WEST COAST. Any dichotomy between gang graffiti on the East Coast and the West Coast of the United States is merely contrived for comparative purposes. However, various gang graffiti on both coasts, and other parts of the country, have far more in common than that which differentiates them. All gang graffiti on both the East and West Coasts have the same overarching purposes of symbolic representation of cultural and geographic identities, as well as symbolic representation of inter-gang conflicts. These two major themes manifest in gang graffiti from different types of gangs on both the East and West Coasts.

Although gang graffiti embodies much of the same meanings and purposes in different parts of the country, three major types of gang graffiti can be identified in the literature, the first being Chicano gang graffiti, originally from California. The second being African American gang graffiti of the **Crips** and **Bloods** gangs, also originally from California. The third being Peoples and Folks gang graffiti, originally from Chicago. Although these three predominant gang types originate in California and Chicago, they have been exported across the nation and one, two, or all three of them can be found in cities on both coasts. For example New York City is home to Chicano gangs from southern California like Mara Salvatruca (MS13), African American gangs from Los Angeles like the Bloods and Crips, and Chicago-based gangs like the **Almighty Latin Kings**. Although Chicago is geographically located in the Midwest, it can be considered to be East Coast for the purposes of analyzing gang culture, as its influence is mostly directed east to cities such as New York and Miami.

Gang graffiti has received less attention from academic sources than have other aspects of gang life such as violence or drug use, although a few outstanding treatments of the gang graffiti phenomenon have been published, some more in-depth than others. Perhaps the first treatment of the gang graffiti phenomenon in academic literature, published in 1974, is from a geographical perspective on the gang graffiti in Philadelphia. Ley and Cybriwsky differentiate between gang graffiti and what would later be called hip hop graffiti done by graffiti "kings" such as the infamous Cornbread of the late 1960s and early 1970s. With regard to gang graffiti, Ley and Cybriwsky present the most basic and obvious purpose of gang graffiti, which is to delineate and demarcate gang territories. Gang youth, who have little legitimate control over urban spaces, use graffiti as a way to define the areas under their de facto control. Unlike the graffiti "kings" who wander far and wide writing their names, these spaces marked with gang graffiti are more permanently identified with the gangs who claim these spaces as their territory. Although these spaces are continually contested by rival gangs, gang turfs are coherently marked by the gangs that occupy them so that anyone who knows what they are looking for can easily identify where they are in the geography of gang territories. Ley and Cybriwsky also suggest the use of graffiti in symbolic conflict between rival gangs in boundary or contested areas.

In his descriptive analysis of Chicano gang culture in Los Angeles, Vigil suggests that gang graffiti is one element of an array of different cultural demarcators that gang members use to identify themselves and to express their "cholo" image. In addition to styles of dress, gestures, mannerisms, language, posture, tattoos, monikers, and car and music preferences, graffiti is another cultural marker that gang members use to adorn the spaces they inhabit and to assert their own unique cultural identities.

Hutchison provides the only academic comparison to date of California and Chicago gang graffiti and finds stylistic differences in the way cultural identities and symbolic representations of inter-gang conflict are portrayed by gang members through the use of graffiti. Hutchison finds that Chicano gangs in California utilize a number of highly stylized and canonical forms of script to represent their gang identities. These graffiti are known as "placas" and represent names and locations of specific Chicano gangs as well as names of their members. Innumerable combinations of initials and euphemisms in Spanish, English, and a combination of the two are used by Chicano gang members in California to identify themselves and their gangs and to boast their supremacy over rivals. Symbolic representations of inter-gang conflicts most often take the form of crossing out each other's "placas" and writing one's own "placa" over the graffiti or in the territory of rivals. Hutchison points out that the use of symbolic imagery is rare in Chicano gang graffiti in California and the use of symbolic images to represent individual gangs is almost unheard of (with the exception of the Playboys gang, which uses the Playboy bunny to represent itself).

In contrast, Hutchison finds that the use of symbolic imagery to represent individual gangs and families of gangs and to symbolically represent inter-gang conflicts in Chicago is ubiquitous. Chicago gangs regularly use a combination of writing and symbolic images. For example a five-pointed crown or a five-pointed star is used to represent the Latin Kings gang. These images, combined with writing the names and initials of gangs and their members are the most common form of gang graffiti found in Chicago. Hutchison found that just as symbolic imagery is used to represent one's own gang, gang members in Chicago manipulate the symbolic images of rival gangs in order to symbolically denounce and disrespect them. For example the Latin Kings destroy the symbolic images of their Latin Disciple rivals in their own graffiti; a six-pointed star can be symbolically destroyed by being torn in two, and a pitchfork can be turned upside down as a symbol of disrespect. In addition, written denunciations of one's enemies further the disrespect shown for bitter rivals. Following the previous example, Latin Kings gang members often write the initials "DK" for "Disciple Killers" in or next to their own graffiti.

Conquergood provides a much more descriptive analysis of Chicago gang graffiti in his 1997 piece, *Street Literacy*. He provides a rich and exhaustive description of the different gangs and families of gangs in the Chicago area and the myriad symbolic images they employ, and destroy, to symbolically represent their own identities and symbolically represent conflicts with rival gangs. Whereas African American gangs in California are split into two main families of gangs, the Crips and the Bloods, Conquergood points to a similar dichotomy among Chicago gangs, Peoples and Folks Nations (the Latin Kings being an example of a Peoples Nation gang, and the **Gangster Disciples** being an example of a Folks Nation gang). As described by Hutchison, Conquergood points to the essentiality of symbolic images and the manipulation of these images and the names and initials of rival gangs in order to symbolically denounce and disrespect them. However, he goes a step further in his analysis, arguing that gang graffiti is itself a symbolic representation of the struggle between gang members and mainstream society, from which gang members are perpetually marginalized. This is an analysis that can just as easily apply to gang graffiti in other parts of the country as gang members in most every community suffer the same forms of degradation and marginalization.

Phillips offers a comprehensive description of both Chicano and African American gang graffiti in Los Angeles in her book, *Wallbangin'*. As in other works on gang graffiti, Phillips emphasizes gang graffiti both as a symbolic representation of cultural and geographic identities, and as symbolic representation of inter-gang conflicts. Gang graffiti is first and foremost a representation of identity and at the same time, a conduit for symbolic representation of actually conflicts that exist between gangs. However, in the streets of Los Angeles, a strict dichotomy exists between Chicano gangs and African American gangs. Chicano gangs tend to use very elaborate scripts in their graffiti that follow a very strict canton in terms of form and style. Chicanos pride themselves on the quality of their visual representations and the demonstration of a skilled graffiti writer is a point of prestige among Chicano gang members in Los Angeles. As has been pointed out before, they very rarely use symbolic images either to represent their own gangs or to disrespect rivals. Rather, Chicano gang members use a complicated combination of abbreviations, letters, and numbers to represent their barrios. Inter-gang conflict is played out on the walls of Los Angeles by crossing out or otherwise defacing the graffiti of rival gangs, often in their own neighborhoods. Phillips also suggests that graffiti is a source of great pride among gang members who represent not only the names of their gangs and themselves, but often all the members of their gangs in long and elaborate roll-calls, which are comprised of lengthy lists of names of members of a gang headed by the name of the gang itself.

Phillips found that African American gang graffiti representing Crip and Blood gangs is very similar to Chicano gang graffiti. Similar symbolic representations of gang entities and geographical locations abound, as do symbolic representations of inter-gang conflicts by the crossing out or defacing of rival gangs' graffiti. African American gang graffiti shared many of the same elements, such as writing the names of gangs and individual members, crossing out rivals, and writing roll-calls of members' names. However, one distinct difference is that African American gangs do use symbolic imagery to denounce their rivals, if not to represent themselves. For example, enemies of Crips might draw a large crab on a wall and cross it out, as a demonstration of disrespect to rival Crip gangs (crab is a derogatory term used for Crips).

References/Suggested Readings: Conquergood, D. 1997. Street Literacy. In James Flood, Shirley Brice Heath, and Diane Lape (eds.), *Handbook of Research on Teaching Literacy through the Communicative and Visual Arts.* New York: Simon and Schuster; Hutchison, R. 1993. Blazon Nouveau: Gang Graffiti in the Barrios of Los Angeles and Chicago. In S. Cummings and D.J. Monti (eds.), *Gangs: The Origins and Impact of Contemporary Youth Gangs in the United States.* New York: SUNY Press; Ley, D., and Cybriwsky, R. 1974. Urban Graffiti as Territorial Markers. *Annals of the Association of American Geographers,* 64 (4), 491–505; Phillips, S.A. 1999. *Wallbangin'.* Chicago: University of Chicago Press; Vigil, J.D. 1988. *Barrio Gangs: Street Life and Identity in Southern California.* Austin: University of Texas Press.

ROBERT D. WEIDE

GANG IDENTITY AS PERFORMANCE. While conceptualizing identity as performance is commonplace in the social sciences, it is remarkably lacking in studies of gangs. This entry reviews some allusions to gangs and identity in the literature, highlighting the importance of a central interactional mechanism for performing gangs: demanding of another, "Where you from!" Such a challenge creates a lively venue for performing identity and emotional manipulation, for both for the instigator who offers the challenge as well as the respondent. Rather than conceptualizing young people as "gang members" and "gangs" as a static group, we may see how the doing of gangs is strategic and context-sensitive. Such an approach provides an alternative to conceptualizing identity, and especially gang identity, as a fixed personal characteristic, but as a sensual response to a moment's vicissitudes.

Over the past fifty years, social scientists have increasingly turned from essentializing identity as a fixed characteristic, to understanding identity as performance. Building from Goffman's (1959, 1976) seminal work on impression management, and Garfinkel's (1984) and Sacks's (1995) insights into identity as an accomplishment, identity is increasingly recognized not as an obdurate quality, but as a resource whose relevance is strategically, contextually determined. Through dress (Davis, 1992; Entwistle, 2001; Garot and Katz, 2003), mannerisms (Merleau-Ponty, 1962; Young, 1980; Sudnow, 1978), and language (Gumperz 1982; Schegloff, 1992; Widdicombe and Wooffitt, 1995), individuals make and dispute claims to identity based in socially recognized categories, and such claims and contestations become the bases for sustaining interaction. Scholars have examined the performance of class (Willis, 1977; MacLeod, 1995; Granfield, 1992), race and ethnicity (Moerman, 1974; Cohen, 1978; Wieder and Pratt, 1989), gender (Young, 1980; West and Zimmerman, 1987; Butler, 1990; Thorne, 1993; Mendoza-Denton, 1996), and sexual identity

(Queen, 1997; Yoshino, 2006), yet aside from a few exceptions (Conquergood, 1994a, 1994b, 1997; Mendoza-Denton, 1996; Garot, 2007), such insights have rarely been applied to the study of gang members.

According to Cohen (1990, p. 12), "That membership in gangs confers identity . . . could be the single most common proposition encountered in the literature on gangs." Yet this proposition is rather static, concerned with such questions as whether a gang is a primary or secondary group, why young people become gang members, what they do in a gang, or how they leave a gang. Some researchers, such as Monti (1994) and Decker and Winkle (1996) determine gang membership for analytic purposes by asking respondents if they claim, without recognizing how such "claims" are highly variable and dependent on how the respondent reads the local context. Such variability is surely known by gang scholars, although it has been avoided as a topic, since "gangs" are analyzed as a phenomenon in themselves, similar to a club or an institution, rather than as a constitutive feature of a local ecology (see Katz and Jackson-Jacobs, 2004). A "gang" does not exist as an autonomous entity, a force such as gravity, bidding members to do its dirty work. Rather, gang members have agency, and through that agency, they may invoke whether or not a membership category such as "gang member" is relevant in a given circumstance.

Descriptions of invocations of gang membership are a common topic in the gang literature (see Brotherton, 1994). As Jack Katz (1988, p. 141) states, "virtually all ethnographies of street violence among adolescent elites describe fights generated by *interrogations* or spontaneous *declarations* of group membership on public streets." Such declarations include public pronouncements such as "We're the Vice Lords, the mighty Vice Lords!" (ibid., p. 142), "parading" "in apparent unison while displaying . . . insignia of membership" (ibid., p. 142), as well as various means of undermining school authority. Matza (1964) used the metaphor of "drift" to capture the nuances of delinquent activity. Yet the metaphor is not quite apt in regard to gangs, for at times a young person definitely is a gang member, and at other times the same young person definitely is not, without any necessary gradual escalation or deescalation in gang-related behavior. Drawing on the metaphor of performance, we may explore how gang membership is invoked as a members' reification practice, which may just as well dereify gangs.

Young people in ecologies where gangs are active may modulate ways of talking, walking, dressing, writing graffiti, wearing make-up, and hiding or revealing tattoos in playing with markers of embodied identity, to obscure, reveal, or provide contradictory signals on a continuum from gang-related to nongang-related (Conquergood, 1994a, 1994b, 1997; Mendoza-Denton, 1996; Garot and Katz, 2003). One of the primary ways to perform gang identity is through the demand, "where you from" (Garot, 2007). Intended to resolve any ambiguity, it actually becomes merely another resource to be worked in the contingent, variable effort in which young people everywhere engage in molding the self. This emotional challenge to identity is a language game (Wittgenstein, 1953), in an interaction ritual designed to create action and challenge face (Goffman, 1967). Moreover, to question a young person's gang affiliation is not primarily of relevance to gang researchers, but to young people. "Who you claimin'?" "Where you from?" or "What you be about" (Conquergood, 1994a, p. 27) are locally recognized interrogation devices, and central practices for demonstrating a gang identity and forcing the respondent to make an identity claim in terms of gangs. Thus, ecologies of gangs provide fertile ground for grappling with how identity is done. A focus on the accomplishment of such practices, rather than merely their "causes" or "effects," will contribute to an appreciation (Matza, 1969) of the skills (Lyng, 1990) of gangbanging, as opposed to the ongoing criminalization of gang members' artful ways.

References/Suggested Readings: Brotherton, David C. 1994. Who Do You Claim?: Gang Formations and Rivalry in an Inner-City Public High School. *Perspectives on Social Problems*, 5, 147–171; Butler, Judith. 1990. *Gender Trouble: Feminism and the Subversion of Identity*. New York: Routledge; Cohen, Albert K. 1990. Foreword and Overview. In C. Ronald Huff (ed.), *Gangs in America*, pp. 7–21. Newbury Park, CA: Sage; Cohen, Ronald. 1978. Ethnicity: Problem and Focus in Anthropology. *Annual Review of Anthropology*, 7, 379–403; Conquergood, Dwight. 1994a. Homeboys and Hoods: Gang Communication and Cultural Space. In Lawrence R. Frey (ed.), *Group Communication in Context: Studies of Natural Groups*, pp. 23–55. Hillsdale, NJ: Lawrence Erlbaum; Conquergood, Dwight. 1994b. For the Nation! How Street Gangs Problematize Patriotism. In Herbert W. Simons and Michael Billig (eds.), *After Postmodernism: Reconstructing Ideology Critique*, pp. 200–221. London: Sage; Conquergood, Dwight. 1997. Street Literacy. In James Flood, Shirley Brice Heath, and Diane Lapp (eds.), *Handbook on Teaching Literacy through the Communicative and Visual Arts*, pp. 254–375. New York: Simon and Schuster Macmillan; Davis, Fred. 1992. *Fashion, Culture and Identity*. Chicago: University of Chicago Press; Decker, Scott, and Barrik Van Winkle. 1996. *Life in a Gang: Family, Friends and Violence*. Cambridge: Cambridge University Press; Entwistle, Joanne. 2001. The Dressed Body. In Joanne Entwistle and Elizabeth Wilson (eds.), *Body Dressing*, pp. 33–58. Oxford: Berg; Garfinkel, Harold. 1984. *Studies in Ethnomethodology*. Cambridge: Polity Press; Garot, Robert. 2007. "Where you From!": Gang Identity as Performance. *Journal of Contemporary Ethnography*; Garot, Robert, and Jack Katz. 2003. Provocative Looks: The Enforcement of School Dress Codes and the Embodiment of Dress at an Inner-City Alternative School. *Ethnography*. 4 (3). 421–454; Goffman, Erving. 1959. *The Presentation of Self in Everyday Life*. New York: Anchor; Goffman, Erving. 1967. *Interaction Ritual: Essays on Face-to-Face Behavior*. New York: Pantheon Books; Goffman, Erving. 1976. *Gender Advertisements*. New York: Harper and Row; Granfield, Robert. 1992. *Making Elite Lawyers: Visions of Law at Harvard and Beyond*. New York: Routledge, Chapman and Hall; Gumperz, John. 1982. *Language and Social Identity*. Cambridge: Cambridge University Press; Katz, Jack. 1988. *Seductions of Crime: Moral and Sensual Attractions in Doing Evil*. New York: Basic Books; Katz, Jack, and Jackson-Jacobs, Curtis. 2004. The Criminologists' Gang. In Colin Sumner (ed.), *The Blackwell Companion to Criminology*, pp. 91–124. Malden, MA: Blackwell; Lyng, Stephen. 1990. Edgework: A Social Psychological Analysis of Voluntary Risk Taking. *American Journal of Sociology*, 95 (4), 851–886; MacLeod, Jay. 1995. *Ain't No Makin' It: Aspirations and Attainment in a Low-Income Neighborhood*. Boulder: Westview; Matza, David. 1964. *Delinquency and Drift*. New York: Wiley; Matza, David. 1969. *Becoming Deviant*. Englewood Cliffs, NJ: Prentice Hall; Mendoza-Denton, Norma. 1996. "Muy Macha": Gender and Ideology in Gang-Girls' Discourse about Makeup. *Ethnos*, 61 (1/2), 47–63; Merleau-Ponty, Maurice. 1962. *The Phenomenology of Perception*. London: Routledge and Kegan Paul; Moerman, Michael. 1974. Accomplishing Ethnicity. In Roy Turner (ed.), *Ethnomethodology*, pp. 54–68. Middlesex: Penguin; Monti, Daniel J. 1994. *Wannabe: Gangs in Suburbs and Schools*. Oxford: Blackwell; Queen, Robin M. 1997. "I Don't Speak Spritch": Locating Lesbian Language. In Ann Livia and Kira Hall (eds.), *Queerly Phrased: Language, Gender, and Sexuality*, pp. 233–256. Oxford: Oxford University Press; Sacks, Harvey. 1995. *Lectures on Conversation*. Oxford: Blackwell; Schegloff, Emanuel A. 1992. In Another Context. In Alessandro Duranti and Charles Goodwin (eds.), *Rethinking Context: Language as an Interactive Phenomenon*, pp. 191–227. Cambridge: Cambridge University Press; Sudnow, David. 1978. *Ways of the Hand: The Organization of Improvised Conduct*. Cambridge, MA: Harvard University Press; Thorne, Barrie. 1993. *Gender Play: Girls and*

Boys in School. New Brunswick, NJ: Rutgers University Press; West, Candice, and Donald H. Zimmerman. 1987. Doing Gender. *Gender and Society*, 1 (2), 125–151; Widdicombe, Sue, and Robin Wooffitt. 1995. *The Language of Youth Subcultures*. Hertfordshire: Harvester Wheatsheaf; Wieder, D. Lawrence, and Steven Pratt. 1989. On Being a Recognizable Indian among Indians. In D. Carbaugh (ed.), *Cultural Communication and Intercultural Contact*. Hillsdale, NJ: Lawrence Erlbaum; Willis, Paul. 1977. *Learning to Labor*. Aldershot: Gower; Wittgenstein, Ludwig. 1953. *Philosophical Investigations*. Oxford: Blackwell; Yoshino, Kenji. 2006. *Covering: The Hidden Assault on our Civil Rights*. New York: Random House; Young, Iris. 1980. Throwing Like a Girl: A Phenomenology of Feminine Body Comportment Motility and Spatiality. *Human Studies*, 3 (2), 137–156.

ROBERT GAROT

GANG PHOTOGRAPHY. Photography documenting gangs generally falls within the very broadly defined genres of photojournalistic crime reporting or visual anthropology and ethnography. It is not always easy to draw firm distinctions between the two, but in general photojournalists cover gangs as they relate to news events or to the public interest—the obvious examples are crime reporting or crime prevention efforts. This approach begins with the assumption that gangs are a social problem. However "news hooks" for visual journalism involving gangs might include the impact of gang-related violence on public health or the ways gangs are treated by the criminal justice system.

Visual anthropologists begin from a different starting point. Their primary interest is in the formation of gang identity and those visual rites and rituals that define gang culture. Such photography often catalogues the visual signifiers related to gang identity such as tattoos, graffiti, and style of dress, hairstyles, and other rituals that differentiate members of one gang from another.

Because of these distinct starting points the visual anthropologists' approach is often considered less judgmental. Some news photography uses visual signifiers in ways that stigmatize by reinforcing criminal stereotypes. Gang tattoos and tough guy postures become a visual shorthand to imply a serious threat of violent criminal behavior whether or not that is the actual situation in which the photographic image was made.

Documentary narrative photography is a storytelling form that uses aspects of the ethnographic and journalistic approaches in order to more fully contextualize and humanize individual life stories that might enlarge public understanding of how social policy effects individuals and communities. Some photographers explore the social context and impact of gangs through the life stories of individual gang members without glamorizing, denying, or exaggerating the potential for violence or evidence of various kinds of violence including social exclusion in the contexts in which their subjects live.

Some early well-known examples of this kind of humanistic documentary approach to gangs are Gordon Parks's 1948 *Life* magazine reportage on an African American gang leader in the Bronx and Bruce Davidson's work "The Brooklyn Gang 1959." More recent work in this tradition are Joseph Rodriguez's *Eastside Stories* exploring the lives of East Los Angeles gang members in the 1990s, and Donna DeCesare's project "Destiny's Children," chronicling the spread of Los Angles gang culture to El Salvador and Guatemala through the stories of individual gang members whose lives she recorded from mid-1990s to the early twenty-first century.

References/Suggested Readings: DeCesare, D. 2004. Destiny's Children: A Photo Narrative at http://www.destinyschildren.org/index2.html; DeCesare, D. 2003. From Civil War to Gang War: The Tragedy of Edgar Bolanos in *Gangs and Society: Alternative Perspectives*, edited by L. Kontos, D. Brotherton, and L. Barrios. New York: Columbia University Press, pp. 238–314; Rodriguez, R. 2003. On the Subject of Gang Photography in *Gangs and Society: Alternative Perspectives*, edited by L. Kontos, D. Brotherton, and L. Barrios. New York: Columbia University Press, pp. 255–282.

DONNA DECESARE

GANG PREVENTION AND INTERVENTION PROGRAMS. Gang membership increases the likelihood of criminal activities. Members of gangs are also more likely to recidivate than non-gang members (Sherman, 1998). As Reed and Decker (2002) state "the group context of gang behavior may provide support and opportunity for its members to engage in both illegal behavior as well as more serious illegal behavior" (p. 14). Therefore, policies and programs are needed to decrease gang involvement and behavior in order to reduce youth crimes. Most policy approaches such as curfews, suppression, and punitive sanctions are not effective at reducing youth gangs. Programs have been developed by communities and schools to decrease youth violent behavior; however, only a few focus specifically on reducing gang membership and behavior. Even fewer have been evaluated to measure the outcomes of the programs.

The Gang Problem

Gangs have been around since the 1600s, yet there is no universally accepted definition of a gang (Spergel, 1990). Police, policy makers, researchers, and program developers have defined gangs in a myriad of ways. The most widely accepted definition among researchers is articulated by Klein (1971 as cited in Huff, 1989), in which the youth gang is "any denotable adolescent group of youngsters who (a) are generally perceived as a distinct aggregation by others in the neighborhood, (b) recognize themselves as a denotable group (almost invariably with a group name) and (c) have been involved in a sufficient number of delinquent incidents to call forth a consistent negative response from neighborhood residents and/or law enforcement agencies" (p. 528).

Since the early 1980s, gangs appear to have been increasing in the United States. Every state now has gangs and gang violence (Spergel, 1990). According to the 1996 National Youth Gang Survey, there are 30,818 gangs and about 846,428 members (Gaffney, 1999; Daily, 2000). About 71 percent of the members are fifteen to twenty-four years of age (National Youth gang survey of 1996, cited in Venkatesh, 1999). Usually the members of gangs have similar characteristics which range from failure in school, dysfunctional families, behavioral problems, low self-esteem, or a history of family abuse and neglect (Gaffney, 1999).

Most gang members have engaged in crimes before joining a gang. However, their membership increases the likelihood of their involvement in crimes. Gang members actively participate in drug trafficking and violent crimes (Howell and Decker, 1999). They commit a higher proportion of violent crimes compared to those who are not in gangs (Spergel, 1990). Where gangs have a large presence, community members typically rank gangs as a serious problem (Hagedorn, 1991). There have been many attempts to decrease youth crime throughout the years, but few programs focused directly on reducing youth gangs.

Community-Based Prevention Approaches and Evaluations

Community- and school-based programs mainly focus on youth violence, drugs, and crime. However, few programs focus directly on gangs and even fewer have been evaluated on their effectiveness in dealing with gangs. Part of the problem, as Sherman (1998) notes, is that the effectiveness of community-based programs "depends heavily on our ability to help reshape community life, at least in our most troubled communities."

One well-known program is the Neutral Zone, a community-based prevention program established in 1982. The results of one evaluation found that the program was effective during the time the adolescents were in the program. However, it did not reduce gang membership or "gang" behavior. Also, there were no differences in crime rates between the hours of when the Neutral Zone activities took place. At the same time, the calls for service did decrease when the Neutral Zone was in effect. The overall results are somewhat positive since most of the participants (gang youth) stated that they would have been involved in crime if it were not for the program (Thurman, 1996).

Spergel et al. (2002) evaluated the Gang Violence Reduction project in Little Village, California. The evaluation results indicated that gangs did not change in size, but there was a decrease in fights and serious offenses. There was also a drop in gang initiation. Gang members attended school more frequently. Employment increased from 30.9 percent to 63.3 percent. The youth who were provided with more individual counseling were more likely to reduce their involvement in gang activities. Last, suppression activities did not have a significant effect on reduction of gang activities, gang violence or drug use (Spergel et al., 2002).

Riverside's comprehensive community wide approach to gang prevention, intervention and suppression titled BRIDGE (Building Resources for the Intervention and Deterrence of Gang Engagement) was also evaluated by Spergel et al. (2003). The main goal of the program is to reduce youth gang crime as well as increase social development for those in gangs and those at high risk of being involved in a gang. This program was developed around a specific theory (**social disorganization**). It targeted communities with a large gang problem and focused on gang leaders. The results indicate that there was no difference in arrest rates for those in the program and those in the comparison group. The program did lower the yearly levels of both violence and arrests for program youth. However, the comparison group had decreased drug use compared to the treatment group. There was no effect on yearly property arrests. Interviews with gang members indicate that there was not much of an effect on enrollment in gang membership. Police interviews and data indicate an increase in gang sizes in both Arlanza and Casa Blanca (Spergel et al., 2003).

The findings of each of the programs have indicated weak to no reduction in gang membership or activities. This can be due to the weak research designs, for example with no comparison group, poor selection of samples, or not enough time to evaluate the program. On the other hand, it might the case that program could not, even under optimal conditions, solve the root causes of gangs.

School-Based Preventions and Evaluation

Some schools have become the battlefield for rival gangs. According to Spergel et al. (1995), "students who are gang members claim the school as their turf" (Parks, 1995). A report by the U.S. Department of Education and Justice found that the presence of gangs has doubled between 1989 and 1995. Gangs are problematic in schools because they create disruption and violence in and around the schools (Howell and Lynch, 2000). Schools can harbor gangs, but schools have great potential to locus gang prevention (Gottfredson, 1998). The focus of this section is to explain the few school-based gang prevention programs and their evaluations (effectiveness).

Since 1991, a number of studies have evaluated the GREAT (Gang Resistance Education and Training) program. The program's curriculum involves "moral" re-education and behavioral modification. In 1995, an evaluation concluded a "slightly increased ability to resist the pressures to join gangs" (Esbensen and Osgood, 1999). However, that study was flawed. A national study in 1999 was also conducted. Students reported having positive attitudes toward the program. However, the program only had modest effects on reducing gang affiliation and delinquency. There was no effect on victimization, status offenses, or drug sales. Another evaluation in 2002 concluded that the staff's attitudes changed positively toward the program, however, few felt that gangs decreased. Overall, it is a promising program (Esbensen and Osgood, 1999).

The Gang Resistance is Paramount (GRIP) school-based program in Paramount, California, was evaluated on the effectives of outcome measures, specifically educating and reducing gang membership. The program includes twenty-six to twenty-nine lessons throughout the school year. This school curriculum is for second, fifth, and ninth graders. The program also provided parent education, family counseling, and recreational activities (Solis et al., 2003). The results from the community members' interviews found that few knew about the program, but did feel as though illegal gang behavior was decreasing, while others did not see a real change. Community members gave credit to the police and the city for the decrease. Those who did know about the program had positive attitudes of GRIP. Generally, the parents had positive attitudes and felt there was a decrease in gang activity. GRIP participants were more likely to agree that graffiti was destructive, joining a gang hurts family and friends, tattoos create problems for future employment, being arrested is a problem, and it is not okay to hang out with gang members. Further, few students felt that gang membership made them safer.

Both programs are widely implemented in schools to reduce gangs and gang violence in school. Each program was evaluated to determine their effectiveness. The results indicate that the programs have a weak impact on gangs. The GREAT program has been evaluated numerous times with different research designs and the overall conclusion is similar: hardly any reduction in gangs. The youths' surroundings and lack of reinforcement outside of school might be an issue. Students can understand the reasons for not joining gangs, but the pressure still exists in their communities.

The relevant literature has indicated that gangs are a problem and programs have not been as effective in reducing the gang membership or criminal behavior. On a positive note, some of programs have increased school attendance, graduation rate, and changed attitudes and decreased certain crimes by participants.

Discussion

In order to prove effective in reducing gangs and gang crime, programs and projects need to be constantly evaluated and amenable to change in response to research findings. Good intentions are not enough. Delinquent youth need effective programs.

References/Suggested Readings: Daily, W. Jr. 2000. National Gang Threat Assessment. *National Alliance of Gang Investigators Associations*, 1–56; Esbensen, F., and Osgood, D.W. 1999. Gang Resistance Education and Training (GREAT); Results from the National Evaluation. *Journal of Research in Crime and Delinquency*, 36 (2), 194–225; Fritsch, E.J., Caeti, T.J., and Taylor, R.W. 1999. Gang Suppression through Saturation Patrol, Aggressive Curfew, and Truancy Enforcement: A Quasi-Experimental Test of the Dallas Anti-Gang Initiative. *Crime and Delinquency*, 45 (1), 122–139; Gaffney, R.J. 1998. Preventing Youth Gang Proliferation in Suffolk County. *Juvenile Crime Prevention Commission Report*. U.S. Department of Justice; Gottfredson, D.C. 1998. *Preventing Crime: What Works, What Doesn't, What's Promising: A Report to the Congress to the United States Congress-School Based Crime Prevention*. Chapter 5; Gottfredson, G.D., and Gottfredson, D.C. 1999. Survey of School-Based Gang Prevention and Intervention Programs; Preliminary Findings. *Behavioral Science Research and Development*. Gottfredson Associates, pp. 1–16; Hagedorn, J.M. 1991. Gangs, Neighborhoods and Public Policy. *Social Problems*, 38 (4), 529–542; Howell, J.C. and Lynch, J.P. 2000. Youth Gangs in Schools. *Juvenile Justice Bulletin, U.S. Department of Justice*. Office of Juvenile Justice and Delinquency Prevention, August; Huff, R.C. 1989. Youth Gangs and Public Policy. *Crime and Delinquency*, 35 (4), 524–537; Korem, D. 1994. *Suburban Gangs: The Affluent Rebels*. Richardson, TX: International Focus Press; Parks, C.P. 1995. Gang Behavior in Schools: Reality or Myth? *Educational Psychology Review*, (7) 1, 41, 68; Peterson, D., and Esbensen, F. 2004. The Outlook Is GREAT; What Educators Say About School-Based Prevention and the Gang Resistance Education and Training (G.R.E.A.T.) Program. *Evaluation Review*, 28 (3), 218–245; Reed, L.W., and Decker, H.S. 2002. *Responding to Gangs; Evaluation and Research*. U.S. Department of Justice, National Institute of Justice; Sherman, L.W. 1998. *Preventing Crime: What Works, What Doesn't, What's Promising: A Report to the United States Congress*. Communities and Crime Prevention, Chapter 3; Solis, A., Schwartz, W., and Hinton, T. 2003. *Gang Resistance Is Paramount (GRIP) Program Evaluation: Final Report*. USC Center for Economic Development School of Policy, Planning and Development, California, pp. 1–82; Spergel, A.I. 1990. Youth Gangs: Continuity and Change. *Crime and Justice*, 21, 171–275; Spergel, A.I. 1995. *The Youth Gang Problem; A Community Approach*. New York: Oxford University Press; Spergel, A.I., Ming Wa, K., Chio, S., Grossman, S., Jacob A., Spergel, A., and Barrios, E.M. 2002. *Evaluation of the Gang Violence Reduction Project in Little Village, Final Report Summary*. School of Social Service Administration, University of Chicago, pp. 1–99; Spergel, A.I., Ming Wa, K., Sosa, V.R., Son, J., Barrios, E.M., and Spergel, A. 2003. *Evaluation of the Riverside Comprehensive Community Wide Approach to Gang Prevention, Intervention and Suppression—Building Resources for the Intervention and Deterrence of Gang Engagement (BRIDGE)*. Prevention School of Social Service Administration, University of Chicago, 1–381; Standing, A. 2005. *The Threat of Gangs and Anti Gang Policy: Policy Discussion Paper*. Institute for Security Studies, pp. 1–29; Thurman, Q.C., Giacomazzi, A.L, Reisig, M.D., and Mueller, D.G. 1996. Community-Based Gang Prevention and Intervention: An Evaluation of the Neutral Zone. *Crime and Delinquency*, 42 (2), 279–295; Venkatesh, S.A. 1999. Community-Based Interventions into Street Gang Activity. *Journal of Community Psychology*, 27 (5), 551–567; White, R. 2004. Police and Community Responses to Youth Gangs: Trends and Issues in Crime and Criminal Justice. *Australian Institute of Criminology*, 274, 1–6.

CRYSTAL RODRIGUEZ

GANG SYMBOLS. One very important element of a gang is its use of symbols. Gang symbols function as a method of communication (Curry, 2003). They are used to distinguish membership within the gang and can also be used to send messages to rival gangs. Some gangs have become so large that the only way members can distinguish each other from other gangs is their symbols (Decker, 1996). These symbols may be in the form of tattoos, colors, clothes, graffiti, or hand signs. Whichever form they take, gang symbols are a crucial component of the gang.

Tattoos

One important gang symbol is the tattoo. Gang tattoos function as a clear and definite indication of membership. They are often used to distinguish a true member from a wannabe (Curry, 2003). The tattoo itself would be an actual symbol of the gang, in the literal sense of the word *symbol*. Each gang has a picture or group of letters and/or numbers to represent itself. For example, members of the commonly known **Bloods** gang in Los Angeles use the word *Bloods* spelled out across the knuckles of their right hand as one of their symbols (www.tattoojohnny.com/gang-tattoo-designs.asp). The Nuestra Familia gang often uses a picture of a sombrero over a machete dripping blood as their symbol (www.tattoojohnny.com/gang-tattoo-designs.asp). The Nuestra Familia also favor the number 14, the letter N being the fourteenth letter of the alphabet (www.nagia.org/Gang%20Articles/Graffi.htm). The action of a member getting "tagged," as it is commonly referred to, signifies a very serious degree of commitment and involvement in the gang (Curry, 2003). To outwardly mark his or her body with the gang's symbol is viewed as a privilege. This privilege is not extended to every member. Such an important distinction of membership is reserved for the most dedicated and involved members. These chosen members have proved themselves within the gang (Curry, 2003). Naturally, the tattooed members are usually the oldest (Decker, 1996). Not all gang members want to be "tagged," as they are likely to get into more trouble if they have the gang's symbols tattooed on their bodies. The tattoo is a bull's eye for rival gangs as well as the police (Decker, 1996). Due to the widespread research on gangs the police now have an extensive library of photographs depicting gangs and their use of tattoos as symbols. As a result, the trend of "tagging" has died down recently (www.tattoojohnny.com/gang-tattoo-designs.asp).

Colors

A more common gang symbol is the use of colors (Decker, 1996). Gangs have specific colors they wear that signify membership. For example, the Bloods use the color red. Their rival gang, the **Crips**, use the color blue (www.nagia.org/Gang%20Articles/Crips%20and%20Bloods.pdf). Colors are used for identification and reinforce unity, as are all gang symbols. Wearing gang colors shows pride in membership. Gang colors make it easier for a member to quickly recognize someone as an ally or a rival. It is very important that a gang member not be caught wearing a rival gang's color. That mistake could be the difference between life and death (Decker, 1996).

Clothing

Clothing is a very important form of expression and communication of gang members. Hats, handkerchiefs, belts, shoelaces, and beaded necklaces are all accessories that can identify gang members. Certain rules apply to the way a gang member may dress. For example, members of Peoples Nation alliances favor their left side, while Folk Nation alliances favor their right side. Gang members will wear their hats tilted to the left or right according to their gang affiliation. This directional distinction also applies to all other forms of dress. Gang members may roll up one pant leg, or wear jewelry on one side. They have also been known to wear handkerchiefs or bandanas attached to a back pocket or belt loop on their gang's side (www.geocities.com/Athens/4111/nogangs.html). Gangs also prefer certain brands. For example, the Crips wear British Knight sneakers with the logo BK on the back (www.dc.state.fl.us/pub/gangs/la.html). They wear the BK logo to signify "Blood Killers" (www.knowgangs.com/gang_resources/Crips/Crips_001.htm). Gangs will sometimes use professional sports jerseys as symbols also. **Latin Kings** sometimes wear LA Kings clothing (www.geocities.com/Athens/4111/nogangs.html). Some Folk Nation affiliates like to wear Georgetown clothing, the initial G representing "gangster" (www.geocities.com/Athens/4111/nogangs.html). Each gang has its own rules and regulations regarding dress codes. Some gangs may wear their shirts buttoned at just the top of their shirt, while others will wear their shirts completely open (ga .essortment.com/gangsignsands_reyp.htm). As with all other gang symbols, clothing symbols vary from gang to gang.

Graffiti

Another gang symbol widely used is graffiti. Graffiti is a form of communication. Gang members may send messages to rival gangs, or mark their territory with the use of graffiti (Decker, 1996). In some cases gang members will cross out a rival gang's graffiti, or mark over it with phrases such as RIP. Writing RIP over a rival gang's graffiti is a clear and definite death threat (Curry, 2003). Gangs have also been known to use graffiti to memorialize the death of a member (Curry, 2003). Gang graffiti can vary from a simple gang logo such as the three- or five-point crown for the Latin Kings, to an elaborate display or message of past or future gang activity (www.knowgangs.com/gang_resources/Crips/Crips_001.htm). Folk Nation affiliates have been known to use symbols such as a pitchfork, a six-point star, or a heart with wings in their graffiti (www.gangsta411.com/gang_symbols.htm). Peoples Nation affiliates use symbols such a five-point star or crown, a star and moon, or just the number 5 itself (www.gangsta411.com/gang_symbols.htm). Certain gangs have specific ways of insulting their rival gangs through graffiti. For example, the Crips replace the letter B with the letter C in their writing to insult their rivals the Bloods (www.knowgangs.com/gang_resources/Crips/Crips_001.htm). Gangs will also write their rival gangs' logos or symbols upside down as an insult. Peoples Nation gangs do this with the Folk Nations pitchfork, drawing it pointing downward instead of up. This type of insult or form of disrespect can often lead to gang violence (www .gangfreekids.org/gangs.html). Gang graffiti serves as an important element in the classification of a gang. What sets a gang apart from any other group is its involvement in criminal activity, such as graffiti or form of vandalism (Curry, 2003). As popular as graffiti is within the gang culture, it is considered by members one of the lowest forms of criminality. Most gangs are involved in much more severe levels of crime than vandalism (Decker, 1996).

Hand Signs

Hand signs were first introduced to the gang community by black gang members in Los Angeles in the mid-1950s (www.knowgangs.com/gang_resources/handsigns/ menu_001.htm). This mode of communication is essentially their own form of sign language. Gang members manipulate their fingers and hands to form certain combinations of letters. They use hand signs to communicate messages and identify themselves to other members. This is usually referred to this as "flashing" or "throwing" signs (www.slsheriff.org/html/org/metrogang/gangsign.html). Hand signs can communicate serious business for gang members. For example, a Crip member may flash a BK hand sign to convey the statement "kill a Blood" of "Blood Killer" (www .slsheriff.org/html/org/metrogang/gangsign.html). The Bloods have a sign that spells out blood with the use of both hands. They "flash" that sign to identify themselves to other members. The Latin Kings have a five-point star hand sign that they use for identification (www.rapdict.org/Latin_Kings). As with all other symbols, hand signs vary from gang to gang.

Symbols are an integral part of gang culture. They convey messages related to solidarity, identification, pride, membership, hate, threats, insults, and revenge.

References/Suggested Readings: Caffey, Wayn. 2006. *Crips and Bloods.* Retrieved on October 15, 2006, from www.nagia.org/Gang%20Articles/Crips%20and%20Bloods.pdf; *Crips.* Retrieved on October 17, 2006, from http://www.knowgangs.com/gang_resources/Crips/Crips_001.htm; Curry, David G., and Decker, Scott H. 2003. *Confronting Gangs: Crime and Community* (2nd ed.). Los Angeles: Roxbury; Decker, Scott H., and Van Winkle, Barrik. 1996. *Life in the Gang: Family, Friends, and Violence.* New York: Cambridge University Press; Florida Department of Corrections. *Los Angeles Based Gangs—Bloods and Crips.* Retrieved on October 17, 2006, from www.dc.state.fl.us/pub/gangs/la.html; *Gang Signs.* Retrieved on October 16, 2006, from www.slsheriff.org/html/org/metrogang/gangsign.html; *Gang Symbols.* Retrieved on October 15, 2006, from gangsta411.com/gang_symbols.htm; *Gang Tattoos and Tattoo Designs.* Retrieved on October 15, 2006, from www.tattoojohnny .com/gang-tattoo-designs.asp; *Hand Signs.* Retrieved on October 16, 2006, from www .knowgangs.com/gang_resources/handsigns/menu_001.htm; *Latin Kings.* Retrieved on October 16, 2006, from www.rapdict.org/Latin_Kings; National Foundation for Abused and Neglected Children. *Gangs.* Retrieved on October 15, 2006, from www.gangfreekids.org/gangs.html; Parents in Crisis. *Gangs!* Retrieved on October 17, 2006, from www.geocities.com/Athens/4111/nogangs.html; Rae, Janene. *Graffiti: The Newspaper of the Streets.* Retrieved on October 16, 2006, from www.nagia.org/Gang%20Articles/Graffi.htm; Walker, Victoria. 2002. *Gang Signs and Symbols.* Retrieved on October 15, 2006, from ga.essortment.com/gangsignsands_reyp.htm.

SHAWN BOOTH

GANG WORKERS. For five years, 2001–2006, I conducted ethnographic research with gang members and their associates in a large Southwestern city. This city, which I will call D-town, (the city and group names used in this chapter are pseudonyms), was politically different than the place where I originated my gang research back in the early 1990s (Dogden). There were groups in D-town whose goals included community empowerment for the people who were often neglected or mistreated by mainstream institutions. In particular these groups advocated for the civil rights of the Latino and African American community. The local police labeled 95 percent of the people on their gang list as Latino or African American. The activist groups included Area Support for All People (ASAP), Gang Group, People Observing the Police (POP), and Unidos.

ASAP was a local group that held meetings once a week with youth to help decrease the escalating violence between gangs. This group had the potential to offer gang members the greatest intervention because the youth were exposed to older ex-gang members who had left the gang lifestyle behind and remained positive cultural role models. ASAP included a professional staff presence that somewhat hindered gang members' comfort levels to speak freely or at great length. The professional staff offered educational, legal, and medical guidance. When the professional staff members were not present, the gangsters talked more comfortably with the ex-gang members. This group's main problem involved funding and the over-emphasis on instituting the professional staffs' solutions that included psychological behavior modification over the ex-gang members' emphasis on cultural knowledge building. When the group began in the early 1990s it was well attended, but since 2000 many of the participants have been court-ordered to attend. The group needed more ex-gang member or barrio raised staff for culture, gender, and language differences, but do not have the institutional or funding support to make this a reality.

The Gang Group was designed to counter police and media claims regarding gang membership and the disproportionate implications against the Latino and African American community. The group included longtime residents who were middle-aged and deeply concerned about how the police and media claims could result in policies and funding that criminalized and harassed local youth of color. The group sought out the media and presented these issues to the community. They sought to educate and incorporate a wide variety of city council and community members to help stop an initiative for a statewide gang database. The group achieved some of its objectives and members went on to work with various other organizations. Several members' activism resulted in legal troubles. The members' dedication included a higher than average number of media attention.

POP was a group that operated in several other cities across the country. When members of this group observed a police stop or a police presence they walked over and recorded the interactions with camcorders. They often spoke with the police or the person(s) of interest after the encounter and obtained officer names or business cards. The goal of this group was to ensure the individual rights of community residents. The D-town POP group faced problems with illegal police surveillance and a lawsuit was initiated on the group's behalf to stop the police for documenting their non-illegal behavior. A few times when individual officers tried to cause problems for the POP group members they were criticized by their superiors or challenged legally.

Finally, Unidos was a local youth and parent group that attempted to improve K through twelfth-grade education in the city. They conducted surveys, met with media, and helped establish reform committees within several schools. The most important component of this group was its strong youth leadership and its adult member advisement. This locally run group received a lot of local and national support. They confronted stereotypes about Latinos not being interested in their education or future. Many of the youth leaders went on to higher education and remained active in their communities.

Education and policing were two major problems that potential or current gang members faced living in this Southwestern city. These activist groups actively attempted to improve these institutions and how mainstream authority figures related with the Latino and black community by the groups' ability to challenge negative claims and inappropriate treatment. The activist groups attempted to portray a positive image of themselves and the community to the media in order to counter inaccurate stereotypes produced by these mainstream institutions that disempowered the residents.

Division of labor was the major problem that each of these groups faced. One group focused on preventing violence whereas other groups focused on policing, education, or media. Each group worked with its own staff and responded to their own internal funding problems. There was not one umbrella group that could meet the needs of the entire community and therefore play a larger role in removing the importance of gangs.

In the past, D-town had a grassroots organization called the Crusade for Justice that attempted to meet the needs of the entire Chicano/a community with networks and alliances with African American and Native American groups. The organization worked under the philosophy of self-determination and cultural pride. They responded to two primary issues: police brutality and the hostile educational system. The Crusade for Justice became involved in protests (police, schools, Vietnam) and opposing anti-Latino public figures, laws, and policies. By the end of the 1960s, the Crusade created bridges with youths by organizing dances and offering support for their creation of Black and Brown Berets (a national Chicano/a youth group). By 1969 most youth had left their gang involvement to join these activist youth groups (Vigil, 1999). This created for the first time a social group that altered youth gang involvement by fighting discrimination while offering status and approval from peers. The demise of the Crusade and its political presence by local and federal COINTELPRO activities has often been thought by community members to have played a major part in the redevelopment of gangs in this city in the early 1980s.

Many grassroots groups across the United States have created gang programs that have received a wide variety of resistance by police or mainstream authority figures. Two of these groups that come to mind are Homies Unidos and Homeboy Industries (Rappleye, 2000; State of Utah Gang Conference, 1999). The lack of support for gang workers and gang programs seems to have developed from the work of Klein (1971). In the early 1970s Klein (1971) researched the impact of a gang worker program in Los Angeles. According to Klein, the group's goal was to reduce gang delinquency by decreasing gang cohesiveness. But, instead, he found that their project increased cohesiveness and only slightly decreased delinquency. He found that the employment aspects of the project produced the most effective results, demonstrated by the fact that non-working days there were almost twice as many offenses. During the same time Dawley's (1972) research found a more optimistic, but less structured approach for confronting the impact of gangs. He worked in Chicago with an African American street gang, gathering funds for self-help programs that emphasized social and economic empowerment. According to Dawley, they were able to establish an art center, clothing boutique, employment office, management training center, recreation center, and teen center. However, the funding did not continue and shortly after it was cut off the gangs once again became a negative presence. Brotherton and Barrios (2004) have also charted how the **Latin Kings** have worked to transform themselves from a street gang into a group for empowerment. But again this gang has been confronted by a large number of police and legal obstacles to their political resistance.

Historically, there is little evidence to indicate that mainstream United States society will support humanist measures to diminish the gangs in low-income communities of color. And activist groups that are considered too radical are soon destroyed (see Durán, 2006). Groups that are more mainstream are often hindered by bureaucratic self-interests that leave the underlying issues unresolved. The groups that are in place in D-town are making a difference to prevent and intervene with gang membership. However, they lack the individual and organizational coalition building that will bring them to the level of empowerment witnessed by the Crusade for Justice.

In this light, reforming gang members toward assimilation or revolutionary resistance faces extreme difficulty. For one, gangs are in conflict with people who share a similar class, ethnicity, and race. These rivalries are often contained within several distinct neighborhoods. Second, many of these conflicts have been encouraged by local police gang enforcement and federal opposition to self-help groups that desire to improve the overall standing of racial and ethnic minority groups within cities across the United States. Third, there exists great confusion as to how to assimilate gang members into mainstream society without changing their social environment or living situation. For these reasons gang membership remains a viable option in politically and socially distressed neighborhoods. Nevertheless, D-town's activist groups can be seen as an active leader in pushing for improving the lives of Chicanos/as and African Americans in the cities barrios and poverty-stricken neighborhoods. These groups have been observed to challenge the issues that keep gangs present in this city and provide a possible place of insight into providing alternatives to gangs.

References/Suggested Readings: Brotherton, D.C. and Barrios, L. 2004. *The Almighty Latin King and Queen Nation: Street Politics and the Transformation of a New York City Gang.* New York: Columbia University Press; Dawley, D. [1973] 1992. *A Nation of Lords: The Autobiography of the Vice Lords.* Prospect Heights, IL: Waveland Press; Durán, R.J. 2006. *Fatalistic Social Control: The Reproduction of Oppression through the Medium of Gangs.* Dissertation. University of Colorado at Boulder; Klein, M.W. 1971. *Street Gangs and Street Workers.* Englewood Cliffs, NJ: Prentice Hall; Rappleye, C. (n.d.). *Harassing Homies: LAPD Campaigns Against a Church-based Gang-peace Project.* Retrieved from www.street-gangs.com/people/asanchez.html; State of Utah Gang Conference. 1999. *Los Angeles Gangs.* Law Enforcement Only Section; Vigil, E.B. 1999. *The Crusade for Justice: Chicano Militancy and the Government's War on Dissent.* Madison: University of Wisconsin Press.

ROBERT DURÁN

GANGS AND DRUGS. For well over a century gangs and drugs have independently commanded the attention of many groups, including law enforcement, social scientists, and the media. Analyses that connected gangs and drugs were, for the most part, limited to drug use by individual gang members. In the mid-1980s the issue was reconstructed with the explosion of the crack epidemic. Law enforcement, aided by media hype, promulgated the notion that gangs and drug sales were synonymous, evidenced by the following statements from two members of Los Angeles law enforcement: "This narcotics stuff is all a matter of gangs and conspiracy" and "gangs and drugs are almost the same problem" (Klein, 1995, p. 40). The accepted narrative not only had violent posses in control of all drug markets but warned of migrating gangs moving into many neighborhoods with the express purpose of setting up organized drug markets. While the concept of gang dominance over drug sales may seem self-evident to police and be a popular subject for news headlines, social science research has produced a far more complex, and at times contradictory, picture of the gangs/drugs nexus.

There are two broad categories of research focusing on gang involvement in the drug market. One school of thought sees the group as a highly organized, vertical structure reflecting an above-ground corporation, a rational organization, ideal for successful drug sales (Skolnick, 1990; Padilla, 1992; Taylor, 1990; Sanchez-Jankowski, 1991).

One proponent of this view is Skolnick (1990), who distinguishes between "cultural" gangs—southern California Chicano groups, and northern California's African American "entrepreneurial" gangs. Although both sell drugs, Skolnick maintains that the "cultural groups" are neighborhood oriented, concerned with loyalty, tradition, and territory. Drug sales are not integral to the groups' existence. In sharp contrast are the "entrepreneurial" black gangs who not only dominate drug sales in their area but who exist only as a drug distribution group. Skolnick maintains that the "cultural" groups are slowly being transformed into instrumental drug-selling corporations as the lure of drug money replaces neighborhood tradition and family ties. He also suggests that the black Los Angeles gangs are migrating into other Western states for (drug) business purposes. Skolnick's business migration view is refuted by the 1997 National Youth Gang Survey, in which the vast majority of respondents, 70 percent, cite social factors such as families and legitimate job opportunities as their reasons for moving.

The picture of the gang as a well-organized drug-selling bureaucracy is echoed by Taylor (1990) in his study of Detroit gangs: the most highly organized drug groups were termed "corporate" gangs, and the more fluid groups were seen as evolutionary stages on their way to corporate status. Sanchez-Jankowski (1991) also views these groups as well structured and highly organized with drug sales playing a central role in the groups' existences. In *The Gang as an American Enterprise*, Padilla describes a second-generation Puerto Rican street gang, originally started as a musical group, which evolved into a drug-selling clique largely in reaction to the Illinois Controlled Substance Act (1971). The legislation carried heavy penalties for those over eighteen years of age who were caught selling heroin and/or cocaine. The older "owners" turned to neighborhood youth to conduct street sales. The youngsters decided to go into business for themselves and the gang became a source of jobs and status for kids who felt the above-ground economy offered them neither.

Many other studies of the 1980s and 1990s offer an alternate view to the version of gangs as well-organized, violent, and entrenched groups in low-income minority areas, starting to spring up across the United States at the height of the crack epidemic. Relying on both quantitative and qualitative data, this contrasting perspective portrays gangs as loosely organized groups, with little cohesion and transient leadership. Rather than vertically organized and sharing common financial goals (focused on drug sales), these youth are involved in "cafeteria style crime" (Klein, 1995). Individual gang members may sell drugs but the activity is conducted in a disorganized, informal fashion with the rather modest proceeds going to the individual seller, not pooled for the gang. The popular tabloid image of massive financial gains from drug sales is continually disputed by research (Fagan, 1989). When asked by researchers what amount of money would get them to stop selling drugs, respondents answered with an amount slightly above what could be made at a fast food restaurant (Huff, 1998). A three-year study of gang members in St. Louis emphasized the informal nature of street drug sales and their tenuous relation to an organized gang, which was described as a "neighborhood friendship" group (Decker and Van Winckle, 1994); members of the St. Louis group sold drugs as individuals, but did not join the gang for monetary gain and the drug sales were incidental to the group's existence. Hagedorn (1994) describes the young adult males members of a Milwaukee gang as being on an "economic merry-go-round," continually looking for opportunities in the above-ground economy but periodically returning to delinquent activities when licit jobs proved temporary or non-existent. In Hagedorn's typology less than 25 percent of the group's members saw drug sales as a long-term career, and only this small group, termed "new jacks" fully embraced non-conformist values. Prior to a study of street gangs and drug sales in two suburbs of Los Angeles, law enforcement predicted that almost all (over 90 percent) of the drug sales taking place in the two locales was dominated by gangs. The studies focused on both co-caine and non-cocaine sales and found that less than 25 percent involved a gang member. The researcher points out that even if one party to the transaction was a gang member this hardly meant that the gang as an institution exerted control (Max-son, 1995).

One of the principle concerns in the literature of the 1980s and 1990s was an analysis of the assertion by law enforcement and the media that increased violence was an inevitable result of gang involvement in drug markets. Research conducted in Los Angeles, based on police records found that although there was a sharp in-crease in crack sales in the mid-1980s, the market was not dominated by gangs and there were no major changes in sales related violence that could be attributed to gang involvement. In fact, the decrease in gun use was more significant in gang inci-dents than non-gang cases (Klein, Maxson, and Cunningham, 1991). Any increase in gang involvement in the drug cases was thought to be a result of law enforce-ment's definition of a gang crime as any incident where one party had gang "status" (Maxson, 1995). Since most street sales involve small amounts of drugs it would seem pointless to employ strategies, such as violence, sure to command unwanted police and media attention. The consensus of the Los Angeles studies was that the city's crack market in the mid-1980s belonged to "regular drug dealers" not to street gangs (Klein, Maxson, and Cunningham, 1991). A study examining gang homicide police data over a twenty-six-year period (1965–1990) revealed that the most lethal gang violence was due to territory issues not drug dales (Block and Block, 1993). Fagan's (1989) study of three American cities revealed that drug dealing had little impact on the serious crime and violence in those locales. Additional research that contradicts popular media stories connecting gang-dominated drug sales leading to explosive violence is a study conducted by two doctors from the Centers for Disease Control who used police data to examine drug aspects of gang homicides, and ex-plore the relationship between gangs, drug sales, and violence: the reported homi-cides were less likely to involve gang members and gang motivated homicides were unlikely to involve drugs (Meehan and O'Carroll, 1995).

Much of the difficulty in reaching a consensus on the gang drug sales connection is due to the varying definitions used by law enforcement and social scientists to define "gang" and "gang-related crime" but the National Youth Gang Survey in 1996 may be revealing. Sent out to over 3,000 police and sheriff departments across the United States, most respondents felt that gangs could never control nor manage drug distribution in their areas.

Although caution should be urged in generalizing findings about a specific drug market in one locale to others, recent ethnographic data into the heroin markets in New York City found a distinct departure from "corporate" dealing that was said to dominate the market in the 1980s and early 1990s ("Heroin In the 21st Century," NIDA). While the former may have been distinct hierarchies, vertically organized with specific roles for the workers, held together by pursuit of the dollar, the dealers over the last ten years are a marked contrast. These young men are held together by family ties and neighborhood loyalties, perhaps a return to Moore's Los Angeles "homeboys" (Moore, 1978). They are small socially bonded groups deeply embedded in the fabric of the neighborhood. The author has known many of these young men for over a decade and their primary allegiances are to their families and longtime friends. Any income derived from the drug sales go to their parents, "wives," and children (Herman, 2000).

Although media and law enforcement have tended to concentrate on drug use and sales as an inner city, minority phenomenon, self-reports indicate that drug use and sales cut across class and color lines. Perhaps future research should look beyond the inner-city streets and start to focus on white middle- and upper-class use and its form of dealing. The view of the street gang as an omnipotent, violent drug-selling organization belongs in the media headlines of the 1980s.

References/Suggested Readings: Block, Carolyn, and Richard Block. 1993. *Street Gang Crime in Chicago. Research in Brief*. Washington, DC: U.S. Department of Justice, Office of Justice Programs, National Institute of Justice; Decker, Scott, and Van Winkle, Barrick. 1994. Slinging Dope: The Role of Gangs and Gang Members in Drug Sales. *Justice Quarterly*, 11 (4), 583–604; Fagan, Jeffrey. 1989. The Social Organization of Drug Use and Drug Selling among Urban Gangs. *Criminology*, 27, 622–667; Hagedorn, John M. 1994. Homeboys, Dope Fiends, Legits, and New Jacks. *Criminology*, 32 (2), 197–219; Herman, Stephanie. 2000. *A Family Affair: Heron Dealing in West Harlem*. Paper presented at the annual meeting of the American Society of Criminology, San Francisco, November; Herman, Stephanie. N.d. Heroin in the 21st Century. NIDA-funded grant; Huff, Ronald. 1998. *Comparing the Criminal Behavior of Youth Gangs and At-Risk Youth. Research in Brief*. Washington, DC: U.S. Department of Justice, Office of Justice Programs, National Institute of Justice; Jankowski, Martin Sanchez 1991. *Islands in the Street: Gangs and American Urban Society*. Berkeley: University of California Press; Klein, Malcolm W. 1995. *The American Street Gang: Its Nature, Prevalence, and Control*. New York: Oxford University Press; Klein, Malcolm W., Maxson, Cheryl L., and Cunningham, Lea C. 1991. Crack, Street Gangs and Violence. *Criminology*, 29, 623–650; Maxson, Cheryl L. 1995. *Street Gangs and Drug Sales in Two Suburban Cities. Research in Brief*. Washington, DC: U.S. Department of Justice, Office of Justice Programs, National Institute of Justice; Meehan, Patrick J., and O'Carroll, Patrick W. 1995. Gangs, Drugs, and Homicide in Los Angeles. In M. Klein, C.L. Maxson, and J. Miller (eds.), *The Modern Gang Reader*, pp. 236–242. Los Angeles: Roxbury Publishing; Moore, Joan W. 1978. *Homeboys: Gangs, Drugs, and Prison in the Barrios of Los Angeles*. Philadelphia: Temple University Press; National Youth Gang Center. 1999. *1996 National Youth Gang Survey. Summary*. Washington, DC: U.S. Department of Justice, Office of Justice Programs, Office of Juvenile Justice and Delinquency Prevention; National Youth Gang Center. 2000. *1997 National Youth Gang Survey. Summary*. Washington, DC: U.S. Department of Justice, Office of Justice Programs, Office of Juvenile Justice and Delinquency Prevention; Padilla, Felix. 1992. *The Gang as an American Enterprise*. New Brunswick, NJ: Rutgers University Press; Skolnick, Jerome H., Correll, Theodore, Navarro, Elizabeth, and Roger Rabb. 1990. The Social Structure of Street Dealing. *American Journal of Police*, 9, 1–41; Taylor, Carl. 1990. *Dangerous Society*. East Lansing: Michigan State University Press.

STEPHANIE HERMAN

GANGS AND POST-INDUSTRIALISM. What we now recognize as gangs emerged in the late 1800s and early 1900s with the birth of the industrial city, in the context of mass migrations of population to the great cities of Europe and North America. Gangs are the product of populations who are "in between": distant from the social world of their parents, while at the same time their integration into their adopted country is blocked by racism, unemployment, or even the spatial structures of the city itself. Gangs are best understood as a spatial response to social exclusion.

The industrial societies that developed over the twentieth century were shaped by high employment levels, mass consumption, increasingly standardized lifestyles, and mass-based organizations such as trade unions and political parties. They also saw the development of mass-based systems of social security reflecting "nation-building" strategies and class compromises. From this perspective, the rise of full employment and mass-based trade unions suggests that gangs would become much less significant as industrial societies consolidated over the twentieth century and became more and more shaped by class structures and relationships. And this pattern is widely evident, with industrialization in many countries seeing gangs give way to working-class youth cultures. These were explored in particular in the United Kingdom in studies of "teddy boys," "mods," and "rockers," all understood in terms of the impact of social class structures that were experienced generationally. The United States remained an exception: immigration, race, and urban segregation combined to make gangs an ongoing feature of American social life throughout the industrial period, a reality captured in Whyte's *Street Corner Society*.

The key to understanding gangs has been the insight that gangs emerge as a local actor defending its territory. But with globalization societies are becoming more fragmented and diverse. Global flows of finance, images, and power mean that once unified societies are becoming increasingly complex and much less integrated, setting in motion new forms of urban segregation and stigmatization. Some parts of cities are integrated into national economies, while other sections are integrated into global flows of finance, production, and tourism. This is not however generating the classical ghettos that marked the transition to the industrial city. The development of the Internet and mass travel mean that social life less and less corresponds to national borders, so that increasing numbers of people live across borders, pursuing lives in two or more countries at once. Crime is an increasingly important generator of globalization, from the drug trade to the traffic of sex workers.

In the transition period of the early industrial age, gangs were best understood as a spatial response to social exclusion, seeking to produce order in worlds of disorder, often through mobilizing ethnic identities and traditions. In increasingly globalized, postindustrial societies, the shape and experience of gangs is diverging from the traditional model of the defense of a bordered territory. **Graffiti** writers, for example, experience the city in terms of flow and visibility rather than place, and are involved in forms of action that aims at visibility and presence in an urban experience lived fundamentally in terms of flow and image, not locality and tradition.

Gangs historically have been linked to violence, one of the ways through which control of territory is imposed and maintained. Here again there are signs of changing patterns. Important forms of contemporary urban violence, such as the burning of cars in French cities in October 2005, alert us to the extent of urban segregation and stigmatization in France and other European cities. The core of this violence took place in poor neighborhoods where the industrial working class has largely disappeared, and where informal and temporary employment rivals the illegal economy as the main source of income. In these suburbs while there are patterns of confrontation between small groups who defend their territory against others, the large structured groups typical of the gangs of industrial society are absent. Forms of organization are much more fragile, while action takes the form of social explosion rather than the ongoing organization that characterized gangs of industrial society.

Similar patterns of segregation are emerging in Britain, most obvious in the northern cities of England, where different groups find themselves competing for control of the same spaces. But in the contemporary context, these young people do not fall back onto defending traditional community cultures, instead they increasingly embrace dimensions of global culture—from hip-hop music to forms of politicized Islam, these constructions involving travel and extensive use of the Internet. In these cases, what is particularly important are personal trajectories, often involving "born again" type experiences. These young people do not embrace traditional cultures or ethnic identities, but increasingly look to mobilize global cultures that create distance both from their parents' generation and the dominant culture—political Islam being the most obvious example of such a global culture. At times this dynamic can spill into new types of violence represented by contemporary **terrorism**: there is now significant evidence suggesting that at least two of the young men involved in the terrorist bombing in London of July 7, 2005, had been involved in an "Asian gang" which had been involved in defending its territory against white youths, organizing physical fitness and fighting classes, as well being involved in muscled approaches to helping young people get off heroin.

In the 1980s, the studies of urban gangs in emerging global cities undertaken by Manuel Castells suggested that as global flows became more and more important, new forms of defensive gangs would emerge and attempt to control local spaces. Unable to shape the global world, Castells argued, new types of gangs would emerge and build up walls around territories they could control. Castells's analysis of the global cities was prescient, but the emerging forms of urban action that we are witnessing today do not take the form of the defense of a territory, but more and more take the form of entering the increasingly diverging global flows that constitute the global city. This can take the form of visual flows, new mobilities of people, and new forms of global identity constructed against both community and national society. In that sense the "turf" of contemporary gangs is shifting: from the street corner to global flows. This shift will be at the center of gang research as we move into the twenty-first century.

References/Suggested Readings: Castells, M. 1983. *The City and the Grassroots.* Berkley: California University Press; Castells, M. 1997. *The Power of Identity.* Malden, MA: Blackwell; McDonald, K. 1999. *Struggles for Subjectivity: Identity, Action and Youth Experience.* Cambridge: Cambridge University Press; Whyte, W. 1943. *Street Corner Society.* Chicago: University of Chicago Press.

KEVIN MCDONALD

GANGS AND THE MEDIA. The process of demonization and criminalization has been repeatedly analyzed by sociologists and criminologists who have pointed to the government-media stereotyping of young inner-city populations as a practice stretching back through much of this century (Gilbert, 1986). What many of the studies have found is that the violent, bestial, and primitivistic imagery of gang youths (Conquergood, 1992) have been constant themes in crime and community reports and play a powerful role in constructing the symbolic reality for a mass audience, most of whom have little real contact with actual gang members. In effect, such reporting has been an effective tool in fueling if not creating **"moral panics"** (Cohen, 1972) at various stages of the economic cycle, reflected in successive waves of anti-gang legislation at local, state, and federal levels. Thus, around such populist concerns as urban decay, rising immigrant populations, juvenile crime, the **drug** culture, failing public schools, and youth immorality, gangs have been "tagged" (Young, 1971) as a leading contributory factor rather than as a primary symptom of a broader set of structural contradictions. In contemporary terms gang representatives appear in lengthy feature articles as well as television investigative reports where the semiotic equation amounts to gangs = violence = drugs = gang name.

In Erikson's (1966) terms, the use of such "enemies" is an effort by the dominant order to restore society's social boundaries by ensuring that the threatening Other is managed and brought into line (Spitzer, 1975). Not surprisingly, gang members that I have dealt with in the course of research (see Brotherton and Barrios, 2004) felt that they were wittingly or unwittingly another example of "blaming the victim" in U.S. urban social policy.

Jankowski (1991) states that there is a striking similarity in gang-media stories. First, the nature of the group is linked explicitly to "killings," "murder," and brutality and it is presented in a way that such involvements are seen as a defining characteristic of the group. This is done through dramatic headlines. The importance of headline construction is emphasized in the work of van Dijk (1988) on media-ethnic relations. Van Dijk calls them the semantic macrostructure of news narratives and shows how ethnic derogation of certain minority groups is a constant in mainstream corporate news reports. His treatment of ethnic relations is particularly relevant to a treatment of gangs and the media, especially the treatment of large gangs such as the **Latin Kings**, the **Bloods**, the **Crips**, and the Mara Salvatrucha which are almost daily news items somewhere in the United States. In basic terms, the media conceptualization of "the gang" is an unsubtle example of race and/or ethnic derogation which is best captured by Conquergood, in his commentary on the media's treatment of the Chicago Latin Kings:

> "Gang" has become a fantasy-fetish of primitivism that is co-extensive with other colonialist tropes deployed to erect barriers between Self and Other. In our postcolonial world the alien Other has migrated from the margins of empire and is now, in an ironic twist of history, colonizing our cities. The figure of the gang member in multicultural late twentieth-century urban America is an ethnic male member of the migrant and un- and underemployed classes. Like the representations of "natives" in the colonies, representations of "gangs" in the cities are deployed to contain and control the "dangerous classes," "urban primitives." (Conquergood. 1992, p. 4)

However, the media presentation of gangs is not all pure hegemony since the media can be very contradictory and there are openings for groups to influence the media if they have the political will and consciousness. For example, in a study of the ALKQN in New York City (Brotherton and Barrios, 2004) we also saw headlines with more equivocation and ambivalence as to the nature of the group. These headlines demonstrated to the reader that the jury is still out on the legitimacy of the organization which is bolstered by competing quotes from members of the group and law enforcement "experts." We also found a cluster of headlines that hardly featured any of the evocative, inflammatory vocabulary with the representation not done cynically but rather suggestively, leaving the reader to digest the article before making any assumption. We concluded that these were powerful examples of the extent to which a gang or street organization was able to effectively intervene in its own representation over time, not only by affecting the content of the news but by impacting one of the vital instruments of media storytelling: the headline. The Kings' situation was unique, though not without historical precedent and parallels, in that members were engaged in an effort to actively make the news themselves, a feat similar to Barak's (1988) notion of "newsmaking criminology" and Gitlin's (1980) reading of the contradictory relationship between the media and radical social movements in the 1960s.

References/Suggested Readings: Barak, G. 1988. Newsmaking Criminology: Reflections on the Media, Intellectuals, and Crime. *Justice Quarterly,* 5, 565–587; Brotherton, D., and Barrios, L. 2004. *The Almighty Latin King and Queen Nation.* New York: Columbia University Press; Cohen, S. 1972. *Folk Devils and Moral Panics: The Creation of Mods and Rockers.* London: McGibbon and Kee; Conquergood, D. 1992. *On Reppin' and Rhetoric: Gang Representations.* Paper presented at the Philosophy and Rhetoric of Inquiry Seminar, University of Iowa; Erikson, K. 1966. *Wayward Puritans: A Study in the Sociology of Deviance.* New York: Wiley; Gitlin, T. 1980. *The Whole World Is Watching.* Berkeley: University of California Press; Glibert, J. 1986. *A Cycle of Outrage: America's Reaction to the Juvenile to the Juvenile Delinquent in the 1950s.* New York: Oxford University Press; Jankowski, M. 1991. *Islands in the Street: Gangs in American Society.* Berkeley: University of California Press; Spitzer, S. 1975. Toward a Marxian Theory of Deviance. *Social Problems,* 22 (June), 641–651; Van Dijk, T. 1988. How They Hit the Headlines: Ethnic Minorities in the Press. In G. Smitherman-Donaldson and T. van Dijk (eds.). *Discourse and Discrimination*, pp. 261–262. Detroit, MI: Wayne State University Press.

DAVID C. BROTHERTON

GANGS AND THE UNDERGROUND ECONOMY. The economic activity of gang members forms part of an informal economy that is interrelated with other economies, in particular, the formal societal economy and the wider global economy, each of which shapes and impacts its constituent sub-economies. The economic activity of gangs began with property crimes such as robbery and theft, and then moved into drug sales and sex trading, has recently expanded into a variety of other activities, including alien smuggling, weapons sales, and identity theft, depending on the race/ ethnicity of the gang. Indeed, each of these activities has become defined and shaped by gender, ethnicity, and race, fueled by the exclusion brought by globalization, and manifesting a political resistance and cultural production, itself amplified by mass mediated images and the conflicting ideologies and diversity of individual gang members.

Types of Underground Economy

Any economic activity operating outside the formal, regular economy, and hidden from government taxation system, is considered part of the informal or underground economy, aspects of which have also been referred to by a variety of terms including hidden, unofficial, irregular, social, and criminal. While these terms are rarely used with definitional precision, there is general agreement that the informal/hidden economy contains three interconnected sub-economies, each of which overlap with the fringes of the formal or regular economy. These sub-economies are differentiated by their degree of illegality. The least problematic "social economy" includes non-monetary barter exchange between networks of friends and neighbors, such as car repair for house repair or various kinds of mutual aid and support. The more problematic "irregular economy" (also called the underground economy) generally refers to off-the-books employment, or work outside of formal employment that avoids government taxes by having its exchanges transacted in cash. Both the social and irregular economy violate taxation laws, and the irregular economy may also violate social security, health, and safety laws and local ordinances; both are considered quasi-legal, but illicit. In contrast, the third and most serious underground sub-economy is the "criminal economy." This is itself comprised of three sub-economies. The first sub-economy of the criminal economy is occupational or workplace crime involving embezzlement, pilfering, sabotage, and fraud. This is often overlooked in gang research as its character, like that of college fraternities, defies the stereotypical characteristics of the street gang. However, it typically contains loose or more organized employee subcultures focused on systematic theft from clients and employees, as Gerald Mars demonstrated in his 1982 classic *Cheats at Work*. Moreover, the underground activities of these employees connects to a wider network of economic distribution, and can be the source of an amateur criminal fencing operation as Stuart Henry illustrated in his 1978 study of *The Hidden Economy*. Moreover, applied to higher echelons of corporate hierarchy, "gangs" of corporate executives can share a subculture that legitimates fraud against customers, clients, and investors and that facilitates a vast, and highly lucrative, corporate underground economy using coercion, political bribery, and "creative accounting," to conduct its illegal business, that can result in massive corporate frauds such as seen in Enron.

The second sub-economy of the criminal economy is **organized crime**, including and merging with street-level gang activity, involving a violation of criminal and racketeering laws. This sub-economy includes everything from more familiar street drugs trading, weapons trading, such as guns, knives, and explosives, vice, sex and pornography, racketeering, loan sharking, gambling, protection and extortion, burglary, robbery, theft (auto theft and shoplifting), and fencing, to the more recently established activities of identity theft, and trading in human parts, exotic animals, expensive pets, children, and babies. While many of these activities are conducted by organized crime, and operate at a global/international level, the extent to which local and national street gangs are involved defines the scope of the underground economy that relates to gangs. Moreover, while the precise economic activities of gangs varies, depending upon the race, ethnicity and gender of the gang, research in 1995 by Ronald Huff has revealed that the most frequently reported criminal economy activities by gang members across the four cities he studied are, in rank order: drug sales (65 percent); non-auto theft (61 percent), auto theft (55 percent); selling stolen goods (49 percent); shoplifting (49 percent); burglary (36 percent); mugging (31 percent); drug theft (30 percent); drug sales in schools (29 percent); robbery (22 percent); credit card theft (19 percent); and burglary from occupied dwelling (15 percent).

Finally, the third sub-economy of the criminal economy is the prison inmate economy, which is largely run by either indigenous prison gangs or gangs imported into the prison from ghetto neighborhoods, and as such, is a variant of the street gang underground economy.

The Relationship between Formal and Informal Economies

In general, informal economy activity has a number of intrinsic rewards relative to formal work and regular economic trade. Apart from providing additional income or savings for the participants, these activities provide a degree of social and political liberation for their members. In particular, they provide a sense of control over one's life, flexible working or trading hours, status and prestige derived from being a part of a network, excitement from working outside or on the margins of the law, and social rewards from helping friends to bargains or goods and services that they otherwise could not obtain. As a consequence, informal economic activity cannot be seen outside of its relationship to the formal political economy.

The second economy in communist states and the former Soviet Union demonstrates the extent to which government and party-political control over an economy produce a vibrant informal sector, matched in degree only by the global corporate capitalist exclusion of the majority of Third World peoples. Indeed, studies of the "Exclusive Society" by Jock Young suggest that the global capitalist exclusion of vast sections of the underclass in Western societies into ghettos of poverty and alienation, is one of the major reasons for informal economic activity in general, and gang activity in particular. Echoing Merton's strain theory and his related concept of "relative deprivation" in producing alienation and disaffection, Young describes the emergence of the "Bulimic Society," which culturally includes yet physically excludes.

Yet, as studies by Felix Padilla and Phillipe Bourgois have shown, gang activity is about more than simple adaptation and survival strategies to structural constraints. It comprises creative entrepreneurial alternative means to earn social respect. Insofar as the formal political economy provides routine, monotonous work, deprives employees of autonomy and creativity, and restricts access to meaningful employment, goods, and services, the informal economy, whether as a substitute for disrespectful low-income service work, or as a supplement to uncreative, bureaucratic executive work, will serve as an attractive alternative. Increasing control over the formal workplace, and restrictions on the availability of products, or limiting access to certain products for specific segments of the population because of class, race, or gender stratification, will produce a demand for informal economic activity and present entrepreneurial opportunities for its products and services, especially among excluded segments. But the desire to participate in informal economies is also about the meaningful excitement of defying the system and outsmarting it, at whatever level, with all the honor, prestige and respect that successful business brings, with the added thrill of the "edgework" that is implied.

This is not to suggest a romantic view of gangs and the informal economy for as 1950s delinquency researchers Cloward and Ohlin noted, distribution of work and rewards in informal economies, particularly gang economies, is no less hierarchical than in the formal economy, with those who do not possess entrepreneurial or marketable skills in the formal economy, or whose roles are restricted by race and gender, also losing out to powerful members of the informal economy. As an illustration, Lisa Maher's studies of Asian-Australian gangs demonstrate that traditional and cultural gender stratification can leave males in dominant roles as "providers" for the gang through robbery and drug sales, while **female** members of the gang are restricted to traditional roles of "housekeeping," cooking, and cleaning. She has shown that where female members break off to form their own gangs, their economic self-provisioning activity is restricted to a spiral cycle of sexed work and drug consumption, and is not only vulnerable to client violence, but also can be dominated by the intervention of relatives in male gangs who use violence to control female gang members.

Dana Nurge's study of Boston women's gangs, however, shows that females' gang activity "was neither wholly dependent on—nor solely focused around satisfying—gang males." Like Ann Campbell's study of *The Girls in the Gang*, which found that girl street gangs provided temporary refuge from underclass poverty, drudgery, and abuse, Nurge found that gangs provided a sense of mutual aid, therapy, and liberation from their oppressive surroundings, and a degree of short-term economic independence, even while being connected to male gang members. Yet she also found that the female gang was limiting, and provided only a temporary refuge for its members' problems. Importantly, Nurge's research shows how female gangs demonstrate the often-neglected interface between the criminal underground economy and the social economy. Thus it provides members with "strength and self-esteem" and with "physical, social, and economic security that they deemed necessary and otherwise unavailable at the time of joining."

Street Gangs and the Drug Economy

While Huff and others have shown that drug sales are the most frequently reported informal economic activity of gangs, other research reveals mixed findings with regard to the role of the gang in drug sales. Research by James Vigil in his 1988 work *Barrio Gangs* and John Hagedorn's 1988 *People and Folks* suggests that the recreational use and sale of drugs may be part of gang life, but that gang-related drug sales are not highly organized or entrepreneurial, but rather, generally run on a small scale (if at all), by individual members or small sub-groups of members within the gang. Most researchers argue that street-based youth gangs lack cohesion and are too loosely organized to effectively traffic drugs; rather, their primary function is to provide youth with opportunities for protection, status, family, and belonging.

Although most gangs are not engaged in high-level drug sales, gang members may see the opportunity to make money through the sale of drugs as an attractive feature of gangs. Scott Decker and Barrik Van Winkle's 1996 research on St. Louis gangs revealed that although members did not identify gang-based drug sales as a key reason for joining their gang, they did identify gang drug profits as a powerful incentive to remain involved. While they noted the difficulties of accurately assessing the amount of drug money earned, they indicated that members earned about $500/week.

Hagedorn's Milwaukee research suggests that the "jobs" provided through gang-based drug sales are an important source of urban economic survival, as fewer living-wage jobs are available in the local labor market. His findings indicate that gang members are holding on to gang ties longer (and former gang members may renew their affiliations) due to a lack of legitimate work opportunities in the formal economy. There is also some evidence that the age range of gang membership is expanding; instead of "aging-out" in their late teens and early twenties, gang members may stay involved well into adulthood.

A few studies such as Martin Jankowski's *Islands in the Street* and Sudhir Venkatesh's *American Project,* have revealed much more organized and profitable gang-based drug structures but these "corporate" gangs seem to be more of the exception than the rule.

A growing body of research on female gang members and their involvement in drug sales and other illicit activities reveals inconsistent findings. Whereas some research (such as Lauderback and colleagues' San Francisco study) shows women to be playing a more central and independent role in gang-based drug sales, other research, such as Venkatesh's 1998 Chicago research on gang drug sales, finds women's involvement to be largely linked to, or controlled by, gang males, and others find that women's drug sales and gang-based economic activity varies along ethnic/racial/cultural lines. For example, both Dave Brotherton's San Francisco research and John Hagedorn and Mary Devitt's Milwaukee study, revealed that African American girl gangs were more independent and self-organized than were the Latina groups they studied.

Other Underground Economic Activity of Gangs

Decker and Van Winkle's study of St. Louis gangs confirms previous research, which suggests that the majority of gang members' time is spent "hanging out" and engaging in typical teenage rather than criminal activity. However, gang members admitted engaging in a variety of property crimes, especially theft; approximately two-thirds said they stole things with their fellow gang members. The most common items stolen in descending order of frequency were cars, clothes, and electronics. Consistent with Malcolm Klein's 1995 research, which found that gang members' criminal activity is of the spontaneous "cafeteria-style" kind, most of the St. Louis gang members' acts of theft were opportunistic and unplanned.

Importantly, the nature and extent of gang members' illicit economic activity is influenced by myriad factors, including illegitimate and legitimate market dynamics within the community. Mercer Sullivan's 1989 research on gang/clique-involved youth in three different New York neighborhoods revealed that distinctive criminal opportunities were available to youth in each community: "Neighborhoods varied in how openly drugs and stolen goods could be sold on the street and in their particular combinations of diffuse and specialized markets. Some neighborhoods contained specialized fences for gold, auto parts, and other goods; all neighborhoods contained diffuse markets, based primarily on personal networks, in which youthful suppliers could sell illegal goods and services to ordinary residents for their own use."

Race, Ethnicity, and Control as a Factor in Gang Economic Activity

Not only are there variations in the underground economic activities of gangs in different geographical locations (Huff, for example, found that in Broward County, Florida, theft, auto theft, and selling stolen goods were the leading economic activities of gangs, whereas in Cleveland and Denver, drug sales top the list); but also important, ethnic gangs engage in different economic enterprises. For example, Asian gangs' economic crimes are wide-ranging, including extortion, home invasion, prostitution, gambling, and drug trafficking. **Chinese gangs** studied by Ko-lin Chin, Jeffrey Fagan, and Robert Kelly in New York City show that the formation of gangs was shaped and harnessed by established highly organized Chinatown community organizations and associations, which acted as major power centers and maintained social order. Chin and Fagan show that there are both legitimate and illegitimate social orders regulating political, economic, and social activity, and that the Chinese gang stands midway between the street gang and the organized crime syndicate. While most community associations are involved only in maintaining the legitimate social order, some are involved in criminal activities as well. Certain territorial rights to such activities as loan sharking, alien smuggling, and drug trafficking, are established within the context of the illegitimate order.

Given the fact that Chinese communities in urban areas are separate entities, because of language and cultural differences, the established associations run these enclaves. Disputes are handled within the confines of these areas. In instances where disputes cannot readily be resolved (e.g., territorial or business disagreements), gang members essentially become the "enforcement arm" of the various associations. It is either in intra- or inter-association disputes about protection payments, loans to association members, political differences between associations and loyalty of members, all issues not easily resolved, where gangs were often used to threaten or enforce association dictates at times through acts of violence. **Vietnamese gangs** tend to show a limited range of economic activity, with an emphasis on threats of violence around issues of extortion and home invasion targeting women and children.

Globalization, Capitalism, and Street Gang Underground Economies

With regard to the criminal economy and gangs, it has been argued that those neighborhoods that produce street gangs are those whose members have been excluded from the mainstream economy and who join together for protection in face of the predatory dangers from others similarly formed. Research by Hagedorn in his 2006 work *Gangs and the Global City* shows that the global city encloses socially excluded spaces, divided by walls of exclusion and segregation along racial lines resulting in "resistance identities" that are influenced by nationalism and religious fundamentalism. The cultural and economic exclusions from the formal economy have, says Hagedorn, produced "an informal economy, including a new global criminal economy," which has become "a mainstay for institutional gangs."

In this context the criminal economy of street gangs within global cities provides their members with many of the rewards and satisfactions that accrue from informal economic activity in general, such as identity, status, and prestige from being a member of an exclusive group, a means of economic exchange and communication through exchange, an alternative way of earning an income and of creating wealth and power, a mechanism to control the exclusion/alienation and chaos of their neighborhoods, and the safety and protection of a substitute family replacing that which has been fragmented by the forces of national capitalism reinforced by globalization. Hagedorn argues that "gangs are conscious organizations within poor communities responding to the conditions of globalization, just as they responded to the conditions of industrialization."

Gangs, Control, and Criminal Justice

An early indication of the nature of the relationship between the underground economy, gangs, and criminal justice can be found in the history of one of the first organized criminal activities in London established by Jonathan Wild. He set himself up in London as "Thief-Taker General of Great Britain and Northern Ireland" in 1712. Wild began his "business" by offering to track down and return lost or stolen property to its rightful owners, for a fee. He did this by developing relationships with burglars, pickpockets, and thieves, serving as a fence. However, instead of laundering stolen property and selling it to others, Wild would advertise for the return of "lost" property. His business escalated into having his gang of thieves systematically steal from London citizens in order to create the "need" for his services. He controlled reluctant and troublesome gang members by turning them into the courts for prosecution, and so providing a steady flow of convictions that kept the courts and the policing of the time satiated, and so gained legitimacy to continue his nefarious underground trade as the first organized criminal operation in London until his arrest and imprisonment in 1725.

Because policies of incarceration and control developed as part of the modern liberal state's "war on drugs," and "war on gangs," the operation of gang-related underground economies has become divided between gangs in the ghetto and gangs in prison, mediated by popular cultural exploitation, movie exportation, and state criminal justice practices. The primary area of ghetto gangs is, as it always was, on the street in local neighborhoods, with gangs claiming their named identity from the streets in their local neighborhoods. The secondary, but interrelated area of increasing gang activity is inside prison, as part of the inmate economy or prison gang economy. While the underground criminal economy of major gangs such as **Crips** and **Bloods** primarily includes drugs, vice, prostitution, and gambling, each of these activities also occurs inside prison.

Paradoxically, while prison officials formally crack down on contraband exchange, research in the 1970s in inmate economies by David Kalinch showed that allowing a degree of inmate economic activity can serve to symbolically satisfy incarcerated offenders. Participants become followers of prison rules since those prisoners successful at buying and selling contraband generally avoid causing problems. These "merchants" and "politicians" attempt to protect the order and stability of their realm to avoid discovery or disruption of their enterprise and paradoxically share the prison administrations' desire for order, and may even become "the major source of institutional security."

Importantly, as with the relationship between formal economic control and informal economic activity, so is there a relationship between formal control of gangs in prison, their cohesion, and proliferation and the expansion of their economic markets. Randall Sheldon has pointed out that not only does incarceration strengthen gang cohesion and improve recruitment, especially from new, fearful short-sentenced prisoners but also that increased prison security produces increased gang activity. It follows, therefore, that increased formal controls/security in prison will increase gang-related economic activity in prison. As with the relations between formal and informal economies, whereby each requires the other to facilitate their existence, says Klein, so it is with gangs and rival gangs. As rival gangs exist in solidarity and growth in relation to each other, and as they develop protected turf and wealth in prison, so the attempt by authorities to control prison gang economic activity through the use of transfer, informers, isolation and monitoring of mail and phones, affords informal economy opportunities to prison officers and other prison officials. These officials can provide a conduit to the outside in return for favors, not least the control of troublesome prisoners by deals with powerful gang members inside of prison. As Kalinch observed, information comes to corrections staff from inmates seeking favors or who "inform on competitors to protect their own market." Thus, security controls on the inside produce increased value for trade with the outside facilitated by those with connections to the outside, usually those working for the prison system (although criminal, this activity by prison staff would be seen as part of the criminal sub-economy of occupational crime/workplace crime). As Kalinch has said, "Prison gangs that deal drugs may become powerful and impossible to manage. Because of the enormous amount of money that may be generated from illegal drug sales, staff may become corrupted." Indeed, the relationships between prison officers, and rival gangs to facilitate the inmate economy is an important dimension of the continued proliferation of this economy, as it is on the outside between rival gangs and police/control agencies, and as it was from the outset in the eighteenth century of Jonathan Wild.

References/Suggested Readings: Bourgois, P. 2005. *In Search of Respect: Selling Crack in El Barrio*. Cambridge: Cambridge University Press; Campbell, A. 2006. *The Girls in the Gang*. Cambridge, MA: Blackwell; Chin, K. 1996. *Chinatown Gangs—Extortion, enterprise, and ethnicity*. New York: Oxford University Press; Chin, K., Fagan, J., and Kelly, R. 1992. Patterns of Chinese gang extortion, *Justice Quarterly* 9(4) December, pp. 401–422; Cloward, R. and Ohlin, L. 1961. *Delinquency and Opportunity*. Glencoe, IL: Free Press; Decker, S., and Van Winkle, B. 1996. *Life in the Gang: Family, Friends and Violence.*

New York: Cambridge University Press; Hagedorn, J.M. 1998. *People and Folks: Gangs, Crime and the Underclass in a Rustbelt City*. Chicago: Lake View Press; Hagedorn, J.M. 2006. *Gangs and the Global City*. Chicago: University of Illinois Press; Kalinch, D.B. 1980. *The Inmate Economy*. Lexington, MA: Lexington Books; Klein, M. 1995. *The American Street Gang: Its Nature, Prevalence, and Control*. New York: Oxford University Press; Maher, L. 1997. *Sexed Work: Gender, Race and Resistance in a Brooklyn Drug Market*. Oxford: Oxford University Press; Nurge, D. 2003. Liberating yet Limiting: The Paradox of Female Gang Membership. In L. Kontos, D. Brotherton, and L. Barrios (eds.), *Gangs and Society: Alternative Perspectives*. New York: Columbia University Press; Padilla, F.M. 1992. *The Gang as an American Enterprise*. New Brunswick, NJ: Rutgers University Press; Sanchez Jankowski, M. 1991. *Islands in the Street: Gangs and American Urban Society*. Berkeley: University of California Press; Sullivan, M. 1989. *Getting Paid: Youth Crime and Work in the Inner City*. Ithaca, NY: Cornell University Press; Venkatesh, S. 2000. *American Project*. Cambridge, MA: Harvard University Press; Vigil, J. 1988. *Barrio Gangs: Street Life and Identity in Southern California*. Austin, TX: University of Texas Press; Young, J. 1999. *The Exclusive Society: Social Exclusion, Crime, and Difference in Late Modernity*. London: Sage.

STUART HENRY AND DANA NURGE

GANGS AS SOCIAL AND ECONOMIC ORGANIZATIONS. Gangs may be defined as any social group with the following characteristics: relative permanence over time (one year or longer), implicit rules separating members from non-members, shared membership identity, and engagement in activities that are considered illegitimate from the standpoint of general social norms and values in which these groups operate (for a list of characteristics frequently used to define gangs see Esbensen, 2000).

The size of gang activity in the United States can be estimated by the data from the National Youth Gang Survey commissioned by the Office of Juvenile Justice and Delinquency Prevention, a Department of Justice agency. In the latest survey (2002) it is estimated that there are over 21,000 gangs comprising more than 700,000 members (Egley, Howell, and Major, 2006). These numbers do not include adult gangs, motorcycle gangs, **hate groups**, or prison gangs such as the Aryan Brotherhood or Mexican Mafia, which operate both in detention facilities and in the streets.

In political and popular discourse gangs seem akin to what communism was during the Cold War—a buzzword or label frequently used for political effect, yet eluding a clear definition of what the problem actually is. This is not to deny that gang-related activities pose a real and serious problem to law enforcement agencies, especially in large metropolitan areas, but to underscore how the view of gangs as forms of social organization is rather murky. Numerous attempts by federal law enforcement agencies and researchers to provide a universally accepted definition of the concept have so far been unsuccessful. As a result, different jurisdictions use different definitions, frequently tailored to meet specific law enforcement objectives (Egley, Howell, and Major, 2006).

Gangs are frequently associated with criminal activity, ranging from burglary to illegal drug trade, and to homicide (for types of crimes attributed to gang activity see Howell, Egley, and Gleason, 2002; Egley, Howell, and Major, 2006). Consequently, the public discourse on gang activity typically occurs in the context of criminal or deviant behavior. This approach tends to focus on individuals who are gang members, and the factors that predict their engagement in criminal or deviant activity and joining gangs. The most frequently quoted risk factors associated with gang membership is ethnic minority origin (Latino and black), male gender, residence in a single-parent household, peer influence, as well as broader structural factors, especially poverty, high unemployment rates, and community disorganization (Esbensen, 2000).

Yet, this criminal-justice centered perspective tends to miss a seemingly obvious distinction between activities of an organization and those of its members. Any organization, from labor unions and employer associations to charities and churches may attract criminal elements, but that does not automatically mean that the organization itself has a criminal purpose. In fact, most of them are recognized as legitimate entities that only incidentally have been misused for criminal purposes by individual members.

The key feature distinguishing between activities of individuals and those of an organization is how the proceeds from those activities are distributed. If the proceeds are retained only by those directly involved in their procurement—e.g., drug dealers retaining profits from drug sales for themselves—this indicates criminal activity of individual members. If, on one hand, the proceeds are transmitted to the organization and distributed according to membership status rather than direct involvement in their procurement (for a discussion of the organizational structure of "corporate" gangs see Venkatesh and Levitt, 2000; Venkatesh, n.d.)—this suggests activity of an organization in addition to that of individual members.

In the case of gang activities, that distinction is often blurred or difficult to establish due to their largely informal, illegal, and secretive nature. Yet it remains as a theoretical possibility that can be confirmed or rejected by empirical evidence, i.e., the actual mode of operation of specific gangs.

This distinction becomes particularly important in determining under what broader class of organizations gangs should be classified. Inasmuch as gangs engage in criminal activities as organizations—the criminal or illicit purpose is a distinct characteristic that sets gangs apart form all other types of organizations. However, if the criminal activity is carried out by individual members on their own account, and gangs as organizations simply act as social clubs providing social and "occupational" support for individuals who happen to engage in illegal activities, such as contacts with potential business partners, sharing relevant experiences and information, socializing, expression of shared identity, etc., gangs are fundamentally no different from other types of membership associations (fraternal lodges, social clubs, profession or trade associations, Boy Scouts, Lions, Rotary Clubs, etc.).

From that point of view, it may be useful to determine if gangs share structural characteristics of membership organizations (for a discussion of gangs as social clubs, see **Thrasher**, 1927; Venkatesh, n.d.). The focus on structural characteristics rather than on purpose or even legal status of an organization is necessitated by the fact that membership organizations by their very nature represent a wide variety of purposes and missions that have very little in common with one another. An obvious example is labor unions and employer associations that serve mutually contradictory goals, yet both are considered legitimate organizational forms. Organizations championing various civil rights or environmental causes are seen as a noble form of civic engagement by the supporters, and as semi-criminal rackets by their detractors, yet such organizations enjoy legal protection and a tax exempt status under the IRS Code (Section 501(c)(4)).

The five structural characteristics of membership associations, which they share with a still broader class of civil society organizations, include the following: (1) having some form of organizational structure, which at the minimum requires the existence of formal or customary rules defining membership, and relative permanence or continuity of the entity even if individual members change over time; (2) being institutionally separate from government; (3) not distributing profits to shareholders; (4) being self-governing (i.e., institutionally separate from other organizations); and (5) being non-compulsory, that is, individuals able to choose to become or cease to be members (Salamon and Anheier, 1996; Salamon et al., 1999; Salamon, Sokolowski, and Associates, 2004; United Nations Statistics Division, 2003).

Most gangs have some form of organizational structure. They have formal or informal rules defining their membership and collective identity, and institutional permanence that continues beyond involvement of specific individuals. They also have a clearly articulated shared identity that distinguishes their members from other gangs or groupings (Esbensen, 2000).

Second, gangs are obviously institutionally separate from government as well as from other organizations, such as other gangs or more legitimate establishments. Even if there are informal connections or relationships between a legitimate establishment and gangs, such relationships are usually "at arm's length" due to the illicit nature of gang activity.

Third, gang membership is voluntary, as individuals join gangs on their own, and leave them after a relatively short period of time, usually one year or less after joining (Esbensen, 2000). The voluntary nature of gang membership must also be compared to membership in associations that is seldom is free from external influences. For example, there are often strong social pressures within various communities to join "appropriate" fraternal lodges or associations and membership in professional associations or labor unions may be needed or required as a condition of a successful professional practice or getting a job. Yet all those pressures notwithstanding, individuals ultimately retain a choice of not being members of these associations, even if exercising that choice may entail personal cost. Likewise, despite pressures to join gangs, most members of "at-risk" communities either choose not to or give up their membership after a relatively short period of time.

As to the non-distribution of profits criterion, a distinction must be made between activities of the organization and those of its members that are carried out on their "own account." Clearly, criminal activities are "for profit" by definition. However, inasmuch as gang members engage in such activities as individuals, that is, do not share their proceeds with the organization that distributes them among other members, gangs as organizations meet the nonprofit distribution criteria. On the other hand, organized rackets, in which the organization and its structure is essential for distributing proceeds from criminal activity to eligible members according to their status within the organization, does not meet the nonprofit distribution criterion, and should be considered as for-profit business. Again, distinguishing between these two types of gang activity may prove difficult in practice, due to the informal nature of the organization and the secrecy surrounding its operations, but these two aspects of gang operations are conceptually separable.

In sum, many if not most gangs can be considered membership associations that belong to a broader civil society sector, although some of them act more like corporations that distribute dividends (profits) to their "shareholders." Of course, to determine which part of a gang is a part of "civil society" and which is a part of the business sector can only be done by scrutinizing a particular gang's activity, which is generally problematic due to limited access to verifiable data.

The idea that gang activities should be seen as a part of the civil society sector may sound counter-intuitive to most readers. After all, "civil society" is generally associated with the promotion of public benefits, such as education, culture, charity, shared interests, civil rights, etc., of which gangsterism would appear to be the antithesis. One needs to remember, however, that concepts like "public benefit" or "civility" are substantially affected by subjective factors, such as cultural background, political views, or even self-interest. For example, the notion of "charity," highly regarded in Anglo-Saxon countries, is generally scorned in Scandinavia as a form of paternalism by the wealthy, and thus antithetical to democratic values. Likewise, groups like the Ku Klux Klan or Hamas are considered "civic associations" and "charities" by supporters, and criminal or terrorist gangs by its opponents. The same is to a large extent true about labor unions or civil rights and environmental organizations. Therefore, the subjective perceptions of "public purpose or benefit" can be misleading as an empirical characteristic determining whether an entity belongs to a certain institutional sector.

Yet the actual or perceived illegitimacy of a group's activities seems to be the most salient characteristic that separates gangs from other types of membership organizations and the public's mind. That approach to defining gangs, while undoubtedly grounded in empirical reality, is nonetheless conceptually misleading. One result of this misconception is to see all gangs as being similar and consequently responding to them with heavy-handed criminal justice measures. A more nuanced approach distinguishing between potentially "good" and "bad" gangs (i.e., those that provide largely social support for individuals who engage in delinquent or criminal activities versus those that engage in criminal activities as organizations) may be useful in using that organization to control individual criminal behavior which is largely due to personal or community factors.

Another benefit of this approach is that it allows placing gangs on a conceptual map of nationwide institutional and economic activities. One such conceptual map has been developed under the 1993 System of National Accounts (United Nations Statistics Division, 1993) adopted by virtually every country in the world for the purpose of economic reporting. This system recognizes four sectors: corporations (non-financial, such as manufacturing or service establishments, and financial, such as banks and similar money lending operations), general government (central and local), households (i.e., activities of individuals and families), and nonprofit institutions serving households, or alternatively, nonprofit institutions (for a discussion on sectoring see United Nations Statistics Division, 2003).

Although gang activities are not reported in economic statistics, they could be included, at least in principle. If they are included in the institutional framework developed for the SNA, they could be allocated to two institutional sectors: nonprofit institutions serving households and the corporate sector. While the complex nature of gang activities may render the practical aspect of their sectoral allocation difficult, this is a broader problem shared by all multi-purpose units, both licit and illicit. This problem is typically solved by allocation based on the primary economic activity (i.e., one that uses most of the organization's resources) or their primary source of income (i.e., sales of goods and services, government grants, or private donations).

An alternative approach to defining gangs is therefore needed, one which is focused on their structural organizational characteristics rather than on the legitimacy of their purpose or intent. From the structural organizational perspective, gangs are a subset of either nonprofit institutions (or more specifically, membership associations), or the business sector, depending on whether members engage in (usually illegal) profit making on their own account, or organizations engage in profit distribution.

This is not to dismiss the seriousness of the criminal aspect of gang activity, but rather to separate a value-neutral structural analysis from value judgments and politically motivated rhetoric. The usefulness of this value-neutral approach to conceptualizing gangs is twofold. First, it makes it possible to place of gangs on a broader conceptual map of social and economic institutions nationwide, and eventually assess the economic value they add to the national economy. Second, conceptualizing at least some gangs as membership associations that are not fundamentally different from other civil society organizations opens the possibility of viewing these organizations as an institutional force that can potentially be harnessed to control criminal or delinquent behavior in "at-risk" populations.

References/Suggested Readings: Egley, A., Howell, J.C., and Major, A.K. 2006. *National Youth Gang Survey, 1999–2001, Summary*. Office of Juvenile Justice and Delinquency Prevention Publication NCJ (209392); Esbensen, F.A. 2000. Preventing Adolescent Gang Involvement. *Juvenile Justice Bulletin,* September; Howell, J.C., Egley, A., and Gleason, D.K. 2002. Modern-Day Youth Gangs. *Juvenile Justice Bulletin,* June; Salamon, L.M., and Anheier, H.K. 1996. *The Emerging Nonprofit Sector: An Overview*. Manchester: Manchester University Press; Salamon, L.M., Anheier, List, R., Toepler, S., Sokolowski, S.W., and Associates. 1999. *Global Civil Society: Dimensions of the Nonprofit Sector*. Baltimore, MD: Johns Hopkins Center for Civil Society Studies; Salamon, L.M., Sokolowski, S.W., and Associates. 2004. *Global Civil Society: Dimensions of the Nonprofit Sector* (vol. 2). Kumarian Press; Thrasher, F.M. 1927. *The Gang: A Study of 1,313 Gangs in Chicago*. Chicago: University of Chicago Press; United Nations Statistics Division. 1993. *System of National Accounts, Rev 4*, Series F, no. 2. Available online at unstats.un.org/unsd/sna1993/toctop.asp; United Nations Statistics Division. 2003. *Handbook on Nonprofit Institutions in the System of National Accounts,* Series F, no. 91. Available online at unstats.un.org/unsd/publication/SeriesF/SeriesF_91E.pdf; Venkatesh, S., and Levitt, S.D. 2000. Are We a Family or a Business? History and Disjuncture in the Urban American Street Gang. *Theory and Society,* Autumn; Venkatesh, S. n.d. *Community Justice and the Gang: A Life-Course Perspective*. Available online at www.jcpr.org/povsem/venkatesh_paper.pdf.

S. WOJCIECH SOKOLOWSKI

GANGS IN PRISON. Some jails, prisons, and penitentiaries are literally run by gangs (Stastny and Tyrnauer, 1982; Camp and Camp, 1985). Even if convicts want to "do their own time" and be left alone, there are strong pressures to join a gang for self-protection. In situations like these, unaffiliated individuals are subject to routine victimization and they may not be able to defend themselves. Gang members may extort or coerce material possessions or services from convicts. Alternatively they may have their material possessions stolen by inmates conducting a cell invasion, in which they simply run into the victims' cell and grab anything of value (Hassine, 2002).

Prison gangs typically coalesce around race, ethnicity, nationality, and neighborhood. One of the most common distinctions is among African American, Hispanic, and white gangs which dominate many correctional facilities. Gang members basically "hang together." This means eating as a group in the cafeteria, walking the yard together, pumping iron (lifting weights), and sticking close to each other at work assignments or in housing units. In some prisons convicts need to affiliate with a group for mutual protection. The loners—the people without social skills or friends—are vulnerable to being physically attacked or preyed upon (American Correctional Association, 1993; Ross and Richards, 2002).

The Different Types

A number of ethnic and racially based prison gangs exist (ACA, 1993). In these milieus there is often considerable diversity. Among the African American gangs in prison are members of the Black Guerrilla Family, the **Vice Lords**, the **Crips**, and **Bloods**. Hispanic and Latino gangs have included **Asociación Ñeta** and **Latin Kings**, which are predominantly Puerto Rican and Hispanic, and the Mexican Mafia and La Nuestra Familia, mainly Mexican American. Some, like the Colombians (many of whom are affiliated with drug cartels) are multiracial, which makes trying to identify groups based solely on skin color difficult.

Most of these organizations have been around for decades and have long histories. Gang membership often evolves and spreads geographically. The black gangs of the 1970s, like the Crips and Bloods, first started on the West Coast in Los Angeles. Soon they spread to other cities in California, then made their way across the Midwest to the East Coast, where they became established in New York City, Boston, and Philadelphia (Moore, 1979). In the Californian institutions, some of the Blue Birds and Hell's Angels of San Quentin (motorcycle gangs) eventually became the white supremacist Aryan Brotherhood.

The public generally thinks that members are teenagers and young adults, but gangs, in fact, include all different age groups including junior gangsters, gang warriors (i.e., "gang bangers"), and older gang members (Klein, 1997). These groups also include "wannabes," associates (family or friends who are loosely connected to the members), and auxiliaries (lady friends). A few of the senior members may have established legitimate businesses that employ high-powered accountants and lawyers and have the resources to buy judges, politicians, and their way out of prison.

Some members of the **Hell's Angels,** for example, are now corporate presidents or businessmen who own golf courses or car dealerships. Ultimately, gangs are a form of **organized crime** (Lavigne, 1989).

There are different kinds of gangs: Some exist primarily for economic gain (focusing on business activities like selling drugs, theft, and extortion), while others are formed for mutual self-protection, and some gangs are more violent than others. Gang culture is often an extension of street life into the penitentiary. Traditions learned on the street are often "imported" into correctional facilities (Irwin and Cressy, 1962).

Gang affiliation will depend on the region of the country in which convicts have to do time. For example, in Illinois and New York, you will find a disproportionate number of Hispanic gangs such as Latin Kings or Vice Lords, or black gangs such as El Rukn or black **Gangster Disciples**. In California and Texas, you will typically find the Mexican Mafia. Much like political parties, gangs have different factions or divisions. In the Mexican organizations, for instance, there are both urban and rural components.

Joining a Gang

Gangs recruit new members on the street, in jail, and in prison and have colonized many state and federal pens (Hagedorn, 1988). A gang may serve as a surrogate family providing social and emotional needs for its members, both on the street and in prison. In fact, members often refer to the gang as their family.

Joining a gang carries many obligations and responsibilities including feuds, revenge, and retaliation against rival factions. These conflicts may extend from the "hood" to the penitentiary and last for years. An important aspect of all gang affiliations is respect. Young men and women who grow up in inner-city neighborhoods want to be respected and not "dissed" (Anderson, 1990). And the way respect is typically displayed in the ghetto and barrios is often through style (e.g., Ferrell, 1993; Ferrell and Sanders, 1995; Miller, 1995), by the clothes you wear, the money you spend, and the car you drive. In the institution, gang members are known by the ways in which they carry themselves, including altering their uniforms, sharing their food and drugs, and the individuals they hang out with in the chow hall and yard (Bourgois, 2002).

Gang members often expect to go to prison. When they go to the correctional facility, they try to make themselves comfortable. This means that they want new uniforms that are sharply pressed and a locker full of cigarettes and commissary food. Some want nothing more then to watch sports channels like ESPN every day.

How They Work

Gangs are organized to carry out business, not only on the street but also in prison. They are primarily responsible for bringing contraband into the penitentiary. These items such as cigarettes, alcohol, drugs, sex, and gambling, are the components of the "inmate economy."

Gangs use many methods to get illegal drugs into prisons. The most common way is to have visitors bring dope into the visiting room. Another way is to simply throw the drugs over the wall or fence in a tennis ball or to use slingshots to propel the projectile. Another method is air drops, in which drugs are released from small airplanes that fly over the institution at night (Ross and Richards, 2002).

Gang members may also recruit or coerce correctional officers to bring drugs into prison. They may compromise the guards by threatening to turn them in for illegal behavior they observe or hear about. Another way to "get the goods" on these officers is when prisoners observe them drinking on the job, doing drugs, or having sex with a prisoner. Alternatively, a convict may successfully threaten an officer's family by finding out where he lives. Still, some correctional officers—because they are paid so little or want to make extra cash—smuggle contraband into the institution.

In many prisons, it is not uncommon to find that black gangs focus a lot of their attention on sports betting. Since the standard currency in prison is a carton of cigarettes, this is usually the minimum bet placed. On the other hand, convicted dope dealers who are used to "living large" and having a lot of money will bet $10,000 to $20,000 on a game. The loser will need to have the money sent in from the outside. If he is lucky, his girlfriend or "old lady" will mail the money in, and if it is not stolen in the process, it will be put on his commissary account. Then he needs to go to the commissary and purchase items on a regular basis to pay his gambling debt. Alternatively, if he owes $1,000, he may have a buddy on the street pay it to the gang on the outside.

Finally, a sophisticated gang may actually get new gang members or wannabes (who do not have a criminal record) to apply for a job as a correctional officer with the state Department of Corrections (DOC). Some jurisdictions appear so desperate to hire and have such low qualification requirements that they will employ anyone who does not have a felony conviction. If hired, the person then acts as the go-between to smuggle drugs and other forms of contraband into the prison (Hagedorn, 1988).

Solutions

Many prison systems have tried to implement gang prevention programs. Most corrections departments educate correctional officers in how to identify gangs

(Gaston, 1996; Valentine and Schober, 2000). During classification DOCs try to determine membership and if possible separate gang members from the general population so that they do not threaten other inmates. "Texas has gone even further in its attempts to control gangs. Managers have designated gang intelligence officers in each prison who gather gang-related information and identify gang members and leadership. Active cooperation in the sharing of information with other criminal justice jurisdictions has prevented the recruitment they try to put gang members in administrative segregation" (Buentello, 1992). Other options are to place gang leaders in super-max prisons where they will have minimal or no contact with fellow inmates. Gang treatment and rehabilitation is another option. Occasionally DOCs institute these kinds of programs. For example, in 1993, the Hampden County Correctional Institution in Massachusetts tried the following. After segregating gang members, the DOC then gives them a cognitive training program (Toller and Tsagaris, 1996a, 1996b). In some prison systems, like those in New York State, programs led by inmates are implemented. The Alternatives to Violence Program (AVP) which started in 1975 is run by lifers who hold workshops and teach younger inmates about the causes of violence, how it can escalate, and how to avoid it.

References/Suggested Readings: American Correctional Association. 1993. *Gangs in Correctional Facilities: A National Assessment.* Washington, DC: U.S. Department of Justice; Anderson, E. 1980. *Streetwise: Race, Class, and Change in an Urban Community.* Chicago: University of Chicago Press; Bourgois, P. 2002. *In Search of Respect: Selling Crack in El Barrio* (2nd ed.). New York: Cambridge University Press; Camp, G., and Camp, C. 1985. *Prison Gangs: Their Extent, Nature, and Impact in Prisons.* Washington, DC: U.S. Department of Justice; Ferrell, J. 1993. *Crimes of Style.* Boston: Northeastern University Press; Ferrell, J., and Sanders, C.R. (eds.) 1995. *Cultural Criminology.* Boston: Northeastern University Press; Fong, R.S. and Buentello, S. 1991. "The detection of prison gang development: An empirical assessment. *Federal Probation* 55(1), pp.66–69; Gaston, A. 1996. *Controlling Gangs through Teamwork and Technology.* Large Jail Network Bulletin. Washington, DC: U.S. Department of Justice, National Institute of Corrections; Hagedorn, J. 1988. *People and Folks: Gangs, Crime and Underclass in a Rustbelt City.* Chicago: Lakeview Press; Hassine, V. 2002. Prison Violence: From Where I Stand. In Rosemary Gido and Ted Alleman (eds.), *Turnstile Justice: Issues in American Corrections*, pp. 38–56. Upper Saddle River, NJ: Prentice Hall; Irwin, J., and Cressey, D. 1962. Thieves, Convicts and Inmate Culture. *Social Problems*, 10, 142–155; Klein, M. 1997. *The American Street Gang.* New York: Oxford University Press; Lavigne, Y. 1989. *Hell's Angels: Three Can Keep a Secret if Two Are Dead.* Toronto: Lyle Stuart; Miller, J. 1995. Struggles over the Symbolic: Gang Style and Meanings of Social Control. In J. Ferrell and C.R. Sanders (eds.), *Cultural Criminology*, pp. 213–234. Boston: Northeastern University Press; Moore, J.W. 1978. *Gangs, Drugs and Prison in the Barrios of Los Angeles.* Philadelphia: Temple University Press; Ross, S.I., and Richards, J.C. 2002. *Behind Bars.* Indianapolis, IN: Alpha Books; Stastny, C., and Tyrnauer, G. 1982. *Who Rules the Joint? The Changing Political Culture of Maximum-Security Prisons in America.* Lexington, MA: Lexington Books; Toller, W., and Tsagaris, B. 1996a. A Comparison of Gang Members and Non-gang Members in a Prison Setting. *Prison Journal*, 81 (2), 50–60; Toller, W., and Tsagaris, B. 1996b. Managing Institutional Gangs: A Practical Approach, Combining Security and Human Services. *Corrections Today*, 58 (6), 110–115; Valentine, B., and Schober, R. 2000. *Gangs and Their Tattoos: Identifying Gangbangers on the Street and in Prison.* Boulder: Paladin.

JEFFREY IAN ROSS

GANGS IN U.S. SCHOOLS. Beginning in the late 1980s, as street gangs became more visibly involved in acts of violence in many U.S. cities and "gang wars" among rival groups vying for control of the new market in crack cocaine played out in L.A. and New York, "gang violence" became a dominant theme in popular media both in news and fiction. So much attention was focused on youth gangs, drugs, and urban violence (each of which were routinely conflated with the other) that news articles on other violence in and around the schools would often specify that the events were *not* believed to be gang-related. "Out of the extraordinary attention of media and state institutions, street gang activity has become depicted as a signature attribute of ghetto life," Sudhir Venkatesh has noted (1995, p. 82). In this atmosphere, school officials and criminologists began to observe gang-related activity among school children in some high schools and even junior highs. The fear of gangs in the schools has led to the formation of anti-gang units in schools and the tracking of incidents of organized violence among students in New York City, Los Angeles, Chicago, and elsewhere. Also in response to the perception of gang activity within schools, many districts dramatically increased their security presence in the schools, including routine use of metal detectors at entrances, locker inspections with drug-sniffing dogs, prohibitions against backpacks, and new policies against a wide assortment of potentially threatening behavior.

While the feared epidemic of violent drug-dealing youth gangs failed to materialize, research has confirmed an increase in the presence of gangs and gang affiliations in schools. Chandler et al. (1998) found that the percentage of students *reporting* gang activity in their school nearly doubled between 1989 and 1995, only some of which can be explained by the rising popularity of the term "gang" to describe any group conflict or violence. Most such studies rely on surveys of the student population, presume the presence of gangs, and seek to measure their pervasiveness. For example, a recent analysis by James C. Howell and James P. Lynch (2000) concluded:

> Gangs are very prevalent in schools. More than one-third (37 percent) of the students surveyed in the 1995 SCS reported gangs in their schools. This number included nearly two-thirds of Hispanic students, almost one-half of black students, and one-third of white students. Students in middle to late adolescence who lived in households with incomes of less than $7,500 and who had been victimized personally were most likely to report gang presence. These students were most likely to attend public schools that they (or their parents or guardians) had chosen in cities with populations between 100,000 and 1 million. These largely urban schools employed a large number of security measures, had high rates of victimization, and were places where drugs were readily available. The most criminally active gangs were reported by 15- to 17-year-old students of either gender.

"Descriptions of American street gangs vary markedly from one generation to another," Klein (1992, p. 80) has observed. "But it is not clear whether the differences are a function more of the gangs or of their research observers." Similarly, many contemporary studies correlate gang behavior to social and demographic variables (race and ethnicity, geographic location, family structure and income, etc.), while few studies go beyond these statistical correlations to explain the mechanisms that lead to them.

Gangs

The notion of a "gang" carries considerable symbolic meaning, generally implying threat, organized power and violence. In research and other writings, however, it is not often clearly defined or described, contributing to the confusion over the nature and extent of the "gang problem." While "youth gangs" have in some documented cases become "drug gangs," the two are not synonymous, as drug gangs tend to be more entrepreneurial while youth gangs are more "social" (Venkatesh and Levitt, 2000). But distinctions among types of gangs are not clear or reliable. Suggestions that street gangs were organizing nationwide drug distribution networks were popular during the 1980s with the emergence of crack cocaine and new drug gangs, but this does not appear to have been an accurate assertion. The "gang" form itself has changed over time, further complicating typologies. Some groups may cultivate a more gang-like image without living the "gang life," while others may more thoroughly emulate the form in practice. While some street gang members may be of school age, or in school, it also does not appear likely that typical street gangs routinely operate in public schools. Instead, smaller "block gangs" of school youth and other "gang-like" groups may account for a significant portion of the organized violence characterized by police and others as gang activity in the schools. We have studied block gangs in New York City schools, and our findings are discussed in detail below.

Social Organization of Adolescent Conflict in the Neighborhood

In urban neighborhoods where street gangs or drug gangs have a dominant presence, their territorial boundaries affect the social organization of the community at many levels. Younger residents in New York define their "hang-out areas" within these territories, and understand their street blocks to be within the "turf" of a particular gang. The school-age kids often organize their activities on a gang-like model, with names (usually the block name), and mutual obligations to the group. Students in block gangs "represent" their blocks, and conflicts between blocks may often turn violent. Most of the obligations to the block gangs are imposed on school-age members of the blocks, and most of their conflicts primarily involve the block gangs on nearby streets. A fight between members of different block groups almost automatically becomes a fight between two block gangs, as the students have the obligation to back up anyone in the group. Having the block "watching your back" protects students in certain circumstances or locations, but introduces conflicts elsewhere.

In general, block gangs organize for physical protection and as a means to protect their dignity in a violent environment. Research on gangs has identified "respect" as the focal commodity guiding gang behavior and determining when violence is called for (Bourgois, 1995; Horowitz, 1983). Student block gangs also reproduce this ideology. Blocks "lose face" when members back down from the threat of violence; force is often met with greater force, as threats become fights and fights lead to greater numbers and the use of weapons. Guns and other weapons are often used to settle disputes between blocks, and older gang youth will often become involved when the violence escalates to that level. Block gangs also negotiate alliances with other blocks. In our research in one New York City junior high school, students were able to recite and explain the unfolding history of conflicts between their blocks and neighboring blocks as various alliances were formed or dissolved, and key "beefs" called for "payback" or the escalation of violence (Mateu-Gelabert and Lune, 2003).

Block gangs resemble street gangs in many ways and may be seen as somewhat supportive of them and possible sources of future recruits. We found there to be a loose connection between block gangs of the middle school and early high school kids and gangs of late teens and young adults. These block gangs had a very loose two-tier system: "very young kids" (middle school and early high school) and older kids (later high school, early twenties). The middle school kids represented their blocks and "had beefs" with other blocks, with some minor incursions into crime. Older youth and young adults associated with the block gangs may act as foot soldiers for the drug dealers. But the block gangs are not necessarily training grounds for later gang activity. School kids who are mostly involved in block gang activity might "graduate" into the older gangs, but most give up on the gangs when they leave school, as they see it as "kid's stuff."

The Effects within the Schools

Block gang conflicts carry over into the schools. Students represent their blocks both at home and at school. Belonging to a block provides protection and power to students, which they draw on when they are away from the block, but it also obliges them to continue to enact conflicts with fellow students whom they would normally avoid outside of school. Fights which, in school, appear to have broken out spontaneously or with little provocation often have their origins in clashes between blocks. Two students who have no personal animosity may trade words over a block fight, which can easily and quickly escalate into violence in which both sides bring their "props." School officials and students tend to label such incidents as "gang" violence.

The rest of the students, the vast majority of whom do not represent a block, also have to worry about block gang activity in the schools. Outside, they may know which blocks to avoid, but in the school they do not have the opportunity to do so. Block gang members may threaten or intimidate others who cannot afford to risk a violent conflict with the entire block. Other forms of conflicts, challenges, and "play-fights" can lead to retaliation or escalation when one student feels disrespected. Students who stand up for themselves against a member of a block gang may be targeted by that student's "peeps," his people from the block who can be counted on to back him up.

Although block gangs are not the same as the street gangs that run drugs, steal cars, or fight with police, they nonetheless create a gang presence in the schools, occasionally involving knives and guns. Once block gang activity becomes predominant in schools, members may feel that their norms concerning violence and competition take precedence over the school's. In Mateu-Gelabert and Lune (2003), a gang member in the eleventh grade explained the way he deals with the problems he and "his people" (friends and other gang members) face at their high school: "The only way people understand in [high school] is with the fist. If you don't get respect people will walk all over you, they will push you around. . . . You got to show that you are not weak."

When those street behaviors become normative in school, all of the disruption associated with "gang violence" may follow. Block gang members concerned with their own authority will challenge that of teachers and administrators. Those worried about fights and threats in school will give little or no attention to education. And the chaos and apparent loss of control that then permeates the school undermines attempts by other students and teachers to maintain a "normal" classroom environment. The majority of the students have little to do with any of this, or gangs, but feel—and report on surveys—that their schools are being run by gangs.

The problem of gangs in the school, therefore, is not a yes or no question. It is a matter of degree. The kids in block gangs clearly identified with "representing" their block and fighting out their conflicts with other blocks. But at the end of the day, most would go home do their homework and go to bed. The block gangs are violent; threats and even "play-fights" have led to serious beatings. But even this violence often seemed to stem from the "gang-like structure" that the kids learned elsewhere. While excessive role identification is clearly not the entire source of the problem, it plays a part.

Schools respond both to the presence of block-gangs and to the label of "gangs in the schools." But the prison-like security systems in some schools do not alter the perception that gangs have infiltrated the premises. Indeed, the cultures of schools have been shown to foster conditions that may increase levels of violence and/or encourage gang activity. Studies of bullying and research following the well-publicized suburban school shootings indicates that schools often have complex social hierarchies maintained in part by violence, threats, and intimidation. Zero-tolerance policies that focus on guns without addressing the social sources of group conflict reify these hierarchies and conflicts. When schools fail to ensure a safe environment, students will seek support from their peers. Representing is about safety. The social organization of such support will often mirror the kinds of structures that students see on the street.

Presumably, therefore, there are more effective ways to provide a safe environment for the students than treating them like potential gang members. Some schools have reduced gang presence, providing a steady presence of caring adults, alternatives to violent conflict resolution and after-school programs (Mateu-Gelabert, 2002). Such an approach would seem naive in applied to a hardened criminal gang, yet is plausible when dealing with lesser versions such as block gangs. Many of the junior high students in the block gangs we studied choose to study in high school rather than participating in more gang activities. They saw that as a part of their childhood that they were growing out of.

Summary

Neither research nor preventive measures are served when every form of organized conflict or violence is attributed to either the expansion of drug markets or the **Crips**. Gangs are neither monolithic nor interchangeable, and many gang-like social groups could be redirected toward others forms, if their underlying needs for security were otherwise addressed. We have not studied block gangs in other cities. It is likely that in urban areas such as Los Angeles where the physical organization of the city is different, the social organization will also be unique. Yet given our findings so far, it would be surprising if the school-based youth gangs in other parts of the country were not also fairly independent of the larger street gangs operating there. We do not need to hypothesize that "street gangs" are taking over the schools in order to account for organized violence among school kids. On the other hand, we do need to understand the students' perceptions and priorities if we are to help them find a better way to deal with the inevitable conflicts that condition their lives.

References/Suggested Readings: Bourgois, P. 1995. *In Search of Respect: Selling Crack in El Barrio*. Cambridge: Cambridge University Press; Chandler, K.A., Chapman, C.D., Rand, M.R., and Taylor, B.M. 1998. Students' reports of school crime: 1989 and 1995. Washington, DC: U.S. Departments of Education and Justice (NCES 98-241/NCJ169607); Horowitz, R. 1983. *Honor and the American Dream: Culture and Identity in a Chicano Community*. New Brunswick, NJ: Rutgers University Press; Howell, J.C. and Lynch, J.P. 2000. Youth gangs in schools. Pub. No. NJC 183015. Washington, DC: Office of Juvenile Justice and Delinquency Prevention; Klein, M. W. 1992. Review: The New Street Gang . . . Or Is It? *Contemporary*

Sociology, 21 (1), 80–82; Klein, M.W. 1995. *The American Street Gang: Its Nature, Prevalence, and Control.* New York: Oxford University Press; Mateu-Gelabert, P. 2002. *Dreams, Gangs, and Guns: The Interplay between Adolescent Violence and Immigration in a New York City Neighborhood.* Vera Institute of Justice, April; Venkatesh, S.A. 1995. The Social Organization of Street Gang Activity in an Urban Ghetto. *American Journal of Sociology*, 103 (1), 82–111; Venkatesh, S.A. and Levitt, S.D. 2000. Are We a Family or a Business? History and Disjuncture in the Urban American Street Gang. *Theory and Society* 29, 427–462.

PEDRO MATEU-GELABERT AND HOWARD LUNE

GANGSTER DISCIPLES

Early History: The Devil's Disciples, Black Disciples, and the Gangster Disciples (Early 1960s to Mid-1970s)

The Gangster Disciples (and later, the Black Gangster Disciple Nation) has its origins in the Devil's Disciples, a Chicago-area street gang. Depending on the source, the Devils Disciples can be traced back to the 1950s (Hagedorn, n.d.) or early 1960s, and was founded by David Barksdale, Jerome "Shorty" Freeman, and Don Derky (*United States v. Irwin*, 1998; Knox, 2001). In 1966, Barksdale formed the Black Disciples as a splinter group and became "King" David Barksdale, alluding to their religious structure (Knox, 2004). Evolving into an enormous organization, the Black Disciples controlled over fourteen different factions (including the original Devil's Disciples, see Emery, 1996), and invested into the community through their development of social programs with support from local businessmen and politicians (Hagedorn, 2005).

Chicago gangs have had a history of political involvement and the "dual character" of community investment with the civil rights movement and crime is evident in the 1960s for most of the major gangs (Hagedorn, 2005). During this period, the "LSD" coalition was formed, which stood for the three major gangs at the time: the "Lords [Vice Lords], Stones [Blackstone Rangers] and Disciples [Black Disciples]," and had ties to political entities such as the Black Panther Party, the Reverend Jesse Jackson, and Martin Luther King Jr. (Hagedorn, 2005; Emery, 1996). As part of the Federal War on Poverty Programs, the Office of Economic Opportunities' Youth Manpower Project allocated funding to both the Black Disciples and the Blackstone Rangers (Jacobs, 1977). It has been suggested that some of this money never made it to the wider community. It instead stayed with Barksdale and the Blackstone Rangers' (later to become the Black Peace Stone Nation and eventually El Rukn) leader Jeff Fort (Chicago Crime Commission, 1995). It has also been argued that the politicization of these groups was nothing more than a method of gaining wealth, power, and organizational growth (Jacobs, 1977). Drug distribution continued as a major source of income in the neighborhoods (Emery, 1996), with reports of corresponding turf wars between the groups. Though no data were gathered, the Chicago Crime Commission estimates that the gang wars between the Black Disciples and the Blackstone Rangers were "bloodiest during that period [of 1966 to 1970]" (Chicago Crime Commission, 1995). In 1969, Barksdale was severely wounded by gunfire, which would eventually lead to his death five years later.

Around the same time, a young man named Larry Hoover, who was formerly involved with the Devil's Disciples, formed another group called "The Family" on the south side of Chicago (Hagedorn, n.d.). Along with one of its subgroups, the Supreme Gangsters, this organization became the Gangster Disciples. The Gangster Disciples grew rapidly, and Hoover was recruited by both Fort and Barksdale to join the Blackstone Rangers (which later changed its name to the Black Peace Stone Nation) and the Black Disciples, respectively. Fort offered Hoover a subordinate position as ambassador in the Black P Stone Nation, which Hoover rejected. According to the Gangster Disciples, Barksdale also approached Hoover, and offered his new vision for an equal-partnership merger between the two organizations. Hoover accepted, and the Black Gangster Disciple Nation was born with two "kings," Barksdale and Hoover (Emery, 1996). However, neither would remain in their neighborhoods for very long. Hoover, convicted in 1973 for the murder of a local drug dealer, was sentenced to 150 to 200 years in the Illinois Department of Corrections, and Barksdale's old injury from the shooting led to his death in 1974 (Knox, 2001).

From Military to Corporate Structure (Mid-1970s to Late 1980s)

With both of its leaders not directly present on the street, the Black Gangster Disciple Nation did not last long. It split into factions: the Gangster Disciples, still headed by Hoover, and the Black Disciples, which were made up of older original members, was headed up by initial founder Jerome "Shorty" Freeman (Chicago Crime Commission, 1995). The Gangster Disciples retained the name of the Black Gangster Disciple Nation. Thus, some scholars argue that the Black Gangster Disciples did not formalize until the death of Barksdale in 1974 (Hagedorn, n.d.; Knox, n.d.). This implies that an equal partnership never existed between Barksdale and Hoover, but rather that the latter merely stepped in and attempted to claim leadership since it and the accompanying narcotics territory was "up for grabs." In this light, Hoover's Black Gangster Disciples was little more than a cosmetic makeover of the original Gangster Disciples, controlled by Hoover in prison (Knox, 2001).

Over the next few years, Hoover gained much control within the prison, and has been partially credited with the development of the "Folks" and "People" nations, which were created for the purpose of "coalition building" in the prisons (Chicago Crime Commission, 1995). Logically, Hoover and other gang leadership concluded that conflicts between groups must be avoided in prison, since the only "victors" would be the corrections staff (Jacobs, 1974). While general peace was kept between the separate gangs, this "politicization" also manifested itself in power struggles between the prisoners and corrections staff. Hoover himself was rumored to have masterminded a 1978 prisoner inmate uprising, which was only one of the many inmate/corrections staff conflicts to occur, and left three officers dead (Jacobs, 1977; Chicago Crime Commission, 1995). During the early 1980s, perhaps due to the increase in levels of organization within the prison community itself, Hoover decided to reorganize the Gangster Disciples around a corporate organizational model (Hagadorn, n.d.). Hoover became "Chairman of the Board," with the Board of Directors, the Institutional Coordinators, and other positions obstinately replacing the formerly militaristic-structured ones (*United States v. Irwin*, 1998, Knox, 2004), although some followers thereafter used "King" and "Chairman" interchangeably (Decker, Bynum, and Weisel, 1998). This "New Concept" allowed Hoover to eventually embark on the Gangster Disciples' continuing transformation into a politically motivated entity (Knox, n.d.). This transition was also mirrored by Chicago's other "supergangs"; not only were the leaderships politicizing the membership of their groups inside prison by "coalition building," but they were also transforming their internal structures. For example, the Black Peace Stone Nation changed their name to "Moorish Science Temple of America, El Rukn tribe," and their organizational structure followed a religious organizational model (as opposed to the Gangster Disciples' shift to a corporate organizational model; see Williams, 2001).

This 1980s transformation was furthered by Hoover's organizational development of the Brothers of the Struggle (BOS), intended for the Gangster Disciples in prison (Knox, n.d.). Directions were issued by memorandums, which included showing respect for correctional officers, taking jobs inside the prison, education, voter registration for those outside prison, etc. During this period, Hoover's Executive Memorandums reflect a number of regulations and a public-relations spin, possibly with the dual purpose of increasing cohesion of the group and reaching out to outsiders for support (for detailed analysis of Hoover's memorandums, see Knox, n.d.). In a 1984 memo, Hoover asked the Gangster Disciples to help him in gaining parole. Hoover's transfer in the late 1980s to a low-security facility allowed him to communicate further with Gangster Disciples outside. During this period, as well as today, it is unknown the extent to which Hoover controls the Gangster Disciples outside prison (Donaldson, n.d.).

Rebirth of a Political Movement (The Early 1990s): 21st Century VOTE and Growth and Development

A second attempt at political involvement from street organizations formed around the early 1990s. For Chicago, this culminated in the 1992–1993 gang truce through the "United in Peace" organization between the **Vice Lords,** the Back P Stone Nation (now El Rukn), the Gangster Disciples, and other major street gangs and street organizations. Many officials, however, saw the United in Peace organization as merely another front group for gangs, vying for positive media attention (Chicago Crime Commission, 1995, p. 10).

The Gangster Disciples also progressed politically in two major ways: by changing the organization to "Growth and Development," and by launching 21st Century VOTE (Voices of Total Empowerment). The first was meant to "allow prison inmates to become socially acceptable to society," and outlined the six principles of Growth and Development: love, life, loyalty, knowledge, wisdom, and understanding (Emery, 1996). Because the timing of transforming the Gangster Disciples into Growth and Development as a political action campaign coincided with Hoover's 1993 parole hearing, most corrections officials saw it as a publicity stunt to that end. Not only was Hoover's parole denied, but he was transferred to a higher-security facility (Knox, n.d.). However, support from churches, schools, community groups and politicians poured in, and it "converted thousands of gangbangers at least temporarily into true believers" (Donaldson, n.d.).

Simultaneously, 21st Century VOTE was launched as a political action organization. It was immediately labeled by law enforcement as a "self-styled 'political action committee' that we see as being little more than a 'Trojan Horse' to further the aims of imprisoned gang leaders" (Chicago Crime Commission, 1995). Critics also argued that VOTE was funded by illegal drug sales by the Disciples, which was estimated at about $100 million per year (Tyson, 1996; *United States v. Irwin,* 1998). Whatever the case may be, 21st Century VOTE was a powerful and legitimate political vehicle in which many disempowered residents could have their voices heard: one major accomplishment includes a 10,000-person rally that ended a conflict between teachers and the city of Chicago (Donaldson, n.d.). Principal in these two political movements was a former enforcer for the Gangster Disciples and childhood friend of Hoover's, Wallace "Gator" Bradley. In 1994, Bradley ran for City Alderman for the

Third Ward, which encompasses much of the Disciples' neighborhood. Many community members in the area, both members and nonmembers of the Gangster Disciples, chose to become politically active by voting and assisting in the campaign. However, it was an uphill battle: with Hoover's name, an underfunded campaign, and allegations of drug-trafficking funding and Gangster Disciple ties, Bradley lost the runoff election.

Criminalization (1995 to Present)

The following years marked another turning point for the Gangster Disciples, when the District Attorney indicted Hoover and thirty-eight other members in "Operation Headache": a twenty-five-year conspiracy charge for extortion and distribution of narcotics. Hoover was directly indicted for running the thirty-five-state, 30,000-member organization from the Joliet State Prison in Illinois (Tyson, 1996; U.S. Drug Enforcement Administration, 1997). Some federal law enforcement likened the Gangster Disciples' drug distribution to a pyramid scheme based on "innovative theories of Japanese management," and warned that exiting members from prison were more highly educated and physically stronger than before (Lindberg, 2001). This image of **organized crime** was used as justification by law enforcement to implement both aggressive policing and legal tactics to prosecute Hoover and others. Federal agencies implanted recording devices in unknowing visitors' name tags (Robinson, 2002). Additionally, prosecution relied on the use of the Continuing Criminal Enterprise Act, which is similar to RICO (Lindberg, 2001). Hoover was convicted in 1997, and is still serving time in a "supermax" facility with no outside contact (Revolutionary Worker #905, 1997).

With the silencing of Hoover, it appears that the Gangster Disciples have since become operationally more decentralized, and are less of a presence in their former neighborhoods, working more as associated networks (Knox, n.d.). Additionally, other gangs have had an increased presence throughout the city of Chicago such as the Vice Lords, the **Latin Kings,** the **Crips, Bloods,** and other factions of the Disciples. Moreover, the associated political organizations have lost steam, with potential leaders being placed in isolation units within prison where communication with the outside world is made to be almost impossible, or other highly visible leaders removing themselves from the scene to avoid the possibility of a similar fate.

References/Suggested Readings: Chicago Crime Commission. 1995. *Public Enemy Number One: Gangs.* Chicago Crime Commission; Decker, S.H., Bynum, T., and Weisel, D. 1998. A Tale of Two Cities: Gangs and Organized Crime Groups. *Justice Quarterly,* 15 (3); Donaldson, G. (n.d.). *Twenty-First Century V.O.T.E.* Retrieved March 4, 2006, from gangreserach. net/ChicagoGangs/BGD/vote21.html; Emery, R. 1996. *From Gangster Disciple to Growth and Development "The Blueprint."* Elgin, IL: Growth and Development; Hagedorn, J. (n.d.). *Black Gangster Disciple Nation.* Retrieved March 4, 2006, from gangreserach.net/Chicago-Gangs/BGD/bgdhomepage.html; Hagedorn, J. 2005. Gangs and Politics. In L. R. Sherrod, C. Flanagan, and R. Kassimir (eds.), *Youth Activism: An International Encyclopedia.* Portshouse, NH: Greenwood Press; Jacobs, J.B. 1974. Street Gangs behind Bars. *Social Problems,* 21 (3); Jacobs, J.B. 1977. *Stateville: The Penitentiary in Mass Society.* Chicago: University of Chicago Press; Knox, G.W. (n.d.). The Impact of the Federal Prosecution of the Gangster Disciples. *National Gang Crime Research Center;* Knox, G.W. 2001. The Gangster Disciples: A Gang Profile. *National Gang Crime Research Center;* Knox, G.W. 2004. Gang Threat Analysis: The Black Disciples. *National Gang Crime Research Center;* Lindberg, R.C. 2001. A Study in Power: The Dismantling of Larry Hoover and the Black Gangster Disciples. Retrieved March 20, 2006, from www.search-international.com/Articles/chicagomob/powerstudy.html; Revolutionary

Worker #905. 1997. Larry Hoover in the Court of Justice. Retrieved March 20, 2005, from rwor.org/a/v19/905/hoover.html; Robinson, M. 2002. Feds Crack Down on Gangs: *Gangster Disciples Rounded up on West Side.* Retrieved March 20, 2006, from www.streetgangs.com; Tyson, A.S. 1996. How Nation's Largest Gang Runs its Drug Enterprise. *Christian Science Monitor,* July 15, 1; *United States v. Irwin,* 95 C.R. 509. 1998; U.S. Drug Enforcement Administration. 1998. *Larry Hoover and the Gangster Disciples.* Retrieved March 20, 2006, from /www.dea.gov/major/hoover.htm; Williams, L. 2001 (October). *The Almighty Black P. Stone Nation.* Lecture presented at University of Illinois School of Public Health, Chicago.

MARISA OMORI AND DOUGLAS E. THOMPKINS

GANGSTER WANNABES. Street gangs are in all American cities. Researchers have estimated that there are up to 21,500 gangs having more than 730,000 members (Triplett, 2004). These gangs have been associated with copious acts such as auto theft, extortion, murder, rape, and so on. While many people immediately think of the **Crips** and **Bloods** when criminal gangs are discussed, a fairly recent phenomenon has emerged involving young teenagers who emulate real gang members (Monti, 1994; Triplett, 2004). These individuals are known as gangster "wannabes."

Characteristics and Activities of Wannabes

The primary distinguishing characteristic of gangster wannabes is that they are not involved in the most serious forms of gang-related crime. While some criminal activity is committed, the level of severity is much lower than acts committed by hard-core gang members (Monti, 1994; Small, 2000). The primary activities of gangster wannabes are:

- graffiti
- vandalism
- school disruptions
- intimidation
- general community annoyances
- serves as gophers/runners for actual gang members
- weapons holders
- lookouts
- attempts to impress (both gang members as well as community members)
- minor theft (e.g., cell phones)
- use/possession of handguns (used to enhance reputation) (Small, 2000; Sheldon, Tracey, and Brown, 2000; Hagedorn and Macon, 1998).

Judging from the list of typical gangster wannabe behaviors, it is clear that these individuals pose a far lesser risk to the community but their activities still warrant societal responses. The justification for a suppressive societal response to wannabes is that it is not uncommon for them to progress to become more dangerous criminals (Richie, 2006). Also, their antisocial behavior is simply intolerable and its eradication a desirable aim in and of itself.

Several authors have attempted to profile gangster wannabes, both demographically as well as by various other personal and/or group level traits. Wannabes tend to be substantially younger, for example, than hard-core gangsters. The typical age for gangster wannabes is in the early teens. They also tend to mimic various aspects of hard-core gang members. Gangster wannabes copy the style and dress (e.g., disheveled appearance, certain types of color combinations, bandanas, language, hand signs, as well as symbols in the use of graffiti; Monti, 1994; Small, 2000).

Another distinguishing characteristic is that gangster wannabes are extremely disorganized relative to their hard-core role models. There is no known hierarchy/chain of command, leader, or meaningful group name (although some police departments have noted recently that some wannabes have attempted to unite with their like-minded friends and create quasi-gang names; Geng, 2000; Wells, 2006).

Another characteristic of gang wannabes is that while hard-core gangsters are primarily urban, wannabes are divided between urban and suburban settings. In fact, many wannabes are middle-class juveniles living in far more affluent neighborhoods than is typically expected from their hard-core counterparts. This is another trait suggesting that suppression via deterrence is a viable response to this phenomenon. Other characteristics of wannabes are:

- A lack of self-confidence
- A lack of a fuller understanding of the gangster lifestyle and its consequences
- The expression of gangster values (e.g., an emphasis on physical prowess over intellectual aims)

Causal Factors Associated with Wannabes

Traditionally, the causes of gang development are cited as poverty, perceptions of racism, abuse in the family, failure in school, lack of parental supervision, and no father in the home (Sheldon et al., 2000). While these factors are undoubtedly associated with wannabes in poor urban areas, other factors more accurately explain the popularity of becoming a gangster wannabe in suburban areas.

For example, young, alienated adolescents go through a process beginning with the wannabe stage and ending up as hard-core gangsters (see Coffey, 1997; Foster, 1996; Monti, 1994). Major factors associated with wannabes include: (1) gangsta rap; (2) a mass media that glorifies violence committed by those wearing gang-related clothing; (3) action movies that desensitize adolescents to violence; (4) desire/lust for power, respect, friends, and security associated with a gangsterism; (5) the fun associated with providing the "shock effect" (i.e., values, mannerisms, speech, clothing that offends middle-class America); and (6) weak societal responses to early manifestations of gang-related behavior. These factors represent Stage 1 of gang wannabes.

Stage 2 consists of societal responses such as the use of the phrase wannabe. After all, who would ever react positively to being called a wannabe regardless of whether it is associated with gangs or anything else? During Stage 3, the adolescent is tagged as a wannabe, then recognizes that he/she is not being taken seriously by authority figures, neighbors, teachers, and so on. If gang clothing, symbols, offensive music and language, and intimidation do not get them taken seriously, wannabes may be forced to resort to more severe behavior. Stage 4 finds the wannabe confronted by a dilemma of increasing the intensity of offensive behavior or accepting the pejorative label. Most affected teens probably grow up and recognize that sagging jeans, hand gestures, and gangsta rap music are puerile in nature and threaten their future status in school and society. They then discontinue the wannabe lifestyle. However, for some (including middle-class kids) the progression continues. In Stage 5, the wannabe escalates behavior and this leads to academic problems (although this could be a causal factor as well), police intervention, and a criminal label. This individual is well on the way to being part of the throwaway population of hard-core gangsters.

Responses to Wannabe Gangsters

Deterrence theory application may not be amenable to hard-core gangsters. This is because their commitment to crime as a way of life is too strong to be overcome by fear of punishment and being locked up can actually improve one's "rep." Hard-core gangsters' lives may be so disadvantaged and the gang lifestyle so ingrained as to make these individuals poor candidates for deterrence.

However, wannabes have characteristics that readily lend themselves to deterrence from crime via fear of punishment. Brown, Esbensen, and Geis (2004) illustrate differential deterability by crime type and personality characteristics. Those with these characteristics tend to be higher in deterability than those with opposite characteristics:

- future oriented
- high self-control
- low risk takers
- authoritarians
- higher social class
- higher stakes in conformity
- property offenses
- mala prohibita offenses
- public offenses

It can be argued that wannabes, particularly those in suburban and/or middle-class neighborhoods, have many of these traits (when compared to their poor, urban counterparts) and therefore they are more amenable to deterrence via fear of punishment. Clearly, middle-class adolescents are higher in socioeconomic status, have more stakes in conformity, and are likely to have higher levels of self-control although they might engage in more property offenses. Further, most deviant behavior engaged in by wannabes is public and regulatory in nature as opposed to intrinsically evil/mala in se. These factors suggest that a suppression-oriented response to wannabe gangsters might be more effective than for hard-core gang members. In sum, gangster wannabes who have not become immersed in a criminal lifestyle may be salvageable and can be deterred from deviant behavior through stricter penalties for the act of emulating hard core gang activities.

References/Suggested Readings: Bridge, M. 2005 (December). Police Say Gangster Wannabes behind Gun Rise. *Vancouver Sun*. Retrieved from www.canada.com/vancouversun/story.html; Brown, S., Esbensen, F., and Geis, G. 2004. *Criminology: Explaining Crime and its Context*. Cincinnati: Anderson Publishers; Coffey, R. 1997. *Military Police, Gangs, and Extremist Groups: A Handbook for Commanders, Parents, and Teachers*. U.S. Army pamphlet. Retrieved March 25, 2006, from 134.11.61.26/CD8/Publications/USAREUR/USAREUR%20Pam/USAREUR%20Pam%20190-100%2019970310.pdf; Foster, K. 1996. *Gang Wannabes Are Gonnabes*. Retrieved March 25, 2006, from www.gangwar.com/textonly/news11.htm; Geng, S. 2005. *The Changing Face of Gangs: Dramatic Increases in Gang Activity Nationwide Include a Strong, Rising Female Presence*. Retrieved March 25, 2006, from silverchips.mbhs.edu/inside; Hagedorn, J., and Macon, P. 1998. *People and Folks: Gangs,*

Crime, and the Underclass in a RustBelt City. Chicago: Lakeview Press; Monti, D. 1994. *Wannabe: Gangs in Suburbs and Schools*. Cambridge, MA: Blackwell; Pardington, J. 2006. *Signs Here of Gang Wannabes*. Chatham News Publishing. Retrieved March 25, 2006, from www.thechathamnews.com/archives/Nov24/index.htm; Ritchie, J. 2006. *Preventing Wannabes from Becoming Gang Recruits*. Retrieved March 26, 2006, from www.iuinfo.indiana. edu/homepages/0920/0920text/gang.htm; Sheldon, R., Tracey, S., and Brown, W. 2000. *Youth Gangs in American Society*. Belmont, CA: Wadsworth; Small, M. A. 2000. *Gangs in South Carolina: An Exploratory Study*. Clemson: Clemson University, Institute on Family and Neighborhood Life; Triplett, W. 2004. Gang Crisis: Do Police and Politicians have a Solution? *CQ Researcher*, 14 (18), 23–36. Retrieved March 22, 2006, from www.lib.msu.edu/harris23/ crimjust/gangs.htm; Wells, K. 2006. Cops Say and Wannabes Pose Dangers. *Times Herald Record*. Retrieved March 25, 2006, from www.recordonline.com/archive.

BILLY LONG

GERMAN GANGS

Definition of "Gangs" in the European Context

The term "gang" that is commonly used in the American literature may be confusing when looking at the European gang phenomenon. Scholars on both continents have had a lot of difficulties comparing European to American gangs because of the structural differences within gangs and the contrasting neighborhood settings in which gangs evolve and operate. Therefore, scholars on both sides have preferred to speak about "troublesome youth groups" or have completely denied the existence of gangs in the European context (Decker and Weerman, 2005). German youth groups, for example, are not known for defending their territory as is commonplace among American gangs, and firearms are generally absent. Additionally, European gangs use symbols such as names, colors, and **graffiti** out of a different reason than American gangs. For them, American symbols are part of the international youth culture which identifies the symbols as the latest fashion. Since their use is not directly connected to a particular gang, the police could not take advantage of them in order to destroy gangs as the American law enforcement agencies tend to do (Van Germert, 2002).

In order to approach these differences between American and European gangs, the Eurogang program instigated by Malcom W. Klein in 1997 agreed on a definition for European gangs that differentiated them from American gangs. According to this definition, "a [European] street gang is any durable street-oriented youth group whose involvement in illegal activities is part of their group identity" (Decker and Weerman, 2005, p. 148). When reading about gangs in Germany, these distinctions should be kept in mind.

Gangs in Germany

Gangs in Germany are not a new phenomenon: the 1950s were the years of the hooligans, the 1970s the years of the rockers; punks and **skinheads** shaped society in the 1980s and 1990s. In the late 1980s and early 1990s, the first immigrant gangs became known (Tertilt, 1996). Nowadays, even though there are various youth subcultures that mainly define themselves through different styles of music, there are four major types of gangs in Germany who are known for criminal and violent behavior: skinheads, hooligans (though these two tend to overlap), gangs of second- and third-generation immigrants (mainly of Turkish and Moroccan decent), and

Russian teenagers of German descent. This article will focus on two of these gangs, skinheads as well as second- and third-generation immigrants.

Skinheads

Even though Germany does have a long history of gangs, there is not a great body of literature on the topic, and reports about gang incidents are very limited and restricted. In 1990, when the first journalists and academics reported about racism and skinheads in Eastern Germany, no one wanted to know about these prevailing problems as people were still excited and enthused by the reunification. Apparently, admitting that Eastern Germany might be a breeding area for disappointed right-wing people who are creating major problems would have diminished the state of ecstasy.

An open discussion about skinheads arose in 2006 when the former government spokesman Heye warned about "no-go areas" for colored people in East Germany (Perger, 2006). Even though Heye became the declared hate figure for many Germans accusing him of setting a wrong signal for Germany before the soccer world championship, his predictions about hate crimes committed by skinheads are actually in line with the recent numbers released by the Federal Department of the Interior, which state that assaults against foreigners and left-wing people committed by skinheads have risen to a total of 322 assaults and one attempted killing in 2005 (Bundesministerium des Innern, 2006). According to the Federal Office for the Protection of the Constitution (Bundesministerium für Verfassungsschutz, 2006, p. 5), 50 percent of Germany's skinheads are Eastern Germans, even though the population of East Germany amounts to only 21 percent of Germany's total population. Apparently, there is a strong belief in East Germany that foreigners take away jobs, are responsible for high crime rates and participate in Germany's prosperity without being citizens (see Ostow, 1995). As such, the results of a survey in a comparative assessment across seven nations are not surprising: 28.4 percent of all East Germans strongly agree and an additional 39.5 percent agree with the statement that "immigrants increase crime rates"—more people than in any other nation (Lynch and Simon, 2002).

Research suggests that Eastern German skinheads have experienced great frustration from unemployment and feel left behind by the promises of politicians, the prosperous West, and also by East Germans who have moved to West Germany after the changeover (*Wende*). The Westernization in post-unification left many Eastern Germans unprepared for the new democracy regime which did not provide jobs or help for everyone as people were used to from the former socialist GDR regime (Gress, 1991). The desire of East Germans to share the West's materialistic prosperity has not come true for everybody, and many East Germans feel the threat of foreigners on their turf who supposedly take away what should belong to them (see Ostow, 1995; Gress, 1991).

Skinhead gangs in East Germany mainly consist of young frustrated teenagers who feel that they do not have anything to look forward to in the unified Germany. Seventy-five percent are under the age of twenty-five and predominately male. Most of them have joined the gang during puberty (see Wahl 2003, p. 259ff.). On the one hand, they can be divided into various subgroups ("Hammerskins," "Blood and Honour," "White Youth," etc.) and have different opinions on the Third Reich: some of them use Nazi material only to gain public attention, yet do not truly believe in Hitler's ideas (see Ostow, 1995), whereas others still proclaim that the Third

Reich was the only true form of government. On the other hand, they all share outrageous hate of foreigners, Jews, gypsies, capitalists, and communists, listen to racist-motivated music, wear characteristic clothes and use certain symbols as identification (Bundesministerium für Verfassungsschutz, 2006). Most skinhead gangs only operate in their own district and tend to have a lose structure without a specific hierarchy, resulting in group affiliation that is mainly based on kinship ties or long-term personal relationships to other members of the local gang (Bundesministerium des Innern, 2006). However, there are also inter-gang connections with gangs from other areas and even a structure that connects gangs within the entire country (Wahl, 2003).

Not all skinheads are members of the various political right-wing parties, nonetheless, these parties recruit their voters mainly in East Germany whereupon the skinhead groups make up a fair amount of their constituency (Bundesministerium für Verfassungsschutz, 2006). Although there is a rise of assaults and robberies against foreigners and other disliked groups in Germany, the main focus of the skinhead gangs tends to be "hanging out," listening to right-wing music, and attending illegal skinhead concerts (Bundesministerium des Innern, 2006; Wahl, 2003; Farin, 1993).

Second- and Third-Generation Immigrants

Immigrant gang incidents have been denied to an even greater extent than those of skinheads. Germany had only a very short gang era that strongly resembled American gangs in the late 1980s and early 1990s. These gangs consisted of second- and third-generation immigrants of mainly Turkish, Italian, former Yugoslavian, and Moroccan background who were fighting over territories and turfs influenced by media reports on American gangs (Tertilt, 1996). After the police had seemingly approached these gang formations successfully, newspapers reported only on rare occasions about gang incidents with immigrants. However, the plea of a Berlin school principal in 2006 to close her school after a situation with violent second- and third-generation immigrant students (since they were beating German students and threatening teachers) was a wake-up call for many Germans who could have never imagined that these problems existed (Von Randow, 2006). One can only speculate why German media and politicians have denied the increasing problem of immigrant teenagers over such a long time. The most appealing reason may be found in the history of Germany and the strong sense of general guilt that does not allow society to speak openly about violent teenagers with Turkish, Moroccan, or Albanian background. Germany does not want to be viewed as a racist or excluding country and therefore, only a few politicians admitted and spoke openly about these teenagers—not without having to face severe criticism. Additionally, Germany has never considered itself an immigration country in the past (though it has the highest immigrant population in Europe). Instead, Germany identified their foreigners as "guest workers" who would soon leave the country again and return to their home countries (see Schiffauer, 1983; White, 1997). Therefore, kindergartens, schools, and other agencies were completely unprepared for immigrant children and their specific needs (Radtke, 2002). Moreover, politicians have continuously denied the existence of integration difficulties as the integrating process itself has never been planned (White, 1997). Moreover, the children are not granted German citizenship even though they are born and raised in Germany. Additionally, they are still considered and labeled as "migrants" in the public debate as "migration" has the notion of moving around whereas "immigration" would imply the destination in the country (see White, 1997).

Nowadays, the immigrant groups are the most pressing gang issue that Germany is facing, and the country has finally recognized and accepted the inevitable problems that come with 10 percent of the teenagers (Bundesministerium für Bildung und Forschung, 2004a, p. 8) who are not granted German citizenship or who have migrant backgrounds which limits their life chances.

On the other hand, many in the general public hold the view that most second- and third-generation teenagers do not have the ambition to be integrated into mainstream society. According to this perspective, they (young immigrants) refuse to assimilate and lack the qualities that are needed for surviving in the German formal economy: on average, these teenagers have low high school achievement records, possess deficient language skills, and lack the willingness to be part of hierarchical systems as demanded by employers. As the Program for International Student Assessment (PISA) has shown, there is no other country besides Germany that has so many difficulties with integrating immigrants (www.destatis.de/basis/d/biwiku/schultab16.php). The gap in school performance between students from an immigrant background and native Germans, and the gap between those from a poor socio-economic background compared to those from a wealthier one, is greater than anywhere else in the world. Apparently, teenagers from immigrant families almost always have both preconditions: being immigrant and having a poor socio-economic background. Therefore, their chances of success in the German system are limited from the outset (Bundesministerium für Bildung und Forschung, 2004b, p. 79f.; OECD, 2004, p. 14f.)

Nonetheless, these teenagers survive within the system. One can even go further and say that money does not seem to be their primary concern. The very opposite is the case: some of them do have the newest cell phones, the hippest clothes, and even cars. One way of satisfying their needs is through trafficking in drugs and/or stealing. Those that choose this route have formed their own system of values and norms that conflicts with their parents' views and those of mainstream German society: their status in a group is heavily influenced by factors such as physical strength, the willingness to unconditionally vouch for friends, financial resources and being a successful fighter or drug trafficker (see Miller, 1958).

Gangs of second- and third-generation male immigrants of Turkish, Moroccan, former Yugoslavian, and Albanian backgrounds can be found in any big city of Germany. The first-generation parents of these teenagers continue to cherish traditional Islamic values and norms, and they consider their stay in Germany to be a transitional phase in their lives for they had never rationally planned or consciously decided to stay in Germany (Schiffauer, 1983; White, 1997). The teenagers, however, are torn between two cultures—even though they were born in Germany and have been exposed to German lifestyle, culture, and especially consumerism, they have very mixed feelings about returning to their "home country," e.g., Turkey. In Germany they are labeled and stigmatized as "Turkish," in Turkey, however, people call them "Almancilar," which means "Germaner" (Tertilt, 1996; White, 1997). Even though they often glorify their home country in conversation with others, ethnographic studies have shown that they want to remain in Germany (Bucerius, 2007; Tertilt, 1996).

Having been raised or having grown up together is the most important criterion of group affiliation for these teenagers. They have known each other since their early childhood as they used to play soccer in the backyards or hang out together in the streets. The common experience of segregation and structured social exclusion has led the teenagers to construct a hybrid system of values and norms in which ethnicity is not important anymore, realizing that they all share a mutual experience as marginalized populations in Germany. This common experience binds migrants together as distinct from native Germans. Earlier generations of migrants were mainly born in their country of origin, but younger migrants have little or no reference to their country of origin, and more significantly, they no longer believe that they will return to their homeland. As such, they feel imprisoned in their parochial world and see no room for progress. Moreover, being born in Germany as second- or third-generation migrants, few of them have a realistic chance of being granted German citizenship. Consequently, they neither feel that they truly belong to Germany nor to their country of origin and thus, in this position as second-class citizens, they recognize their commonality with others in the same situation who are struggling to define their identity. The hybrid culture that they have created is driven by a fundamental need to belong somewhere, and it helps to create such a place. The street seems to provide a rare opportunity to gain self-esteem by demonstrating and staging masculinity, and to accumulate money. The main activity of these various gangs is a quite deedless form of "hanging out" at local youth centers, street corners, and parks in the district. Additionally, personal and family honor continue to be quite important, as losing honor is one of the greatest disgraces for Muslims (see Tertilt, 1996; Levine, 2003). If one of the gang members feels the need to restore his personal, family, or even the gang's honor, other gang members might help out in these often very violent acts.

Although the public may think that these teenagers are completely disconnected from the outside world and not interested in politics, their stance is actually very clear and firm. Their biggest object of hate is Jewish people and consequently, calling someone a Jew is the greatest curse. Moreover, they are anti-American and anti-Israel, which clearly differentiates them from German mainstream publics (see also van Germert and Fleisher, 2005). Recently, some of Germany's bigger cities have experienced a rapid growth of diasporic ghettos which has been unknown in Germany so far, and society, police, and political establishment now faced with neighborhoods in which Germans are a clear minority. At the same time, violent acts and assaults by second- and third-generation immigrant gangs against Jews but also against Germans have arisen in these neighborhoods and will probably continue until Germany guarantees that these marginalized teenagers have the same opportunities as their German counterparts in order to have a future in Germany—the country in which they were born and raised.

References/Suggested Readings: Bucerius, Sandra. 2007. Vor was soll ich denn Angst haben. In Bernd Werse (ed.), *Handeln, Dealen, Checken. Drogendistribution in Frankfurt.* Wiesbaden: VS-Verlag; Bundesministerium des Innern. 2006. *Verfassungsschutzbericht 2005.* Berlin, Bonn: Volz & Partner; Bundesamt für Verfassungsschutz. 2006. *Verfassungsschutz gegen Rechtsextremismus.* Berlin: BfV; Bundesministerium für Bildung und Forschung. 2004a. *Migrationshintergrund von Kindern und Jugendlichen—Wege zur Weiterentwicklung der amtlichen Statistik.* Berlin: BMBF; Bundesministerium für Bildung und Forschung. 2004b. *Berufsbildungsbericht 2004.* Berlin: BMBF; Decker Scott H., and Weerman, Frank M. (eds). 2005. *European Street Gangs and Troublesome Youth Groups.* Lanham, MD: Alta Mira Press; Farin, Klaus, and Seidel-Pielen, Eberhard (eds.). 1993. *Skinheads.* München: C.H. Beck-Verlag; Germert van, Frank. 2002. Moeizame Marokkaanse medewerking; Cultuur als verklaring voormethodologische obstakels. In Hanneke Houtkoop-Steenstra and Justus Veenman (eds.), *Interviewen in een multiculturele samenleving—Problemen en oplossingen.* Assen: Van Gorcum; Germert van, Frank. 2005. Youth Groups and Gangs in Amsterdam: A Prestest of the European Expert Study. In Scott H. Decker and Frank M. Weerman (ed.s), *European Street Gangs and Troublesome Youth Groups*, pp. 147–168. Lanham, MD: Alta Mira Press; Germert van, Frank, and Fleisher, Mark S. 2005. In the Grip of the Group. In Scott H. Decker and Frank M. Weerman (ed.), *European Street Gangs and Troublesome Youth Groups*, pp. 11–30. LanhamMD: Alta Mira Press; Gress, David. 1991. The Politics of German Unification. *Proceedings of the Academy of Political Science*, 38 (1), 140–152; Levine, Kay. 2003. Negotiating the Boundaries of Crime and Culture: A Sociolegal Perspective on Cultural Defense Strategies. *Law and Social Inquiry*. 39–86; Lynch, James P., and Simon, Rita J. 2002. A Comparative Assessment of Criminal Involvement along Immigrants and Natives across Seven Nations. In Joshua D. Freilich (ed.), *Migration, Culture Conflict and Crime*. Aldershot: Darmouth; Miller, Walter B. 1958. Kultur der Unterschicht als Entstehungsmilieu für Bandendelinquenz. In Fritz Sack and Rene König (ed.), 1979: *Kriminalsoziologie*, pp. 339–359. 3. Auflage. Wiesbaden: Akademische Verlagsgesellschaft: Seite; OECD. 2004. *Messages from Pisa 2000*. Paris: OECD Publications; Ostow, Robin. 1995. Ne Art Bürgerwehr in Form von Skins: Young German on the Streets in the Eastern and Western States of the Federal Republic. *New German Critique: East, West and Other*, 64, 87–103; Perger, Werner A. 2006. Betreten auf eigene Gefahr. In *Die Zeit* 22. Hamburg: Zeit-Verlag; Radtke, Frank-Olaf, and Gomolla, Mechthild. 2002. *Institutionelle Diskriminierung—eine Herstellung ethnischer Differenz in der Schule*. Opladen: Leske + Budrich; Randow von, Gero. 2006. Unter Polizeischutz. In *Die Zeit* 14. Hamburg: Zeit-Verlag; Schiffauer Werner. 1983. *Die Gewalt der Ehre*. Frankfurt: Suhrkamp; Tertilt, Herman. 1996. *Turkish Power Boys. Ethnographie einer Jugendbande*. Frankfurt: Suhrkamp Verlag; Wahl, Klaus (ed). 2003. *Skinheads, Neonazis, Mitläufer—Täterstudien und Prävention*. Opladen: Leske & Budrich; White, Jenny B. 1997. Turks in Germany. *American Anthropologist*, 99 (4), 754–769.

SANDRA M. BUCERIUS

GODFATHERS. Italian **organized crime** has been called several things in its sordid history. The Mafia, the outfit, and Cosa Nostra are common names for this criminal enterprise that traces its roots to the small island of Sicily off the southern coast of Italy. Cosa Nostra was not originally a criminal enterprise; rather it was formed as way to help the citizens of Sicily. The island had been exploited for centuries by the Normans, Germans, French, and Spanish Bourbons (Gage, 1973). In order to control the peasants, the Bourbons formed a pseudo-police force that was made up of ruthless members, some of whom were criminals who were saved from the gallows if they agreed to join in the oppression of the Sicilian peasants (Gage, 1973, p. 68).

Under such barbarous rule the citizens had no choice but turn to the "men of honor," the Mafioso, to protect them and exact retribution for their losses of property and family members (Barzin, 1971). The origins of the Mafia can be traced to the city of Palermo, Sicily, in 1282. It was then that the natives of the island rose up against the French. The rebellion is known as the Sicilian Vespers (Gage, 1971). The name Mafia is said to come from the Vespers' motto "Morte alla Francia Italia anela" (Death to the French is Italy's cry). Taking the first letter in each word of the motto spells MAFIA (Gage, 1971, p. 30). It is believed that the Mafia was formed to protect the citizens of Sicily from future conquests and oppression.

After the Vespers rebellion the Mafia stayed powerful in Sicily, offering protection to the peasantry and acting as a mediator for local disputes. Their power base grew throughout Sicily until the small island ran out of financial opportunities. Some of the more industrious Mafioso sent men to seek new opportunities in America. In the early 1900s, there was an explosion of Italian and Sicilian immigration. Most of these new Americans banded together in small neighborhoods in major cities like New York and Chicago. Along with the hard-working Italians and Sicilians came the criminals and minor Mafioso. Many of the early Italian criminals formed small extortion gangs that were called **Black Hand** gangs. Some of the other criminals started providing the same services to the poor Italian and Sicilian immigrants that were available in the old country such as protection, mediation of disputes, and revenge for hire. These were the predecessor to the American Cosa Nostra, referred to as Mustache Petes. The most notable of the Petes was also the most powerful, Giuseppe "Joe the Boss" Masseria. Joe and the rest of the Petes were very conservative in their business dealings and were unwilling to change with the times.

Joe the Boss's conservative business practices restricted his lieutenants from making huge profits. Salvatore Lucania, better known as Lucky Luciano, thought he could do better. His ambition was seen by Joe as a threat and an attempt was made on Lucky's life. He survived and teamed up with Jewish gangster Meyer Lansky and Joe's competitor Salvatore Maranzano to seek revenge on Joe the Boss. Joe was killed and his death helped end the Castellammarese War that had been raging between Maranzano's and Joe's men. With the war concluded, Maranzano declared himself "Boss of all Bosses" in New York with five New York families under his control. Maranzano wanted to expand his control over the entire United States, but in order to do that he would first need to eliminate the only two men he thought could ever challenge his power: Lucky Luciano and Chicago's Al Capone. True to his moniker, Lucky learned of Maranzano's plans and had him executed before he had a chance to carry them out.

Luciano was now at the height of power and used his influence to control the other families through a murder for hire team called "Murder Inc." These stone-cold killers eliminated any Mafioso that did not live by the code of ómerta. This code forbade any member from speaking about the organization and from working with the authorities. Lucky ruled over New York and built casinos in Havana before Castro and communism took over. Luciano organized the families into a commission wherein all the Mafia families could work out disputes and discuss new members. Lucky was eventually arrested for his part in organizing prostitution and was sent to prison to serve a thirty- to forty-year sentence. His imprisonment was cut short when Naval Intelligence had him pardoned. In return, Luciano used his influence to insure that the Navy's ships would be safe in New York harbor. Luciano later returned to Sicily where he received tributes from the American Mafia members until a heart attack took his life in 1962.

While Luciano ruled over New York, Al Capone was the Godfather of Chicago. Alphonse Capone was raised in New York and by all accounts was a well-behaved child. As a young man he became involved with local gangsters Johnny Torrio and Frankie Yale. When Torrio went to Chicago in 1920, Capone followed. There Capone started working with the Chicago Mafia involving himself in prostitution, racketeering, and bootlegging. What separated Capone from other Mafioso was his willingness to work with non-Italians. His best friend and closest confidant was a Jew named Jack Guzika, who acted as a mentor for young Capone. Capone and Torrio made an excellent team and after only a few years were some of the most powerful men in Chicago. When Torrio was seriously injured in a failed assassination attempt, he saw it as a sign for him to leave the life of crime. He turned the entire empire over to Capone, making him one of the biggest gangsters in all of Chicago.

His empire expanded due to Prohibition. The Capone organization used old cigarette smuggling routes to sneak booze into the States. Their speakeasies were great money makers for them, providing a place to sell booze while encouraging prostitution and gambling.

With so much money to be made, Capone was faced with a great deal of competition. Capone used force to squelch most competitors, including the bloody St. Valentine's Day Massacre, which killed off nearly all of the competition. This made Capone the King of Chicago. He began living lavishly in Chicago's best hotels and even hired a press agent to cultivate his image as a great man. However, all the publicity only made law enforcement concentrate on him more, earning him the status of public enemy number one. In the end, Treasury agent Eliot Ness brought Capone down for tax evasion. Capone was jailed and sent to prison in Atlanta, then moved to Alcatraz until his November 1939 release after only six years and five months. He then moved to Florida where he died a free man.

After Capone left, Anthony Accardo, former wheelman to Capone, took over as head of the family. He remained in control of Chicago until he was pressured out by mounting FBI scrutiny. He appointed his underboss, Sam "Momo" Giacana, to take the reins as King of Chicago. Momo started out as a bootlegger in Capone's organization and worked his way up to trigger man, becoming close to Capone himself. This association with Capone allowed him to move up the ranks quickly, attracting the notice of Accardo, who eventually would promote him to boss of the Chicago outfit. Momo made millions for his organization through skimming money in casinos in Las Vegas and Havana. What makes Momo Giacana such an interesting example of a Godfather is the amount of scandal in which he was involved. It is claimed that John F. Kennedy owed his presidency in part to the work Momo did garnering support for Kennedy's presidential run in Chicago. Interestingly enough, Momo was also named as a possible conspirator in the killing of Kennedy, as well as a possible conspirator in an assassination attempt on Fidel Castro. Following the Kennedy assassination, Momo moved to Mexico to run his businesses. The Mexican government eventually forced him out in 1974. He was summoned to testify before the Senate Select Subcommittee on Intelligence, a summons he would not attend as he was killed in his home on June 19, 1975.

There have been many great Mafia bosses: Luciano, Capone, Accardo, Albert Anastasia, Carlo Gambino. Some recent bosses, such as New York's John Gotti, have earned just as much fame, if not the same level of success. The boss of the family is the Godfather. He rules over the family, his orders cannot be questioned. His will must be done. All major decisions of the family go to him. The Godfather is in the position of having the most power, he also gains the most from the family's illegal enterprises. He is the "big fish" that law enforcement wants to arrest. Without a strong Godfather in charge, family members tend to pursue selfish goals that may not be in the best interests of the family. It is the Godfather who must protect the family from outside threats such as rivals and law enforcement, while at the same time protecting the family from its own selfishness through control of the members. The Godfather of a Mafia family is a job similar to the head of a major corporation, with the exception that retirement for a Godfather often comes with a bullet.

References/Suggested Readings: Abandinsky, H. 1997. *Organized Crime*. Chicago: Nelson-Hall; Barzini, L. 1971. *From Caesar to the Mafia: Sketches of Italian Life*. New York: Library Press; Gage, N. 1973. *Mafia USA*. New York: Dell Publishing.

DAVID HOHN

GRASP (GANG REDUCTION AND AGGRESSIVE SUPERVISION PAROLE).

The GRASP program was implemented by the New Jersey State Parole Board in February 2002, in response to a growing street gang population in New Jersey. The increased emphasis on gang related criminal prosecutions by law enforcement in the previous decade had led to a significant increase in the number of gang members being incarcerated statewide, and a corresponding increase in gang members released on parole supervision after serving the custodial portion of their sentence. This growth in gang members being released in the early 2000s necessitated a coordinated response from Parole and Corrections officials in New Jersey; and that response was the creation of the GRASP program. The primary goal of the GRASP program is to afford paroled gang members every opportunity to renounce their gang affiliation through education and diversion, and hopefully guide them to adopt a more productive pro-social lifestyle. The GRASP officer is tasked to provide knowledgeable supervision and appropriate intervention, with the anticipated result of reducing parole revocation and recidivism rates for gang member parolees.

Gang Identification and Security Threat Groups

The GRASP program is designed to provide an increased level of supervision for paroled gang members, and every New Jersey parolee assigned to the program has been identified as a member of the one of the following gangs: the **Bloods**, the **Crips**, the **Almighty Latin King and Queen Nation**, the East Coast Aryan Brotherhood, the Five-Percenters (also known as The Nation of Gods and Earth), **Asociación Ñeta**, and the Prison Brotherhood of Bikers. These seven gangs are the most prevalent in the New Jersey correctional system, and have been classified by the New Jersey Department of Corrections as Security Threat Groups (STGs). STGs can be briefly defined as groups whose activities pose a threat to the safety of institutional staff and other inmates, and to the security of a correctional institution. Every STG inmate placed under the parole supervision of the GRASP program must first meet specific gang identification criteria. The identification criteria include self-admission of gang membership, tattoos or branding, possession of gang recruitment literature or manifestos, letters from other gang members, or photos of the offender with other identified gang members. Gang members can also be identified based on information provided by another law enforcement agency as part of the GRASP intelligence-sharing initiative. The identification process has become much more challenging in recent years, as street gangs are becoming much more sophisticated, and many are now concealing their gang affiliation from law enforcement officials. Members who had previously boasted openly about their gang affiliation now routinely deny gang membership to avoid institutional and parole sanctions, and many do not wear their gang colors openly in the community, in an effort to avoid increased scrutiny from law enforcement.

Training

It is critical to the success of the GRASP program that officers assigned receive regularly updated training to keep abreast of the continuously changing and evolving world of street gangs. Training is essential for officer safety. It is also believed that this training can enable the officers to communicate with gang members more effectively, and also to help the officer better understand the unique problems and obstacles facing gang members upon their return to the community. Each GRASP officer must receive a minimum of forty hours annually in gang related training.

A GRASP officer must have over 250 hours of gang training to be eligible to be a training officer. GRASP training officers provide gang training to other law enforcement agencies, as well as providing gang awareness training to local schools in New Jersey communities.

Multi-Agency Anti-Gang Initiative

The GRASP program was instituted by the New Jersey State Parole Board as part of a multi-agency task force targeting the street gang parolee populations in several urban areas in New Jersey. The law enforcement objectives of GRASP were to reduce the criminal activity of paroled gang members through intensive directed supervision, and to develop an inter-agency intelligence and information sharing network with other law enforcement agencies throughout the state. As the GRASP initiative grew, the role of the parole officers was expanded to include multi-agency suppression sweeps targeting violent gang members, surveillance of suspected gang activities, and participation in criminal investigations. GRASP parole officers soon transcended the traditional boundaries of casework supervision to become an integral part of New Jersey's anti-gang initiative and have been involved in numerous high-profile gang suppression initiatives throughout the state.

Intervention

As stated previously, the GRASP program is a specially trained unit of parole officers, supervising caseloads of high-risk gang member parolees utilizing pro-active casework techniques. Pro-active parole supervision may entail diversion by placing the gang member to a community-based treatment facility if there is evidence of a return to CDS/alcohol usage; or it may necessitate returning the gang member to prison if the violation of parole was deemed to be of a serious or persistent nature. Ideally this intervention is done before the gang member has the opportunity to commit a new criminal offense. This pro-active intervention policy is based on the belief that paroled gang members, upon their return to the street gang environment with the likelihood of an increased exposure to drugs and weapons, may have a higher likelihood to re-offend than non-gang offenders, released to the same or similar environment at the same time. Based on this understanding of the environmental obstacles facing gang members, the GRASP program is committed to the objective of reducing gang-related violence by utilizing this educated proactive approach to casework supervision.

GRASP Supervision

Gang members are held to strict supervision conditions as part of the GRASP program. They are prohibited from recruiting for gang purposes, they can have no unauthorized contact with other gang members, they cannot wear their gang colors in public, and they cannot possess any prohibited gang-related literature or photographs. Evidence of any of these prohibited activities can result in immediate return to custody. GRASP parole officers conduct frequent after-hours curfew checks, often as part of a larger multi-agency gang operation, and are authorized to search the residences of gang members at any time if they have reasonable suspicion to believe that the parolee may have renewed their gang affiliation or returned to criminal activity.

References/Suggested Readings: Butler, Richard and Venessa Garcia. 2006. The Parole Supervision of Security Threat Group Members: A Collaborative Response. *Corrections Today*

(April); Klein, Malcolm W. 1995. *The American Street Gang.* New York: Oxford University Press; Knox, G. 2000. A National Assessment of Gangs and Security Threat Groups in Adult Correctional Institutions: Results of the 1999 Adult Corrections Study. National Gang Crime Research Center Report; McGloin, Jean Marie. 2005. Policy and Intervention Considerations of a Network Analysis of Street Gangs. *Criminology & Public Policy* 4: 607–636; New Jersey State Police. 2005. *Gangs in New Jersey: Municipal Law Enforcement Response to the 2004 & 2001 NJSP Gang Surveys.* Retrieved October 19, 2005, http://www.njsp.org/info/pdf/ njgangsurvey-2001-2004.pdf; Spergel, I. 1994. Office of Juvenile Justice and Delinquency Prevention. *OJJDP Research Summary 1994. Gang Suppression and Response: Problem and Response.*

RICHARD BUTLER

H

HATE GROUPS. A hate group is an organized movement or group that centers its activity on hostility or violence toward individuals of a particular race, ethnic group, religious affiliation, disability, or sexual orientation. Hate groups like the Ku Klux Klan, White Aryan Resistance, **skinheads**, and National Socialists often commit bias-motivated crimes. But not all of the existing hate groups pursue the exercise of violence. Some of them, such as People for the American Way, and Americans for Truth, focus instead on the compilation and redistribution of defamatory information on the people and communities that are the objects of hate.

The Federal Hate Crime Statistics Act of 1990 recognized hate crimes as a specific category of crime for the first time. In less than five years, a total of thirty-seven states had passed legislation against this type of crime. In addition, there are several organizations in the United States that aim to dismantle intolerance, lobbying for more anti–hate crime legislation and promoting positive images of minorities. Three of the most important ones are the Anti-Defamation League (ADL), the Southern Poverty Law Center (SPLC), and the Center for Democratic Renewal (CDR). The Web sites for these organizations offer a list of supremacist and extremist groups connected to hate crimes.

Physical attacks on minorities are often preceded by the exercise of verbal violence. The concept of verbal violence refers to the use of hostile language as a tool for diminishing the sense of self-worth of the victim. "Hate speech" is a qualified form of verbal violence, which tries to denigrate a minority group or individual, and tends to encourage violence toward the subject of hate. Ultimately, hate speech has the intended result of making minorities feel that their lives are in jeopardy, that their physical or mental integrity will be diminished if they refuse to relocate. Some individuals move beyond hate speech, into the realm of physical violence. But even when it is not a precursor of physical aggression, hate speech may cause profound psychological harm, and it must therefore be recognized as aggression in its own right.

The FBI Law Enforcement Bulletin of 2003 outlines the evolution of a typical hate group (Schafer, 2003). A hate group typically goes through seven evolutionary stages (see below). The report makes a clear distinction between individuals who feel satisfied by engaging in verbal attacks, and those who move further to the physical terrain. The outlined stages are:

- Stage 1: Grouping. Members of hate groups seek others with similar animosity toward a community, in search of peer validation. Grouping favors the empowerment of the hater, whose feelings are supported by other members.

- Stage 2: Self-definition. Hate groups generate particular sets of symbols or rituals. These codes serve to reinforce a common identity and to establish a secret form of communication among group members.

- Stage 3: Disparaging the target. Hate groups depict their victim as an inferior "other." In this way, hate groups also succeed in raising their own self-esteem and status.

- Stage 4: Taunting the target. Members of hate groups accentuate the manifestation of their hatred toward minorities, becoming more vocal and offensive.

- Stage 5: Attacking without weapons. At this stage, there is a clear split between those individuals who only advocate for verbal violence and those who decide to engage in physical aggression. Once the aggressor moves beyond hate speech, he or she is commonly isolated form mainstream society. Ultimately, anger accumulates and violence escalates accordingly.

- Stage 6: Use of weapons. Violent individuals have a tendency to commit hate crimes with close-contact weapons or firearms. These weapons allow the victim to see up close the identity of the attacker, which aggravates feelings of helplessness.

- Stage 7: Destruction of the victim. The object of hate must be finally destroyed. In fact, hate groups typically perceive members who are willing to kill for their cause as heroes.

Sociological Explanations of Bias-Motivated Crimes

There are many theoretical explanations of bias-motivated crimes. As explained by Grattet and Jenness (2001), the following theories are most popular among sociologists.

1. Competition over scarce resources (Grimshaw, 1969);
2. Long-standing social rituals (Nieburg, 1972);
3. Early socio-psychological trauma (Sterba, 1969).

These theories focus on the motivation for the hate behavior. Common to each of them is the idea that the victim of a hate crime is deemed the cause behind a series of lost opportunities or economic failure that the aggressor has gone through in the past. The violent act can be expressive (for personal satisfaction) or instrumental (to get rid of the victim).

According to the Center for Democratic Renewal, hate groups actively recruit youths. Young people are predisposed to join hate groups when they have a history of physical abuse at school or at home; suffer from paranoid fear against members of races or cultures different from one's own; are religious fanatics; and need to find a scapegoat for their own failures or the general problems of society.

Sometimes it is hard to determine the nature of the violent crime, but certain details can easily identify a hate crime as such. These signs are use of racist language, lack of provocation or economic motives, and timing (e.g., religious holiday). The Justice Department has introduced federal initiatives designed to aid in the prevention and identification of hate crimes. The establishment of the special unit known as the Community Relations Service (CRS) is one of them. The CRS serves as a mediator for community conflicts that originate on the basis of race, color, and national origin. It was created by the Civil Rights Act of 1964, and its role (as stated on the Justice Department Web site, www.usdoj.gov/crs), is "preventing and resolving racial and ethnic tensions, incidents and civil disorders." Professional conciliators within this organization train local leaders and promote interracial and interethnic dialogue.

References/Suggested Readings: Berk, Richard, Boyd, Elizabeth, and Hamner, Karl. 1992. Thinking More Clearly about Hate-Motivated Crimes. In G. Herek and K. Berrill (eds.) *Hate Crimes*, pp. 123–143. Newbury Park, CA: Sage Publications; Grimshaw, A. 1969. *Racial Violence in the United States*. Chicago: Aldine; Grattet, Ryken, and Jenness, Valerie. 2001. Examining the Boundaries of Hate Crime Law: Disabilities and the "Dilemma of Difference." *Journal of Criminology and Criminal Law* (Spring) 91 (3), 653–698; Nieberg, H. 1972. Agonistic Rituals of Conflict. In J. Short and M. Wolfgang (eds.), *Collective Violence*, pp. 82–99. Chicago: Aldine; Schafer, John R. and Navarro, Joe. 2003. The Seven-Stage Hate Model: The Psychopathology of Hate Groups. *FBI Law Enforcement Bulletin* (March); Sterba, R. 1969. Some Psychological Factors in Anti-Negro Race Hatred. In A. Grimshaw (ed.), *Racial Violence in the United States*, pp. 408–413. Chicago: Aldine.

YOLANDA MARTIN

HELL'S ANGELS IN CANADA. The Hell's Angels motorcycle club gained its name after a B-17 bomber group referred to one of their fighter planes as *Hell's Angels* during World War II. As a result, the nickname grew in popularity by the time the war ended in 1945. An American pilot returning to California mentioned the name to his biker friends who adopted it as a moniker. The official symbol of the Hells Angels is known as the "Death Head"—a screaming skeleton with a helmet and feathers. The official colors of the club are red and white. Members reach a milestone when they are granted a "full patch."

Background

The first official chapter of the Hell's Angels motorcycle club was created in San Bernardino, California, in 1948. By this time, the American Motorcycle Association (AMA) had officially distanced themselves from the bikers, referring to them as "hoodlums and troublemakers" (from the Hell's Angels Website: www.hells-angels .com). The AMA also stated that 99 percent of bikers were law-abiding citizens, which led Hell's Angels members to refer to themselves as the "one-percenters."

The club gained notoriety in 1969 after being hired to work as security for an outdoor concert featuring The Rolling Stones and Jefferson Airplane in Altamont, California. During the performance of the song "Under My Thumb" by The Rolling Stones, a man named Meredith Hunter was stabbed to death by Angels member Alan Passaro. In court, Passaro claimed that he had simply been defending himself. He was eventually acquitted on the grounds of self-defense. However, after this incident the Hell's Angels received a tremendous amount of negative publicity. This led Ralph "Sonny" Barger, who began the club's Oakland chapter in 1957, to appear on a radio station in defense of the club's conduct during the concert. The organization now had a public profile.

Into Canada

In 1977, the Hell's Angels finally made their way into Canada through the province of Quebec. A chapter was established in the small town of Sorel, which is located just outside of Montreal. The Quebec Nomads chapter was run by Maurice "Mom" Boucher, who is currently in prison and appealing a life sentence. By 1984, the Angels had added another chapter in Sherbrooke, Quebec, as well as one in Halifax, Nova Scotia, and four in British Columbia.

It is now generally acknowledged that the response of Canadian authorities to the club's expansion was poor. While the club's presence in Canada was growing during the late 1970s and throughout the 1980s, politicians and law enforcement agencies were slow to respond. "No one was targeting them from a law enforcement perspective," stated Andy Richards, an inspector with British Columbia's Organized Crime Agency. "By the time we all collectively woke up in the early nineties, we're going, 'Holy Shit, we have a problem here'" (Sher and Marsden, 2003). One of the first serious attempts to crack down on the Angels occurred in 1995 when the Quebec provincial government announced the creation of a special task force called "Wolverine" to go after the bikers' alleged illegal activities. Wolverine was established following the tragic death of an eleven-year-old boy named Daniel Desrochers, who died as a result of injuries sustained from a car bomb that was planted during the biker war between the Hell's Angels and enemy biker group Rock Machine. In the end, Wolverine failed due to corruption and infighting among the officers who were assigned to the operation. Following the failure of Wolverine, a royal commission, headed by former Quebec Superior Court Chief Justice Lawrence Poitras, was created to investigate what went wrong. In 1998, the Poitras Commission issued a 1,700-page report which described incompetent, corrupt, and unprofessional conduct on the part of police officers. One example involved interrogating sources at expensive hotels while ordering extravagant food and then billing it as an expense. Another more serious example involved allegations of planting incriminating documents on Hell's Angels members in an effort to prosecute them.

The man considered widely responsible for expanding the Angels across Canada is Walter "Nurget" Stadnik, who was born and raised in Hamilton, Ontario. Although he always maintained a residence in Hamilton, Stadnik spent much of his time in Quebec and became a Nomad. He paid frequent visits to Winnipeg, Manitoba, in the early 1990s and created small "puppet" motorcycle clubs with a vision of eventually flipping them over as official chapters of Hell's Angels. By 1997, Stadnik had convinced one of the main motorcycle clubs in Manitoba, called Los Brovos, to flip over to the Hell's Angels. Earlier that same year, the Hell's Angels welcomed the Grim Reapers biker club in Alberta. By this time, the Angels were said to be involved in a variety of illegal activities in Canada, all of which generated money for the organization. This included a near monopoly on the cocaine trade in the province of Nova Scotia and control of smuggling through Vancouver-area ports in British Columbia. The club was also linked to various types of money laundering operations with the apparent assistance of unethical bankers, stockbrokers, and lawyers. Moreover, the Hell's Angels were also linked to narcotics trafficking, prostitution rings, protection rackets, and loan sharking.

The breakthrough in Ontario that the Hell's Angels were looking for came in 2000 primarily through signing up members of the biker club Satan's Choice. Simply by taking over chapters that had been established by Satan's Choice, the Hell's Angels gained immediate access to communities all over Ontario, including Thunder Bay, Sudbury, Simcoe County, Keswick, Kitchener, Oshawa, and the eastern part of Toronto. The club also gained locations in central Toronto and Woodbridge. On January 12, 2002, Hell's Angels members booked a weekend in a downtown Toronto hotel to celebrate their anniversary in the province. Former Toronto Mayor Mel Lastman was approached by Hell's Angels member Tony Biancaflora. As Lastman shook Biancaflora's hand, the news media took photographs which were widely published across Canada the next day and generated a hostile reaction toward the Toronto mayor. Lastman added fuel to the fire by appearing on national television afterward and stating, "You know, they really are just a nice bunch of guys." After considerable pressure from the public and the media, Lastman later admitted that shaking Biancaflora's hand was probably a mistake. Regardless, there were 260 estimated Hell's Angels members in Ontario by the end of 2003.

Arrests and the Anti-Gang Law

In 2001, law enforcement agencies across Canada began to use a relatively new federal anti-gang law (Bill C-95) to crack down on the organization. (The federal government revised the anti-gang law in an effort to further strengthen its language in 2002—the current, revised version is Bill C-24.) Operation Hammer occurred in Halifax, Nova Scotia, and Operation Springtime led to arrests in Quebec. Some of the organization's most prominent members were arrested during these initiatives in addition to more isolated, local arrests of Angels members.

On September 13, 2004, Walter Stadnik and fellow Quebec Nomad Donald Stockford were each imprisoned for twenty years and fined $100,000 for drug trafficking, gangsterism, and conspiracy to commit murder. Earlier that year, three other Hell's Angels were convicted on charges of drug trafficking and gangsterism. In addition, an Ontario court rejected the legal application made by lawyers representing two Hell's Angels members charged with extortion. The application had argued that Canada's new anti-gang laws violated the members' constitutional rights, as outlined in the Canadian Charter of Rights and Freedoms.

Most recently, in January 2006, Operation Husky resulted in the arrests of twenty-seven suspects, including five "full patch" Angels from eastern Canada. This successful cooperation between law enforcement agencies, including the Royal Canadian Mounted Police, the Ontario Provincial Police, and the Surete du Quebec, has led some to speculate that the club's presence in Canada may be on the decline. That remains to be seen. What is known for certain is that the Hell's Angels have been in Canada since 1977 and have expanded considerably since. In the spring of 2002, there were thirty-seven known chapters across the country with nearly 600 members.

References/Suggested Readings: B.C.'s Hell's Angels: Rich and Powerful. Available online at www.canada.com; Biker Gangs. 2006. CBC News Indepth. Available online at www.cbc.ca; Cherry, Paul. 2005. *The Biker Trials: Bringing Down the Hell's Angels*. Canada: ECW Press; Hell's Angels Official Site. Available online at www.hells-angels.com; Sher, Julian, and Marsden, William. 2003. *The Road to Hell: How the Biker Gangs Are Conquering Canada*. New York: Seal Books.

ANGELO KONTOS

J

JAPANESE ORGANIZED CRIME AND GANGS. Organized crime groups first appeared in Japan over 300 years ago. What can be considered the start of organized crime groups began when the feudal Japanese monarchs did away with Samurai warriors. The new government leaders saw no need for these inordinate soldiers who had served Japan's feudal barons during the sixteenth and seventeenth centuries. The once proud Samurai warriors found themselves cast adrift by the leaders that they would have sacrificed their lives for. These brave soldiers of fortune soon became an undisciplined group of mercenaries who were unable to contend with peaceful times. Many of these warriors found themselves roaming the countryside committing crimes against local merchants and farmers to support themselves (Kata, 1964). Eventually, the Samurai members were to become a major part of what today is known as the Yakuza (a gambling term for numbers that are considered worthless or useless).

Groups known as the Tekiya or Yashi (street traders) or Bakuto (street gamblers) were formed while a larger group, the Borvokudan (violent ones), which has been in existence for over 300 years and at one time was committed to old customs and the cultural traditions of Japan. Many of the early members of Boryokudan regarded themselves as direct descendants of the Samurai warriors. The Boryokudan recruited a vast majority of their members from the Buraku (ghetto) who constantly complained that they were abused and discriminated against by the rest of Japanese society. Another ghetto group that became a part the Boryokudan was the Eta, meaning "much contamination." They worked jobs that the majority of the members of Japanese society considered the most repugnant drudgery (slaughtering animals, washing and dressing dead bodies). This group was stigmatized with the name "sangoku-jin" or third country people. The ghetto associates were comprised of different ethnic members including Chinese and Korean who were seeking ways to rid themselves of poverty. These ghetto-bred individuals quickly became the most violent members of the Boryokudan.

Prior to World War II, members of the Yakuza adopted the American gangster dress style and strut. The majority of gang participants have a plentiful amount of ornate tattoos all over their bodies. A large portion of these tattoos relate to the Samurai warriors who most members identify as the original founders of the group. One must also remember that tattooing was initially used in feudal Japan to classify the criminal elements in their society. The gang embraced the tattooing as an additional trademark of their mobster image. These modern-day criminals are known as "koika boryokudan" or the chic, stylish, and classy violent ones.

When the leader of the Yakuza group decides that one of the members has violated some type of group policy, the member must atone for his mistake by cutting off the joint of his last finger (a ceremonial ritual known as yubitsume) and presenting it to his boss. It is then up to the boss to decide whether or not all is forgiven. This type of action may be required with other fingers any time a mistake is made by a "koban" soldier and the reparation is accepted by the leader. If the cutting off of a finger is not acceptable as atonement by the boss, then the member might have to commit "seppuku" (suicide by self-disembowelment). Many of the gangs portray themselves as "mutual aid societies," but most people are aware of this deceptive measure.

At the conclusion of World War II there was a large quantity of social and economic problems and the Yakuza quickly gained control over the newly created black market. They then extended their activities to include gambling, extortion, prostitution, labor racketeering, and drug trafficking. A number of new gangs, most of them consisted of delinquents known as "chimpira," started to appear in Japan. Some of these newly organized gangs were known as "gurentai" or "seishonen-hryo dan." There was a significant amount of turbulent contention among the new and old gangs. Ultimately these new groups were assimilated into either the "bakuto" or "tekiya" (U.S. Customs Service, 1993).

The Yakuza permanence lies in the gang's ability to control power and money and the major purpose of this group is to increase the organization through force. Presently, there are approximately 2,300 Yakuza gangs that contain about 87,000 members. A gang member's rank is decided by that person's productivity as a procurer of assets for his bosses. The higher the person's status in the organization, the larger the amount of funds that are allocated to him, despite the fact that he is still responsible to the higher ranking officials in the group. The Yakuza maintains a very competitive association that is designed to provide tension on each member so that he will maintain a high level of productivity. Yakuza members are always seeking ways to create new ventures to gratify their bosses. One must remember that the two most important functions of Japanese gang members are their ability to remain loyal and productive to their superiors and the obligation of being responsible to their specific group.

References/Suggested Readings: Kata, K. 1974. *Japanese Yakuza*. Tokyo: Daiwa Shodu; U.S. Customs Service. 1993 (June). *Asian Organized Crime Organizations*.

SEAN GRENNAN

JEWISH GANGS AND GANGSTERS. Historically, crime in American society has seldom been associated with Jews. Even though anti-Semitic stereotypes about devious or materialistic Jews were part of American popular culture, the idea of Jewish criminals was not (Joselit, 1983, p. 1). But back in the 1920s and 1930s, some of the most feared gangsters were Jewish—men like Abner "Longy" Zwillman, Meyer Lansky, Benjamin "Bugsy" Siegel, and Louis "Lepke" Buchalter. The influence of

Jewish gangsters was seen in such organizations as Murder Incorporated, which carried out contract killings for crime bosses in New York, or in the Purple Gang, which terrorized the city of Detroit. Some Jewish gangsters had their own mainly Jewish mob, while others worked in tandem with Italian and Irish mobsters. Jewish gangs made their presence felt in bootlegging, bookmaking, racketeering, and gambling. They infiltrated labor unions and became enforcers for corrupt union bosses as well as for unscrupulous factory owners. Not all the gangsters were men: on the Lower East Side of Manhattan, prostitution was dominated by a madam named "Mother Rosie" Hertz, who also fenced stolen goods for her gangster friends (Joselit, 1983, p. 47). And while there are still a small number of Jewish gangsters today, the majority of whom seem to come mainly from the former Soviet Union, the era of Jewish dominance in criminal enterprises ended in the 1950s.

The large numbers of European Jews who emigrated to America beginning in the 1880s were, like other immigrants, hard-working. Many started off as peddlers or small shop-keepers, and although they had to make compromises about working on the Jewish sabbath, they tried to remain faithful to their religious traditions (Rubin, 2002, p. 1). At first most of the newcomers lived in poverty in crowded tenements, under conditions which could sometimes lead to drinking or fighting, but by all accounts, the majority of the Jewish immigrants were law-abiding. Thus, the fact that a few Jews became so heavily involved in **organized crime** is a subject that sociologists are still trying to explain. It's also a subject that makes some Jewish people uncomfortable—after all, it's better to be remembered for giving the world Albert Einstein or Jonas Salk or even Mel Brooks, as opposed to giving the world somebody who performed murders for hire or helped to fix the 1919 World Series. Noting that it wasn't until 1980 that anyone tried to write a history of Jewish gangsters, Joe Kraus writes, "The old neighborhood concept of 'a shonder fer de goyim' ('it's all right for us [Jews] to talk about it, but don't let the Gentiles know') was—and to some extent remains—persuasive" (Kraus, 1995, p. 62).

Kraus's translation of the Yiddish phrase does not convey fully that it was considered something shameful (a shonder) or humiliating to admit to non-Jews that your people had been involved in criminal activity. And even when talking to other Jews, the subject of Jewish delinquents or gang members could be embarrassing. That may explain why in the early 1900s, the Jewish press completely ignored the subject, perhaps in the hope that it was just a passing phase. But by 1912, it was obvious that Jewish criminality was not going to vanish, at which point the major Jewish newspapers began to editorialize, offering possible reasons why young Jews in America were losing their way. The religious newspapers blamed American materialism, or the lack of a good Jewish education. The secular newspapers attributed Jewish crime to economic factors: impoverished immigrants with large families had to work long hours, and their children were often left unsupervised; the crowded tenements became breeding grounds for petty crime. But none of the Jewish newspaper editorials had a simple solution. They just wished the problem would go away (Joselit, 1983, pp. 78–79).

Similarly, for Jews whose relatives had been involved with crime, it was not something to brag about. In fact, it was usually quite a shock to discover that a family member or relative had at one time been a gangster. "Like most people born after World War II," writes Joseph Kraus, "I had only the vaguest idea that there had ever been anything like Jewish gangsters. Jews weren't tough; we were cerebral. We didn't own guns; we lobbied our congressmen for gun control." And then one day he found out that his grandfather had been involved with "guns, gangs, and Al Capone" (Kraus, 1995, p. 53). It was an embarrassing revelation, and certainly not what he had expected from what began as an innocent conversation with his mom about her childhood in Chicago. Some social historians have suggested that Kraus's ambivalent reaction—he later went on to say that some of his grandfather's gangland exploits sounded rather exciting—is very typical of how most American Jews felt about the phenomenon of the Jewish gangster. Until fairly recently, there has been a reticence to delve too deeply into the subject of American Jews and crime. For one thing, as Kraus stated, there has long been a belief that Jews don't do that sort of thing. Jewish kids went to college, not to prison. And even in a culture that still had casual anti-Semitism, the perception that Jews were law-abiding and honest was acknowledged, including by American magazines which routinely praised the Jews for having a strong moral and ethical code (Rubin, 2002. p. 1; Joselit, 1983, p. 1). But a better reason for avoiding the subject of Jewish criminality may stem from the insecurity that many American Jews have felt about their place in America. Many feared "that criminal Jews would tarnish the reputation of all Jews, thereby fanning the flames of antisemitism and preventing a comfortable entry into American society" (Rubin, 2002, p. 4). It was thus better to pretend that Jewish gangsters didn't exist.

There are no easy answers to why some American Jews turned to crime. But historically, many people seemed to expect the worst from Jews. In Europe, a pervasive thread of what would later be called anti-Semitism was woven into the fabric of the popular culture, a byproduct of the teachings of the Christian religion, which reviled the Jews for their refusal to accept Jesus. The most common myth spread by the church hierarchy was that Jews only cared about money, making them inherently greedy, unethical, devious, and dishonest. Attitudes about the Jews were also gendered: Jewish women were supposed to be bossy and lacking in morals, while Jewish men were supposed to be sickly and weak, lacking in manliness. Although Jews had little political power and were restricted in what occupations they could enter, the populace often accused Jewish shop-keepers of cheating their customers, and whenever there was an unsolved murder, some people were sure to assume a Jew must have committed it. In nineteenth-century Europe, stereotypes of the treacherous and mercenary Jew could be found in popular songs, illustrations in books, and characters in stage plays. And when a number of European Christians emigrated, they brought some of these beliefs with them to the United States.

But in turn-of-the-century America, where freedom of religion was enshrined in the Constitution, some Jewish immigrants were becoming successful, and they decided it was time to challenge the ancient myths. So they created what came to be called "muscular Judaism." It can be traced back to an 1898 speech given by Max Nordau at the Zionist Congress in Switzerland, in which Nordau called for a new emphasis on physical strength, courage, and boldness in order to change the image of the Jew in the popular culture (Hoberman, 2005, p. 175). In America, the muscular Judaism movement took the form of an emphasis on athletics and physical fitness, as Jewish men (and even some women) attempted to prove to their Christian antagonists that Jews were as physically strong and capable as anyone else. In earlier times, some Jewish men had tried to re-define Jewish masculinity by joining the military. But many more Jews of the early 1900s became caught up in physical fitness, joining the Jewish equivalent of the YMCA, the YMHA. Even synagogues built community centers and gymnasiums. Gradually, the image of the "typical Jew" began to change. The end result of these efforts was that by the 1920s, "American Jews were heavily represented in, and excelled at, several important sports—notably boxing, basketball, and track—during the three decades preceding World War II" (Norwood, 1999, p. 409). In fact, as Steven Riess observes, Jewish men had become so successful as boxers that "non-Jews sometimes adopted Jewish names for the ring" (quoted in Norwood, 1999, p. 410). Becoming a boxer had the advantage of teaching young Jewish men how to protect themselves from an attack, as well as enabling them to earn prize money if they won enough professional fights. Interestingly, a West Coast mobster named Mickey Cohen had some success as a boxer before he finally settled on a career in organized crime. But ironically, while boxing was at first presented to Jews in a positive light, the sport was soon infiltrated by organized crime. By the mid-1930s, as Jewish young men from the middle class were able to attend college, varsity sports like basketball replaced boxing as a more socially respected way to show manhood (Sachar, 1992, p. 352, 375).

"Muscular Judaism" was a useful strategy for some Jews of the early 1900s, but there was another group of Jewish men who were proving their manhood in an entirely different way—by joining gangs. This was not easy at first. New immigrant Jews who arrived in America knew nothing about going to the local YMHA, and working long hours in sweatshops left little time to learn how to box. For the young Jews who were getting beaten up by Irish or Italian toughs, there was little protection available, since not many gangs had any Jewish members who could stand up for them. But this slowly began to change. By 1912, a sensational gangland murder case called attention to the fact that there were Jewish mobsters. Gambler Herman Rosenthal was shot dead in July 1912, and a New York gang, led by "Big Jack" Zelig was suspected almost immediately; the word was that Rosenthal had become a police informant. Zelig himself was killed in October before he could testify about Rosenthal's murder. Four members of Zelig's gang, including Harry (Gyp the Blood) Horowitz and Louis (Lefty Louie) Rosenberg, were tried and convicted for the Rosenthal slaying; they were executed at Sing Sing in 1914. And while the gangland killings got most of the headlines, evidence was also becoming available that more Jewish women were turning to crime: a 1912 survey of women sent to prison in New York found that 19 percent of the prostitutes were Jewish (Joselit, 1983, p. 48).

One response to the growing number of young Jews behaving badly was to offer them a chance at rehabilitation. As early as 1907, Jewish philanthropists like Jacob Schiff, along with community leaders and social workers had secured funding to open up a training school for New York City's delinquent Jewish boys. The hope was that a good education, often offered by editorialists as one way to prevent future criminal acts, and a location far away from the slums would help to turn young Jewish delinquents into productive citizens. This noble experiment, the Hawthorne School, opened in upstate New York, in a setting that looked more like a private school than a reformatory, featuring a gym and a baseball diamond, residential cottages, and a scenic view overlooking the Hudson River (Joselit, 1983, pp. 14–16). By 1912, there was a similar school for Jewish girls. Called Cedar Knolls, it was located near the Hawthorne School. But while both schools were widely praised for their innovative approaches by judges and by journalists, there continued to be a growing number of Jewish delinquents, often far more than either school had room for.

Despite the fact that anti-Semitism still permeated American culture, often fueled by anti-immigrant sentiments, most mainstream newspaper coverage of Jewish criminals did not assert that their Jewishness was "proof" of inherent Jewish evil.

In reporting on the gangland execution of gambler Herman Rosenthal, journalists seemed puzzled that young men from good homes would turn to crime. One editorial pointed out that among the four men convicted of the Rosenthal murder, "Lefty Louie" Rosenberg came from a very educated and religious family which had never broken the law, while "Gyp the Blood" Horowitz had an equally normal middle-class upbringing—and yet several of his brothers had already gotten in trouble and been arrested. It seemed there was no "one size fits all" explanation as to why some young men ignored parental discipline and religious precepts to become murderers ("Criminal Biographies," *Chicago Tribune*, April 12, 1914, p. A4).

Sociologists who have studied the phenomenon of Jewish gangs suggest that a pattern existed: "[Jewish gangsters] started out as neighborhood kids clearly going bad, getting into fights with older boys, and then getting into fights with boys from close-by ethnic neighborhoods. When they'd won enough fights, they 'ran' the neighborhood, and such businesses as the numbers games, election slugging, and small protection rackets fell into their laps" (Kraus, 1995, pp. 56–57). Social workers of the early 1900s often suggested that the harsh environment of the tenement was a factor in why some of these boys "went bad." However, that theory does not explain why the majority of Jewish boys who were raised in tenements and beaten up by neighborhood toughs chose to stay out of trouble and either go to college or learn a skilled trade. There is no simple explanation for Meyer Lansky, who by all accounts came from a fairly typical immigrant family yet turned to petty crime when still in his teens and ultimately graduated to an honored position as one of the few Jewish members of the Mafia. Nor is there a simple explanation for Arnold Rothstein, whose father was a successful and widely admired merchant, known for his honesty. Arnold began gambling when he was still in junior high school. He never liked school and quit at age sixteen. He became known in underworld circles as "The Brain," one of the most influential bookmakers and loan sharks in New York City. He told a reporter that he especially loved gambling because it was so exciting (quoted in *New York Times*, October 27, 1963, p. 47); he would get into games with other mobsters in which large sums were won and lost. He once lost over $300,000 and was subsequently killed by another gambler to whom he owed money. Rothstein was reputed to be one of the men involved in the bribery of the Chicago baseball players in the notorious Black Sox scandal in 1919, although just how involved he really was is not entirely clear (Sachar, 1992, p. 347). He certainly bet on the games and the fact that he knew the Series was fixed led to his making a sizable profit on those bets.

And what explanation is there for the brutal mob boss Lewis "Lepke" Buchalter? Lepke came from a large family, like many immigrants, but while his father never made a lot of money, both of his parents were respected in the community and tried to give their children a normal life. Yet by his early teens, Lepke was already engaged in petty theft and fell under the influence of Big Jack Zelig's gang (*New York Times*, March 5, 1944, p. 30). This did not happen to other members of the Buchalter family, all of whom were raised in the same poverty as Lepke.

Whatever the reason becoming a gangster appealed to certain Jewish young men, they rapidly became successful at it. A few individual Jewish gangsters can be found as far back as the 1890s, but the heyday of the Jewish gangster was the era of the Roaring Twenties and Prohibition. In that period from 1919 to 1933, "50 percent of the country's leading bootleggers were Jews, and Jewish criminals financed and directed much of the nation's narcotics traffic. Jewish gangs also dominated illicit activities in a number of America's largest cities, including Cleveland, Detroit, Minneapolis, Newark, New York and Philadelphia" (Rockaway, 2001, p. 113). In 1924, Herbert Mayer, a police reporter for *McClure's* magazine, wrote an article called "Murder and Robbery as a Business." In it, he observed that New York's criminal gangs had divided the city up into districts. "The modern gangster," he wrote,

> is nearly always a Russian or Polish Jew, a Sicilian, or a low-caste Italian. The devil-may-care Irish . . . gangs have vanished. The Italians and Sicilians specialize in . . . extortion, bootlegging, robbery and dope peddling and furnish many of the most skillful knife and gun men. The Jewish gangsters . . . specialize in labor disputes, fighting on one side or another and sometimes on both at the same time, but bringing always the spirit of terrorism and thuggery into ordinary strike situations. (Mayer, 1924, p. 2)

Mayer's article may have been an oversimplification, but it expressed a belief that was shared by law enforcement and even a few politicians, one of whom suggested that the recent wave of immigrants contained a lot of bad apples, with "the Jews furnishing the brains and the Italians the brawn" for the gangs (*Chicago Tribune*, July 2, 1930, p. 3). Stereotypical or not, in a number of cities throughout the era of Prohibition, Jewish gangs terrorized the population the same way that gangs from other ethnic groups did, and often Jewish mobsters did join up with their Italian counterparts. Of the gangs dominated by Jewish members, the most notorious one was Detroit's Purple Gang. According to historian Robert Rockaway, the gang resulted from the merger of two gangs—one was the Oakland Sugar House Gang, which was active in bootlegging. Their members included "Charles Leiter, a distillery owner and the mob's leader, Harry Fleisher, a hefty youngster who started out as a driver for the gang and later became a vicious thug and killer; [and] Henry Shorr, a former potato sacker at a produce market, who was the gang's financial genius and business head." Then there was the Purple Gang, which "was originally formed by Sammy Cohen, a stout gunman and enforcer who was also known as 'Sammy Purple.'" In the early 1920s the leadership of the gang was assumed by the four Bernstein brothers—Abe, Joe, Isidore, and Ray—who immigrated with their parents to Detroit from New York (Rockaway, 2001, pp. 117–118).

There is some debate about how the Purple Gang got its name—was it from the custom of early members to wear purple swimming trunks, or was it because one young member liked to wear a purple sweater, or was it as the *Detroit News* once asserted, the result of a comment by a police officer that "Their characters are off-color. They're purple like the color of bad meat" (Rockaway, 2001, p. 118). But what was beyond dispute was the viciousness of the newly formed gang. They soon came to dominate the bootlegging trade, supplying liquor to the so-called bling pigs (known in other cities as a speakeasy, this was an establishment that sold liquor illegally during Prohibition). They also extorted money from local merchants, and may have killed as many as 500 members of rival gangs. There were Chicago detectives who believed the gang did not just restrict itself to greater Detroit: they were certain that some of the Purples had worked with Al Capone and were involved in the St. Valentine's Day Massacre (*New York Times*, February 17, 1929, p. 1). And while some modern gangster movies may romanticize the gangster lifestyle, Rockaway and others are quick to point out that Jewish gangs had no loyalty to other Jews—they would steal or extort from Jewish merchants as quickly as they did from non-Jewish merchants (Rockaway, 2001, p. 116). They also had no fear of law enforcement: they would intimidate potential witnesses, kidnapping them if necessary.

Those who were believed to be snitches were shot dead. And when in the summer of 1928 some members of the gang were put on trial, the courthouse was bombed, injuring twelve people (*New York Times*, June 19, 1928, p. 1). At their highest point of influence, around 1928, they had over fifty members. Ultimately, their own carelessness, coupled with the growing strength of the Sicilian mob and a concerted effort by police led to a majority of the Purples being arrested, tried, and convicted; other members were killed by the Sicilians. By 1933, what had been one of Detroit's most powerful gangs had been rendered nearly irrelevant.

The other well-known gang that had many Jewish members came to be known as Murder Inc. Its leader was Lepke Buchalter, a New York racketeer whose criminal career began when he was still in his teens. (His nickname was the Yiddish version of his name—it meant "little Lewis." Quite a few Jewish mobsters used their Yiddish name as their nickname. For example, Buchalter's right-hand man in the gang was Phillip "Little Farvel" Cohen.) At the height of his power, Lepke commanded as many as 200 gang members; they were originally involved with loan sharking and extortion, especially with the "protection" racket, where gangsters would force merchants to pay up or their shop would mysteriously be burned to the ground. Buchalter's gang expanded into another kind of protection, where they promised factory owners they could prevent workers from going on strike. This was achieved by threatening and intimidating workers, or from infiltrating their unions. But Buchalter also provided murder for hire—contract killings for other mob bosses. Murder Inc. operated from about 1928 to 1940, and during that time, Buchalter struck fear into the hearts of even his own men, who called him "The Judge" and did not want to disobey him. Still, even though several unsuccessful attempts were made to prosecute him, he was finally convicted and sentenced to death. Newspaper reports referred to Lepke as "frightened" and "subdued" at the end, a far cry from the confident gangster who believed he would never be caught and never pay for his crimes (*New York Times*, March 5, 1944, p. 1). He died in the electric chair at Sing Sing in early March 1944. Several of his henchmen, Emanuel (Mendy) Weiss and Louis Capone, were also executed for their role in Murder Inc. And Little Farvel, who turned state's evidence and testified against his former boss, was ultimately executed gangland style in 1949.

While New York was the center of many of the Jewish gangs, there were other influential Jewish gangsters in other cities. One was Charles "King" Solomon, often known as "Boston Charlie," who owned a controlling interest in several Boston night clubs. His specialties were extorting money and benefiting from the illegal liquor trade. He was shot dead in early 1933, and like many gangland murders, his killers were not found. Yet while police reports stressed that he was a racketeer, over 3,000 people attended his funeral, as mourners spoke of him as a legitimate businessman and a good employer (*Boston Globe*, January 28, 1933, p. 1). In Cleveland, a successful gang of bootleggers and money launderers was led by Morris "Moe" Dalitz. Despite being identified by the FBI as being the head of the Cleveland crime syndicate, Moe managed to avoid ever being prosecuted for his gangland activities, always staying one step ahead of law enforcement. He moved his enterprises, which included illegal casinos, to Detroit, and then to Las Vegas, where he eventually became part owner of the Desert Inn and Stardust Hotel. In his later years, he bought an interest in a California winery, and also became known for philanthropy, always insisting he was an honest businessman.

In New Jersey, the king of organized crime was Abner "Longy" Zwillman. (His nickname referred to the fact that he was tall.) He prospered during Prohibition, and "flourished in a world of corrupt policemen, judges and politicians" (Mappen, 1991, p. 23). In fact, he became a major player in Jersey politics, helping certain candidates get elected. He was known to be a colleague and friend of New York gangsters like Lucky Luciano and Bugsy Siegel, but he carved out his own fiefdom in northern New Jersey, with a controlling interest in a number of corrupt unions, as well as a profitable vending machine business. And out on the West Coast, Meyer "Mickey" Cohen made a name for himself, coming from an impoverished childhood in East Los Angeles to become a feared racketeer. Mickey was quite a character, by all accounts. He could be ruthless and brutal when he felt threatened by a rival mobster. Yet he loved publicity and cultivated relationships with certain crime reporters, feeding them stories and giving them quotes (as long as he was not implicated in the particular crime). By the 1940s, he and his gang had a dominant role in West Coast gambling.

But undoubtedly, the two best known Jewish gang leaders were Benjamin "Bugsy" Siegel and his friend Meyer Lansky. Siegel got some of his early training in crime from Lepke Buchalter in New York, and became sufficiently well known to have his name mentioned on the popular radio program *Gangbusters* (Burke, 2005, p. 168). When Prohibition ended, Siegel and Lansky continued their involvement with gambling. They opened several casinos (which were still illegal back then) in the South and made huge profits, before going to the West Coast. Bugsy (whose friends called him "Benny") joined the mob in Los Angeles, but he was interested in Las Vegas because it was legal to gamble there. Known for having a roving eye, Siegel had both a wife and a mistress, as well as expensive tastes. He liked to spend money, and this would lead to his downfall. Siegel was first involved in racketeering and bookmaking, especially sports betting, and he had some involvement in the narcotics trade as well. He extorted money from movie studios and forced them to hire his friends. He finally was able to achieve success in Las Vegas in late 1946 when he founded the Flamingo Hotel; it was one of the first gambling resorts on what became the Strip. But his lavish lifestyle plus the belief that he was skimming money from the hotel's profits made the mob think he was a liability. There is reason to believe his friend Lansky ordered the "hit" on him, something Lansky always denied. Siegel was shot to death in June 1947 at his mistress's home. After he died, Mickey Cohen took over his territory. Interestingly, a 1991 movie about Siegel's life, which starred Warren Beatty, treated him as almost a sympathetic figure, rather than the mobster he really was (Schiff, 2003, p. 60).

As for Meyer Lansky, he started his criminal career as a bootlegger and became a good friend of Italian gangster Lucky Luciano. Lansky went on to be involved in gambling but became known for doing money laundering for the Mafia. (A character in the movie *The Godfather II*, Hyman Roth, is modeled after Lansky.) Despite his association with the mob, he was never directly implicated in any murder or violence; he was always able to get others to do the dirty work for him. In fact, throughout his life, he always maintained an image as an articulate businessman, who had made good investments and gave to charities. Unlike some mobsters, he did not brag about his criminal activities; in fact, he was unwilling to acknowledge any involvement with crime at all. He was once quoted as saying that "organized crime" was a myth (*Syracuse Post-Standard*, January 17, 1983, p. 2). He was both feared and respected by those who knew him. And although he was arrested a number of times, he seemed to always beat the charges against him. Unlike those mobsters whose deaths he was alleged to have ordered, Lansky died of natural causes in 1983. But the public seemed unsure about whether he really was as bad as law enforcement officials claimed. In the book *Everything You Need to Know About American Jews*, one of the questions the author is asked is whether Lansky was a good guy or a bad guy. The author, while acknowledging that Lansky raised millions for charities (including the United Jewish Appeal) also noted that Lansky was beyond a doubt the brains behind numerous mob enterprises and benefited from them (Rosenberg, 1997, p. 192).

Coverage of Mickey Cohen's final years (he died of cancer in 1976) showed similar mixed emotions—when he went out in 1975 to do interviews in support of a book he was writing, reporters and the general public seemed fascinated by the old former mobster and loved listening to his stories. Cohen had always cultivated certain media sources, and he liked to be seen with the rich and famous. Even his obituary referred to him as a former "Hollywood celebrity" (*Pasadena CA Star-News*, July 28, 1976, p. A7). One wonders if the victims he beat up or intimidated over the years found him equally personable.

In Hollywood, a number of gangster movies were made in the period when the Jewish and Italian mobs were fighting for control, but these films had to contend with a strict movie code that forbade directors from glorifying crime or letting the bad guys win. These days, crime movies can be as revisionist as they wish, romanticizing the Bugsy Siegels of gangland. And while Jews no longer have reason to fear that the existence of Jewish criminals will cause a loss of status for Jews in society, there is still ambivalence about how much attention to give to the subject of Jewish gangsters. In the early 1900s, Jewish newspapers were reticent to speak about the growing number of Jews going into crime. Then, in 1911, a strongly worded piece in New York's *Jewish Daily News* chastised the Jewish community for looking the other way and not acknowledging the problem. It found such denial especially inappropriate given that many of the Jewish gangsters were extorting money or robbing other Jews *Atlanta Constitution*, May 21, 1911, p. B7).

Some denial has persisted even in modern times. In 1997, a museum in Michigan was planning a photographic tribute to the Jews of Detroit in the 1920s and 1930s, but three groups refused to donate any photographs when they found out a number of the pictures in the exhibit would show members of the Purple Gang (*Jerusalem Post*, October 12, 1997, p. 3). And in Israel, critics have complained that not enough attention is being paid to Russian Jewish mobsters, who are involved in some of the same crimes that Bugsy Siegel and Meyer Lansky were known for (Heller, 2006). It has often been only in movies or in works of fiction that Jewish gangsters are made visible (Schiff, 2003, pp. 85–86). The problem with that, of course, is as Krauss points out: using fictional representations of Jewish gangsters only adds to the myth and legend that already surrounds these people's lives, and it does not lend itself to serious to analysis of the place of Jews in American life (Krauss, 1995, p. 58). So should the subject of Jewish crime be ignored, for fear that it would be "bad for the Jews" or for fear that impressionable young people might find the gangster life appealing? Or is talking about it the first step to addressing the problem? Whether discussing the Jewish gangsters of the past or the ones who may be around today, this remains a contentious subject, one that still has no easy answers or explanations.

References/Suggested Readings: 35 Years Ago, Arnold Rothstein Was Mysteriously Murdered. 1963. *New York Times*, October 27, p. 47; Burke, James Lee. (2005, Winter). Why Bugsy Siegel Was a Friend of Mine. *Southern Review,* 41 (1), 167–179; Cohen, Rich. 1998. *Tough Jews: Fathers, Sons and Gangster Dreams*. New York: Simon and Schuster; Criminal Biographies. 1914. *Chicago Tribune*, April 12, p. A4; Crowd of 3000 at Funeral of Solomon in Brookline. 1933. *Boston Globe*, January 26, p. 1; Graft and Gangland Murder 50 Years Ago. 1962.

JEWISH GANGS AND GANGSTERS

Wisconsin Rapids (WI) Daily Tribune, July 16, p. 10; Heller, Aron. 2006. Extradition of Top Mob Boss to U.S. Draws Attention to Israel's Underworld. *Associated Press*, March 6. Accessed from Lexis/Nexis, August 1, 2006; Hoberman, John. 2005. Review of "Legacy of Rage: Jewish Masculinity, Violence, and Culture" by Warren Rosenberg. *Shofar* (Winter), 23 (2), 175–177; Howe, Irving. 1980. *World of Our Fathers*. New York: Bantam; Jewish Gangs Spread Terror. 1911. *Atlanta Constitution*, May 11, p. B7; Jewish Protectory for Boys Opened. 1907. *New York Times*, May 13, p. 9; Joselit, Jenna Weissman. 1983. *Our Gang: Jewish Crime and the New York Jewish Community 1900–1940*. Bloomington: Indiana University Press; Kefauver, Estes. 1951. Cleveland Area: Middletown of Crime. *Fredericksburg (IA) News*, November 22, p. 3; Kraus, Joe. 1995. The Jewish Gangster. *American Scholar*, 64 (1), pp. 53–66; Lane, Winthrop D. 1914. What Makes Murderers? Putting Gunmen under the Lens of Cold Science. *Atlanta Constitution*, April 5, p. D4; Mappen, Marc. 1991. Jersey-ana: A Gangster Who Went from Being on Top of the World to Death in a Basement. *New York Times*, February 10, p. NJ23; Mayer, Herbert. 1924. Underworld News. *Lincoln (NE) State Journal*, June 17, p. 2; Michigan Jewish History Exhibit Draws Fire Over Gang Photos. 1997. *Jerusalem Post*, October 12, p. 3; Norwood, Stephen H. 1999. Review of "Sports and the American Jew." *American Jewish History*, 87 (4), 409–411; Private Rites for Mobster Mickey Cohen. 1976. *Pasadena (CA) Star-News*, July 30, p. A7; Rockaway, Robert A. 2001. The Notorious Purple Gang: Detroit's All-Jewish Prohibition Era Mob. *Shofar*, 20 (1), 113–130; Rosenberg, Roy A. 1997. *Everything You Need to Know about America's Jews*. New York: Plume; Rubin, Rachel. 2002. Gangster Generation: Crime, Jews and the Problem of Assimilation. *Shofar*, 20 (4), 1–17; Sachar, Howard M. 1992. *A History of the Jews in America*. New York: Knopf; Schiff, Ellen. 2003. Sinners, Scandals, Scoundrels, and Scamps on the American Jewish Stage. *American Jewish History*, 91 (1), 83–96; Walsh, Denny. 1976. The Mob "Takes a Bath" in Wine. *Fresno (CA) Bee*, October 21, p. A1.

DONNA L. HALPER

K

KING BLOOD. King Blood, whose real name is Luis Felipe Fernández Mendez, was the founder of the New York branch of the Latin Kings and Queens that became known as the **Almighty Latin King and Queen Nation**. Details of Blood's early life are few except that he was born on May 11, 1961, in Habana, Cuba and that his mother, Esterina, was a sex worker, his father, Gilbert, was unknown to him, he had a brother, a son called Duane, and an ex-wife called María. According to Blood, other than his son, who lives with his grandmother in Spain, and his ex-wife who lives in New York City, he has no living relatives. In an interview with a journalist Blood reveals the following about his journey from Cuba to the United States:

> One morning in 1979, he was making his way home when he felt the cold barrel of a gun behind his ear. He escaped, ran behind a car, pulled out a .38 revolver, and fired several shots. "I shot the guy in the arm," he says. "But before I had a chance to run away from la policia, they arrested me and charged me with attempted homicide. I got 10 years."
>
> By the next year, Cuba seemed overtaken with lawlessness and desperation. That's when Castro opened his prison cells and freed the "undesirables". King Blood became one of the lucky ones, setting off across the Straits of Florida in a rickety boat made of inner tubes and old furniture. More than 100 refugees traveled together in a ragtag flotilla, their fate in nature's indifferent hands. He remembers seeing a fin cutting through the water just before the raft next to him was rammed, throwing an old man overboard. The sharks ripped him apart, filling the water with magenta clouds. "I felt like a prisoner of the sea," says King Blood. Six years later, he wrote in the Latin Kings' manifesto, "You don't even know if you will survive the present night. But the biggest risk of all is living and dying, and as a King this is our eternal companion."
>
> Felipe landed in Miami two days later, traveled to Key West, then to Puerto Rico, and eventually wound up in Chicago. There he reapplied his street skills, dealing cocaine and heroin and developing a reputation for ruthlessness . . . he joined a renegade faction

called the Pee-Wee Kings. "I was about gangbanging then," he says, "I shot people, I killed people, I have been shot and killed myself." (Rivera, 1997)

While in Chicago, Blood rose in the ranks of the Latin Kings to be the President of the Brynmar and Winthrop chapter, a working-class neighborhood in the gang's "Northside" homeland. In 1981, he moved to the South Bronx in New York City, an area that had become synonymous with poverty and racial discrimination, and where he resumed his criminal career. In 1982, after becoming involved in what he describes as a "drunken accident," he was charged with shooting his girlfriend through a door and found guilty of second-degree manslaughter, for which he received nine years in the New York State correctional system. After moving from institution to institution, Blood found himself in Collins Correctional Facility, a medium security prison with a reputation for brutality. Surrounded by a system dominated by "black gangs and white guards," Blood set about establishing the first branch of the Latin Kings in the New York State prison system in 1986, with himself as the Inka, First Supreme Crown and President. He did this by writing his own manifesto, a departure from most other Latin King branches. This new "bible" is a mixture of his own interpretation of Latin Kings ideology along with a history of the New York group's beginnings and the primary rules of the organization laid down by Chicago Motherland. In time, this manifesto is added to by other leading prison members of the group which is later supplemented by writings from its civilian membership.

In 1989, King Blood was paroled, but less than a year later he was rearrested for car theft and sent back to Attica in 1991 for another five years. During his prison stay Blood was regularly disciplined by the authorities and, by 1993, he had already spent four years in the "box," i.e., in a part of the prison that is segregated from the general population of inmates and where much of the time is spent in solitary confinement. In fact, until his final conviction in 1996, Blood had spent almost half of his incarceration time under the prison regime's most punishing physical and psychological conditions.

By the time Blood's final trial date approached, he was thoroughly institutionalized. Meanwhile his beloved Latin Kings are no longer a small clique of Latino inmates in "the system" but a city-wide organization that is growing rapidly throughout the state as more and more inmates are released onto the streets. By now, Blood is a revered and legendary founder of the group and in the eyes of the members he is a prophet-like figure, a teacher of the oppressed and a fearless leader who has withstood the prison's most punishing conditions while upholding the mantle of Latino solidarity and manhood.

Nonetheless, in the eyes of the criminal justice system he is nothing but a pathological and ruthless gang leader who has brought the infamous Latin Kings to New York with its cult-like dogma and paramilitaristic rules. In 1995, a federal grand jury indicted some fifty members of the Latin King on a series of charges, including racketeering, extortion, and the murders of three of its own members and the attempted murder of four others during the years 1993–1994. According to the prosecution, Blood was guilty of conspiracy, for it was he and he alone, as day-to-day leader of the group, who could have ordered the executions and the attempted murders. The primary evidence against King Blood and the rest came from two star informers or "snitches," Alex Figueroa (King Al) and Nelson Torres (King Nel), who were formerly leading members of the New York City organization and who themselves played a major role in all of the homicides.

The plea bargains of the two informers with the prosecution saved their own lives but condemned those of the others to sentences ranging from fifteen to thirty years. Blood, however, decided not to go the way of his followers, and opted to face a trial by his peers. The charge that he ordered the killings from his jail cell was supported by the testimony of the two federal witnesses; the letters he wrote to his colleagues (some 1556 of them were intercepted, photocopied and summarized by the prison authorities); and his phone calls, which were all taped.

On September 9, 1997, at the U.S. District Court in Manhattan, King Blood was sentenced to life for the murder conspiracies (a total of 100 years) plus 45 years for weapons possession. He would probably have received a death sentence, but this was not allowed under federal sentencing laws on conspiracy. Then the presiding federal judge outlined the following unusual stipulations for his incarceration:

1. The first forty-five years of King Blood's sentence are to be spent in solitary confinement;

2. There will be no mail between King Blood and anyone except through his lawyers; and

3. The only people who will be allowed to see King Blood are his two lawyers, Lawrence Feitell and Mr. L, a paralegal secretary who works on the case in Manhattan, and Father Luis Barrios.

The punishment did not stop there. To complete the process, the state ruled that King Blood would keep company with the most celebrated deviants of society's adjudicated individuals. From the time of his sentencing until the present, King Blood is in Florence, Colorado, at an Administration Maximum Facility (ADX) or a "super-max" facility built by the Department of Corrections. The facility contains an assortment of confinement units with the worst being the super-isolation cells where he is held for twenty-three hours a day. His fellow inmates have included Timothy McVeigh, one of the Oklahoma City bombers, Ted Kaczynski, the Unabomber from California, and Ramzi Ahmed Yousef, the so-called mastermind of the first World Trade Center bombing. Since his sentence, only his lawyers have been able to visit him.

References/Suggested Readings: Rivera, Lucas. 1997. Anatomy of a King. *Jibe*, July, 167–169.

DAVID C. BROTHERTON

KINGISM. In the sociological literature there is some consensus that a relationship exists between the construction of identity and collective action (Melucci, 1989; Calhoun, 1991; Calderon, Piscitelli, and Reyna, 1992; Escobar, 1992; Castells, 1997; Della and Diani, 1999). Yet little attention is paid in sociology to the construction of collective identity within the types of groups that are labeled gangs. For the most part, the importance of identity is restricted to the notion of "risk factors," whereas gangs are increasingly perceived and defined as socially pathological. As Branch (1997) states, many functions are normally attributed to the gang by sociologists; but it has never been seen as the kind of support system that could foster a gang member's transition to mainstream life, nor one that could transform itself. This conventional wisdom requires scrutiny. The following entry on Kingism is based on an ethnographic study with the **Almighty Latin King and Queen Nation** (Brotherton and Barrios, 2004).

Collective Identity

Can a collective identity emerge from a street subculture that makes possible their transformation in a pro-social direction? To answer this question, it is necessary to look at a group's "meaning system" to excavate what "sources of meaning" (Castells, 1997, p. 6) are prioritized over others and eventually become internalized. As social agents, group members struggle to recognize what Latin American liberation theologists describe as their *realidad humana* (human reality). This concept refers to the process by which group members become aware that their personal struggles take place against a dominant culture that seeks to both neutralize them politically and assimilate them culturally. Many respondents, particularly those of the second generation (the New York Chapter of the ALKQN was founded in 1986), discussed the quest for their own ethnicity with reference to the traditions and struggles of their parents.

Assertions of ethnic self-affirmation and continuity, while they reflect efforts to resolve identity issues at the level of the individual are carried out in conjunction with the entire membership, becoming an integral part of the group's collective agency. This point is crucial and distinguishes the ethno-political development of this group from other street subcultures, i.e., from groups that, while claiming ethnic solidarity, leave it undeveloped, parochial, and particularistic (for example, the notions of mi barrio, or cholismo among West Coast Chicano gangs).

The Latin Kings' Manifesto contains only a few paragraphs in which the concept of Kingism is outlined. Nonetheless, members claim to possess a system of beliefs and a "way of life" that are distinct morally and politically from that of other gangs and mainstream groups. Kingism revolves around the claim that the Latino community is represented only by tokens who are installed by dominant groups (the "white man") in order to ensure unequal opportunity and outcomes, to stifle dissent, and to offset linkages with other ethnic groups and communities. In response, the Kings claim the ability and the right to "represent" the Latino community in socio-cultural resistance. The audacity of the group contradicts the tendency, so rampant in the popular discourse on American social justice, that human and political rights are essentially a black and white "thing" (Munoz, 1989).

On a range of ideological, organizational and cultural levels, the ALKQN was dedicated to resisting and ending processes of social-psychological subjugation that is the modus operandi of colonial social control. One important facet of this resistance orientation was the commitment of the group's members to (1) make themselves and "their people" visible, and (2) reject all attempts by the dominant culture to successfully label the group as criminal and pathological. These tasks were extremely difficult, given the history of political and economic subordination of most Latinos/as in New York City, the number of members returning to civil society from incarcerated settings, and the past criminal actions of the group which haunted its every move.

In effect, the ALKQN, members are "coming out" as Latino/as, unafraid to represent who they are in any social gathering. This is done in various ways, but in particular it is carried out through what Hebdige (1979) calls "cultural style," including their (1) attire (e.g., black and gold bandanas, black, gold, and sometimes red beads, yellow/gold shirts sometimes with black ribbing, yellow leather boots sometimes with black laces, etc.); (2) demonstrative hand gestures, greeting rituals, and prayer performances; and (3) verbal self-identifications, e.g., "Amor de Rey," "Amor de Reyna," or "ADR."

Such an orientation to everyday life is confrontational, to be sure. Members announce their presence boldly and in places where they are feared or loathed. This orientation embodies the quality of what Freire (1970) calls the power to imagine, i.e., the capacity to think and act beyond the boundaries of our enforced social, economic, and cultural location.

For the most part, however, the hopes and dreams of the members are conventional, expressed in terms of achieving the "American Dream"; moving out of the projects; sending their children to decent schools; getting an education for themselves (i.e., finishing their General Equivalency Degree, aspiring to college, or finishing college); having a government (usually at the city level) that is accountable to the people; and surviving the rigors of debilitating and sometimes fatal diseases.

Thus, Kingism, as ideology and "imagination" is not particularly utopian, even though the rhetoric of the group is relatively grandiose. Rather, it is concretely related to accomplishing the goals of members in their everyday lives through small, incremental achievements that give their existence meaning in a world which is racially fragmented, hyper-competitive, and ideologically empty. Sometimes the leadership would grow impatient with these limited ideals, charging the rank-and-file with complacency and a lack of imagination. Nonetheless, to habitually approach the world from a position of optimism instead of resignation, or to harbor a set of expectations in which the individual member routinely sees him or herself as an agent in the creation of the everyday (Flacks, 1991), was and is still an extraordinary psycho-social development for most members and infected the entire organization with an upbeat mood. But there is also another aspect of identity that has to be addressed and helps to explain how the political animus of the group was maintained over time.

In the construction of their identity the ALKQN does not restrict its spiritual praxis to mere contemplation or a series of internal abstractions but rather it consciously uses this aspect of its identity construction to urge members to reflect on their realidad humana through rituals and ceremonies which highlight the daily experiences of poverty, unemployment, police brutality, and racism. This approach to cementing the group's identity within the members' religio-cultural histories played an important role in the reform process and helped to reinforce key tenets of the group doctrine. For King Tone, the group's leader and former street preacher, the discourse and rhetorical style used to expand this politicization are often borrowed from standard religious practices, and became his stock-in-trade as an innovative promoter of the group's ethno-spiritual project.

Therefore, in meeting after meeting that I attended, Tone produced countless renditions of biblical narratives in the form of prayers, anecdotes, and parables to refer indirectly to some of the tensions facing the group internally, to illuminate challenges to the group from external sources and to emphasize the need of the organization to keep focused on its possibilities for growth and regeneration. This process of linking the group's collective identity to the pursuit of a radical and action-oriented spirituality was a determining characteristic of the organization and proved an effective strategy for solidifying the identity of members and helping the group to withstand the pressures of the struggle.

In my analysis, spirituality is one of the main driving forces behind the group's collective identity, encouraging members to engage in an ongoing reflexive relationship with the structures of their everyday life through a "human re-encounter" with the creation of God. This is carried out first, by giving members permission to seek an alternative consciousness; second, by convincing them of the moral need to subvert the present social order; and third, by making them responsible for dismantling their realidad humana: e.g., their political oppression, helplessness, exploitation and exclusion. Further, the foundation of the group's spirituality is always manifested in a specific time and space and grounded in the struggle for dignity, justice, and respect in daily life (Barrios, 2000, 2003, 2004, 2006). Therefore, in Kingism, spirituality is an integral part of the meaning system through which a "resistance" identity is constructed and regenerated, and functions as a powerful bulwark to the pressures of the dominant society's ideological penetrations and corrupting moralities.

In conclusion, Kingism is the ideological and spiritual experience through which empowerment solidarity is achieved within the group by urging its members toward a critical class consciousness, on the one hand, and prompting the socio-political transformation of the organization on the other. This manifestation of a subversive spirituality becomes a social phenomenon concretely related to subjectivity, identities, meanings, experiences, and actions. A substantial part of the data I gathered shows that both the collective and individual identities that emerge out of ALKQN members' commitment to the group are embedded in a resistance project that Castells has begun to highlight, but no one has yet applied to the case of gangs. These findings point again to significant gaps in the gang research literature where identity formation is largely considered a window into group and/or individual acculturation processes rather than a novel psycho-social pathway into communal levels of empowerment.

References/Suggested Readings: Barrios, L. 2000. *Josconiando: Dimensiones sociales y políticas de la espiritualidad.* Santo Domingo: Editorial Aguiar; Barrios, L. 2003. The Almighty Latin King and Queen Nation and the Spirituality of Resistance: Agency, Social Cohesion, and Liberating Rituals in the Making of a Street Organization. In L. Kontos, D.C. Brotherton, and L. Barrios (eds.), *Gangs and Society: Alternative Perspectives,* pp. 119–135. New York: Columbia University Press; Barrios, L. 2004. *Pitirreando: De la desesperanza a la esperanza.* San Juan: Editorial Edil; Barrios, L. 2006. A Spirituality of Liberation that Understands Our "Realidad Humana" without Avoiding Our "Solidaridad Humana": An Experiment Identified as the Almighty Latin Kings/Queens Nation. In J. Hagedorn (ed.), *Gangs and the Global City: Understanding Worldwide Gangs through the Lens of Globalization.* Chicago: University of Illinois Press; Branch, C. 1997. *Clinical Interventions with Gang Adolescents and Their Families.* Boulder, CO: Westview Press; Brotherton, D., and Barrios, L. 2004. *The Almighty Latin King and Queen Nation: Street Politics and the Transformation of a New York Gang.* New York: Columbia University Press; Calderon, F., Piscitelli, A., and Reyna, J.L. 1992. Social Movements: Actors, Theories, Expectations. In A. Escobar and S.E. Alvarez (eds.), *The Making of Social Movement in Latin America: Identity, Strategy and Democracy,* pp. 19–36). Boulder: Westview Press; Calhoun, C. 1991. The Problem of Identity in Collective Action. In J. Huber (ed.), *Macro-Micro Linkages in Sociology,* pp. 51–75. London/Beverly Hills: Sage; Castells, M. 1997. *The Power of Identity.* New York: Blackwell; Della, P., Diani, D., and Diani, M. 1999. *Social Movements: An Introduction.* Malden, MA: Blackwell; Escobar, A. 1992. Culture, Economics, and Politics in Latin American Social Movements Theory and Research. In A. Escobar and S.E. Alvarez (eds.), *The Making of Social Movements in Latin America: Identity, Strategy and Democracy,* pp. 62–85. Boulder: Westview Press; Flacks, R. 1992. *Making History: The American Left and the American Mind.* New York: Columbia University Press; Freire, P. 1970. *Pedagogy of the Oppressed.* New York: Seabury Press; Hebdige, D. 1979. *Subculture: The Meaning of Style.* London: Methuen; Melucci, A. 1989. *Nomads of the Present.* Philadelphia: Temple University Press; Munoz, C. 1989. *Youth, Identity, Power: The Chicano Movement.* New York: Verso.

LUIS BARRIOS

KOREAN ORGANIZED CRIME AND GANGS. Korean involvement in **organized crime** dates back to the early 1800s when an organized group of Korean businessmen was formed to smuggle jewels and drugs out of China to be used by the Korean nobility. It was not long after the formation of this group that other criminal associations started to appear in Korea. The Japanese occupation of Korea during World War II promoted the development of many of these criminal associations in Korea by supplying an incentive type of atmosphere that let corruptive types of activity control the environment. These types of conditions ultimately led to the evolution of one of the most powerful Korean organized crime groups in the mid-1940s (U.S. Customs, 1994). This group, the Samurai Pa gang, became the most powerful force in Seoul by taking over control of the central business district and the entertainment area known as Chong No. A major portion of the membership of this gang was made up of ethnic Japanese with the minority group being comprised of Koreans who were in low ranks of the gang. The Samurai Pa gang was protected by the Japanese army because they cooperated with the military and provided the army with certain services such as call girls, and the gang also gathered information related to the activities of the Korean freedom fighters for dissemination by the Japanese military rulers. Another Korean gang was quickly formed when Tu Hwan Kim, a radical Korean independent freedom fighter, reappeared with his associates in Korea and quickly formed the Chong No Pa gang. There was immediate conflict between the Samurai Pa and the Chong No Pa gang. Most of these hostilities evolved over control of the Chong No district in Seoul. The strife continued until the Chong No Pa defeated the Samurai Pa and took over control of the Chong No district.

At the end of World War II, Korea was hit with an unusual amount of societal chaos. This outcome of all this turmoil was an expansive increase in the number of unemployed workers that produced an expansion in the number of vagrants, beggars, and criminals within Korean society. During these cataclysmic times the criminal element within this society, especially Chong No Pa, continued to prosper. This led to an increase in the number of gangs in Korea. A number of these new gangs started to appear throughout Seoul with a major portion of the membership being recruited from among the unemployed workers. Most of these gangs concentrated on recruiting membership from a specific region, town, or village or the same clan in an effort to firmly create the area they would control. Gang activity and recruitment was extremely intense in the Cholla do section of the Korean peninsula. These new gangs had problems with previously entrenched rival gangs such as the Chong No Pa. This led to most of these gangs operating on a hit-or-miss basis on local businesses and stores. This type of activity lasted until the gangs were finally able to take over some of the territories previously controlled by the Chong No Pa (FBI, 1993).

Some of the gangs that survived all of these trying times and ultimately emanated out of these unstable times were Myong Dong, Tong Dae Moon Pa, Sodae Moon, and Mookyo Done Pa. All of these gangs regulated different areas of Seoul, including sections from which these groups took their original names. Each one of these gangs is a separate entity that functions as broad and adaptable organized crime system working either together or apart. During the 1950s, Korean organized crime syndicates began to be classified into two different categories, one a political type of gang and the other a street gang.

Political Gangs

The most dominant gangs in Korea are the political gangs because of their attachment to corrupt politicians. These gangs were categorized as political groups because they were employed by corrupt politicians to use whatever method necessary to make opposing bureaucrats withdraw from an election race, relinquish their elected position, or throw their support to the criminal syndicates.

Most political gangs, besides being dominant, were well established organizations that were substantially well connected with government officials. This put the political gangs in a favorable position because it left the Korean National Police (KNP) in a position where they were left ineffective against the gangs. In fact, the KNP very seldom interceded in any activities involving the gangs.

Once police interference was eliminated the Chong No Pa, the Mookyo Dong Pa and the Tongdae Moon Pa could do whatever they pleased without any interruptions. These criminal syndicates were able to operate all of their illegal activities (loan sharking, prostitution, gambling, smuggling). During this time investigations by the KNP and the Korean Central Intelligence Agency indicate that the Korean gangs, specifically the Chong No Pa, renewed their relationships with the **Japanese gangs**. Although contact with the Yakuza was established, the effect of thirty-five years of occupation and poor treatment at the hands of the Japanese during their reign in Korea, the in-roads made due to this contact were basically insignificant. A working relationship between the Japanese and the Koreans was finally reestablished in the 1960s and firmed up in the 1970s (U.S. Customs, 1994).

Street Gangs

The second form of Korean gang is the street gangs. These groups of paltry lawbreakers roamed the streets of Korea victimizing local businesses and amusement areas. The street gangs' major method of financing their operations is by extorting funds from businesses within the area of their operation and having the rights to black-market goods. Street gang members were characterized as street urchins by both the citizens and the police of Korea. In most cases, the Korean street gangs did not create the same major type of violent threat to society like present-day street gangs.

Gangs on the Run

Early in 1961, a military coup took over South Korea with General Park Chong Hee as the new Korean leader. Park immediately commanded his underlings to arrest all known gang members and place them in military camps to be reeducated on how to get out of the criminal lifestyle. The military rounded up hundreds of gang members and petty criminals and sent them off to an desolate island off the coast of Inchon. A large portion of the gang leaders and their membership were either put to death by members of the military or opposing gang leaders or died because of the poor prison conditions. The reeducation programs created by General Park Chong Hee were basically unsuccessful and the only thing that these camps accomplished was the killing of numerous gang leaders and members. Ultimately, those who did not die in these camps were released by the government in early 1964 (U.S. Customs, 1994).

New Gangs

The Korean governments attempts to quell gang activities was short term because once the government started releasing gang members from the prison camps the gangs, once again, started to sprout up all over Korea. San-chong Sin, a camp releasee and a prior member of Chong No Pa, quickly established a new gang the Cholla Do Pa whose new membership included hundreds of one-time Chong No Pa members. Within a short period of time this gang had taken over control of almost all parts of the Cholla do business and entertainment area in Seoul. Within a short period of time another gang the Bon Gae Pa was formed by Chong-sok Pak, a former captain in the Chong No Pa. The Bon Gae Pa (the lighting faction) gang was soon to become the major rival of the Cholla Do Pa. These two groups continually battled over control of the main business and entertainment areas in Yongdongp'o, Cholla do, and other similar areas in the major cities of South Korea. After several years of hostilities the Bon Gae Pa took a major action by attacking the headquarters of the Cholla No Pa and killing Cholla leader San-chong Sin and many of his underbosses. This action helped the Bon Gae Pa become the strongest and most feared gang in Seoul. During the mid-1970s the Bon Gae Pa membership increased so much that the gang was divided into three different groups the Sobang Pa, the Yang Un Pa, and the Ob Pa with Chong-sok Pak in charge of all these gangs (KNP, 1994).

Pak delegated the power to run these new gangs to several of his underbosses. Tae chon Kim and Chong chol Oh were appointed as leaders of the Sobang Pa. While the Yang Un Pa was named after and controlled by Yang un Cho who had participated with Pak in a political gang prior to being imprisoned by the military. The leader of the Ob Pa gang was Tong chae Yi who also ran the Ho Rang Yi Pa (the tiger faction) gang. Yi took over the leadership of the Ob Pa gang by murdering Pak while Pak was visiting one of his criminal operations in Kwangju, Cholla-do. A short time later, Tong chae Yi moved his headquarters along with most of his Ob Pa gang to Seoul. Yi made sure he would to remain in control over his unlawful activities in Kwangju by leaving a sufficient number of Ob Pa gang members in Kwangju to supervise operations there (KNP, 1994).

References/Suggested Readings: Federal Bureau of Investigation. 1993. *Organized Crime in America.* October; Korean National Police. 1994. *Report on Organized Crime in South Korea.* July; U.S Customs. 1994. *Asian Organized Crime: Korean Groups.* September.

SEAN GRENNAN

L

LABELING THEORY. Labeling theory presents the hypothesis that people assume and accept the labels society places on them, thereby affirming the basis upon which those labels are applied. This is not unlike the age-old idea of the "self-fulfilling prophecy." Labeling theory is particularly focused on how people assume deviant roles in society. It suggests that deviant behavior is reinforced and deviant identities are solidified by deviant labels that are placed by society on those who engage in deviant behaviors. People can become what they are labeled as being, even if they were not so prior to the application of the label. Rather than looking for the cause of deviance, labeling theory argues that society itself creates deviance by labeling certain behaviors and persons who engage in them as deviant. This argument, by default, suggests that no behaviors or persons are inherently deviant.

Labeling theory is commonly associated with the work of sociologist Howard Becker. However, the ideas that underlie this theory can be traced to previous scholars. The precursor to Becker's labeling theory was Charles Cooley's *Human Nature and the Social Order,* which was first published in 1902. In this work, Cooley develops the theoretical concept of "the looking glass self." He suggests that people perceive themselves as if they were looking through the eyes of others, forming judgments about themselves according to this imaginary perspective of what others might think. The essential idea being that people define their own identities according to how they believe others perceive them. Although not mentioned by Becker, this idea is the basis of what later developed into labeling theory.

Frank Tannenbaum is widely credited with asserting the first form of labeling theory in 1938. In his study of juvenile delinquency, Tannenbaum offers a novel analysis of deviant behavior and deviant identities. He suggests that juveniles do not define their deviant behaviors in a negative light, rather negative perceptions of their deviant behaviors are imposed on them by society. According to Tannenbaum, a juvenile delinquent is "tagged" with a deviant identity by society upon being caught and punished for his delinquent behavior. He then assumes the deviant identity he has been tagged with and strives to conform to the deviant role to which he has been assigned. Tannenbaum refers to this process as the "the dramatization of evil." Tannenbaum argues that rather than dissuading a juvenile delinquent from a life of crime, the dramatization of evil compels juvenile delinquents to become further committed to a life of deviance.

The second widely recognized manifestation of labeling theory with regard to deviance was presented by sociologist Edwin M. Lemert in 1951. Lemert suggests using the theoretical categories of primary and secondary deviance to better understand deviance. According to Lemert, deviant behaviors are considered primary so long as such behaviors can be rationalized as functions of a socially acceptable role. If such behaviors do not threaten a person's socially acceptable role, they will not lead to a deviant career. However, when deviant behaviors are visible and repetitive enough to provoke severe social repudiation, they move into the category of secondary deviance. With secondary deviance, the deviant reorganizes their conception of themselves such that they reject previously held socially acceptable roles and assume a new deviant identity based on the deviant behavior that was subject to social rebuke. Unlike the primary deviance that the person once engaged in, this new secondary deviance is both intransigent and pervasive in the new deviant role.

Howard Becker is widely credited with explicitly developing labeling as a theory of deviant behavior in his 1963 book, *Outsiders: Studies in the Sociology of Deviance*. His classic study of jazz musicians and marijuana smokers suggests that in developing a deviant career, the most important step is being labeled with, accepting, and assuming a deviant identity. Becker argues that no behaviors are inherently deviant, rather, certain behaviors are labeled as being deviant by moral entrepreneurs who have an interest in doing so.

However, engaging in any particular deviant behavior is not in itself enough to create a deviant identity. In order to cement a deviant identity as a master status, one must be caught committing a deviant act and become publicly labeled as a deviant. According to Becker, it is this public labeling that creates a more permanent deviant identity and self-perception in the mind of the deviant. By being publicly labeled as a deviant, one is permanently cut off from other socially accepted roles with which one might previously have identified. This fissure with acceptable society necessarily leads the deviant to further involvement with deviant behavior and deviant groups and solidifies the deviant's own self-perception. The deviant role is thus seen as a master status, one that supersedes all other statuses and is the basis of all future assessments of the deviant's character.

Becker views these deviants as essentially different from members of mainstream, rule-abiding society. According to Becker, this difference leads most deviants who have been so labeled to accept and embrace their deviant roles, thereby rejecting and devaluing societal norms. The final step in assuming a deviant career is entry into a deviant subculture or group, where the behavior that has led to one's deviant label has a positive perception.

References/Suggested Readings: Becker, H. 1963. *Outsiders: Studies in the Sociology of Deviance*. New York: Free Press; Cooley, C.H. 1922. *Human Nature and the Social Order*. New York: Scribner; Gove, W. 1975. *The Labeling of Deviance: Evaluating a Perspective*. Beverly Hills: Sage Publications; Lemert, E.M. 1951. *Social Pathology*. New York: McGraw-Hill; Tannenbaum, F. 1938. *Crime and the Community*. New York: Columbia University Press.

ROBERT D. WEIDE

LATIN GANGS IN BARCELONA. On October 28, 2003, Colombian teenager Ronny Tapias was murdered in Barcelona. According to the police investigation, the murder was an act of revenge by gang members (the Ñetas) who supposedly mistook Ronny as a member of another gang (the **Latin Kings**) with whom they had had a fight some days before in a dance club. This case resulted in the "discovery" by the media of a new social problem, "Latin Gangs," and led to a wave of **moral panic** that has not ceased yet. This event and others in Madrid and Barcelona followed by an alarmist reaction in the Department of Home Security and by sensationalist coverage in the media, served to demonize Latin American youth. Against this backdrop it is easy to ignore the fact that thousands of boys and girls of Latin American origin have been coming to Barcelona since the late 1990s through different processes of family reunification, exiled from their hometowns and social networks in one of the most difficult moments in their lives (the always complicated transition to adult life). Upon reaching their destination, they confront terrified adults (over-employed mothers, often absent fathers, insecure teachers and social workers, fearful neighbors). In this disturbing scene, there are new forms of youth sociability crossing geographical and temporal borders to build global identities that we still confuse with traditional gangs.

Despite the murder of Ronny Tapias as a pivotal event, a reference, the first news linked to Latin gangs appeared at the beginnings of 2003 in Madrid and Barcelona. Small actions attributed to those groups (fights among groups of Latin American boys) allowed the media to present a public image of those gangs. Stereotypes about groups of Latin American youth "encroaching" on public spaces were now commonplace. In September 2003, a month before Ronny's death, there were media accounts about the presence of Latin gangs in Barcelona. The accounts, based exclusively on police sources, served as a warning to society: "A dangerous youth gang alerts the police in Barcelona. The police say that minors are lured in high schools and that they commit aggressions" (*El Periódico*, September 10, 2003). Such news became the basis for more of the same, creating a "wave" from disparate events and stereotypes. The look was (and still is) a crucial element in the media creation of gangs, presenting a boy wearing a black bandana, preferably gold, blue, and black clothes, hip-hop music and style, and tattooed crowns (in the case of Latin Kings). Much was also made of the way "gangs" were organized—their pyramidal structure—and their violent orientation—toward members, rival gangs' members, and non-related people. The scary image citizens received from the mainstream media was that of maladjusted and problem kids that are inherently antisocial and that seek to take over public spaces: "Youngsters with severe problems of social integration, coming from dysfunctional families and with a high rate of school drop-out that evidence lack of control and absence of rules of behavior" (*El Mundo,* July 16, 2004).

First Intervention Strategies

While this type of news about gangs was spreading, some social and law enforcement agencies developed alternative approaches to the phenomenon. Barcelona's local police was the first agency interested in this issue, about the middle of 2002, after discovering some conflicts between groups of teenagers of Latin American origin who were said to belong to the Latin Kings, Ñetas, and Masters. This discovery led the agents to try to document the origin of those groups in the United States, their journey to Latin America and their recent settlement in the Spanish territory.

The planning of social and educative measures, at that first moment, was deeply biased by the impact of news, at the same time, filled the void of direct information most professionals were facing. This is an important element, because besides law enforcement, very few professionals and agencies had direct knowledge of the gangs, and they faced many difficulties in diagnosing the "gangs situation" in Barcelona's context without referring to the media or to some urban legends:

> We talked to the board (in a school). There were twelve or thirteen people who were shit-scared. They were scared, and I don't exaggerate, that someday, going out of school, there could be some boy with a gun waiting to shoot them. "Excuse me, calm down, nobody is going to wait for you around the corner, this is not a Calabria-style mafia . . ." And I say it without knowing how gangs work, but the fear they had is the one of the movies, "The Godfather" . . . as if these were Mafia-style gangs. (Interview with a local policeman)

Teachers, outreach workers, members of agencies—people with a lot of valid information when speaking about education, families, and social issues around Latin American youth—were seemingly at a loss when asked about the organizations. They repeated "I don't know . . . ," "I don't know but I heard that . . . ," "I have read . . ." These adults explained that the youngsters didn't speak about it, that they didn't find the adults reliable enough, and that the professionals themselves avoided the issue, sometimes because of fears and doubts, sometimes as an intervention policy.

On the other hand, the appearance of Latin gangs prompted professionals to evaluate the intervention programs for the large community of Latin American teenagers arrived in Barcelona during the last years, as a result of family reunification processes. It could not be helped noticing the shortcomings of the integration policies for Latin American adolescents at school (Carrasco 2004), job placement programs, access to social resources. This had important consequences for the marginalization of certain groups, specially those teenagers at an age on the borderline between compulsory education and the minimum age for employment (in Spain school is compulsory until age sixteen, the minimum age for employment is also sixteen, and the majority age is reached at eighteen), and those young adults in a situation of legal exclusion (Canelles, 2006). Similarly, the lack of stable links between Latin American teenagers and socio-educational agencies placed those youngsters in leisure and relationship places apart from those used by the native youth population. Streets became the main leisure environment, and the presence of the "Latinos" in parks and squares started to be seen as controversial, both by neighbors and authorities.

The emergence of gangs in the agendas of different agencies unveiled some problems related to social and educational intervention in the city of Barcelona; failures in coordination and articulation of policies between educational, social, juridical, and other fields; opaqueness in relationships between different departments, mistrust about the use of information, etc. Despite those not being new problems, they became more relevant when talking about gangs, since the moral panics surrounding the issue amplified the sense of un-coordination.

In this context, strongly influenced by the media alarm, the first intervention strategies with gangs logically tended to favor therapeutic and police work, since the basis for intervention was a stereotyped definition of those groups as criminal organizations and cult-oriented. In addition to identifying gang members and prosecuting their crimes, law enforcement initiated rehabilitation procedures for members of organizations whose parents asked for it. The task of therapeutic intervention assumed by a private agency traditionally devoted to overcoming addiction to cults, now taking "gang cases" transferred by social services and high schools in the city. Their function was counseling the family and the teenagers, providing clinical diagnosis, and helping members quit their organizations. Later, a protocol to be used in high schools and social services was promoted by Prevention Services of the City Council of Barcelona. This protocol formalized the transfer to the above-mentioned agency, so they could start their intervention with teenagers involved in cannabis consumption, vandalism, drug trafficking, fights, etc.

References/Suggested Readings: Brotherton, David C., and Barrios, Luis. 2004. *The Almighty Latin King and Queen Nation. Street Politics and the Transformation of a New York City Gang.* New York: Columbia University Press; Canelles, Noemí. 2006. Modelos de Intervención. In Carles Feixa (dir.), Laura Porzio and Carlolina Recio (eds.), *Jovenes Latinos en Barcelona: Espacio público y cultura urbana.* Barcelona: Anthropos; Carrasco, Silvia. 2004. Infancia e inmigración: proyectos y realidades. In Carmen Gómez-Granell et al. (coords.), *Infancia y familias: realidades y tendencias,* pp. 205–231. Barcelona: Instituto de Infancia y Mundo Urbano; Cerbino, Mauro. 2005. Movimientos y máquinas de guerra juveniles. *Nómadas,* 23, 112–121; Cerbino, Mauro. 2006. *Jóvenes en la calle. Cultura y conflicto.* Barcelona: Anthropos; Esteva Martínez, Juan Francisco. 2003. Urban Street Activists: Gang and Community Efforts to Bring Peace and Justice to Los Angeles Neighborhoods. In Louis Kontos, David C. Brotherton, and Luis Barrios (eds.), *Gangs and Society. Alternative Perspectives,* pp. 95–115. New York: Columbia University Press; Feixa, Carles. 1998. *El reloj de arena.* Mexico: IMJ; Feixa, Carles. 2006. De Jóvenes. Barcelona: Bandas y Tribus; Feixa, Carles, and Muñoz, Germán. 2004. ¿Reyes Latinos? Pistas para superar los estereotipos. *Newspaper El País,* December 12; Hagedorn, John M. 2001. Globalization, Gangs and Collaborative Research. In Malcom W. Klein et al. (eds.), *The Eurogang Paradox,* pp. 41–58. London: Kluwer,; Klein, M.W., Kerner, H.-J., Maxson, C.L., and Weitekamp, E. (eds.). 2001. *The Eurogang Paradox. Street Gangs and Youth Groups in the U.S. and Europe.* London: Kluwer; Matza, David. 1973 [1961]. Subterranean Traditions of Youth. In H. Silverstein (ed.), *The Sociology of Youth: Evolution and Revolution,* pp. 252–271. New York: Macmillan; Queirolo Palmas, Luca. 2005. Verso dove? Voci e pratiche giovanili fra stigmatizzazione, cittadinanza e rifiuto dell'integrazione subalterna. In Luca Queirolo Palmas and Andrea T. Torre (coords.), *Il fantasma delle bande. Giovani dall'America Latina a Genova,* pp. 279–328. Fratelli Frilli Editore Genova; Reguillo, Rossana. 1995. *En la calle otra vez. Las bandas: identidad urbana y usos de la comunicación.* Guadalajara: ITESO; Sánchez-Jankowski, Martin. 1991. *Islands in the Streets. Gangs and American Urban Society,* Berkeley: University of California Press; Salazar, Alonso. 1990. *No Nacimos Pa` Semilla. La cultura de las bandas en Medellín;* Bogotá: CINEP; Urteaga, Maritza. 1996. *Por los territorios del rock.* Mexico: IMJ; Valenzuela, José Manuel. 2002. De los pachucos a los cholos. Movimientos juveniles en la frontera México-Estados Unidos. In C. Feixa, F. Molina, and C. Alsinet (eds.), *Movimientos Juveniles en América Latina. Pachucos, malandros, punketas.* Barcelona: Ariel.

NOEMÍ CANELLES AND CARLES FEIXA

LATIN KING BIBLE. The Latin King Bible consists of a manifesto, lessons, rules, poetry, and other kinds of writing. Several passages contained therein liken the history of Latinos in American society to that of Native and African American people. They are assumed to share the same enemies: "capitalists," "sell-outs," "traitors," and "the white man." There are also passages that liken the participation of the **ALKQN** in the underworld to that of European ethnic groups, whose economic and political power is attributed to a history of violence and organized crime.

In this narrative the ALKQN must "endure" the underworld and eventually abandon it. The stated objective is to assume a "rightful place" in the Latino community as a political vanguard, and to establish businesses that provide employment opportunities and cultural centers for the re-education of Latino youth. Each generation of members, in this narrative, is "struggling" not only on its own behalf, but to pave the way for future generations whose lives can then be freer of contradictions that must now be lived, and battles that must now be fought.

There is also in this text an account of earlier attempts in the history of the group to leave the underworld. The failure of such attempts is attributed to state repression (with emphasis on the FBI's counter-insurgency program, COINTELPRO), as well as a lack of solidarity and the existence of "cowards" and "traitors" among the ranks of the group—who misled it or caused setbacks. This account of events provides the rationale for hundreds of rules and procedures that comprise the bulk of the Latin King Bible. Members are instructed, for instance, that they are not to talk to any outsiders about the affairs of the organization, not to trust anybody outside the organization, and not to accuse anyone within the organization of wrongdoings in the absence of concrete evidence ("court documents"). Against the same backdrop of recounted instances of treachery and betrayal, particular members are identified as especially heroic and/or gripped by a form of inspiration that privileges their voice. They are designated as "knowledge builders," their writings now canonized in the text of the Latin King Bible.

There are several versions of this literature (bounded as a single text) in circulation. No distinction is made therein between original and supplemental materials, including revisions. Nor is it always clear what has been rewritten—what has been changed, when, why, and by whom. In one version of the Constitution, for instance, there are references to TOS ("terminate on sight") as a penalty for certain forms of rule violation, namely "snitching" and violating the oath of secrecy; whereas, in another, the penalty ranges from demotion to expulsion. Another revision appears around the symbol of the crown. In one version (apparently the most recent) it "represents the following "five points" (each depicted in emblems and drawings as a point of a crown): respect, honesty, knowledge, unity, and love; whereas an earlier (undated) version contains obedience and loyalty in place of honesty and unity.

There are also disparate and incompatible accounts of the origins of the organization within this literature. In one account, the Kings trace their origins to a Chicago-area gang named Noble Lords. This group is said to have been founded in the 1930s and to have changed its name to Latin Kings in the 1940s. One of its members, King Cookie, is said to have thought up the new name and, at some point, to have become the leader of the new organization. "King Cookie is known to have baptized us with the name Latin Kings. He was also considered the first godfather of the Nation." In another passage on "origins," the Kings are said to have been "born by the realization of one man who saw the struggles and deaths of our Latin brothers and sisters." This member, referred to only by the name Supremo, is supposed to have selected "five other Latin brothers whom possessed the awareness of their Latin brother whom possessed the awareness of the people's predicament." Supremo supposedly also created five "principles" for the newly formed organization: respect, honesty, unity, knowledge, and love (i.e., the later version of "five points").

Formative Events

In the 1960s the Kings appeared to put these principles into practice and to make good on some of their professed commitments to the community. As recounted in the Latin King Bible, the Chicago Kings "fought for many Latino rights. Soon businesses opened. A Latin King newspaper was in circulation. Facilities and stores owned by Kings were being operated. [. . .] However the government did not like what they saw. They feared Latinos so they put obstacles in our way. Forcing the Almighty Latin King Nation to go underground." The Kings were not alone among established gangs in the 1960s to either become politically active or try to gain recognition as a community organization. (During this same time, for example, the Blackstone Rangers and Disciples received the bulk of a federal grant of $927,341; Short, 1972, p. 142).

Coinciding with the end of its political phase the group took the name Almighty Latin King Nation and began to refer to the contents of its literature as religious—its religion being **Kingism**. The new name of the group and the name Kingism are credited to King Crazy Dino who "claim[ed] rank and started passing out positions[,] thus forming a crown structure" (LKB). While serving time in prison for a "sacrifice for the Nation," King Crazy Dino also provided the official definition of Kingism in a passage by the same name.

> Kingism as a belief, as a way of giving our blessing to the Almighty and as a way of showing love and respect to ourselves as a Latin nation did not take form or was revealed to us until 1969 at the State Ville correctional center in Chicago to King Crazy Dino. While at the State Ville, serving 25–40 for a sacrifice for the Nation, it was revealed unto him that the trials and tribulations, we as Kings were having was the work of our creator to test those of us who were chosen. . . . Kingism shall be a religion unto itself. It shall be a cry unto itself. It shall be a cry of unity, love, and respect to the lost Latino Nation. . . . We are the Sun People of the Lion Tribe, the strong tribes that were lost and now found. We stand upright with our fist across our hearts for up to 360 degrees of wisdom, knowledge, and understanding, proclaiming "I'll die for my brother."

This passage is followed by a reiteration of central themes, including that Latinos need to be educated as to their history, culture, and the nature of their problems and struggles; and that the Kings must assume the roles of leader and educator of "the people." "Therefore, it's our goal to educate the Latin community at large, that we may come together from all sides and establish one people, one nation under one leadership; and one that has been striving for years for its people, and that can only mean—only be the A.L.K.N" (Note the Q (Queen) was, at some point, added to the names and literature of several East Coast state chapters. There is no reference in the literature regarding the circumstances of this change of name, and it has not been adopted by other state chapters.)

References/Suggested Readings: Brotherton, David C. and Luis Barrios. 2004. *The Almighty Latin King and Queen Nation*. New York: Columbia University Press; Kontos, Louis. 2003. Between Criminal and Political Deviance: A Sociological Analysis of the New York Chapter of the Almighty Latin King and Queen Nation. In David Muggleton and Rupert Weinzierl (eds.), *The Post-Subcultures Reader*, pp. 113–147. Oxford: Berg; Short, James F. 1972. Gangs, Politics, and the Social Order. In *Delinquency, Crime and Society*. Chicago: University of Chicago Press.

LOUIS KONTOS

THE LATIN QUEENS. From its inception, gang research has focused on the behavior of males, often neglecting or distorting females' roles in street gangs. The first truly large and intensive formal academic study on gang members involved a survey of 1,313 separate gangs by **Frederic Thrasher**. Thrasher (1927) included only one page of discussion about female gang participation, and claimed that he found no evidence of female gangs. Thrasher concluded that females lacked the "ganging instinct" and that their role was mostly limited to the destruction of the gang, that is either by acting as sexual objects or pulling males away from the gang by encouraging marriage. Contemporary researchers generally, with few exceptions, characterize female members as maladjusted tomboys or sexual deviants who, in either case, are no more than appendages to male gang members (Joe and Chesney, 1995).

These traditional and stereotypical views contrast sharply with recent research into the social processes and consequences of females' involvement in gangs. That is, recent research indicates that female gang members are increasingly taking an active, independent role in the gang (Joe and Chesney, 1995; Brotherton and Salazar, 2003; Brotherton and Barrios, 2004).

We can gain some insight into the motivations of female gang membership and the roles females play in the gang by taking a look into the lives of a particular group: the female members of the New York Chapter of the **Almighty Latin King and Queen Nation (ALKQN)**. The Almighty Latin King and Queen Nation of New York has a unique history, which includes a period of reform (1996–1999). During this time, members called themselves a street organization. Brotherton and Barrios (2004, p. 23) define a **street organization** as

> A group formed largely by youth and adults of a marginalized social class which aims to provide its members with a resistant identity, an opportunity to be individually and collectively empowered, a voice to speak back to and challenge the dominant culture, a refuge from the stresses and strains of barrio or ghetto life, and a spiritual enclave within which its own sacred rituals can be generated and practiced.

The unique history of the ALKQN underscores the importance of gaining a better understanding of its female members.

The New York State Latin Queens were founded in 1991 after a manifesto was written for them by **King Blood**, who held the position of First President of the New York State Latin Kings. Prior to that there had been no organized group for women who wanted to join the Latin Kings. From 1991 to 1996, the Latin Queens expanded and grew to include approximately sixty members. Toward the end of this period, the group changed its name to the Almighty Latin King and Queen Nation, reflecting the increased role of females in the organization. After 1996, the role of the Latin Queens began to expand even more with the ascension of King Tone to the position of President. Under his leadership, the rules of the Queens were amended and for the first time the Queens began to put forward their own demands. By 1998, the Queens had grown to more than 200 members throughout New York State. By the time the reform period of the ALKQN ended, tensions between the Kings and Queens were very high due to the Queens' resistance to double standards.

Brotherton and Salazar (2003) describe the motivations of females joining a gang in terms of push/pull factors. The "push" factors encompass a broad array of influences, including psychological, political, and cultural. The "pull" factors are narrower, yet still powerful. They include economic benefits, the feeling of protection, as well as the social benefits of power and prestige. Brotherton and Salazar integrated these push/pull factors into five major themes: (1) issues of identity, (2) family pressures, (3) economic survival, (4) community/family networks, and (5) working-class/underclass experiences.

First, regarding issues of identity, Brotherton and Salazar found that the Latin Queens described themselves as having autonomy and being the "backbone" of the Nation. They prided themselves on motherhood and their ability to support and care for their children. They also strongly identified with their Latin roots and rejected the notion of being American. In many ways joining the ALKQN was an act of "coming out" as Latinas.

Second, nearly all of the twenty-eight Latin Queens interviewed by Brotherton and Salazar studied came from traumatic and abusive households. Many Latin Queens joined the ALKQN as a way to escape their homes and feel safe and secure. Other researchers have also found that escaping harmful family situations is a major motivating factor for young females who join gangs (Moore, 1991; Miller, 2001; Fleisher and Krienert, 2004).

Third, only a few of the Queens appeared to have joined the group for access to illegal activities. However, economic survival was at issue for each of them. The ALKQN offered its members economic aid in the form of holding baby showers so that new babies would have clothes and furniture, babysitting for single mothers so that the mother could go to job interviews, providing temporary housing for homeless Latin Queens, formally and informally adopting younger females who ran away from their abusive homes, and short-term loans from the Latin Queens welfare fund.

Fourth, community/family networks provided a source of motivation. That is, many females joined the ALKQN as if it were simply a natural thing to do, since many had friends, boyfriends, and family members already in the gang.

Fifth, Brotherton and Salazar found that members share a working-class/underclass experience. Female members, just like their male counterparts, are described by the authors as looking for dignity, recognition, and respect in their neighborhoods and schools. Other research studies have argued that gang members gain their power and respect by their leverage over others and their willingness to make good on their threats (Decker and Van Winkle, 1996). Brotherton and Salazar found that in the ALKQN dignity and respect is acquired by gaining "inner strength." It is this aura of self-respect and collective strength that attracts many females into the ALKQN. Brotherton and Salazar also found that many females who were struggling with drugs and alcohol abuse joined the ALKQN in order to regain their self-control and stay clean, since they knew that their fellow Kings and Queens would help and support them.

Contradictions

Brotherton and Barrios (2004) found that the Latin Queens were not only formally organized but also had well-defined roles, a deep sense of commitment to the group, were highly motivated by both personal and collective goals and maintained their own autonomy within the organization. The ALKQN claimed that it had created a strong organization around common goals and aspirations. It also claimed that increasing the autonomy of the Latin Queens and strengthening their positions in the gang was a major goal of the group during their reformation period. Yet there was much sexism and many double standards.

Part of the problem can be traced to cultural traditions, particularly **machismo** and "marianismo." Marianismo refers to the sacred duty a female has to her family. The female is expected to be the strong, stoic, and loyal anchor of the family. Marianismo restricts women's values to motherhood and caretaking. Being the backbone of the organization is not the same as being a leader in the organization (Brotherton and Barrios, 2004).

The affirmation of marianismo within the ALKQN can be seen with regard to several sexist double standards. Prior to the reformation period, the Kings were allowed to have wives and mistresses, but the Queens had to be faithful or risk being punished with expulsion (Brotherton and Barrios, 2004). During the reform period the rules were amended so that both Kings and Queens had to be loyal to each other. However, Brotherton and Barrios (2004) found that while several females were expelled from the organization for committing adultery, not a single punishment was ever given to a King for being unfaithful. The Latin Kings obviously felt that they had a right to be sexually promiscuous, whereas Latin Queens taking part in the same behavior were seen as immoral and punished.

Another example of the double standards that existed within the organization pertains to dress codes. The Latin Queens were required to dress "respectfully" during all meetings. They were not allowed to wear short skirts or tight clothing or reveal cleavage or their bare stomachs (Brotherton and Barrios 2004). If the females did not abide by these dress codes they were punished—which usually entailed being placed on "probation." In contrast, the Latin Kings did not have the same constraints.

Many Latin Queens joined the ALKQN in search of support, safety, and empowerment. The organization provided its female members with emotional, social, and spiritual support. It gave them the opportunity to express their individual identities and embrace their heritage. However, sexist codes and double standards were never fully eliminated.

References/Suggested Readings: Brotherton, D., and Salazar, C. 2003. Amor de reina! The Pushes and Pulls of Group Membership among the Latin Queens. In L. Kontos, D. Brotherton, and L. Barrios (eds.), *Gangs in Society: Alternative Perspectives,* pp. 182–209. New York: Columbia University Press; Brotherton, D., and Barrios, L. 2004. *The Almighty Latin King and Queen Nation: Street Politics and the Transformation of a New York City Gang.* New York: Columbia University Press; Campbell, A. 1984. *The Girls in the Gang.* Oxford: Basil Blackwell; Decker, S., and Van Winkle, B. 1996. *Life in the Gang.* Cambridge: Cambridge University Press; Fleisher, M., and Krienert, J. 2004. Life-Course Events, Social Networks, and the Emergence of Violence among Female Gang Members. *Journal of Community Psychology,* 32, 607–622; Joe, K., and Chesney L.M. 1995. Just Every Mother's Angel: An Analysis of Gender and Ethnic Variations in Youth Gang Membership. *Gender and Society,* 9, 408–438; Miller, J. 2001. *One of the Guys: Girls, Gangs, and Gender.* New York: Oxford University Press; Moore, J.W. 1991. *Going Down to the Barrio: Homeboys and Homegirls in Change.* Philadelphia: Temple University Press; Thrasher, F. 1927. *The Gang: A Study of 1,313 Gangs in Chicago.* Chicago: University of Chicago Press.

MILADY T. PADILLA

LITTLE BROTHER SYNDROME. The Little Brother syndrome is a term that was first popularized in New York City in the mid-1990s as social scientists sought to make sense of steep declines in crime and crack use that were evident in inner cities across the United States. The most popular explanation for the drop in crime and hard drug use was that law enforcement strategies begun in the late 1980s were finally paying off (see, for example, Silverman, 1999). The Little Brother syndrome, on the other hand, argued that one important reason that inner-city youths began to desist from criminality and hard drug use was that they had witnessed the multiple horrors that had befallen their older siblings and parents—drug addiction, disease, death, and high rates of incarceration—and they were determined not to succumb to the same fate (Curtis, 1998).

The new generation of local youth—the little brothers—had grown up in the worst of times, and for many of them, the world built by their predecessors—the "old heads" in Elijah Anderson's (1999) words—was socially and culturally bankrupt. The "old school" attitudes and behaviors that were rooted in the violent 1980s provided a counterpoint against which many young men sought to define themselves. The new identity to which many aspired explicitly repudiated the excesses of the crack era. Youngsters no longer aspired to be big-time drug dealers, and even some drug dealers no longer wanted to be identified as such. Gone was the "Mr. T" look characterized by gaudy jewelry and garish clothes. In their personal habits, they believed in keeping a tight rein on the use of mind-altering substances. For many, marijuana was the only substance they consumed because they felt it allowed them to keep their wits about them regardless of how much they smoked. Even alcohol, once aggressively marketed in minority neighborhoods in forty-ounce bottles of malt liquor, was shunned by many youth who disliked its stultifying effect. Crack or heroin use was strictly taboo, and while sniffing cocaine was tolerated, users were not lionized by their peers as they were in the 1980s. Indeed they were praised for their ability to show restraint at the end of the night when the compulsion to buy more was strongest. Clearly, some important shifts were taking place in the thinking and behaviors of the little brothers in these neighborhoods.

In many New York City neighborhoods, where the phenomenon was first noticed (see, Sviridoff et al., 1992), large corporate-style drug selling organizations had also influenced the attitudes, orientations, and behaviors of the little brothers. These large organizations had dominated the economic landscape in poor neighborhoods since the early 1970s, and they were once seen as lucrative businesses that offered minority youths economic opportunities that were denied to them in the legitimate world of work. Many young men aspired to be "gangsters" and "managers" in these businesses. To them, an added bonus was that participation in drug selling carried with it a subversive quality, an element of resistance to the state's attempt to regulate and control unruly, working-class minorities who live in the inner city. By the early 1990s, however, the entrenched management structures and brutal track records of many corporate-style drug distribution organizations were increasingly seen by youths as offering few real economic opportunities for entry-level employees, and they no longer even offered a feeling of resistance to the state. Instead, the organizations bred and relied upon a culture of subjugation and fear to dominate local markets.

The shift in local attitudes against the drug-selling organizations was solidified by their increasingly frequent public use of violence as a management tool to keep employees in line. Adding to their sense that these drug distributors had betrayed the community, young community residents stood witness as building after building was run down by the incessant drum-beat of business; the streets were constantly filthy with drug paraphernalia from the heavy traffic; children could not play on sidewalks as distributors and users stood shoulder to shoulder until late into the night; vicious fights were a daily occurrence; and most of the young men from the neighborhood had been locked up and left to fend for themselves in the criminal justice system as an outcome of their involvement with the businesses. The taste of drug money that had initially been so attractive had clearly soured in many people's mouths, and there was no longer any illusion that working for the drug organizations was a source of anything but trouble. By 1993, a tipping point was reached in many inner-city neighborhoods. The little brothers saw how former street-level drug workers suffered at the hands of their bosses and the police: the "owners" of drug businesses did not bail them out of jail, hire lawyers, look after family, or compensate them for the time in prison. Participation in corporate-style drug distribution had come to symbolize adherence to a destructive hedonism that was blind to family and community suffering, and many youths wanted no part of that.

In New York City, technologically informed zero-tolerance policing policies were hailed as the backbone of the miraculous drop in crime, but other cities like Dallas, Miami, and Seattle also achieved substantial reductions in crime over this same period while actually decreasing per capita police staffing levels. Lacking a critical self-examination that seeks answers at the intersection of social, cultural, economic, and political currents flowing through a city, the resulting vacuum of ideas has been filled with plausible-sounding explanatory devices: civility did not percolate from the bottom up, but rather, was imposed from the top down by the more clever application of state power in managing people, especially around the linchpin problems of disorder. Clearly, however, people have agency and they do not always respond in ways that are anticipated by social scientists, policy makers, or professionals. The case of the Little Brother syndrome is one such example of people confounding the experts.

References/Suggested Readings: Anderson, E. 1999. *Code of the Street: Decency, Violence, and the Moral Life of the Inner City*. New York: Norton; Curtis, R. 1998. The Improbable Transformation of Inner-City Neighborhoods: Crime, Violence, Drugs and Youth in the 1990s. *Journal of Criminal Law and Criminology*, 88 (4), 1223–1276; Silverman, E.B. 1999. *NYPD Battles Crime: Innovative Strategies in Policing*. Boston: Northeastern University Press; Sviridoff, M., Sadd S., Curtis R., and Grinc, R. 1992. *The Neighborhood Effects of New York City's Tactical Narcotics Team on Three Brooklyn Precincts*. Vera Institute of Justice.

RIC CURTIS

M

MACHISMO. Similar to the term "male chauvinism," the Spanish noun *machismo* describes a virile, overconfident, and dominating male. The adjective *machista*, "the person who embraces machismo and acts upon it," is etymologically related to macho. Macho translates as "male," and in the Spanish language it is most commonly used for animals. In addition, Spanish-speaking people often use this noun in order to qualify a person as exceptionally strong or brave, yet positive connotations of the word machista are rare, as it is usually perceived as derogative. Although the origin of the word is unknown, it is a conspicuous term in scholarly discourse of status, women's rights, men's roles, and moral judgments. Evelyn Stevens (1973, p. 90), in what has become the most frequently cited definition, described machismo as a "cult of virility" whose chief characteristics are "exaggerated aggressiveness and intransigence in male-to-male interpersonal relationships and arrogance and sexual aggression in male-to-female relationships."

Historically, machismo has been closely intertwined with street gang culture. Traditional gender roles are usually stressed within the street gang, in which men serve as the "protectors" of their subservient women. As a consequence, the term machismo has long had conflicting connotations throughout society. Nevertheless, although this sort of street culture can be considered negative in creating rebels and delinquents, it can also help enhance the perspectives of youth on issues of influence, power, and social status. For example, some African American gang members, according to Majors and Billson (1992, p. 4), aim to make their masculinity visible, in a society that disempowers black youth. Therefore, machismo in the street gang framework may promote youth empowerment in a society characterized by endemic joblessness for the lower classes. Yet Messerchmidt (1993, p. 182) presents street warfare as a direct result of idealized image of hegemonic masculinity. Confrontations between rival gangs, then, serves to bring about recognition of a macho reputation and status.

Latino gangs are another common example of the interconnection between street gangs and machismo. In fact, machismo is a conspicuous trait of the Latino street gang culture. Acting as a macho signifies protecting one's honor by any means necessary, even making use of violence to solve disputes. Street gang fighting is one of the manners in which gang members gain power and respect from their peers. Furthermore, success within the gang often depends on the youth's ability to defend his masculine image. Indeed, Latino gang members overemphasize masculinity as an attribute required for both survival and effective leadership. But in certain situations, machismo also implies an emphasis on the male role as the provider for the household, or the guardian of the family well-being. In this case, men are expected to take charge of their responsibilities as fathers and husbands. As a result, a cultural trait like machismo can be the foundation for both socially sanctioned behavior, and actions that are socially disruptive (like domestic battering or criminal gang activity).

In summary, machismo has been traditionally accepted as a cultural element of typically patriarchal societies. It permeates the polity, the legal system, as well as everyday social interactions in and outside the home. Machismo predisposes a community toward authoritarian attitudes from the individual and/or from the ruling elites in relation to others. It usually involves the subjugation of women by economic, physical, or emotional means. Machismo, therefore, is associated with a patriarchal and conservative worldview, which gives rise to countless problems of domestic abuse and street violence.

References/Suggested Readings: Majors, R., and Billson, J.M. 1992. *Cool Pose: The Dilemmas of Black Manhood in America*. New York: Touchstone; Messerschmidt, J.W. 1993. *Masculinities and Crime: Critique and Reconceptualization of Theory*. Lanham, MD: Rowman and Littlefield; Stevens, Evelyn P. 1973. Marianismo: The Other Face of Machismo in Latin America. In Ann Pescatello (ed.), *Female and Male in Latin America*. Pittsburgh: University of Pittsburgh Press.

YOLANDA MARTÍN

MEXICAN GANGS. The presence of street gangs in Mexico has a long history, whereas their public relevance is related to the emergence of *chavos banda* (youth gangs) in the 1980s. They were young people from urban-popular environments, often unemployed or employed in the underground economy; *esquinas* (street corners) were their living spaces, and they marked them through *pintas* (**graffiti**). They were passionate about rock-and-roll and were dressed with jeans and stamped T-shirts. The *banda* "grandparents" were the *pachucos,* a youth style born in Los Angeles in the 1940s among Mexican American youth, which later spread to other cities in the Northern frontier and the center of the country. The *banda*, "parents," also called *chavos de onda*, a youth movement born at the end of the 1960s that in Mexico included the *jipitecas*; politically concerned students who suffered the slaughter of 1968; and young *rocanroleros* from working-class origins who lived in the Avandaro Festival in 1973 their particular Woodstock. In the periphery of Mexico, and in other urban settlements, the banda is part of the neighbourhood's daily landscape, and its historical background is traced in this text.

Olvidados and Palomillas

In big modern cities like New York, Paris, London, there are plenty of miserable homes where children are undernourished, lack hygiene measures, are not attending school, are hidden behind the magnificent buildings—a real seedbed for future offenders. Society supposedly tries hard to amend this evil, but success is limited. Only in a near future will the children and adolescents' rights be claimed, so that they become useful for society. Mexico, the big modern society, is no exception to this universal rule. This is why this film based on real facts is not optimistic and leaves the solution to these problems to the progressive forces of society (Buñuel, 1980, p. 5).

Los Olvidados, released in 1950, is one of the first films by Buñuel in his Mexican period. The director explained that in his first idle times in Mexico City he wandered through the slums, observing how street gangs proliferated in a world of deprivation and distress that inspired his film. He did some research in the archives of a reformatory and chose non-professional actors. Unlike other films about marginal youth, Buñuel managed to avoid the prevailing tendency of moralization, and also managed to involve the audience in the tragic picture of the suburb. It was not usual to see the contrasting scenarios of urban poverty pictured in the cinema, revealing the human costs of the fast-moving rural-urban migration and the growth of Mexico City suburbs since the 1940s. Young gang people were the hidden side of the American dream. They were lost and forgotten like dogs without a collar. Institutions and official agencies were guilty of their oblivion, and literature and human sciences were accomplices of the first (only the police and sensationalist press "remembered" them regularly). Buñuel managed to find the hidden keys of this oblivion: forms of generation sociability substituting the family, particular language (the *caló*), characteristic clothing, occupation of urban space, consensual leadership, use of leisure time, integration through conflict, etc. These are similar keys to the ones analyzed by the authors of the school of Chicago that had studied North American city street gangs a few decades before (the poet Jacques Prévert, in a passionate praise of Buñuel's film, defined the main characters as "little wandering plants from the Mexican suburbs, prematurely pulled out from their mother's womb, from the earth and misery's womb"). But by focusing on the gruesome psychology of young men like Jaibo, the filmmaker ignored the relationships that the "forgotten" had with power and institutions, which largely explain their position in Mexican urban society.

Buñuel's portrait has remarkable parallels with the work developed by Oscar Lewis a few years later around the same scenarios, which would lead to his well-known notion of "culture of poverty." Lewis also wanted to make a work of social denunciation, by rescuing the poor of the big cities from academic oblivion and by putting forward in a realistic way their personal and social drama. Lewis also tried to explain this situation in psychological and cultural terms. It is however remarkable, that the author concentrates from the very beginning on the persistence of gangs among the poor. The existence of *palomillas* was one of the concomitant features of the "culture of poverty": "the neighbourhood gangs that went beyond the local boundaries" is regarded as one of the scarce signs of the organisation of the poor beyond the family (Lewis, 1986, pp. 112–113). The North American anthropologist described the environment in the center of Mexico City in the mid-1950s:

> The young people go to the same schools and belong to the "palomilla" of Casa Grande, they are friends forever and are loyal to each other. On Sunday nights there are balls in some patios, organised by young people and people of all ages go there. . . . Street fights are common among "palomillas." (Lewis, 1986, pp. 567–568)

Youth street gangs and stigmatizing images about them are not new phenomena in Mexico's history, although their emergence in the 1980s signals the birth of new and more persisting social metaphors. In order to outline the general situation of gangs, we will assess some of the mentioned structuring factors: generation, class, gender, ethnic, and territorial identities manifested by some contemporary Mexican youth styles.

Pachucos and Cholos

It is well known that pachucos are youth gangs, usually of Mexican origin, living in Southern cities of the United States. They are noted for their clothing and for their behavior and language. North American racists have often vented their anger against these instinctive rebels. But pachucos do not claim their race or their ancestors' nationality. Although their attitude reveals an obstinate and nearly fanatical will, such will does not affirm anything in particular, just the ambition—an ambiguous ambition, as we'll see—of being different. Pachucos do not want to go back to their Mexican origin; they don't want to mix with the North American life either—or so it seems. They deny themselves; they are full of contradictions, enigmas (Paz, 1990 [1950], p. 13).

Zoot Suit (1981), a film of the Chicano director Luis Valdez, explains the story of Henry Reyna, a young North American Mexican arrested and accused of murder in 1942, the same day he had joined the Marines. The film starts in a dance club in Los Angeles, where Henry's friends madly dance the mambo, the boogie-boogie, and the swing. They speak a strange caló (mixture of Spanglish and marginal argot) and their clothing is somewhat extravagant. Boys wear wide wing hats with a feather on one side, they have square-cut long hair, long jacket with big shoulder pads, black or pink shirt, a belt with an enormous buckle, the end of their trousers fastened to their ankles, and heavy sole shoes (it is the famous zoot suit clothing, similar to the one used by Harlem's blacks). Girls have short hair or a "rat" style tuft, jumper, short skirt, striped tights, and dancing shoes or "ballerinas." They are all "pachucos," characteristic youth subculture spread at the beginning of the 1940s made up of second-generation immigrants in California. After arguing with another gang, some Marines go to the party where a murder takes place. In spite of the lack of evidence, Henry is arrested, judged, and declared guilty. The film is based on real facts that brought pachucos to the foreground of public life. The totally tampered process was a great aggression against the rights of minorities, and marked the criminalization of pachucos. The public prosecutor even attributed their aggressiveness to "the Indian element that has come to the United States in big numbers, and that for their cultural and biological background is prone to violence, all they know or feel is the desire to use a knife or any lethal arm" (quoted in Valenzuela, 1988, pp. 43–44).

Pachuco became a popular evil image for Anglo-American society, but it became a symbol of national identity among Mexicans. Octavio Paz dedicated his first chapter of *El laberinto de la soledad* to pachucos (1950). In *El pachuco y otros extremos*, the author describes his arrival to Los Angeles in the 1940s, where there were already over a million Chicanos. There was a sort of "Mexicanity" floating in the air, very clearly to be seen in the attitude to life and "disguise" used by the street gangs of young pachucos, who had spread there. Between the culture of origin and the culture of destination, between the will of being different and the will of being equal, between infancy and adult life, the pachuco phenomenon seemed a "hybrid solution" to social anomie. His interpretation of them as "an extreme that Mexicans can grow to be" is classical now. Their response is hostile and distorted in front of a society that is rejecting them. They also try to create an "identity" that they cannot search in their community of origin any more. This identity turns into a "disguise that protects them and, at the same time, points them out and isolates them; hides them and shows them off" (Paz, 1990, p. 14). A series of repressing and assimilating processes are implemented in what Paz has called the inevitable "redemption" of the pachuco. But at the same time, their image is gaining prestige: their stigma is turning into an emblem, and their style is quickly spread though the South of the United States, the North frontier cities, and even Mexico City. The pachuco is a symbol of a time and of a country: Mexican identity in the beginning of urbanization, migration processes, mass culture; their resistance is also the whole country's resistance against assimilation. This is why chavos banda nowadays demand the recognition of their footprint as a generational precedent, as Ome Toxtli, a *chavo* from Neza says:

> In the '40s, when my parents were young, there were pachucos: baggy trousers, with the chain hanging here, gangster hat, shoulder pads and long jackets with wide sleeves, white shirts with a spot here. Pachucos were the street gangs of the '40s to the North of the country. It is a reaction to the culture mixture, the culture crash, I think it rose from the fights at the border after the revolution: they took the Chamizal, then they gave it back, *villistas* or *cristeros* pushed *gabachos* back home with their rifles, and so on. *Pachucos* looked after the border like no-one else. (Feixa, 1998).

By the end of the 1960s, Chicano gang members adopted a new style of clothing, talking, moving, tattooing, and making graffiti, which was inherited from the pachuco style, and was called *cholo* (traditionally used in different parts of Latin America to designate partially uneducated indigenous). Cholos would be the object of similar demonization processes (not racism-free) spread through the boundaries to various Mexican cities. The research by James Vigil (1990) about youth street gangs in the Mexican American neighborhoods in southern California does not allow the reader to consider them a temporary phenomenon. By undertaking the functions of the family, the school, and the law, Chicano youth gangs constitute one of the main instruments for second generation Mexican immigrants in the United States to construct their precarious social identity. Therefore, their syncretic, mestizo character, the mixture of clothing and music tendencies, sometimes irreconcilable (from rock music to ranchera) are not surprising. A young Zapoteco emigrant to Los Angeles talked to me about them:

> Cholos are sometimes born there, or they emigrate very young and then they join the Cholos. They have their own language, their own sounds and their own signals, and all these identify them. When someone does not identify, then they know it's the enemy. They want to release their youth energies, they want to be aggressive. From fifteen to eighteen you want to release your aggressiveness, do rough exercise. Sometimes they can't find a job, they search the union within the group, they search people with equal taste. They dress in the same way: baggy trousers, loose-fitting shirts, a handkerchief (tied to their head), a little hat, or maybe black glasses, or they cut their hair leaving little tails, or very short. There are many styles. Their tattoos: protest, panoramas, girls, tears, the Virgin of Guadalupe, they are usually on their heart, and sometimes they design a little snake. Even their cars are different: they have wide rims, different headlights, half painted in two different colours, very noisy. They like noisy music: heavy metal, black music, that one which is only talking, music you dance in the street, street music. They speak Spanglish. It's a mixture. Then, when they talk, they have to move in a certain way, it's like a sort of droning. Blacks also do this. They rock, even when they walk they have to swing. They take things from the black, the white, and the Mexican. Some Cholos now are in three colors: they have blacks, they have whites, and they have Mexicans. (Ric)

Chavos Banda and Chavos Fresa

From the beginning of the 1980s, a new youth style is present: the chavos banda. They appeared in the public stage in 1981, when the Panchitos from Santa Fe sent to the press their now famous manifesto. Unlike the *olvidados* ("forgotten") the chavos banda seem able to turn the stigma of their social condition into an emblem of identity. It is mostly the second generation of immigrants who are involved in this movement. And it is mostly the popular colonies around Distrito Federal where street gangs emerge. For their social origin and for their style, they were opposed to "chavos fresa," middle-class young people worrying about fashion and consuming who gathered at the discos in the "pink area."

While chavos banda are associated with a determined ecological context (the popular colony), with a way of dressing (jeans and leather jackets), with a certain music (rock and its variants), to an activity (unemployment or underground economy), with a way of having fun (the gig) to a meeting place (the corner) to their big rivalry with *la tira* (the police) and with a critical appropriation of the North American influence (rock and roll), chavos fresa's image evokes a different ecological context (residential districts), a way of dressing (according to the commercial fashion trends), a certain music (a sweetened pop and some Mexican music), an activity (studying), a way of having fun (the disco), a meeting place (the pink area, and the fashionable bars) and an imitation of the North American trend (football and consuming). While chavos banda make compact, permanent, territorially based group structures, based in the street, chavos fresa construct diffuse, individual, temporary sociocultural environments, which are not territorially based, but school or leisure based, and their meeting place is not the street, but bars and homes. While chavos banda have been stigmatized by the dominant culture as rebels without a cause, violent, and drug addicts, chavos fresa are seen as conformist, passive, harmless, and healthy, but in fact, they present non-stigmatized forms of diversion, violence, and intoxication.

Both styles gather cultural features from the social layers they are brewed in, and their extreme polarity is an expression of the social dualism that features in Mexican society (widened by the crisis). Cultural images do not always correspond to social conditions: there is a cultural circulation that makes urban-popular young people identify—or be identified—with chavos fresa, and that other middle-class young people identify with the gang. Many chavos banda are in high school or doing vocational training, and many young workers in the service sector adopt the fresa style. In the words of a chavo from Nezahualcóyotl City:

> There's everything here: *chavos banda, chavos fresa, chavos popis*. What are *chavos fresa* concerned about? Just getting the North American group gig, get discos close at six in the morning, 'cause three is too early, have Rod Stewart or Billy Joel playing live, so that they can spend half a worker's month wage getting to a gig. Some *chavos* among us are spiritless too. You can tell by the way they have fun. *Chavos fresa* go to the disco. There are three or four discos and some very expensive night clubs. In some discos they don't let you in if you wear sports shoes and trousers. The love for the American: Levis jeans. They are also understood and respected. But you tend to identify with your own people. (José Asunción)

Aida is a twenty-year-old business administration student at ITAM, one of the most renowned Mexican universities (where the local bourgeoisie are schooled).

Her opinion about chavos banda and chavos fresa contrasts with the ones heard so far:

> They call *fresa* anyone. For instance, I go to the disco and they offer me a drink: "No, thanks" "Don't be *fresa*!," If you're not in the craic, if you're quiet then you're a *fresa*. In the past, *fresas* used to be the ones who had money, but I like to deal with people from all social backgrounds. If you're in a lower social class and you know upper-class people are called *fresa*, well, even if you don't have the money, you have the prestige. . . . What do I think about *chavos banda*? I think they are out of line; they don't really know what they want, and this makes them aggressive. But I think they are also envious. They scratch good cars but, why do they do that? Because they don't have them. So it's a repressed society. . . . They are mostly lower class. There are also some high class, but they are really harsh girls.

Quinceañeras and Machinas

> I want to have my new mind / I don't want to be chained to your hands / I want to live my own life / I want to know what goes on without a lie / I want to tell you the truth about my ideas / because I am getting out of your repressing idea / I just want to live my own life. (Chavas Activas Punks, no. 3, 1988)

The articulation between youth cultures and gender in the Mexican case can be dealt with from two paradigms: the *quinceañera* (fifteen-year-old) and the *machina*. The quinceañera represents the pure, obedient, radiant young woman presented in society in the "age of illusion," as the transit to adult age and availability for marriage. Quinceañeras are a clear example of cultural appropriation and re-elaboration of rituals that belonged to the elite from subaltern classes. It is significant that this is exported to indigenous areas as a symbol of modernity. A young Zapoteca woman says:

> We didn't celebrate the *quinceañera* party in the past. People say: "What do they make this party for? It's a useless expense. They'd better become housemaids, they should pay for a good Mass and make a good expense." But nowadays most people do it. This is becoming a modern habit. This was not known here before. This is copied from other peoples, from other places, with the fifteen-year-old girls going to dance her waltz. This is an urban habit which we didn't do in the past. Some people go to Mexico, see how they celebrate the fifteen years of age, then they come back: "Guess what: we're going to celebrate the fifteen years of age for my daughter." But we just don't have this habit here. (Porfiria)

Quinceañeras are a model of construction of youth identity that accepts the role of the woman in society. Opposed to this model, there is an equivalent inverse model: the machina, which is the most radical way to become a chava banda (although many quiceañeras become machinas after a while, and the banda take part in many quinceañeras parties). *Machín* is the name of the leader of a gang, usually the most "skilled for punching" or the best strategist to "move" (lead) the gang in its daily activities. The term identifies "young" with "male." By extension, chavas that join the gang (who start "getting into" rock and roll and "popping in" gigs) can be called "machinas." Youth cultures are a reflection of the subaltern position of the woman in the Mexican society, according to the rhetoric of the official male chauvinism.

Since belonging to the gang demands full-time dedication, the girls' domestic duties make them play a secondary role. A chava banda from Neza told me:

> There are hardly any women in the gang. It's hard to know why there are so few *chavas*. Many of them gather and they are pure *chavas*. A few used to meet here, and I used to join them. I saw them for a few days, but then I didn't like their chat. I just didn't fit. They talked about boys all the time, and not about interesting things like books, or music or gigs: "Look, my boy left me, and Bicho asked me out, and such told me such and such," . . . I just find it boring. When *chavas* join the *banda* it's because they know someone there, or because they are with someone: "Hi, how are you doing?" And then they talk, and go to gigs with them. (Diana)

But the presence of chavas in gangs has not been specifically studied. Casuistry is diverse. It is necessary to analyze the place of chavas in gangs that are composed mainly by males (chavas can be their girlfriends, sisters, or neighbors). There are also gangs where the ratio of male to female members appears somewhat balanced, and some that are composed by females only (with revealing names like "Las castrado-ras" [The castrators], "Las viudas negras" [The black widows], etc.)—and their behaviors are sometimes more aggressive than those of male gangs. The feminist trend had its peak expression in the groups created by the punk gang in the mid-1980s, like *Chavas Activas Punk* (CHAPs) from which a few music groups of *puras chavas* emerged. The best known was *Virginidad Sacudida* (Shaken virginity). Why this name? Zappa, group leader and one of the most clear-thinking members of the gang says:

> In that time there were a few *chavas* who believed that by giving up virginity they should be mothers. No way! I sustained that women had other rights, not just this, this is a myth. . . . A few thought in the same way as me, and we tried to remove this sort of thinking. (quoted in Urteaga, 1998)

Indigenous and Paisarockers

To talk about the indigenous has always meant to talk about the leaders or chamans, prayers or healers, artisans or *milperos*, *mayordomos* or *macehuales*. The indigenous subject in ethnological texts has always been the adult male . . . very little has been said about Indian children . . . adolescents and young people belonging to ethnical groups have not been involved either, although they make up the future grown-up population, both in economic and cultural terms. Their possible concern about the constant and increasing worsening of the possibilities of socio-economic improvement has not been taken into account. (Acevedo, 1986, pp. 7–8).

The ethnical presence in the youth culture takes us to the indigenous peoples, to the "deep Mexico" which remains in cities as in the country. There are many parallels between young people and the indigenous. They are both subaltern groups; they are both under the state tutelage; they are both seen as immature and childish; they are both organised in community structures; both of them show exotic clothing and language; and both of them tend to have rituals and parties. From this perspective, it is surprising how little study has been devoted to the indigenous youth situation, in a country where indigenousness has become the official ideology (and where most indigenous people are under age twenty). This oblivion can be due to the fact that most indigenous cultures have never acknowledged in their history a life phase equivalent to what "youth" would be in the Western society. The young people's "invisibility" in ethnical communities can be explained by the subordinated status of young girls, by the early integration of boys to economic activities, and by the lack of specific signs of identity of adolescents, for instance in clothing. Many indigenous languages do not have a specific term to define youth, since the fundamental change of stage is from childhood to adulthood (through work and the "charge system") and from single to "citizen" (through marriage). In the words of an adult Zapoteco:

> The young people that were born during the '38, '40 up until the '50s had a much harder life than today's young people. I worked as hired hand in the ranch since I was ten years old. Natives from Santa Ana start serving since childhood, since they are ten, more or less. The steward is in charge of going from house to house: "I'm here to tell you that your boy has to participate with a third of the firewood in the next party," I had to gather firewood and bring it here. This was done in three occasions, and then another three times I had to take ocote wood to participate in the party that takes place in August. Then we must also join the religion: clean a corner in the temple and place an image. . . . Then we must serve as auxiliaries when we are about sixteen: guard the Municipal Palace, public buildings and we also patrol inside the city, street after street, as if we were the night watchmen (*serenos*) in big cities, in Oaxaca. I spent one year as an auxiliary when I was sixteen, and then, at the age of seventeen I had my first post as L/corporal. (Don Román)

Nowadays this situation has changed for many reasons: on the one hand, youth culture symbols (from music to fashion) reach the most remote areas in the country thanks to mass communication media, and it is possible to find youth indigenous who like rock music; on the other hand, most of the young people in certain areas emigrate to the United States, and when they come back to their communities they bring along some cultural elements that they learned there. It is not a simple assimilation but rather a syncretic process of adaptation. Sometimes the tension between the old and the new takes the form of generational conflict, but it also happens that the contact with the "outside" reinforces the young people's ethnical awareness (the leaders of Indian movements are usually university-educated people). In the words of Ric, a young Zapoteco who emigrated to Los Angeles, and who has temporarily come back to his Oaxaca town for the Patron's fiesta:

> Emigration has influenced society quite a lot. It started around 1975, when young men and upper-class people started to emigrate. In that time you could still count the number of people who emigrated from this town on the one hand. But once people got to see that young men went away, and found jobs, the rest tried to go too. Around '82, '83 the first mass escapes took place. Every August festival many young people left, because a relative came back for the festival, and took two or three of his cousins with them. The social effect has been big, because in this town, cultural and sports activities had started to increase, and then they started to go down. For instance, in the town square, many young people went to play basketball and the place wasn't big enough. There were even two basketball courts, and that wasn't enough. Today you go and you're bound to see no one playing. The street corners were full of little groups of friends, and you can't see them any more. They're all gone. There used to be a great respect for older people. They always greeted them with both hands. Now they don't do it any more. They see an adult and: "There you are!" Good manners, greetings are being lost due to the influence of TV. Many of these things started to come from there to here, and also from the people that come from the USA. (Ric)

Some data suggest the existence of indigenous street gangs where communities of origin maintain a certain cohesion (in different conferences and seminars I heard about *totonac* gangs in Xalapa, *otomies* in Querétaro). These gangs can maintain their ethnical terms of sociability (*la "bola"*) disguised with some of the urban youth culture (rock music). Often though, it is incompatible to be a street gang and to be indigenous (I heard that when a Totonaca young man became a militant rock and roller he was rejected by his community). The entrance of indigenous youth in street gangs and the change in their clothing habits can be seen as an expression of giving up their Indian identity. But let's not allow appearances to lead us: for certain chavos, you can be in a gang without giving up being Indian.

Some people come to Neza from the province. They are called *chundos*, an indigenous abbreviation.

> People in the neighbourhood are often racist: "Look at those *chundos*!" I don't feel like this: I think we're all the same, flesh and bone. They dress very humbly, they still wear their *huaraches*. Some of them still even wear hats. The women wear long dresses. Local girls wear short skirts and high boots to look prettier, or wear jeans, whereas the other ones are humble: they wear tire sandals, long dresses, and braids. They look very different. And the way they speak is different too. They speak in their own language among themselves. Then we meet at the *Diablillos* corner on Sundays and some *chundos* join. They only meet for drinking. Then they look for the Mafia, because they like marijuana and this is another reason for being in contact. They're a gang also, then they stay for a while. There was a *chundo* that also stayed with *Diablillos*, they called him *Tieso*. When someone dies, all the neighborhood sort of get together and comfort each other. Some of them make little cases, like rucksacks, and they give them to us. They also know how bad we are. They prefer the Northern music, the music from their side, the groups that play more sentimental music. Some of them are in the city and start to wear jeans, but the rest stay like this. It's for the money: if they earn little, a pair of jeans cost half the salary. (Podrido)

Jipitecas and Punketas

Mexican *jipitecas* searched in indigenous villages and cultures (the other) for the possibility of "becoming themselves." To approach "the other" was also to get to know and learn part of the Indian archaic cosmic vision (in the sense of circular and repetitive). Indigenous rituals were like doors that open into other sides and dimensions of time and space. The desire of being what one wants to be, beyond the myth (Urteaga. 1998).

Not only has youth culture influenced the indigenous world, indigenous cultures have also left their print on the youth culture. This syncretism can be clearly seen between jipitecas and *punketas*, Unlike European or North American hippies, for whom the rhetoric of the "savage" was purely ideological, for Mexican jipitecas the Indian factor was next to them and they could observe it to broaden their life experience (Monsiváis, 1977). This happened, especially, through experiences with hallucinogens (Maria Sabina's mushrooms and Don Juan's peyote attracted hippies from all over the world) and through clothing and garments.

Here in this country, hippies took up many of the indigenous crafts: *nahuas, mixes, seris, apaches, navajos, mayas, totonacas, chichimecas*. . . . Since hippy was a return to nature, love and peace, they took many of the indigenous clothing: wool trousers, indigenous-style colored clothes, guaraches, their guitar, their earrings; you could see women wearing *huipiles*, with woven bands of *huichol* origin. They were very religious also, the vibes of their amulets, full of pendants of a pre-Hispanic style. Many of the hippies in the past are now Mexicanist, they claim the Náhuatl culture. Even the jipis craftsman tradition has passed to the nowadays punk gang (Ome Toxtli).

It is more difficult to perceive indigenous presence among chavos banda. Some forms of community gang organisation—consensual leadership, co-operative (*cooperacha*) to buy beer or drugs, festive cycle of gigs (*tocadas*)—remind us of indigenous institutions of mutual help—like the "tequio" and the "guelaguetza." The Virgin of Guadalupe is present in the gang's collective imaginary (the gang is Guadalupana). Some chavos pilgrim to sanctuaries like Chalma and their belief in popular medicine is as deeply rooted as it is in their parents. Death (so present in punk symbols) is also connected to Indian and mestizo rituals. Walking through Chopo, the market that gathers thousands of young people from Mexico City weekly, one gets the impression of being in an indigenous *tianguis* (street market): goods and *changarrítos* (small stores) are in very good order, every tribe has its own space; even some Marias—indigenous women—do their selling while they hold their children. Exchange is not an exotic thing to do.

Another connecting field is the indigenous influence on Mexican rock music, analyzed by Urteaga (1998). In the 1970s, some of the best-known rock music groups had names like Náhuatl, Ritual, Coatlicue, Los Yaqui. In the 1980s the so-called ethno-rock appears as a syncretic musical fusion of a re-created/reinvented Indian identity (its maximum expressions would be Jorge Reyes, Chaac Mool, and Tribu, who experience new sound dimensions, usually well accepted by the gang). It is impressing to attend a Reyes gig in a magic place like the sculpture park at UNAM, or the ritual ceremonies of solstice and eclipse. For many punks—symbolic vanguard of chavos banda—the ethnic reinvention articulates some of their forms and contents. In some fanzines you can read that the first punk was Cuauhtémoc (last Azteca emperor, hero of the resistance against Hernán Cortés), both for his physical aspect and for his fierce attitude. The punk fierceness resembles the fierceness of pre-Hispanic cultures, and the resistance to assimilation reminds us of the "deep Mexico" so reluctant to integrate into the "national culture." Even the *pogo*—punk dance—is seen as a "savage dance." The community forms of organization, the promotion of craftsmanship, their liking of marijuana, their apocalyptic vision of the future are seen by young people as correlating factors between past and present Indians.

From Defé to Neza York

We now call it Nezayork, in a kind way. Neza is the third biggest city in the country. It's got like . . . four million? It's to point out its cosmopolitan feature, like to give it a distinction, but it's got nothing Saxon in it. Since we make a *caló* for many things, we're also calling Neza a nickname. New York is a mad city, with big buildings and smart people, and Neza is right the opposite, it's just at its dusk in industry, in economy, in culture, in everything. And to make an irony, we call it Neza York. (Ome Toxtli)

The phenomenon of youth cultures has been ascribed to the metropolitan area in Mexico. More exactly in FD and Mexico State. Since the times of jipitecas, the gang is said to be *chilanga*. A certain dialectics is acknowledged with urban areas in the north border (Tijuana and Ciudad Juárez). But the presence of gangs and groups in medium-size inland cities has not been studied so deeply, and youth identities in the South have been studied even less. Chavos bandas' initial ties to a certain territory (popular colonies in the big cities) seem undeniable. But as the communication circuits reach everywhere, styles and forms of organization settle in many other contexts like medium-sized and even small villages (Reguillo, 1993). In recent colonies where inhabitants are not fully settled yet, they don't have meeting spaces and they don't share signs of identity yet gangs replace other factors of sociability in the construction of a local identity, and neighbors appreciate them. Among cholos, for instance, the "natural" way of organization is the district.

The district represents the geographical boundaries controlled by a number of young people. Association starts at a very early age, and some districts started in a trial to organize children's clubs or sports teams. Some districts appeared from the splitting of a colony, and of some districts. For instance, when people moved from a colony, the young people that had left their district made up another cholo district in their new settlement (Valenzuela, 1988, p. 80).

Another model of organization are the so-called *colectivos* promoted by the punk scene in the 1980s. The colectivos have the aim of trespassing territorial boundaries and getting organized according to common tastes and activities. This formula turned out to be very positive in order to overcome internal rivalry, and they ended up in the solidarity movement after the earthquake in 1985. But with time, district identities emerged again. Colectivos also had their space of meeting—the market of El Chopo:

> A group can become a community by respecting every one's individuality. They all have the right to change, to evolve, to grow and enrich with the own experiences, and not just with what's given by the socialising institutions. . . . They all have the right to open their affective and intellectual horizons with the male or female friends they wish (read: no sectarianism product of the narrow-mindedness that most *chavos banda* from the neighbourhood suffer). (Urteaga, 1998, p. 8)

In Mexico City, the territorial dialectics of youth cultures is seen in the contrast between FD and the "lost cities" of Mexico State. Ciudad Nezahualcóyotl is an enormous dormitory city east of FD in Mexico State. The city is famous for the amount of local street gangs. There are always empty walls in the street where they can put a new name to their city as "nezayork" (or "nezallorc"). The Mierdas Punk is one of the best-known gangs in Neza. They started in 1981, after the confluence of a few gangs, and by the mid-1980s they had over 600 members (organized in sectors in different locations of the city). Most of the gang members are second-generation immigrants. Their parents "made it" when they migrated to FD, they built their houses, got a steady job, fought in the MUP, etc. Nearly all chavos are born in FD, therefore, they are urban, radically urban. You can tell they're urban by their style, which is different from the style in more recent parts of the city, where there's a bigger presence of pachanguero and paisarocker: "Mierdas brought a style of their own: a combination between Mohican and Sid Vicious. Even doing makeshift things: shoulder pads, screws, pieces of boot embedded in their clothes, Mad Max style T-shirts, were part of the Mierda style" (Ome Toxtli). Ethnic identity is therefore expressed as opposed to indigenous and rural, but also as opposed to the "gabacho," in their preference for the European punk, like the attitude of seasonal workers that come back from the North.

> When they talk about "the Bronze race" they talk about Mexicans, especially about indigenous and mestizos. It is a sort of nationalism, like the Nazis with Aryan race, something like that happened here with the Bronze race. The ones that move to the North claim this. Just like there is a Bronx race, Chicanos have a trend that is still Bronze race. When some of them come back, they bring this trend along, paint their walls, they sort of show off. (Ome Toxtli)

Mierdas feel clearly mestizo, they distinguish from mulattoes or the indigenous in Neza, although in the beginning some of the founders spoke Náhuatl. Ethnical distinctions within the gang are often only certain "racial" features: if one has more indigenous features has a nickname accordingly (Oaxaco, Negro). But territorial ties seem to prevail over the ethnic ones.

> In Neza there are indigenous youngsters too. They all belong to gangs now, there aren't any big differences. Maybe there are indigenous *chavos* gangs, but we don't even know if they really are indigenous. The difference does not come from there. You can't divide them according to their ethnicity. For instance, if someone from the South arrives, and gets mixed with the craic in the centre, they grow to adapt to the mess here. They very rarely continue to use their language. Maybe some of the big ones, those who were in a gang fifteen or twenty years ago still speak Nahua. (Ome Toxtli)

To a certain extent, the gang is the result of a process of "creolization," by which different ethnical and generation expressions present in Neza meet in a highly expressive style. The history of mierdas is also emblematic for their capacity of turning the changing social conditions of Mexican youth into metaphors. In the first stage, from 1981 until 1985, the predominant ideology was self-destruction, which is expressed by an aggressive aesthetic, tendency to violence, and massive drug consumption. Toward 1986, along with the emergence of civil society in the post-earthquake and the pre-election, the gang gave a big shift: from self-destruction to construction. MP changed to be "Punk Movement" and, together with other gangs, they promoted the constitution of BUN (Bandas Unidas de Neza, Neza United Gangs). All this brought along a manifold of cultural initiatives: fanzine releases, work with street children, promotion of cooperatives, constitution of Mierdas Films, participation in the university movement in 1986, exhibitions, gigs, creation of BAT (Brigadas Anti Tiras, Anti Cop Brigades) to raise awareness about human rights, organization Germen (supporting the different rock and roll groups), organization of courses for adults, gigs, etc. By the end of the decade, this trend coincided in general causes (trial from institutions to attract gangs, crash of popular urban movement after the electoral fraud in 1988) and particular causes (loss of the facilities where most of the initiatives took place, the older members leaving the gang, the numerical crisis of MP, and going back to territorial gangs).

Chavos banda are product and producers. They are the product of a specific space and time (the popular neighborhoods of the urban Mexico in a decade of crisis). They are producers of cultural artifacts (forms of sociability, music, leisure spaces, jargon, elements of a visual culture, tattoos, etc.) In this sense, they move at the crossroads of two big issues: parental cultures (most of their parents are indigenous peasants who migrated to cities) and the hegemonic culture (communication media, government institutions, police). In these crossroads, integration usually prevails over open conflict with institutions. This is why defiance usually happen at the symbolic level: contestation can be the disguise to hide the values of the traditional culture. But disguises are not always harmless: powers that be are always wary of Carnival, although this party will never change the structure of domination. This is exactly what chavos and chavas banda do: dramatize social change, represent in the public stage the contradictions of contemporary Mexico. Since the 1990s other gangs and youth lifestyles and have entered the Mexican scene: *darketos* (gothics), *raperos* (hip-hop), *raztecas* (a mixing between rastafarians and Aztec revitalism), *skatos* (skateboards), *vaqueros* (a kind of cowboy lover of Latin music styles), and finally *mareros* from Central America (see Reguillo, 2000; Nateras, 2002; Urteaga and Feixa, 2005). Nevertheless, the barrio-centered bandas have continued to be present in the social realities and imaginaries of Mexican postmodern cities, and to attract the teenagers of the following generations.

References/Suggested Readings: Acevedo, C. 1986. *Estudios sobre el ciclo vital*. México: INAH; Buñuel, L. 1980. *Los olvidados*. México: Era; Feixa, C. 1998. *El Reloj de Arena. Culturas juveniles en México*. México: Centro de Estudios e Investigaciones sobre la Juventud; Lewis, O. 1986. *Ensayos antropológicos*. México: Grijalbo; Monsiváis, C. 1977. La naturaleza de la onda. *Amor perdido*, 225–252; Nateras, A. (ed). 2002. *Jóvenes, culturas e identidades urbanas*. México: UAM; Paz, O. 1990. El pachuco y otros extremos. *El laberinto de la soledad*, 9–25; Reguillo, R. 1991. *En la calle otra vez. Las bandas: identidad urbana y usos de la comunicación*. Guadalajara: ITESO; Reguillo R. 2000. *Emergencia de culturas juveniles. Estrategias del desencanto*. Buenos Aires: Norma; Urteaga, M. 1998. *Por los Territorios del Rock. Identidades Juveniles y Rock Mexicano*. México: Culturas Populares/Causa Joven; Urteaga, M., and Feixa, C. 2005. De jóvenes, músicas y las dificultades de integrarse. In N. García Canclini (ed.), *La antropología urbana en México*, pp. 265–306. México: Fondo Cultura Económica; Valenzuela, J.M. 1988. *¡A la brava ése!. Cholos, punks, chavos banda*. Tijuana: El Colegio de la Frontera Norte; Vigil, J.D. 1990. *Barrio Gang. Street Life and Identify in Southern California*. Austin: University of Texas Press.

CARLES FEIXA

MORAL PANICS. It is 1964 on an English beach at Easter in the small seaside town of Clacton; the weather is cold and wet as usual, two groups of kids—Mods and Rockers—get into a spat, some bikes and scooters roar up and down the Front, windows are broken, some beach huts are wrecked. There was not a great disturbance—the TV footage looks derisory—but there was an extraordinary disturbance in the mass media commentary and among members of the public. "There was Dad asleep in the deckchair and Mum making sandcastles on the beach" said *The Daily Express*—one pictures them relaxed, pink in the sun, Dad perhaps with the traditional handkerchief tied around his head, and then suddenly a "Day of Terror" with the "Wild Ones" who "Beat Up The Town." This pattern was reported over a two-year period involving other seaside towns, roaming gangs of Mods and Rockers "from London" periodically "invaded," caused mayhem, displayed their arrogance and new affluence, insulted decent people, and were in a memorable phrase "sawdust caesars" puffed up with their own cowardice and aggression.

One reading of this series of events (and many like it) which is encountered frequently in the literature is that an event occurred (for a reason which is unimportant), that it was in itself of little consequence, but it was mistakenly reported and exaggerated by the mass media and consequently generated a feeling of fear and panic in the general public. All of this is, in part, true but such a simple liberal, linear model from media down to public scarcely captures the notion of moral panic. What are missing are both the sense of energy and intensity of this happening and, rather than a one-way process, this is a collective endeavor, for the youth, the media, the moral entrepreneurs, the control agents, and the public are, so to speak, accomplices in the action.

Stan Cohen's third edition of *Folk Devils and Moral Panics* reminds us of the continued importance of its contribution to deviancy theory. It is a richly analyzed text of much greater complexity and subtlety than many of the summaries and studies of moral panics which have followed it and it reads today with as much impact as it did in the early 1970s. Let us look more closely at the constituents of moral panic theory:

Symmetry

Both the subculture and the moral panic have to be explained—that is both the action and the reaction. Furthermore, they must be explored symmetrically, using the same model of analysis. Thus both moral panic and subculture are read as narratives where actors attempt to solve problems facing them. For this reason although in the main body of the book Cohen focuses largely on moral panic, in the fascinating introduction to the second edition, Symbols of Trouble, he turns to subculture and finally returns to moral panic in the introduction of the third edition.

Energy

A pulse of energy is introduced at each stage of the process. The kids on the beaches are driven by a creativity and exuberance which generates youth subcultures. They create but they also thrill to transgress: to get up peoples' noses, to annoy, to act out in front of the world's media. Thus Dick Hebdige's surmise in the wonderful *Hiding in the Light*: "spectacular youth cultures convert the fact of being under surveillance into the pleasure of being watched" (1988, p. 8). Furthermore, the public watching the skirmishes are not mere passive spectators: they are morally indignant, they are glad that magistrates and policeman reaffirm the boundaries of decency and propriety (as do the magistrates and police officers themselves). They are not merely manipulated recipients of media stereotypes—they *want* those messages, they read the popular papers, and watch the telly with gusto while the media, in turn, have learned that there is a ready market in winding up audiences—they have institutionalized moral indignation with both enthusiasm and self-righteousness (Cohen and Young, 1973).

The Real Problem, the Real Significance

Cohen is at pains to stress that there is a real problem there and that what is happening is not simply an illusion, a misperception. He touches base with Svend Ranulf's (1964) classic discussion of middle-class moral indignation where such intervention is seen to have a "disinterested" quality—it is a moral anger about something which does not directly affect their interests. Cohen, quite correctly, doubts that the distinction between interest and disinterest is a viable one (2002, p. 16); the hedonism and spontaneity of the new youth culture for the Mods *did* threaten the norms and standards of their elders:

> The Mods and rockers symbolized something far more important than what they actually did. They reached the delicate and ambivalent nerves through which post-war social change in Britain was experienced. No one wanted depressions or austerity but messages about "*never having it so good*" were ambivalent in that some people were having it too good and too quickly. . . . Resentment and jealousy were easily directed against the young, if only because of their increased spending power and sexual freedom. When this was combined with a too-open flouting of the work and leisure ethic, with violence and vandalism and drugtaking something more than the image of a peaceful Bank Holiday at the sea was being shattered. (2002, pp. 161–162)

You cannot have a moral panic unless there is something out there morally to panic about although it may not be the actual object of fear but a displacement of another fear or more frequently a mystification of the true threat of the actual object of dismay. The text of panic is, therefore, a transposition of fear—the very disproportionality and excess of the language, the venom of the stereotype signifies that something other than direct reporting is up. Listen to the much quoted *News of the World* report (September 21, 1969) on the hippie squat in 1969 in an elegant Georgian mansion in Piccadilly,

> Drug-taking, couples making love while others look on, a heavy mob armed with ironbars, filth and stench, foul language, that is the scene inside the hippies' fortress in London's Piccadilly. These are not rumours but facts, sordid facts which will shock ordinary decent living people. Drug taking and squalor, sex . . . and they'll get no state aid etc.

Savor the mixture of fascination and repulsion, attraction and condemnation, of a text which contains fragments of truth, rephrased and contextualized, as they sit there "lit only by the light of their drugged cigarettes" led by the elusive Dr. John, the *nom de guerre* of Phil Cohen who was later to resurface, in a wicked twist of fate, as a leading theoretician of subculture theory (see commentary in Young, 1971; Brake, 1985; and especially Cohen, 1995). If one takes these three "classic" accounts of moral panics: Stan Cohen's study of Mods and Rockers (1972) situated in 1964–1966, my own study of cannabis and hippies in *The Drugtakers* (1971) situated in 1968, and Stuart Hall and his team's study of the mugging panic *Policing the Crisis* (1978) situated in 1972, they all seem to represent major structural and value changes in industrial society as refracted through the prism of youth.

References/Suggested Readings: Brake, M. 1984. *Comparative Youth Culture*. London: RKP; Cohen, P. 1997. *Rethinking the Youth Question*. London: Macmillan; Cohen, S. 2002. *Folk Devils and Moral Panics* (3rd ed.). London: Routledge; Cohen, S., and Young, J. 1973. *The Manufacture of News*. London: Constable; Hall, S., Chritcher, C., Jefferson, T., Clarke, J., and Roberts, B. 1978. *Policing the Crisis*. London: Macmillan; Harrington, M. 1962. *The Other America*. New York: Macmillan; Hebdige, D. 1988. *Hiding in the Light*. London: Routledge; Ranulf, S. 1964. *Moral Indignation and Middle Class Psychology*. New York: Schocken Books; Young, J. 1971. *The Drugtakers*. London: Paladin; Young, J. 1999. *The Exclusive Society*. London: Sage.

JOCK YOUNG

N

NON-RACIST SKINHEADS. Non-racist skinheads began to organize in the late 1980s and early 1990s and frequently find themselves in violent confrontations with racist skinheads. Often referred to as SHARP (Skinheads Against Racial Prejudice) or SAR (Skinheads Against Racism) these groups consider themselves survivalists awaiting natural or politically generated disasters. Non-racist skinheads have been found to reject their parent's racism or were once members of racist skinhead groups (Wooden and Blazak, 2001). The first SHARP organization was created in New York City in 1987 and spread to other U.S. cities, Canada, and Europe by 1990 (Wood, 1999). Non-racist skinheads have organized anti-racist rallies and have challenged racist and neo-Nazi skinheads on the streets and in the media.

References/Suggested Readings: Wood, R.T. 1999. The Indigenous, Nonracist Origins of the American Skinhead Subculture. *Youth and Society*, 131–151; Wooden, W.S., and Blazak, R. 2001. *Renegade Kids, Suburban Outlaws: From Youth Culture to Delinquency.* Wadsworth.

ALBERT DICHIARA

O

OPERATION CEASEFIRE. Focused deterrence or pulling levers approaches to preventing gang violence (and other related crimes) emerged from the Boston Gun Project in the mid-1990s (Kennedy, 1997, 1998). The Boston Gun Project was a problem-oriented policing exercise conducted by a partnership of Harvard University researchers, front-line law enforcement practitioners, gang outreach workers, community figures, and others (Braga et al., 2001). Its research into serious youth violence in Boston revealed a pattern of cyclic violence within a small, highly active population of gangs and street drug crews, a diagnosis consistent with the larger gang literature and since replicated in a number of different jurisdictions (McGarrell and Chermak, 2003; Braga, Kennedy, and Tita, 2002; Wakeling, 2003; Tita et al., 2003; Dalton, 2003). Operation Ceasefire, the first focused deterrence intervention, was implemented in Boston in 1996 in response to this analysis. These strategies deploy enforcement, services, the moral voice of communities, and deliberate communication with offenders and groups of offenders in order to create a powerful deterrent to particular behavior by particular offenders.

Their basic elements include

- Selection of a particular crime problem, such as youth homicide or street drug dealing;
- Pulling together an interagency enforcement group—typically including police, probation, parole, state and federal prosecutors, and sometimes federal enforcement agencies—and a parallel group of service providers and community figures;
- Conducting research, usually relying heavily on the field experience of front-line police officers, to identify key offenders—and frequently *groups* of offenders, such as street gangs, drug crews, and the like—and the context of their behavior;
- Framing a special enforcement operation directed at those offenders and groups of offenders, and designed to substantially influence that context, for example by using any and all legal tools (or "levers") to sanction groups such as drug crews whose members commit serious violence;

- Matching those enforcement operations with parallel efforts to direct services and the moral voices of affected communities to those same offenders and groups;

- Communicating directly and repeatedly with offenders and groups to let them know that they are under particular scrutiny, what acts (such as shootings) will get special attention, when that has in fact happened to particular offenders and groups, and what they can do to avoid enforcement action. One form of this communication is the "forum," "notification," or "call-in," in which offenders are invited or directed (usually because they are on probation or parole) to attend face-to-face meetings with law enforcement officials, service providers, and community figures.

In Boston, for example, probation officers pulled members of street drug groups into meetings with authorities, service providers and community figures in which they were told that violence had led to comprehensive enforcement actions—such as federal drug investigations—against several violent groups, that violence by their groups would provoke similarly focused enforcement actions, that services were available to those who wished them, that the affected communities desperately wanted the violence to stop, and that groups that did not act violently would not get such unusual, high-level enforcement attention. Similar efforts in other jurisdictions followed. "Pulling levers" has been a central theme in the Justice Department's Strategic Approaches to Community Safety Initiative and Project Safe Neighborhoods initiative, and the basic ideas are increasingly showing up in local operations (see Dalton, 2003).

These interventions do not lend themselves to the kind of high-level random-assignment experimental designs that would give the strongest evaluations of their impact, and academic debate about their effectiveness continues (for a review of this discussion, see National Research Council, 2004). Evaluations from Boston and Indianapolis show city-wide reductions in homicide of around 50 percent, with larger effects on the younger, minority, mostly gun victimization at which both interventions were primarily directed. The same pattern has been seen in Minneapolis (Kennedy and Braga); Stockton, California (Wakeling, 2003); High Point and Winston-Salem, North Carolina (Dalton); and Portland, Oregon (Dalton). A weak, only partially implemented, version even appears to have been somewhat effective in east Los Angeles (Tita et al., 2003). An intervention in Chicago, using a quasi-experimental evaluation design, showed similar reductions in homicide in a pool of violent gun and gang offenders (Papachristos, Meares, and Fagan, 2005).

Outside the core matter of impact, the main issue with these strategies concerns sustainability. Many jurisdictions that have mounted apparently successful interventions—including Boston—have subsequently let them fall apart (Kennedy, 2002; Jonas, 2006). Whether and how the interventions can be sustained over time has thus emerged as a key concern of the academics and practitioners working with the approach.

References/Suggested Readings: Braga, Anthony A., Kennedy, David M., and Tita, George E. 2002. New Approaches to the Strategic Prevention of Gang and Group-Involved Violence. In C. Ronald Huff (ed.), *Gangs in America III*. Thousand Oaks, CA: Sage; Braga, Anthony A., Kennedy, David M., Waring, Elin J., and Piehl, Anne M. 2001. Problem-Oriented Policing, Deterrence, and Youth Violence: An Evaluation of Boston's Operation Ceasefire. *Journal of Research in Crime and Delinquency*, 38; Dalton, Erin. 2003. Lessons in Preventing Homicide. Project Safe Neighborhoods Report. Michigan State University, December; Jonas, Michael. 2006. Crime and Puzzlement. *Commonwealth Magazine* (Winter); Kennedy, David M. 1997. Pulling Levers: Chronic Offenders, High-Crime Settings, and a Theory of Prevention. *Valparaiso University Law Review*; Kennedy, David M. 1998. Pulling Levers: Getting Deterrence Right.

National Institute of Justice Journal (July); Kennedy, David M. 2002. We Can Make Boston Safe Again. *Boston Globe*, July 15; Kennedy, David M. and Anthony A. Braga. 1998. "Homicide in Minneapolis: Research for Problem Solving," *Homicide Studies* 2(3) (August); McGarrell, Edmund F., and Chermak, Steven. 2003. Strategic Approaches to Reducing Firearms Violence: Final Report on the Indianapolis Violence Reduction Partnership. Final report submitted to the National Institute of Justice; National Research Council. 2004. *Firearms and Violence: A Critical Review*. Washington, DC: Committee on Law and Justice, National Academies Press; Papachristos, Andrew V., Meares, Tracey, and Fagan, Jeffrey. 2005. Attention Felons: Evaluating Project Safe Neighborhoods in Chicago. Law School, University of Chicago, available online at papers.ssrn.com/sol3/papers.cfm?abstract_id=860685; Tita, George, Riley, K. Jack, Ridgeway, Greg, Grammich, Clifford, Abrahamse, Allan F., and Greenwood, Peter W. 2003. *Reducing Gun Violence: Results from an Intervention in East Los Angeles*. Rand Corporation; Wakeling, Stewart. 2003. *Ending Gang Homicide: Deterrence Can Work*. California Attorney General's Office/California Health and Human Services Agency, February.

DAVID KENNEDY

ORGANIZED CRIME. The history of organized crime in Europe and the United States tends to focus on the role organized crime has played in resistance by oppressed groups such as Italian peasants and ethnic immigrants into the United States. In Italy, organized crime emerged from the experience of peasants whose lives and labor were controlled by absentee landlords. These landlords used overseers, know as *gabellotti*, to manage day to day issues. The gabellotti formed the basis of the Mafia, and used their position to resist the landlords, victimize peasants, and mediate disputes between the two. It is this system of patronage and victimization that is said to have been brought to the United States by Italian immigrants, who modified it to accommodate American culture. For decades, organized crime thrived in the United States, principally among Italian Americans, but also among the Irish and Jewish immigrants in the urban areas. Similarly, African American organized crime developed in cities such as New York City and Los Angeles. Scholars have suggested that organized crime was a "ladder of social mobility" for these downtrodden groups, and as they were able to amass wealth and achieve positions in the middle and upper classes were able to abandon their criminal ways. The long-standing prominence of Italian Americans in organized crime defies this explanation. Some would argue that the Italian tradition of *omerta*, commonly known as the code of silence and non-cooperation, was the key to the success of the Italians. However, while this may be true, Italian American organized crime benefited from the indifference and complicity of the city leaders in New York City who failed to rein in such criminal activity. Italian American organized crime flourished due to the innovations of Lucky Luciano, who is credited with "Americanizing" the business practices of mobsters, who created the five family structure of Italian American organized crime in New York City, and who was responsible for organizing the heroin trade with the Sicilian Mafia. In the 1980s and 1990s the federal government was able to successfully prosecute leaders of organized crime using the Racketeer Influenced and Corrupt Organizations Act (RICO), among other federal statutes, and severely diminish the power of the Italian American Mafia. Similarly, authorities in Italy were able to counter the power of the Sicilian mafia, and other Italian organized crime groups such as N'drangheta and Camorra in the Maxi-Trials and Operation *Mani Puliti* (Clean Hands), which revealed the links between Italian organized crime groups and the Christian Democrat Party.

The recent history of organized crime in the United States and internationally illustrates significant changes in the structure and functions of organized crime groups. Most significant is the emergence of the so-called Russian Mafia, which is more an umbrella term for a variety of Russian and Eastern European/Western Asian crime groups. These groups are characterized by a more fluid organizational structure, unlike the "commission" model that Donald Cressey said was characteristic of the Italians. In addition, these groups specialize in crimes generally not common in traditional organized crime groups. Whereas in the past loan sharking, labor racketeering, extortion, and drug sales formed the core of criminal activities, the Russian groups are more likely to engage in phone card scams, fuel oil scams, medicare and insurance fraud, and other high-tech forms of crime, augmented by traditional extortion and violence. Other groups, such as the Japanese *yakuza,* Chinese Triads and street gangs, Vietnamese gangs, and Latin American drug cartels now populate the ranks of organized crime, bringing with them new traditions and activities.

Internationally organized crime groups have flourished in many countries and have motivated governments to create new legislation to control criminal activities previously unknown to those countries. For example in India organized crime has grown significantly with the change over from a socialist command economy to a free enterprise economy, particularly in the area of real estate. Organized criminal organizations have been noted in a number of countries, however the diversity of the criminal operations of these national groups appears to be limited when compared to the operations of the Italian Americans and the Italians. The changing nature of international organized crime has motivated some to rethink the challenge and control of organized crime by emphasizing the relationships between legitimate business and organized crime and the need to retool law enforcement to accommodate this new reality. The interconnectedness of the world economy makes the idea of national organized crime groups seem rather quaint and some now suggest that rather than thinking in terms of organized crime, we should view this from the perspective of transnational crime that crosses borders and links local criminal activity, such as the drug trade, to larger international criminal structures. This change in thinking has motivated some to call for greater international cooperation and training. The changes in international organized crime show the futility of focusing on ethnicity as a major explanatory variable in organized and directs attention toward the structure of the economy and the available criminal opportunities for groups seeking to gain power and riches through criminal activity.

References/Suggested Readings: Abadinsky, H. 2007. *Organized Crime.* New York: Thompson-Wadsworth; Cressey, D. 1969. *Theft of the Nation: The Structure and Operations of Organized Crime in America.* New York: Harper and Row; Smith, D.C. 1975. *The Mafia Mystique.* New York: Free Press.

ALBERT DICHIARA

OUTLAW BIKERS. Motorcycles, and the "biker" lifestyle, have become embedded within mainstream Americana over the past twenty-five years. The Harley-Davidson Big Twin motorcycle has emerged as a status symbol of sorts, and has been assimilated to contemporary America as symbolic of patriotism, freedom, and autonomy. As the mean age of motorcyclists has risen from thirty-three years to over forty, according to the National Highway Safety Administration, a much greater percentage of motorcycles purchased and operated on the road are now these large-capacity machines, which had theretofore been almost exclusively ridden and favored by those identified as "outlaw bikers." It has become downright trendy for vast hordes of "weekend warriors" to take to the highways each weekend, clad in chaps and heavily leathered, in a quest for the adventure and autonomy they once admired as teenagers of the baby boom generation.

And so it is a bit of a paradox that true outlaw bikers are most often perceived as a menacing, lumpen, and exceedingly dangerous phenomenon—prone to gratuitous, expressive acts of violence, and heavily involved in organized criminal activity. This perception can be misleading and is not accurate in general terms. But to begin with, it is essential to understand the differences between motorcycle enthusiast groups and what are generally referred to or defined as "motorcycle gangs." Gangs can be differentiated from hobbyists, whose activities are devoted to motorcycles in the context of weekend excursions, cross-country touring, or sport riding as exemplified by motocross or track racing. Many of these sport enthusiasts are affiliated with the American Motorcycle Association (AMA), an organization that predates the appearance of what are known as biker gangs. They are mainstream in the worldview, and consider motorcycling a sport. Outlaws, either affiliated with a club or independent, have little interest in gaining acceptance within either the larger community of neither motorcycle enthusiasts nor the wider society. When pressed, outlaw bikers will declare that they "don't fit—and don't care." These are the groups that have become emblematic, in the public eye, of "biker gangs." And from the 1970s through the late 1990s they became known as highly sophisticated **organized crime** networks that were deeply involved in narcotics trafficking, prostitution, the black-market weapons trade, and fencing operations. There is little doubt that a significant number of the most extremist factions of the major biker gangs engaged in these activities during this era, however most attempts by federal authorities to prosecute these activities as widespread conspiracies failed. And club officers, such as former **Hell's Angels** national President Sonny Barger, maintain that any illegal activity that involved Hell's Angels as individuals or even groups did not involve the Hell's Angels as an organization.

Most scholars agree that the subculture of outlaw biker gangism was born in the era following the end of World War II, when large numbers of traumatized and disaffected veterans returned to the United States. The continued estrangement and anomie experienced by many lower and working-class European Americans in the Western states presaged the formation of the first "biker" groups, most notably the Hell's Angels in California. These proto-bikers were characterized by their retention of the militaristic social structure, obsession with power, and dedicated to the formation, maintenance, and integrity of the in-group. The origin of the label Hell's Angels is often misstated in current literature; it has been attributed to the 1927 World War I movie of the same name, directed by Howard Hughes, and also has been traced to a B-17 bomber crew of the same name that served in the 303rd Bomber Squadron in the United States 8th Army Air Force. But in fact the name Hell's Angels was suggested to club members in 1948 by Arvid Olsen, a former commander of a unit of the Flying Tigers fighter group, which also carried the same moniker (Barker, 2005). Olsen was a close associate of the early Angels, though he never formally joined the club.

The root determinants of the rise of bike gangism are in many ways no different than those of urban street gangs in the present time—a reactive phenomenon to the anomie, hopelessness, and exclusion of late modernity. In 1947 approximately 500 largely unaffiliated and loosely organized proto-outlaws disrupted a recreational motorcycle tour sponsored by the mainstream American Motorcycle Association (AMA) in Hollister, California. One of the more organized groups was known as the Pissed Off Bastards. This became known as the Hollister Riot, and inspired film director Stanley Kramer to shoot *The Wild One*, starring Marlon Brando in 1953. The movie created the first popular image of the disaffected, existentially challenged biker-as-deviant. The Pissed Off Bastards are sometimes identified as the parent group of the Hell's Angels, who recently celebrated their fiftieth anniversary.

The 1-Percent Culture

Following the Hollister Riot, the AMA released a statement proclaiming that the participants in the disorder were unrepresentative of the 99 percent of all motorcyclists who were law-abiding and presented no threat to society. By inference, it was the 1 percent on the lunatic fringe that fomented the violence in and alleged takeover of Hollister. Clubs such as the Hell's Angels very quickly appropriated the term "one-percenter" as a badge of honor—it continues to provide a mechanism of boundary establishment between the subculture of bikerism and the wider society. And it is quite true that the 1 percent culture rejects mainstream norms and does not fit, maintaining an alternative social milieu that revolves around a cluster of activities specific to the biker subculture. These activities include:

- The acquisition and maintenance of Harley-Davidson V-Twin motorcycles.
- Organized "runs," or large-scale excursions involving the members of the club or club chapter.
- Activities necessary to acquire and maintain dominance within a particular geographic area. This is more akin to a "jurisdiction" than a street gang's "turf," because other bikers are often tolerated under conditions that symbolize fealty and/or subjugation.
- The maintenance of a clubhouse.
- The organization of the club into a hierarchical, militarized structure. There is in most instances a club "constitution," which establishes a code of conduct and sets the normative expectations agreed upon by the group.
- The "constitution" sets and controls social relations both within the group and as the group may interact with other biker groups and members of the wider society.

Most biker groups require a period of apprenticeship before a new member is admitted. A prospective member first engages in social activity associated with the club, in a sense both the aspirant as well as the club begins the process of discernment. If one or more club members formally nominate the aspirant for membership, he is designated as a "prospect" or a "striker." This status places the prospective member in the category of apprentice member, and can last from six months up to two years. Research indicates that the prospect period is generally shorter in time of conflict. The "prospecting" process often involves hazing rituals and identity re-formation exercises, which are carefully constructed to strengthen the prospect's ties to the group at the same time as they weaken the prospect's ties to the outside world. If the prospect passes through the probationary period, he is then provided with his "colors" in a final initiation ritual.

Colors are symbolic of the essence of what it means to be an outlaw biker. Upon acceptance and initiation, a new member is provided with a blue jean cutoff jacket. It may have been worn through the prospect phase, with some part of the club's nomenclature emblazoned upon it, but when the prospect is admitted to full membership he receives the actual "patch," which is sewn onto the back of the vest. There are sometimes "rockers" that identify the city, region, and/or state where the club or club chapter is located. Only the most powerful of the clubs will "fly colors" that contain a bottom rocker that is labeled with a state—staking that claim signifies dominant status within the state, and if a club seeks to avoid conflict with, for example, the Hell's Angels in the State of California—it would likely identify a city or county on the bottom rocker. Colors are held sacred, and if lost a club member will face serious to extreme sanction. In fact, the Mongols fought a seventeen-year war with the Hell's Angels that was largely based upon the right to wear a bottom rocker emblazoned with the label "California." The Mongols, a gang with roots in Chicano prison gangs in the California penal archipelago, have developed a violently oppositional subculture. And although they are relatively small in numbers in comparison with the Hell's Angels, the Mongols prevailed in their quest to fly colors containing "California." Although the two clubs remain in a state of war, the Angels eventually conceded the Mongols' right to wear the bottom rocker, conceding that they had earned the right (Queen, 2002).

It should be noted that biker gangism is a male-dominated subculture. Women are assigned to one of three categories (Wolf, 1991):

- Old ladies (wives or steady girlfriends)
- Mamas (club groupies)
- Broads (objects of sexual gratification)

Old ladies are afforded the respect due to the club member—she is not subject to advances by other club members and will be protected both external as well as internal interference. Old ladies are relegated to a tightly controlled subordinate status, and in fact are considered "property" in some club constitutions. Mamas are loosely associated with the club culture—socially and in some instances economically. Broads are unaffiliated with the club, and can be arbitrarily exploited and/or abused sexually.

And though there have been some isolated examples of multi-racial biker gangs (such as the Ching-a-Ling Nomads in New York City in the 1970's), biker gangs are largely a domain of lower, to lower working-class European Americans. Along with a small group of Ching-a-lings that remain active in Queens, New York, the East Bay Dragons in Oakland, California, and the Wheels of Soul and Ghetto Riders clubs in New Jersey are notable exceptions. The Mongols are the sole example of a gang with an interstate network of chapters that are multi-ethnic, though Chicanos are the dominant group (Queen, 2002).

Conflict and Innovation

Scholars contend that most outlaw biker groups contain members who fall loosely within two categorical distinctions—radical or conservative (Wolf, 1991; Quinn, 2001). The radicals will be more likely to adhere dogmatically to biker subcultural themes such as independence from any reliance on the wider society, group solidarity, maintenance of boundaries, and the often violent defense of jurisdiction. Scholars argue that the "radical factions" were instrumental to the rapid expansion of what are known as the Big Four clubs in the late 1970s to the 1990s. This process of expansion was born of the need to accumulate power and resources, and has been termed the "retrenchment" period, where the Big Four clubs absorbed most of the more localized groups. The expansion of the clubs was at first a political phenomenon. The battle for survival between the Hell's Angels and the Mongols in California, the Hell's Angels and the Outlaws in the Southern states, and the Hell's Angels and the Pagans in the Northeast necessitated expansion—increased numbers of members provided more available club members for conflict.

It was during this period that many of the smaller outlaw clubs were "patched over" by one of the Big Four. An example of this would be the Dirty Dozen MC in Pima County, Arizona, which was patched over by the Hell's Angels in 1996. But the economic gain reaped from illegal activity and the attendant violence provoked a law enforcement response that unleashed an unprecedented assault on biker gangs. By the end of the twentieth century, there was a discernible shift in the focus of outlaw bikerdom—it became less a counter-culture as the economic gains of the retrenchment era enabled a more secure financial base. Truces and armistice agreements were arrived at by the Big Four, and with exceptions have been maintained. However, the Bandidos, Outlaws, Pagans, and Mongols continue to maintain an alliance against the Hell's Angels and their smaller allies, and on occasion the armed truce is broken.

Bikers and Criminality

It should be remembered that outlaw bikers are primarily concerned with the biker lifestyle and culture. Runs, party activities, and group solidarity are the themes emphasized in the public rhetoric now fashionable among the various outlaw clubs, and have always been central to biker gangism. Participant-observer research is thin due to the difficulty of gaining entry to the secretive, insular, and reactively hostile world of outlaw bikers. But the work that has been done often finds that the overriding concern of outlaws is to be left alone. Biker subcultures represent elaborate and tightly organized social communities; most clubs have created complex constitutions enshrining their normative beliefs, and conduct regular meetings controlled by Robert's Rules of Order. They are governed through the election of Executive Boards, which are organized as hierarchies that provide a mechanism of social control. They engage in economic activities that are necessary to sustain the viability of the group in terms of motorcycle maintenance, housing needs, club facility upkeep, and even provide for welfare and legal defense funds for members. Runs are in essence celebratory manifestations of their culture—ritualistic outbursts of exuberance and solidarity.

Although there is no doubt that members of outlaw clubs, and even radical factions of varying proportionate representation within clubs have and continue to engage in criminal activity that is often violent in the extreme, much of this activity can be directly associated with the survivalist mentality that accompanied the period of intense inter-club warfare that began in the late 1970s and continues today, though at a lower level. Under a perceived state of siege, many club members continue to turn to crime and violence to accumulate financial resources and a greater share of cultural capital. It should be remembered that the collective memories and group subcultures of outlaw motorcycle gangism continue to revolve around the extended family "brotherhood" and the militaristic and hierarchical structures that were developed to preserve it. Some of the most violent groups, such as the Mongols, trace additional roots to the prison subculture and their activities reflect the consequences of the mass incarceration policies of the late modern era in the United States.

In the first decade of the twenty-first century, the largest clubs have begun to represent themselves in the media as less extreme, and groups such as the Hell's Angels,

Bandidos, and Outlaws maintain sophisticated and well-funded public relations efforts that reflect a newly professed desire to enter the mainstream—at least in the economic sense. Web pages advertise apparel and other items for sale to the general public, and some legendary bikers have made careers of appearing in movies and accepting paid speaking engagements. Outlaw bikers donate some of this revenue to mainstream charities, and continue to present an avowedly conservative political ideology.

The term "1 percenter" represents a full-time commitment to participation in club activities and the maintenance of the group as an autonomous, economically viable tribe. Although the Hell's Angels no longer employ the term as they continue to develop legitimate means of income generation, they are still dedicated to maintaining their independence from the wider society. However, there are other biker groups that resemble the 1 percenters in appearance and activities—but on a part-time basis. These groups, sometimes affiliated with national associations that are known as "modified motorcycle associations" (as differentiated from the wholly mainstream AMA) are distinguished by a greater proportion of the membership that hold full-time employment and live in traditional, nuclear family units. Despite a greater commitment to the mainstream, these groups engage in similar activities and often abide by many of the same normative assumptions as do outlaws. These groups might be considered "outlaws light." One example of a modified club might be the Huns of Arizona.

The Big Four Clubs and Their Estimated Numbers in 2005

(Employing Barker's [2005] "best guess" estimate and club Web sites)

- The Bandidos Motorcycle Club (Bandido Nation)
  72 Chapters in 14 states
  81 chapters in 12 countries outside the United States
  Estimated membership:
  United States: 510 to 2,125
  Worldwide: 948 to 4,050
- The Hell's Angels Motorcycle Club
  Up to 65 chapters in the United States (30 listed on the HAMC Web site)
  Up to 35 worldwide
  Estimated membership:
  600 to 2,500 members worldwide
- The Outlaws Motorcycle Club
  80 chapters in 20 states
  116 chapters in 14 countries worldwide
  Estimated membership:
  936 to 3,900 world wide
  396 to 1,650 in the U.S.
- The Pagans Motorcycle Club
  Up to 44 chapters in the Eastern United States
  Up to 900 members
  No reliable estimates are available for foreign expansion activity.

Pagans are said to be suffering from a decline in both members as well as chapter expansion activity due to reclusive cultural identity as well as pressure from law enforcement and inter–club warfare (Barker, 2005).

References/Suggested Readings: Barger, Sonny. 2000. *Hells Angel*. New York: Harper Collins; Barker, Tom. 2005. One Percent Bikers Clubs: A Description. *Trends in Organized Crime*, 9 (1); Queen, William. 2002. *Under and Alone*. New York: Random House; Quinn, James F., Angels, Bandidos. 2001. Outlaws and Pagans: The Evolution of Organized Crime among the Big Four 1% Motorcycle Clubs. *Deviant Behavior: An Interdisciplinary Journal*, 22 (4), 379–399; Thompson, Hunter S. 1966/1967. *Hell's Angels*. New York: Ballantine Press; Wolf, Daniel R. 1991. *The Rebels: A Brotherhood of Outlaw Bikers*. Toronto: University of Toronto Press; Zito, Chuck. 2002. *Street Justice*. New York: St. Martin's Press.

MITCH LIBRETT

P

PATHE (POSITIVE ACTION THROUGH HOLISTIC EDUCATION). PATHE is an integration of services within an existing school management structure intended to produce academic gains and improved behavior. Not solely a "program," it is a structure and process for managing broad school improvement, taking into account each school's strengths and needs. PATHE was originated by educators in the Charleston County, South Carolina, School District and is currently being replicated in Maryland school districts by researchers at the University of Maryland, College Park (Gottfredson, n.d.).

The Office of Juvenile Justice and Delinquency Prevention (OJJDP) describes PATHE as a universal comprehensive school organizational change program that is used in secondary schools to reduce school disorder and improve the school environment, in turn enhancing student experiences and attitudes about school. The program targets all students in middle schools and high schools, serving large numbers of minority youths in both inner cities and impoverished rural areas (Project PATHE, 2002).

The Positive Action program is unique in that it deals with the whole child, teaching physical, intellectual, social, and emotional skills. The goal is to produce positive change in students and schools (Positive Action, 2006).

Components of PATHE

OJJDP, in their article titled "Project PATHE," highlighted five major components:

1. Staff, student, and community participation in planning
2. School-wide organizational changes aimed at increasing academic performance
3. School-wide organizational changes aimed at enhancing school climate
4. Programs to prepare students for careers
5. Academic and affective services for high-risk youth

The program design is unique in its comprehensive coverage and in its simultaneous concentration on organizations and individual level change. The school's climate is enhanced through added extracurricular activities, peer counseling, and school pride campaigns. Job-seeking skills programs emphasize career attainment. At-risk students receive additional monitoring, tutoring, and counseling (Project PATHE, 2002).

Once a site has determined the prevalence of risk factors and the existence of protective factors, programs are selected to help decrease those risk factors while maintaining and building on the protective factors. Positive Action serves both purposes concurrently, and addresses the following risk and protective factors outlined by Hawkins and Catalano in numerous studies on prevention science (Positive Action, 2006).

Protective Factors Addressed

- Individual
  - Recognition
  - Resiliency
  - Competencies and skills

- Social Domains: Family, School, Peer Group, and Neighborhood
  - Bonding
  - Healthy beliefs and clear standards
  - Pro-social opportunities
  - Reinforced for pro-social involvement

Risk Factors Addressed

- Individual/Peer
  - Friends who engage in the problem behavior
  - Early initiation of the problem behavior
  - Early and persistent antisocial behavior
  - Gang involvement

- School
  - Academic failure
  - Lack of commitment to school

- Family
  - Family conflict
  - Family history of the problem behavior
  - Family management problems
  - Favorable attitudes toward the problem behavior
  - Favorable parental attitudes toward the problem behavior

- Community
  - Availability of drugs
  - Community laws and norms favorable toward drug use, firearms, and crime
  - Low neighborhood attachment and community disorganization

Evaluation

The initial project design included four experimental middle schools, one control middle school, three experimental high schools, and one control high school.

Students were predominantly African American and resided in both urban and rural areas. The school was the unit of analysis. Students were surveyed in 1981, 1982, and 1983. In 1981 a random sample of 300 students was surveyed in the participating high schools. The entire student and teacher populations were surveyed in the other years (with response rates of 79 percent to 86 percent). In the fall of 1982 the comparison high school closed. Thus, the evaluation covers a three-year period for the middle schools in the sample and a one-year period for high schools (Gottfredson, n.d.).

Evaluation Outcome

High school students reported significant decreases in delinquency and drug involvement and fewer school suspensions and less punishment than the control group. Students in the program who received special academic and counseling services reported significantly higher grades and were less likely to repeat a grade than students who did not receive these services. High school seniors who received these services were also more likely to graduate than those who did not receive the services (Project PATHE, 2002). For middle school students in the intervention, there were declines in suspensions. PATHE high schools, compared with the control groups, showed that self-reported delinquency (including drug involvement suspensions and school punishments) declined, and school climate and discipline management improved in all the treatment schools. At-risk students showed higher rates of graduation and standardized achievement tests and increased school attendance (Gottfredson, n.d.).

References/Suggested Readings: Catalano, R.F. 1999. *School and Community Interventions to Prevent Serious and Violent Offending.* Washington, DC: U.S. Department of Justice, Office of Justice Programs, Office of Juvenile Justice and Delinquency Prevention; Gottfredson, D. n.d. *The Source Book of Drug and Violence Prevention Programs for Children and Adolescents.* New Jersey: Violence Institute of New Jersey at UMDNJ. Retrieved October 18, 2006, from vinst.umdnj.edu/sdfs/Abstract; Helping America's Youth: Project PATHE. 2002

RACQUEL ELLIS

POLICE REPRESSION TACTICS AGAINST U.S. STREET GANGS. Coordinated and systematic police actions aimed at repressing, containing, and eventually eradicating lower class street gang activities in the United States have been in vogue since the mid-1970s (Jimenez, 2000) when the law enforcement campaign against gangs called TRASH (Total Resources Against Street Hoodlums) was initiated in east Los Angeles. This movement toward a more punitive, paramilitary view of the street gang phenomenon represented a shift from the police-community problem-solving social controls traditionally used for dealing with youth "deviants," particularly in urban areas, since the turn of the century (Thrasher, 1927). Such a shift in tactics mirrored a hardening in attitudes across local, state, and federal governments toward inner-city populations in the post-1960s period. As a progressive, reformist phase of U.S. history waned, an era of neo-conservativism was fully instituted with the first Reagan administration at the end of the 1970s. During the decade that followed, the generalized belief that the increasing crime rate, often reduced to the signifying elements of gangs, drugs, and violence, was indissolubly linked to the pathological character and cultural deficits of the inner-city poor (Bennett, Diliulio, and Walters,

1996), became an ideological mainstay behind calls for more aggressive law enforcement, particularly with regard to lower class, mainly minority street gangs.

While this change in national politics is the foreground to some of the anti-gang initiatives witnessed in recent years, it is also important to note the background factors. In the final two decades of the last century, the United States has seen a massive downsizing of its social safety net, including sustained government cuts in welfare, housing, health, and public education, while tax rates on the nation's wealthiest classes and corporations have shrunk to historic lows. To manage the increase in the numbers of relatively deprived populations of the inner city and the suburbs, from whence gangs draw the bulk of their recruits, sharp increases in the budgets and resources of law enforcement and correctional institutions have been the rule (Wacquant, 2002). This sea change in what some have called population management policies (Spitzer, 1975) has been widely noted by a range of criminologists with Garland (2001), for example, explaining this development as the normalization of a "culture of control," while Young (1999) views these endless crusades on gangs in particular and on poor communities in general as part of a tendency toward an elite-centered "exclusionary society." It is in this political and historical context that the penchant for gang repression among both planners and practitioners of law enforcement has become so prevalent.

As Spergel (1995) notes, California has tended to set the trend in the moral and physical war on street gangs and by the late 1980s strategies of suppression were the most common tactics in local, state, and federal agencies throughout the United States (Curry and Decker, 2003). While California was now throwing ever more funding and personnel into programs such as the Los Angeles Police Department's renamed Community Resources Against Street Hoodlums (CRASH) and the Los Angeles County Sheriffs' Gang Enforcement Team (GET), Chicago was similarly upping the urban ante with its specialized gang task force mushrooming to more than 500 uniformed personnel by 1992. Meanwhile, as anti-gang police units were being formed and expanded throughout the nation anti-gang legal statutes were being passed such as California's Street Terrorism Enforcement and Prevention (STEP) Act of 1988 and a string of gang injunctions such as the City of Chicago's Gang Congregation Ordinance in 1992 (later voided as unconstitutional by the Chicago Supreme Court in 1997), followed by local injunctions against specific street gangs in San Jose, Pasadena, and Redondo Beach. Summing up this barrage of gang repression strategies, Klein (1995) lists five major approaches as observed in California: (1) prosecution, (2) specialized enforcement, (3) specialized probation, (4) targeting of gang members in juvenile detention centers and prison, and (5) gang injunctions. Klein concludes, however, that suppression rarely works and in fact most often leads to the opposite effect, promoting gang cohesion and gang proliferation despite the ongoing arrests and imprisonment of tens of thousands of gang members nationally.

In a recent work by Hayden (2004), the former California state senator, having headed an official inquiry into the Ramparts police department in Los Angeles leading to the prosecution of numerous specialized gang officers and the disbandment of the city's largest and most powerful gang unit, argues that

the apparatus for fighting gangs was institutionalized gradually by the passage of six multi-billon dollar federal anti-crime bills, the drug war's draconian penalties for

possession of crack cocaine, mandatory minimum sentencing laws, three-strikes penalties, and the greatest splurge of prison construction in the nation's history. By the Nineties, every police department in America harbored an aggressive anti-gang unit, was
busy stopping, frisking, profiling and locking up hundreds of thousands of at-risk youth
until the United States, with five percent of the world's population, contained twenty
percent of the world's inmates. (Hayden 2004, p. 23)

Recently, the ineffectiveness of the suppression strategy now in place for more
than twenty years is indicated by data provided by the California State's Department
of Corrections. According to the state's gang identification system for prisons, fully
one-third of California's 160,000 inmates are now members of a gang (Hayden,
personal communication), while William Bratton, Chief of the Los Angeles Police
Department, has publicly stated there has been no diminution in street gang membership and that the continued growth of this population represents the gravest
threat to public order in the United States (Wood, 2004).

Currently, it is common to see gang suppression campaigns organized across a
range of law enforcement agencies, such as occurred in New York City in the late
1990s. During what was called Operation Crown, which targeted the **Almighty
Latin King and Queen Nation**, a New York State street gang/organization, agents
from the New York Police Department, Federal Bureau of Investigation, Immigration
and Naturalization Service, New York State Police, and the federal Drug Enforcement
Agency in May 1998 carried out the biggest police sweep in New York City since the
anti-communist Palmer raids of 1918–1921 (Brotherton and Barrios, 2004). Employing a range of repression techniques including systematic harassment of assumed
members, phone taps, paid informants, stings, and photographic surveillance, the
strategy took on a political character as the administration of Mayor Giuliani repeatedly used the war against gangs to bolster its public image (Brotherton and Barrios, 2004). Although it would be an exaggeration to say that political gamesman-
ship is often behind repressive anti-gang policy, for there are many occasions when
hard-pressed communities are the first to call for tougher measures against local
anti-social elements, the continual spectacle of police repression in everyday life and
the ideology behind purging pathological gang elements from an otherwise healthy
society ultimately undermine the achievement of a safe and stable civil society. As
many criminologists have argued, this form of reactive surgery is no substitute for
prevention and cure. As long as the gang phenomenon is primarily defined as a
criminal rather than as a social problem, public resources will continue to support
repressive gang policy with little to show for it other than short-term hollow victo-
ries and long-term disenfranchised and disengaged "problem populations."

References/Suggested Readings: Bennett, W., Diliulio John, J. Jr., and Walters, John P. 1996.
Body Count: Moral Poverty . . . And How to Win America's War against Crime and Drugs.
New York: Simon and Schuster; Brotherton, D.C., and Barrios, L. 2004. *The Almighty Latin
King and Queen Nation: Street Politics and the Transformation of a New York Gang.* New
York: Columbia University Press; Curry, G., Decker, D., and Decker, S.H. 2003. *Confronting
Gangs: Crime and Community.* Los Angeles: Roxbury; Garland, D. 2001. *The Culture of
Control: Crime and Social Order in Contemporary Society.* Chicago: University of Chicago
Press; Hayden, T. 2004. *Street Wars: Gangs and the Future of Violence.* New York: New Press;
Jimenez, R. 1999. *The Suppression Movement against Gangs: The Case of East Los Angeles.*
Ann Arbor: University of Michigan, unpublished manuscript; Klein, M. 1995. *The American
Street Gang: Its Nature, Prevalence, and Control.* New York: Oxford University Press;

Spergel, I. 1995. *The Youth Gang Problem: A Community Approach*. New York: Oxford University Press; Spitzer, S. 1975. Toward a Marxian Theory of Deviance. *Social Problems*, 22, 641–651; Thrasher, F. 1927. *The Gang: A Study of 1,313 Gangs in Chicago*. Chicago: University of Chicago Press; Wacquant, L. 2002. Deadly Symbiosis. *Boston Review*, May, 1–25; Wood, D.B. 2004. As Gangs Rise, so Do Calls for a U.S.-Dragnet. *Christian Science Monitor*, 1 (February); Young, J. 1999. *The Exclusive Society: Social Exclusion, Crime and Difference in Late Modernity*. London: Sage.

DAVID C. BROTHERTON

Q

QUALITATIVE ANALYSIS AND GANGS. All data in the social sciences involve social meaning. The interpretive method or hermeneutic perspective is a comprehensive term that refers to qualitative analysis, as an approach that is distinct from quantitative analysis, but not disconsonant with it. Qualitative analysis is most closely related to the interpretive method. Interpretivists strive for empathetic understanding, or to use Max Weber's term, *verstehen*, whereby they endeavor to understand the inner lives and viewpoint(s) of gang members and of those associated with them. This is done through the collection and analysis of "soft" or richly descriptive and often nuanced data—interviews, graffiti, photographs, tattoos, emblems, anything that is discursive—as well as accounts of observable behavior. This work is done within the context of field research, case studies, or ethnomethodology. If we want to analyze gangs and their place in North American culture, we might begin, as quantitative analysts, to gather statistics on gangs—the numbers of members, the amount of money generated, mortality rates . . . the potential list is extensive. But this would provide a different body of knowledge from what a qualitative analyst would seek. The interpretive theorist would want to know what a gang member's experience of membership is like. What are the sights, feelings, and emotions of gang membership? What is the experience like?

Qualitative researchers seek to convey what given events mean to their participants rather than trying to interpret those events themselves. Every effort is made to view interactions without the interference of one's own preconceptions. Interpretive researchers' studies are regarded as humanistic, because they value all viewpoints, and endeavor to "give a voice" to people who may be rarely heard (Anderson, 1996). For instance, where only the opinions of authorities might typically be offered, interpretive analysts would include interviews of gang members incarcerated in juvenile detention institutions, thereby affording them a voice.

Qualitative research is not standardized, and the subject and context are treated holistically, rather than being separated into dependent and independent variables.

Qualitative analysis is a craft, such that researchers work within guidelines but without set rules, allowing for great flexibility within which to work. When studying gangs, a researcher using qualitative methods would be free to develop her research questions as she goes along, and as her understanding of the particular gang context increases, rather than formulating these before any contact. Unlike quantitative analysts who use deductive reasoning, qualitative researchers use inductive reasoning, moving from the particular (some observation they happen to make) to more general statements about the phenomena they are studying (Anderson, 1996).

While the interpretive or hermeneutic perspective provides a strong critique of positivist (quantitative) methodology, they share common ground to the extent that both assume that a value-free study of society is possible, and that an objective reality exists independently of the researcher. Qualitative analysis practiced through the interpretive or hermeneutic perspective is valuable for those who wish to remain solidly within the scientific tradition while incorporating aspects of subjectivity into their inquiry (Anderson, 1996, p. 185).

References/Suggested Readings: Anderson, K. 1996. *Sociology: A Critical Introduction.* Canada: Nelson.

ANNETTE BICKFORD

R

RACIST SKINHEADS IN THE U.S. Despite widespread media coverage and consistent monitoring by civil rights organizations, racist skinhead gangs in the United States remain understudied by social scientists. While American skinheads are a relatively small portion of the overall gang picture, they have maintained a continuous presence in the United States for the last twenty-five years and can be found in every region of the country.

Although American skinheads have been neglected in the academic literature, the original British skinheads received considerable scholarly attention. Using a neo-Marxist inspired conception of youth subculture, these studies tended to focus exclusively upon style, which they explained as an attempt to resolve a marginal working-class status in a class-based society. One of the consistent controversies surrounding the study of skinheads has been whether to define them as stylistic subcultures (as British scholars did), gangs, hate groups, or even terrorists. In the United States skinheads have typically been excluded from gang studies on the grounds that they are better understood as "**hate groups**" and/or "terrorists" sharing little in common with traditional street gangs. In contrast to street gangs, racist skinheads have been portrayed as closely organized around an ideological system of "Aryan supremacy" and as lacking traditional gang territorial claims. Moreover, it is commonly believed that skinheads differ from traditional gangs in that they do not spend significant amounts of time "hanging out" on the streets; instead, they are said to be "inside . . . working on their materials; or if outside, they're looking for a target, not just lounging around . . . skinheads are focused, always planning. . . . Skins prefer narrower ranges of trouble."

Yet a careful review of the literature suggests the inadequacy of conceptualizations of racist skinheads as completely distinct from traditional youth street gangs. Stephen Baron's (1997) study of Canadian racist skinheads and Erik Anderson's (1987) study of San Francisco skinheads, for example, found these youth to be neither highly organized nor politicized. Skinhead youth lived on the streets or in other transient circumstances (e.g., crashpads) and often used violent and other criminal means for survival and the settlement of disputes with other urban and suburban youth cliques. This chapter examines the early development of U.S. racist skinhead gangs, their organizational characteristics including the relationship between skinheads and white supremacist groups, and current trends within the skinhead scene.

History of Skinheads in the U.K.

A significant component of skinhead culture is their appearance. Traditionally skinhead style included closely cropped hair or shaved head, work pants or denim jeans, Doc Marten steel-toed work boots, suspenders, and tattoos. As one observer pointed out, skinheads dressed like a "caricature of the model worker." Skinhead culture began in Great Britain and developed in two waves through the 1960s and 1970s. The first skinheads emerged in Great Britain in the late 1960s in response to deteriorating traditional working-class communities stemming from a stagnating economy, competition with immigrants for scarce jobs, and withering neighborhood traditions. While they did not explicitly associate themselves with Nazism, they were ardently nationalist in political orientation and fervently opposed to foreign immigration, which was reflected by their affinity for violently attacking Pakistani immigrants aka "Paki-bashing." The first skinheads "were aware that they attended the worst schools, lived in the poorest districts, and had the worst jobs with the smallest wages. They perceived hippies in the same way as they viewed students, as idle layabouts living off the state."

While the first skinheads defined themselves along themes of nationalism, ultramasculinity, and working-class issues (e.g., lack of economic opportunity), they expressed political sentiments primarily through stylistic imagery, hence, they were not typically involved in traditional, organized political activities (e.g., unions, political parties, marches, etc.). This lack of politicization began to change as a second wave of English skinheads emerged in the late 1970s and tentatively became associated with the National Front (NF) and the British National Party (BNP), extreme right-wing political parties, who saw the utility of drawing disaffected white youth into their ranks. The second wave of skinheads spread beyond Britain and emerged in several other European countries as well as North America.

The Development of American Skinheads

Although the skinhead style spread to America through a process of international cultural diffusion, American skinhead gangs formed in response to changes in local punk rock scenes as well as larger changes in the wider social structure. In the late 1970s, local punk rock scenes starting getting "hard core," which signaled a more violent and suburban trend in punk rock. Hard core referred to a faster style of music and a more hostile attitude, which was expressed through random violence directed at other punks during music shows. For younger suburban kids, hard-core aggressiveness provided an important security device from those antagonistic toward punk style. During this time, the skinhead style evolved from hard core and, similar to hard core, became a popular alternative to kids attracted to an ultra-aggressive style.

In the early 1980s, local youth cliques across urban and suburban areas in the United States began forming skinhead gangs. The first skinhead gangs bonded around identity markers and shared interests (e.g., shaved heads, clothing styles, musical preferences, slang, tattoos, etc.). Skinheads were building a collective identity with organizational names, initiation rites, semi-hierarchical social roles, and non-specialized, "garden-variety" delinquency (e.g., vandalism, under-age drinking, petty theft, and maybe most important, fighting). Yet skinhead identity was also loose, unstructured, and tied to social gatherings that were relatively unregulated, allowing for the innovation needed to create oppositional identities. Most skinheads describe their early participation as involving "street socialization" within urban and suburban locales such as malls, parks, music shows, etc. Street socialization is a street-based process providing peer guidance, creating an alternate set of values and norms among youth who lack parental supervision and positive school experiences. Contrary to what some observers contend, skinhead gangs have not been devoid of local neighborhood-based territoriality which can be seen in their choice of gang names (e.g., South Bay Skins, San Francisco Skins, etc.) and claiming specific locations, such as parks or music clubs by using graffiti "tags" and other more physically aggressive means.

In addition to changes in local punk scenes, skinhead gangs were also forming in response to changes involving the larger socio-political environment. Since the mid-1960s, increasing "non-white" immigration had been significantly altering U.S. demographics. Initially the skinhead response to these changes bore great resemblance to the kinds of conflict that ethnic/racial migration spurred in New York and other large urban centers only a few decades earlier. Race was only implicitly important, in much the way that it was to the punks. The majority of (but not all) punks and skinheads were white youth, and although pockets of explicitly racist sentiments existed among punks and the early skinheads, racist political activism was not a primary emphasis before the late 1980s.

The Organizational Characteristics of Skinhead Gangs

Most skinheads become involved between the ages of twelve and nineteen, are predominantly male (60–70 percent), and tend to coalesce around a unique subculture that is autonomous and distinct from adult hate groups such as the Klan. Because skinheads have maintained a presence in the United States since the late 1970s, there are now skinheads in their early forties, however, very little is known about these "O.G." skinheads or more generally about how aging affects a skinhead's identity or life course trajectory. Many skinhead gangs are short-lived and have overlapping membership (e.g., sometimes a smaller skinhead clique will be completely compromised of members from other larger skinhead gangs). Most skinhead gangs are either organized at the state-level (e.g., West Virginia Skinheads), county and/or city-level (e.g., Orange County Skins, Las Vegas Skins), or even neighborhood and/or school-based (e.g., Milwaukee Eastside Bullies). One of the few exceptions is the Hammerskin Nation (HSN) which is an international skinhead organization that was originally formed in Dallas, Texas, in 1988. Currently the HSN has five regional chapters in the United States (e.g., Northern Hammers, Midland Hammers, etc.) and outside the United States an additional ten countries also have official HSN chapters.

Through much of the 1980s the skinhead scene was an umbrella without clearly demarcated boundaries, allowing fluid forms of participation; yet there emerged within the scene subgroups with clearer boundaries of membership (skinheads often referred to these as "crews"). Over the years as some skinhead gangs became closely aligned with white supremacist groups the distinction between racist and anti-racist skinheads has become relatively clear-cut; however, this was not the case initially, as factions along lines of racial ideology were originally much blurrier. Even today some ambiguity continues to persist as skinheads change allegiances between racist and anti-racist.

One of the skinheads' most interesting organizational characteristics is the segment who does not belong to any specific group but instead prefer an "Independent" status. Independent skins combine the amorphous elements of "youth culture" with informal associational ties to specific gang organizations, but allegiance is situational and generically directed to the skinhead scene. These loosely affiliated individuals defy traditional notions of organizational boundaries and reflect a flexible style of participation that does not require the same degree of loyalty or commitment, yet Independent Skins maintain relationships with multiple gangs and often help facilitate the flow of information between gangs. Although Independent Skins potentially threaten organizational stability by acting as "free riders," they also enrich organizational culture by acting as liaisons between relatively disconnected and sometimes conflictual organizations. Independent Skins also offer a recruitment pool for skinhead gangs attempting to consolidate membership of smaller gangs in order to increase organizational strength and at times the Independent label is used strategically by members of skinhead gangs to deflect law enforcement efforts to identify their affiliation.

Skinhead Gangs and the White Supremacist Movement

By the mid-1980s American skinheads began developing links to various white supremacist groups such as the White Aryan Resistance, Aryan Nations, and factions of the Ku Klux Klan. Some of these links were initiated by skinheads while other links resulted from recruitment efforts among U.S. white supremacist groups, who, like the NF and BNP in England, viewed skinheads as a means to "energize" an otherwise aging movement. Network ties to the white supremacy movement provided skinheads with invaluable political socialization, including racist political literature, organizational affiliations, leadership training, and financial resources. Before forging these ties, some skinhead gangs were racist, but not politically active. As racist skinheads became increasingly aligned with white supremacist groups they started attending rallies and marches and appearing on nationally televised talk shows like *Geraldo* and the *Oprah Winfrey Show*.

Images of shaven-headed, swastika-tattooed, jack booted youth hurling racial epithets at Oprah and breaking Geraldo's nose earned skinheads a "folk devil" status. Skinheads, however, are, arguably, best known for their brutal acts of hate violence while roaming the streets like packs of wolves. Although skinhead violence during the early and mid-1980s was sometimes racially motivated, there is little evidence to suggest that these early skinhead gangs went beyond the long standing pattern of white gangs' defense of racial neighborhood boundaries. Much skinhead violence was directed toward other subcultural groups (e.g., other skin gangs, punks, surfers, etc.) that were also willing participants in the action. Skinheads defined their violence as a means of protecting themselves from aggressive non-skinhead groups.

According to some observers, by the late 1980s skinhead violence was increasingly motivated by their neo-Nazi ideology and facilitated by their links to white supremacist groups like White Aryan Resistance. Clearly U.S. skinheads have committed a variety of horrific acts of violence, but careful analysis of the quality and quantity of skinhead violence is lacking. Catalogs of skinhead violence suggest that much of their aggression is directed toward minority groups, yet the construction of these catalogs are relatively selective and thus it is difficult to compare the proportion of skinhead violence directed toward minority groups with skinhead violence directed toward other targets. Additionally, there has been little effort to systematically analyze long-term patterns and levels of skinhead violence.

Recent Trends in the Skinhead Scene

During the last two and half decades the number of racist skinheads has ebbed and flowed. Recently, some observers report a resurgence of skinhead gangs. This resurgence has spurred the Anti-Defamation League to sponsor the Racist Skinhead Project, a national effort to monitor skinhead gangs across the country. Since their emergence in the United States skinheads have varied greatly from one region to another. This continues to be the case. In some skinhead scenes, emphasis is placed on retaining the "authentic" and traditional appearance of the skinhead style, while in other areas (most notably southern California) some skinheads blend a traditional style with a more contemporary "gangsta" style (e.g., saggy pants, socks pulled up). Still other highly political skinheads encourage their "brothers" to grow their hair out and refrain from getting completely tattooed in order to infiltrate the system which they argue is controlled by a "small cabal of Jews" who are secretly plotting to eradicate the "white race."

Aside from stylistic differences, skinheads also vary significantly in their activities. Some skinheads are involved in an elaborate array of cyberspace practices including chatrooms, designing Web sites, and virtual gaming (Internet-based video and fantasy games). Other skinheads participate in the recently growing white power music scene where music shows are often coupled with festivals that are either organized by racist skinheads (e.g., the HSN's Hammerfest) or that cater to racist skinheads (e.g., the Imperial Klans of America's Nordic Fest). Not surprisingly, the white power music scene is strongest in areas where racist skinheads have maintained a strong presence over the years (e.g., southern California, Pennsylvania, and Portland, Oregon).

Other skinheads focus their energy toward profit-oriented criminal activity which may include manufacturing and distributing methamphetamine, home invasions, illegal gun sales, identity theft, and counterfeiting. In recent years the two largest racist skinhead gangs in southern California have been organized around profit-motivated criminal activity as opposed to a political agenda. Between 1996 and 2000 the Nazi Low Riders (NLR) grew from 28 confirmed members to over 1,500 members in California alone. Today the NLR is essentially defunct, however, another southern California–based skinhead gang, Public Enemy Number One (PEN1), has grown from a few dozen members in the mid-1990s to more than 500 current members. The growth of both the NLR and PEN1 is related to their links to the Aryan Brotherhood, a national prison-based gang that was originally founded in San Quentin in the mid-1960s. Despite these gangs' white supremacist orientation, their predominant focus is on profit-motivated criminal activity designed for personal gain. There is no evidence that these gangs have used the profits derived from criminal enterprises for funding larger political endeavors related to the white supremacist movement. Like early racist skinhead gangs, the NLR and PEN1 do not participate in racist political activism, and while their violence is sometimes racially motivated, they are just as likely to engage in instrumentally motivated violence related to criminal operations or spontaneous violence related to interpersonal disputes.

In some areas (e.g., Phoenix, Arizona) the skinhead scene continues to thrive despite a continuous implosion of specific groups. In other parts of the country skinheads have developed ties to outlaw motorcycle gangs. A few of the areas where skinhead scenes are especially active include southern California, Pennsylvania (especially the corridor between Philadelphia and Harrisburg), Portland, Ohio, Indiana, and New Jersey.

In conclusion, the most important lessons of skinhead gangs involve three points: (1) racist skinhead gangs do not fit neatly in any one particular category—they are diverse and change frequently; (2) despite rapid turnover and group splintering, the U.S. skinhead scene has been able to persist; and (3) although some skinhead gangs have become a branch of the contemporary white supremacist movement, many other skinhead gangs remain oppositional in localized terms without a clear political program for broad social change.

References/Suggested Readings: Anderson, Erik. 1987. Skinheads: From Britain to San Francisco via Punk Rock. M.A. thesis, Washington State University; Baron, Steven. 1997. Canadian Male Street Skinheads: Street Gang or Street Terrorist? *Canadian Review of Sociology and Anthropology,* 34, 125–154; Blazak, Randy. 2001. White Boys to Terrorist Men: Target Recruitment of Nazi Skinheads. *American Behavioral Scientist,* 44, 982–1000; Blush, Steven. 2001. *American Hardcore: A Tribal History.* Los Angeles: Feral House; Brake, Michael. 1974. The Skinheads: An English Working Class Subculture. *Youth and Society,* 6, 179–199; Clarke, John. 1976. The Skinheads and the Magical Recovery of Community. In Stuart Hall and Tony Jefferson (eds.), *Resistance through Rituals,* pp. 99–102. London: Hutchinson; Hamm, Mark. 1993. *American Skinheads.* Boston: Northeastern University Press; Hebdige, Dick. 1979. *Subculture, the Meaning of Style.* London: Methuen; Hicks, Wendy. 2004. Skinheads: A Three Nation Comparison. *Journal of Gang Research,* 11 (2), 51–74; Knight, Nick. 1982. *Skinhead.* London: Omnibus Press; Moore, Jack. 1993. *Skinheads Shaved for Battle: A Cultural History of American Skinheads.* Bowling Green, OH: Bowling Green State University Popular Press; Spitz, Marc, and Muller, Brendan. 2001. *We Got the Neutron Bomb: The Untold Story of L.A. Punk.* New York: Three Rivers Press; Wooden, Wayne, and Blazak, Randy. 2001. *Renegade Kids, Suburban Outlaws: From Youth Culture to Delinquency* (2nd ed.). Belmont, CA: Wadsworth Publishing.

PETER G. SIMI

RAP MUSIC. A history has been constructed that links rap music to the black community, deindustrialization, and the urban poor. It is generally agreed that rap emerged in the Bronx, New York, in the 1970s, with three DJs credited with bringing it into public consciousness: Kool Herc (originally from Jamaica), Grandmaster Flash, and Afrika Bambaataa (founder of the Zulu Nation). The origins are well documented through interviews and direct observations, providing rich detail as to the process by which rap was originally broadcast. Given that these artists lived in abject poverty, rappers moved their music from private to public space by usurping electricity found in abandoned factories and tapping into traffic lights in order to power turntables, speakers, and microphones. Using preexisting recordings to provide music, DJs set up record players and tape recorders on street corners, school yards, and in abandoned buildings in order to perform before live audiences. ("Rapping" has a well-documented history within black community music; see Rose, 1994; Toop, 1992; Perkins, 1996. Also bands such as *The Dead Poets* did perform rap, albeit not at the commercial level of latter rappers.) One area of the Bronx in which this occurred, Morrisania, has a deep tradition of street-level public music that had garnered commercial success in the 1950s musical genre doo wop, which later served to inspire pop music production from the Brill Building.

Reductions in municipal spending in New York, as in many large cities, meant urban neighborhoods had few public spaces in which performances could occur. Deindustrialization left cities without resources bringing an end to public programs such as after-school music lessons, and budget cuts resulted in the redistribution of public school music teachers such as Eddie Bonamere. (Bonamere is credited with teaching hundreds of south Bronx students how to play the trumpet, trombone, flute, and violin. He is cited as one of the caring, special teachers who made lifelong changes within students, a man who cared for and about students both in and out of school; Naison, 2004). Prior to "cost reductions" Bonamere headed the school band at Clark Junior High School and allowed students to take musical instruments home at night and over weekends, offered lessons after school, and sponsored a regular jazz concert in the schoolyard of PS 18 and invited famous musicians such as Willie Bobo. The loss of such teachers was a direct attack on the culture of the Bronx and served to exacerbate neighborhood inequalities and propel the dissemination of rap music.

With limited opportunities for live performances, public community centers were utilized for shows and became safe houses where DJs and rappers could weave their musical products while enjoying a reprise from the hostile environment that was the 1970s/1980s Bronx. Within these and other locations rappers would use constructed beats over which they would "flow" verse in complex melodic ways. Common forms of rap were *toasts*, popular in Jamaica and common in African American culture, where a rapper would follow in the oral tradition and tell stories such as the "Signaling Monkey" (also known as "Signifyin' Monkey") and "Dolemite," often singing chants and rhymes; and *playing the dozens* which is an exchange of verbal wit between DJs. Local fame and reputations grew allowing some the opportunity to put on shows and in so doing attracted a new, young audience to whom rappers and DJs sold their mixed tapes (mixed tapes are a form of music wherein an artist uses prior recordings and alters them to reflect their own musical expression thus producing a new musical product). These tapes were consumed at a local level and were disseminated throughout the United States. In 1978 rap music was launched as a media staple and garnered certified platinum when the Sugar Hill Gang from New York released "Rappers Delight."

Gangsta Rap

Though the evolution of rap is well documented by scholars a debate exists as to when gangsta rap began. Some believe gangsta rap began in the mid- to late 1980s, others that it began in the early 1990s. This is a semantic issue as there is consensus that the artist Todd Shaw, known as Too $hort, was indeed the first to be called a gangsta rapper and began his career in the early 1980s as an independent artist selling made-to-order mixed tapes in high school. (Too $hort's early mixed tapes were made specifically for each customer and cost $10. They contained thirty minutes of glamorizing rap about the customer.) His first commercial project was produced in 1985 and stands as the official beginning of gangsta rap, as NWA (Niggers with Attitude), the group most often credited with creating gangsta rap, did not release their first LP until the following year. Though Ice-T did produce singles in the early 1980s, they did not achieve commercial success. Moreover, once Too $hort coupled with musician-producer Shorty B. gangsta rap gained commercial success and was regularly certified platinum.

Prior to the mass consumption of rap, songs were played in local spaces, cars, and portable stereos that were to be appropriately labeled *ghetto blasters*. The producers and audience sonically reclaimed the local space and provided the soundtrack to the urban environment steeped in economic recession mirroring the East Coast rap scene. While the Bronx was being treated to the pirating of electrical lines by Grand Master Flash and the others who broadcast rap music literally on the streets, Oakland's streets were tuned to Too $hort and later to his colleague Tupac Shakur, the most commercially successful rap artist, with sales of over 73 million worldwide.

Gangsta rap subsequently evolved into a category that described many artists, albeit a West Coast phenomenon, that found an audience in white male adolescents. Even though this genre was supported through various acts the core features of gangsta rap, storytelling, and 1960/1970s funk samples, established by Too $hort and Shorty B., remain central to the genre.

The rappers Ice-T and Ice Cube are often credited with creating gangsta rap due to their high visibility as actors, community leaders, and involvement in the group NWA. In 1988, NWA did land a commercial successful gangsta rap project, *Straight Outta Compton*, however, Too $hort brought gold certification to the gangsta rap community a year earlier, in 1987. Too $hort was born Todd Shaw in south central Los Angeles, in 1966, and like many other rappers was reared amidst the political upheaval of the civil rights movement and the formation of the Black Power paradigm by his mother, an active member of the Black Panther Party. He grew up in a home where music was listened to, especially the radio station KDAY, an Afro-centric station that broadcast black music and whose DJs were often viewed as political leaders of the community and where funk musicians stood as proof of the effectiveness of Black Power as praxis.

Too $hort is, contrary to media depictions, not only a "dirty rapper" telling stories of sexual prowess but is also a social rapper, like his colleague and band-mate Tupac Shakur, and follows a tradition of the social gospel preachers of the past. They tell stories about the black community from an organic perspective; focusing on oppression, racism, poverty, and the conflict in society through the eyes of a poor black youth from California. They speak of resistance to the dominant culture and openly about gang membership as an alternative to societal assimilation, feeling community cohesion, even at the level of the street gang, provides more support than the oppressive society at large. The connection of street gangs to the Black Panther Party is well documented and Too $hort's mother is a member of the Los Angeles branch of the Black Panther Party which was formed by Bunchy Carter, a member of Renegade Slauson gang, that later became the **Crips**.

Too $hort moved to Oakland, California, the seat of the Black Panther Party, when he was twelve years old and was further immersed in Black Power ideology. Talk of capitalism and exploitation were common in the homes of many gangsta rap artists whose parents were active members of the Black Panther Party. And these members identified the political economy as the superstructure which contributed to their lesser status as African Americans and also to the high levels of unemployment within their communities. Consequently, the men that were to become gangsta rap artists were not looking for gainful employment per se. Jobs were in the hands of the racist capitalist ruling class which forced them to react accordingly.

Armed with an oppositional ideology that stressed the importance of self-reliance and distrust of dominant norms as hegemonic (ergo oppressive), Too $hort began his professional music career in high school offering independent cassette mixes for purchase. Then, at age seventeen, he began selling musical product literally out of the trunk of his car. He networked, in the spirit of Theatre Owners Booking Association, within the California black music circuit, between Oakland, Fresno, Bakersfield, and Sacramento, to boost sales and open new markets. These markets, like so many other small, localized ones across the United States, had been overlooked by mainstream music production companies, who were still not producing what would become rap and pandered to rock and country music. When Too $hort with his third independent project, *Players* (1985), sold over 50,000 copies, Jive Records in New York took notice. And in 1986, Too $hort ultimately signed with Jive Records for distribution. At a time when the earned median annual wage in Oakland was under $8,000 (U.S. Census, 2006, Fact Finder), Too $hort could make this amount in less than a week. Without the help of conventional record production, or the established music market, Too $hort became famous and earned more annually than most of his neighbors earned in their combined lifetimes. Moreover this line of work was legitimate yet avoided the trappings of working for the Man.

Living in Oakland, Too $hort met Tupac Shakur, Humpty-Hump (aka Shock-G), Shorty B., Ant Banks, and Pee Wee and began working as a band called Digital Underground. Tupac, whose mother was deeply associated with the Black Panther Party of New York and whose godfather was the infamous Black Panther leader Elmer "Geronimo" Pratt, had moved to Marin City, California, across the bay from Oakland in 1988. Digital Underground became an Oakland-based rap project that included more than talented poets, and was unique in they used a live band in addition to rappers. They created a sound similar to the 1960/1970s Westbound funk bands (i.e., Parliament-Funkadelic, Bootsy Collins, the Ohio Players) and often included guest musicians from these Westbound bands, their heroes, in their recorded projects. Later, in the 1990s, many rappers had begun to emulate the sound created in Oakland and sampled pieces of music from these Westbound funk bands and James Brown. (Many of the samples of James Brown also include Westbound acts such as Bootsy and his brother Catfish Collins, who were members of James Brown Band, and later Bootsy became a member of Parliament-Funkadelic.)

Unlike the West Coast rappers Digital Underground, who included original funk musicians as guests on new products, thus ensuring no legal issue would arise when samples were lifted from original recordings, many rappers such as New York's Biggie Smalls (a name taken from a fictional gangster in a 1975 film *Let's Do It Again*) were taken to court by original funk musicians. In 2006, sales were halted for Biggie Smalls's *Ready to Die* (1994), as a court found in favor of the Ohio Players, whom Biggie had sampled in his title track of the album without permission.

Commercial Rap

The 1990s saw a shift in rap due to commercial success. West Coast producers held the majority of new commercially popular product under the production of Los Angeles–based Dr. Dre and Suge Knight (of the Mob Piru **Bloods** gang of Compton, California; the Pirus broke off from the **Crips** to form the Bloods in the mid-1970s), and Death Row Records. Though Dr. Dre was known to take rap away from the gangsta rap sound, he had difficulty in removing gangs from rap production. Consequently the most successful acts of the early 1990s, such as Snoop Doggy Dogg (Snoop's first LP, *Doggystyle* [1993], went platinum five times), tout gang culture proudly and brought gang symbols such as tattoos, hand signals, colors, clothing, and language to the fore of U.S. culture. It is not until 1998 when Dr. Dre began work with Eminem (Marshall Mathers) that commercial rap shifted from primarily gangsta rap to unashamed mainstream popular music when the song "My Name Is" becomes a crossover hit and earned Dr. Dre and Eminem quadruple-platinum certification. Dr. Dre continued taking rap into the popular mainstream when, in 2005, he produced rapper Eve and pop star Gwen Stefani's commercial success "Rich Girl," a double-platinum certified single that is based on a 1990s English pop hit by

Louchie Lou and Michie, originally covering, "If I Were a Rich Man" from the musical *Fiddler on the Roof*. However, Dr. Dre's work with 50 Cent, a rapper from Queens, New York, brought gangs back into the public image of contemporary commercial rap.

It was during the days of the West Coast domination in the rap industry when the East Coast responded with what has been termed the "East Coast Renaissance": the rise of the Wu-Tang Clan, Nas, and the Notorious B.I.G. (aka Biggie Smalls) put New York rap back into view under the production house of Bad Boy Records. This also launched the career of business student Sean Combs, who later emerged as Puff Daddy to rise in rank as the most wealthy rap artist in the United States to date. Combs attended the private secondary school Mount Saint Michael Academy in the Bronx and Howard University in Washington, DC. After interning at Uptown Records he landed a job as an A&R executive and started Bad Boy Records to produce rap music for commercial consumption. This brought New York back into the arena to compete with California's rap producers.

Tupac Shakur and his Outlawz crew received the lion's share of publicity in the 1990s, thus propelling West Coast gangsta rap into the public consciousness. This status provoked a territorial feud between West Coast rappers and those of the East Coast which was manifested in the East Coast/West Coast War and the infamous assassinations of Tupac Shakur of Death Row Records in 1996 and Biggie Smalls (Notorious B.I.G.) of Bad Boy Records in 1997.

Rap's Reception

Rap music that was once produced at a local level and consumed in small quantities grew into a genre that outsold all other music genres with the exception of rock. However, given the duration of rock it stands as testament to the popularity of rap that sales are only slightly lower for rap than for rock. Even though rap has become the second most popular form of music in the United States, public response has not been favorable.

Magazines with traditional black readership find no harm in rap music; however magazines with traditional white readership find harm. Rap is framed as dangerous to society, and protection of individuals (especially women and children) within society is invoked to combat the harm disseminating from this music (see Binder, 1993).

Among the most notable critics of rap, the Parents' Music Resource Center (PMRC) has been particularly active. Original members of the PMRC include Tipper Gore (wife of Senator and later Vice President Al Gore); Susan Baker, wife of Treasury Secretary James Baker; and Nancy Thurmond, wife of Senator Strom Thurmond. According to a brief written by the ACLU (2006) under the Art Censorship Project, the PMRC started as a collective of fundamental religious and parent groups to "wage a persistent campaign to limit the variety of cultural messages available to American youth by attacking the content of some of the music industry's creative products." The PMRC's collective actions include a demand for a warning label meant to alert consumers of themes within certain products deemed offensive: sex, violence, drug or alcohol use, suicide, or the "occult." Sanctions by the PMRC have included prosecutions of record companies and store owners for distribution of nefarious material.

In 1990 pressure from the PMRC caused the RIAA (Recording Industry Association of America) to administer stickers with the logo "Parental Advisory—Explicit Lyrics" for use on rock and rap products. Industry personnel came in droves to testify against this practice, citing the action's bias against black artists. They argue no standards are offered to guide record companies as to what is explicit content and that the stickers are placed on products within only two genres generally considered black music: rock and rap. (Rap is primarily produced by blacks and rock is well documented as evolving from blues which is considered a predominantly black cultural expression. This fact is debated in Wald, 2004. The common reading of blues as black music is generally agreed upon.) Stickers, many argued, are not required for use on comedy, country, or opera records even though many of their themes are as controversial as those articulated by the PMRC. This treatment was seen within the music production industry as uneven and racist.

Due to the often explicit language found in rap music, especially those of gang members who, in the tradition of the Black Panther Party, refer to police as "pigs" and suggest violence as a rational means to evoke personal and community power, rap artists found themselves defending the First Amendment. The PMRC was only one agency that situated itself against the freedom of speech of rappers. A Florida circuit judge in the 1990s claimed rap music could not be defined as music, because it was not melodic and therefore did not deserve First Amendment protection. And in 2001 a Federal Trade Commission Report listed thirty-five CDs deemed "bad" for children; of these thirty were black artists and only three contained all-white band members (Maya Dollarhide, 2001, The Freedom Forum).

Given the uneven treatment of rap music compared to other forms of entertainment which also provide controversial material (i.e., comedy, theater, literature), one cannot dismiss the effect rap has had upon culture both domestically as well as globally. Rap music is consumed and produced on all continents, in many languages, and by a variety of groups. Additionally rap music has brought new words into the English language such as the *mack*. Probably from the French *maquereau*, using words to hustle or trick, the meaning behind the *mack* is complex and has been shown (Quinn, 2000) to be residual of the African diaspora which has been traced back to the Signaling Monkey folk tale. Three characters make up this tale: a Monkey, a Lion, and an Elephant. The Lion is the ruler and unjust. The Monkey tells the Elephant (a neutral, albeit powerful, third party) a lie, that the Lion is talking badly about the Elephant. This motivates the Elephant to bully (and potentially kill) the Lion. Through wit and clever weaving of language the Monkey resists the will of the Lion and indeed injects his own will, thus wielding power in a situation where he was seemingly powerless. The Lion signifies the dominant forces (often referred to as "Whitey"), the Monkey is the black trickster, and the Elephant is the medium by which the Monkey gains advantage over the Elephant. The trickster has deep meaning in the black community as it relates directly to African deities Esu, Legba, and Anansi. These tricksters are heralded throughout African American culture and are seen in other characters such as Brer Rabbit, as weaving language in clever ways, spinning illusory tales to exert power and gain control in situations where one has no control. This trickster who gains controls over others is manifested in the form of the pimp, also called the mack.

The actor Max Julien was at the heart of a series of films categorized as "blaxploitation" that embrace Black Panther Party values. He starred in the hit film *The Mack* (1973) and wrote the screenplay for *Cleopatra Jones* (1973) which launched blaxploitation film into the mainstream of commercial success. These films use funk music as their soundtracks and were produced in a manner parallel to rap music, locally and funded by "any means necessary" (see Van Peebles's comments regarding gang funding of his 1971 film *Sweet Sweetback's Baadasssss Song* in the 2003 film *Badass!*)

The mack is a code that has held consistent meaning across time and space. The use of the word mack is a function of collective political resistance and was resurrected by West Coast rappers. Supporting this shared meaning of the pimp narrative, commonly referred to as mackin', Too $hort responds, "To me, it's positive . . . It's almost like the Muslims. Being a Muslim is like keeping your mind straight. The mack thing is about keepin' your mind correct. It's a self-esteem thing, if you ask me" (Perkins, 1996).

More than a decade later, in 1988, after meeting Mr. Julien, Too $hort named his album, *Born to Mack*. Then, in 1999, over twenty-five years since the original film, Rappin' 4-Tay recorded *Introduction to Mackin'*, a project produced by Shorty B. and recorded at Celeb Studios in north Hollywood. During the taping of the Rappin' 4-Tay's project, Max Julien was a regular visitor and advisor (Southgate, forthcoming), showing the intent of the producers to invoke his image. Max Julien embodies the very essence of the mack and is a strong and active member in the perpetration of meaning: Black Power in the face of white hegemony.

Rap is often seen as a path for mobility for young people of color with 15 percent of the thirty richest people of black or Hispanic origin under the age of forty reportedly having earned their fortune through the rap music industry (Kroll and Fass, 2006). However, this statistic is misleading when one considers these four individuals: Sean Combs earned his fortune owning Bad Boy Records and not as a rapper; Shawn Carter, aka Jay-Z, earned his fortune owning Roc-a-Fella Enterprises; Jennifer Lopez is a singer, actress, and co-owner of Sweetface Fashion; and Will Smith has had a most lucrative career as an actor though he started as a rapper. It was not rapping that amassed these fortunes.

Though commercial success has changed the soundscape of rap music, it remains the second most consumed music genre in the United States with sales in 2005 of $13.3 million (RIAA, 2006), and spans many styles to include gangsta rap, new jack swing, G-funk, alternative rap, Christian rap, East Coast/West Coast rap, hard-core rap, jazz-rap, Old School rap, Southern rap, dirty rap, Dirty South, political rap, and many other styles. From urban centers steeped in extreme poverty, musicians rose to provide music that impacted the world. Disenfranchised individuals used local power by any means necessary, through gang affiliation and money from illegal means, such as pandering and drug sales, to loans from individuals within the community who saw promise in rap music, to fund a collective movement despite their marginality.

References/Suggested Reading: American Civil Liberties Union. 2006. Popular Music Under Siege. Arts Censorship Project. Public Education Department; Binder, Amy. 1993. Constructing Racial Rhetoric: Media Depictions of Harm in Heavy Metal and Rap Music. *American Sociological Review,* 58, 753–767; Dollarhide, Maya. 2001. "Music Censorship: The Beat Goes On." The Freedom Forum. Accessed January 2003. http://www.freedomforum.org/templates/document.asp?documentID=13981; Kroll, Luisa, and Fass Alison. 2006. Rich Kids: 40 Richest Under 40. *Forbes;* Naison, Mark. 2004. From Doo Wop to Hip Hop: The Bittersweet Odyssey of African-Americans in the South Bronx. *Socialism and Democracy,* 18, 37–49; Perkins, William Eric. 1996. The Rap Attack: An Introduction. In W. E. Perkins (ed.), *Droppin' Science: Critical Essays on Rap Music and Hip Hop Culture*. Philadelphia: Temple University Press; Quinn, Eithne. 2000. "Who's The Mack?" The Performativity and Politics of the Pimp Figure in Gangsta Rap. *Journal of American Studies,* 34, 115–136; Recoding Industry Association of America. 2006. *The Annual Consumer Profile Chart;* Rose, Tricia. 1994.

Black Noise: Rap Music and Black Culture in Contemporary America. Middletown, Connecticut: Wesleyan University Press; Toop, David. 1992. *Rap Attack 2: African Rap to Global Hip Hop.* London: Serpent's Tail; Wald, Elijah. 2004. *Escaping the Delta.* New York: Amistad/HarperCollins.

DARBY E. SOUTHGATE

RESEARCH METHODS. From its Greek origins, "method" denotes a path taken, or ways in which research is conducted. Assertions such as "Gang members are criminals" are arrived at by following particular procedures for gathering and expressing information. These methods are informed by specific ontological and epistemological convictions and thus, different methods have distinct purposes in producing knowledge. For instance, positivist methods are used in order to be able to predict social behavior, whereas interpretive methods are used by qualitative sociologists who wish to gain a certain degree of *intersubjectivity*; and relativist methods are used by sociologists working from a *critical perspective*, who argue that all knowledge is socially constructed. As Anthony Giddens (1991, p. 21) suggests, sociology shares some things in common with science, insofar as sociologists analyze events systematically, but it must be understood that because human beings (as objects of social inquiry) act with conscious intent, sociological inquiry cannot be directly compared to natural sciences such as physics (Anderson, 1996, p. 177).

Since the eighteenth century the notion of objective, value-free research has been upheld as the way toward arriving at Truth; but social scientists have increasingly come to question the feasibility of objective research. While events occur, they are variously interpreted, and in this way, their meaning may be said to be socially constructed. Joyce McCarl Nielson contends that knowledge is explicable only within its cultural and historical context. There is no universally accepted transcendent truth, and the manufacturing of knowledge is a political act (Anderson, 1996).

Intrinsic to research methods are the theoretical perspectives they are rooted in. Theoretical perspectives in sociology are divided into three main categories: positivist, interpretive, and critical approaches. Despite significant differences, proponents of both positivist and interpretive approaches strive to perform value free scientific research in discovering objective reality, and both maintain an underlying assumption of an objective reality that exists independently of the researcher. Moreover, an unmediated relationship is assumed between observer and that which is being observed. There is a growing uncertainty that research can be value free; that there is only chaotic reality that is variously interpreted, and this movement is deeply affecting the discipline of sociology. Given the notion that the world is made not found, groundbreaking knowledge is viewed as constructed rather than discovered. According to Habermas (1971) the production of even scientific knowledge is inseparable from its social interests, and its historical and cultural contexts (Anderson, 1996, p. 177). Those grounded in relativist methods suggest that greater accuracy can be had by allowing for social cultural influences upon our interpretations and the kinds of questions we ask. For example, if we ask about whether gang members are naturally violent, or if this is environmentally caused, the research question indicates more about our own preoccupation with the nature/nurture debate than it does about gang members' behavior. If we study an event such as police treatment of gang members, it is imperative that we are aware of our own assumptions about racialization perhaps, and gang activity, which will necessarily mediate our interpretations of events. Critical sociology advocates the relativist basis of knowledge, and calls for researchers to explicitly integrate personal and political contexts in the data gathering process.

Positivist and interpretive research methods rely on the assumption that with direct observation and rational thought, truly objective researchers can discover the social world and true knowledge (Anderson, 1996, p. 177). Sociologists adopting positivist methods aim to establish universal laws (rather than patterns) about culture and human nature—across time and space. Once discovered, it is believed that this Truth will allow for prediction, and thus, control. Nevertheless, Truth claims may be challenged and made obsolete. Positivist researchers employ deductive reasoning. Here, research questions are formulated before data collection begins (Anderson, 1996, p. 183).

Qualitative analysis is most closely related to the interpretive method (hermeneutic perspective). Interpretivists strive for empathetic understanding, or to use Max Weber's term, *verstehen*, whereby they endeavor to understand the inner lives and viewpoint(s) of the actors involved. This is done through the collection and analysis of "soft" or richly descriptive and often nuanced data—diaries, letters, oral histories, or interviews, as well as accounts of observable behavior. This work is done within the context of field research, case studies, or ethnomethodology (Anderson, 1996, p. 86). If we want to analyze gangs and their place in North American culture, we might begin, as quantitative analysts, to gather statistics on gangs—the numbers of members, the amount of money generated, mortality rates—the potential list is extensive. But this would provide a different body of knowledge from what a qualitative analyst would seek. The interpretive theorist would want to know what a gang member's experience of membership is like. What are the sights, feelings, and emotions of gang membership? What is the experience like?

Qualitative researchers seek to convey what given events mean to their participants rather than trying to interpret those events themselves. Every effort is made to view interactions without the interference of one's own preconceptions. Interpretive researchers' studies are regarded as humanistic, because they value all viewpoints, and endeavor to "give a voice" to people who may be rarely heard (Anderson, 1996). For instance, where only the opinions of authorities might typically be offered, interpretive analysts would include interviews of gang members incarcerated in juvenile detention institutions, thereby affording them a voice.

Qualitative research is not standardized, and the subject and context are treated holistically, rather than being separated into dependent and independent variables. Qualitative analysis is a craft, such that researchers work within guidelines but without set rules, allowing for great flexibility within which to work. There is such a great deal of latitude that interpretive researchers may actually develop their research questions as they go along, rather than formulating these before even beginning to explore the subject matter. Interpretivists employ inductive reasoning, moving from the particular (some observation they happen to make) to more general statements about the phenomena they are studying (Anderson, 1996).

While the interpretive or hermeneutic perspective provides a strong critique of positivist (quantitative) methodology and initially provided researchers with a viable alternative to positivism at a time when this was upheld as the only valid method, they share common ground to the extent that both assume that a value-free study of society is desirable, and that an objective reality exists independently of the researcher. Qualitative analysis practiced through the interpretive or hermeneutic perspective is valuable for those who wish to remain solidly within the scientific tradition while incorporating aspects of subjectivity into their inquiry (Anderson, 1996, p. 185).

Perhaps the most significant shortcoming of the interpretive method and of positivism is that they do not address the issue of power—of social conflict, of social structures, and social change. Positivist and interpretivist methods, while useful, do not enable the researcher to question culturally accepted understandings of the role of gangs in North American society. For such a view, the researcher would need to take a critical stance and ask such questions as, *why* is gang membership sought after in the first place? Who profits and why? Do gang relationships of race, gender, class, and sexuality challenge or ultimately reinscribe those of the dominant culture? Why is this? How is loyalty ensured? Critical theorists might gather statistics (positivist method) and be interested in gang experiences (interpretivist method), but would be most interested in determining relations of power between the various players both within and outside of gang membership. For critical theorists, all knowledge must be viewed in the context of its potential contribution to human emancipation. Relativist methods offer a substantial alternative to the assumptions of value-free research. Unlike the value-free scientific methods, relativist method allows researchers to question the dominant belief system of their society, thereby noticing popular discourses and practices that limit human freedom (Anderson, 1996, p. 190). Discourse analysis and genealogy are a significant aspect of relativist methodology, and Michel Foucault's contribution to research methods in social sciences through discourse analyses is significant. Analyses of discourses—holding our invisible biases, our language, and ways of seeing up to scrutiny often works to dismantle our strongest convictions, but allowing us to develop fresh perspectives. Discourse analyses can show the different ways that power exists in all social relations, in even the minutest of human exchanges. Foucault's method of discourse analysis was genealogical, meaning that he tried to identify variations that occur as social practices are transformed. Whereas historians often may compile facts to describe events "as they really were," researchers using relativist methodology would analyze how discourses played a role in society. Using methods of observation and induction, researchers employing methods of critical theory question the notion that facts are self-evident and simply speak for themselves. Some relativist researchers would go so far as to say that there are no facts, only interpretations. Given this, researchers using the relativist methodology must be willing to tolerate, and even embrace uncertainty (Foucault, 1980, p. 149; Foucault, 1984; Anderson, 1996, p. 194). Relativist research methods move beyond the limitations of positivism and the interpretive approach, allowing for in-depth assessments of cultural discourses, the concomitant analysis of power, and potential for constructive social change. *See also*: Qualitative Analysis.

References/Suggested Readings: Anderson, K. 1996. *Sociology: A Critical Introduction.* Canada: Nelson; Foucault, M. 1980. Body/Power and Truth and Oower. In C. Gordon (ed.)., *Michel Foucault: Power/Knowledge.* U.K.: Harvester; Foucault, M. 1984. What Is Enlightenment? In P. Rabinow (ed.), *The Foucault Reader.* New York: Pantheon; Giddens, A. 1991. *Introduction to Sociology.* New York: Norton; Habermas, J. 1971. *Knowledge and Human Interest* (J. Shapiro, trans.). Boston: Beacon Press.

ANNETTE BICKFORD

RESTORATIVE JUSTICE AND GANG CRIME. The current method of dealing with gang-related crime is based on vengeance, deterrence, and punishment. This approach, known as retributive justice, involves identifying the gang member/perpetrator and adjudicating him/her in open court as part of a status degradation ceremony. Temporary exclusion from society is usually the result. The problem of reintegration, i.e., after the gang member is released from prison, is not part of the logic of the criminal justice system. Although retributive justice maintains a suppression effect (Braga, 2001), supporters of the restorative justice (RJ) model argue that this promotes "a negative peace" rather than truly bringing about positive social change and a genuine desire on the part of the gang member to refrain from criminal activity (Umbreit, Vos, Coates, and Brown, 2003).

Criticisms of retribution-based justice are copious. Attempts to lash out at gang members to cause them to suffer or punishing them for the purpose of special or general deterrence does nothing to address the underlying root causes of gang-related criminality. Retribution and deterrence-based approaches ignore the lack of social opportunities, inequitable distribution of resources in American society, and the lack of education, training, and jobs (Cummings and Monti, 1993; Goldstein, 1993; Hagedorn, 1988; Huff, 1990, 1993; Moore, 1991). Until the basic inequities in the current social structure are addressed, the efficacy of suppression efforts is limited (Whitehead and Lab, 2006).

Applying Principles of Restorative Justice to Gang-Related Crime

Several principles of RJ may be effectively applied to gang-related crime. The following is a summary of RJ principles noted in the juvenile justice literature (see, for example, Ashworth, 2003; Feld, 1999; Kurki, 2000; Bazemore and Umbriet, 2001).

1. Crime is an offense against human relationships and secondarily a violation of law. This means that we must recognize that when gang crime occurs, simplistic punishments motivated by vengeance fail to recognize the root causes of the violation while simultaneously ignoring the victim. The goal should not be to castigate the offender as much as it should be to repair, to whatever extent possible, the harm caused by the offense. This can only be done by viewing gang-related crime as an upheaval of human relationships generally, and by examining the specific relation between victim and offender—which is often long-standing and conflict-habituated. An RJ approach, on the other hand, recognizes that crime is not necessarily the cause of a problem, but rather, crime is a symptom of a larger and more complex underlying problem involving human relationships.
2. Crime control lies primarily in the community, not the formal criminal justice system. This principle implies that it is not the formal criminal justice system that should take priority in dealing with gang-related crime. Rather than using the adversarial system involving the courtroom workgroup (e.g., police, prosecutors, defense attorneys, and judges), community members should be used in resolving disputes. For example, after a gang-related incident has been noted and the victim identified, members of the community should be involved in resolving this dispute. This can include conferencing circles, neighborhood accountability boards, or other community members such as teachers, pastors, neighbors, or police officers. By avoiding an adversarial approach to dealing with incidents—including avoiding, to whatever extent possible, stigma, isolation, and removing the gang member from the community—there is a much greater likelihood of repairing the harm caused by an act. Keeping and bringing the gang member back into the community is the ultimate objective.
3. Punishment alone is not effective in changing behavior and is disruptive to community harmony and good relationships. By treating gang-related crime as an individual

act with individual responsibility that is to be punished, the end result is further alienation of the gang member. Not only does punishment further exacerbate the problem of feelings of detachment from the community, but it also does little to repair the harm caused by the deviant behavior. RJ approaches such as victim-offender mediation (VOM) whereby the victim and offender communicate directly with each other using a trained mediator to facilitate meaningful dialogue, is much more likely to result in a satisfactory conclusion as it relates to repairing harm. Simply meting out punishment to a gang member will not achieve similar results (Bazemore and Schiff, 2005).

4. Victims are central to the process of resolving crime and the offender is defined by a capacity to make reparations. Whereas the current criminal justice system treats victims as detached from the process. For example, victims' primary contribution to the court process is to serve as witnesses who testify as to what the perpetrator did. Subsequently, they are discharged and essentially deemed relatively unimportant for the rest of the process (Whitehead and Lab, 2006). Along the same lines, offenders are defined by "pathologies" (e.g., some deficiency that causes them to become criminal). RJ, on the other hand, seeks to repair the harm done to the victim and this philosophy takes priority in that the victims' needs are deemed important. Also, the offender is not viewed as a flawed, deficient human being; rather, he/she is evaluated in terms of his/her ability to return the relationship to a state of equilibrium. In other words, the offender is viewed as a person who can potentially compensate the victim or otherwise bring about a situation comparable to the one prior to the criminal act.

5. The focus is on problem-solving for the future, not on establishing blame or guilt for the present. Traditional court procedures are flawed because they focus on establishing blame, determining guilt, and attacking the offender. Contrariwise, RJ via VOM attempts to address the underlying relationship problem between the gang member and the victim. By doing so, RJ is much more effective in reducing the likelihood of further attacks against the victim because there is a genuine attempt to have the victim and offender connect in a way that leads to meaningful dialogue and a peaceful settlement. This typically manifests itself by having a trained mediator meet with the victim and perpetrator. The victim is allowed the opportunity to express his/her concerns about the crime and any damages that occurred. Similarly, the offender gets the chance to explain why the crime was committed, and through this exchange the two parties gain a better understanding of the others' perceptions, feelings, and needs. Ultimately, the mediator helps the disputants agree on how best to restore the situation to the pre-crime state (Umbriet et al., 2003).

6. Restitution is the primary means of restoring equilibrium as opposed to the imposition of pain. Simply stated, a peaceful resolution to a dispute between victim and perpetrator is more likely if the offender is encouraged to reconcile and/or compensate the victim. Traditional, formal criminal justice responses usually involve pain to the offender in order to pay them back for past wrongs or to deter others in the future. In sum, if formal criminal justice responses such as retribution and punishment for the sake of deterrence are de-emphasized, RJ principles can achieve several goals. By focusing more on restoring relationships between participants of disputes and keeping the process in the community rather than trying to ostracize the offender, a true state of peace can be achieved. The sequence of events for RJ include (1) expressing disapproval of the offense; (2) promoting forgiveness as opposed to vengeance; (3) encouraging repairs to the relationships between parties as opposed to focusing only on punishment; and (5) reintegrateinghe offender back into the community as opposed to further stigmatizing him or her.

Limitations of Restorative Justice

It must be noted that there are some troubling limitations to the concept of RJ as a response to gang-related crime. Whitehead and Lab (2006) provide a list of limitations:

- inability to engender participation
- problems with identifying appropriate participants
- coercive participation (particularly offenders)
- net widening
- inability of participants to meaningfully contribute
- lack of neutrality by participants and/or mediators
- inability to protect constitutional rights of offenders

In addition, perhaps the most disconcerting limitation is the fact that RJ cannot offset the problems associated with inequities in the social structure. That is, whether the response is one of a formal criminal justice approach or a peacemaking/restorative approach, many gang members still suffer from extreme relative deprivation (Kurki, 2000). It is naive to think that alterations to the responses to gang-related crime that fail to involve the redistribution of wealth downward will have any appreciable effect on gang-related crime rates.

References/Suggested Readings: Ashworth, A. 2003. Is Restorative Justice the Way Forward for Criminal Justice? In E. McLaughlin, R. Fergusson, G. Hughes, and L. Westmarland (eds.), *Restorative Justice: Critical Issues*. Thousand Oaks: Sage; Bazemore, G., and Schiff, M. 2005. *Juvenile Justice Reform and Restorative Justice: Building Theory and Policy from Practice*. Portland: Willan; Bazemore, G., and Umbriet, M. 2001. *A Comparison of Four Restorative Conferencing Models*. Washington, DC: U.S. Department of Justice, Office of Juvenile Justice and Delinquency Prevention; Braga, A. 2001. The Effects of Hot Sports Policing on Crime. *Annals of the American Academy of Political and Social Science*, 578, 104–125; Bureau of Justice Assistance. 2005. *Gang Resistance Education and Training*. Washington DC: Bureau of Justice Assistance. Available online at great-online.org; Cook, P., Moore, M., and Braga, A. 2002. Gun Control. In J. Wilson and J. Petersilia (eds.), *Crime: Public Policies for Crime Control*. Oakland: ICS Press; Cummings, S., and Monti, D. 1993. Public Policy and Gangs: Social Science and the Urban Underclass. In S. Cummings and D. Monti (eds.), *Gangs: The Origins and Impact of Contemporary Youth Gangs in the United States*, pp. 305–320. Albany: SUNY Press; Curry, G., Ball, R., Fox, R., and Stone, D. 1992. *National Assessment of Law Enforcement Anti-gang Information Resources: Final Report*. Washington, DC: National Institute of Justice; Esbensen, F., and Osgood, D. 1999. Gang Resistance Education and Training (G.R.E.A.T.): Results from the National Evaluation. *Journal of Research in Crime and Delinquency*, 36, 194–225; Esbensen, F., Peterson, D., Taylor, T., Freng, A., and Osgood, D. 2004. Gang Prevention: A Case Study of a Primary Prevention Program. In F. Esbensen, S. Tibbetts, and L. Gaines (eds.), *American Youth Gangs at the Millennium*, pp. 351–374. Long Grove: Waveland; Feld, B. 1999. Rehabilitation, Retribution and Restorative Justice: Alternative Conceptions of Juvenile Justice. In G. Bazemore and L. Walgrave (eds.), *Restorative Juvenile Justice: Repairing the Harm of Youth Crime*. Monsey: Criminal Justice Press; Goldstein, A. 1993. Gang Intervention: A Historical Review. In A. Goldstein and C. Huff (eds.), *The Gang Intervention Handbook*, pp. 21–51. Champaign: Research Press; Gray, J. 2001. *Why Our Drug Laws Have Failed and What We Can Do about It*. Philadelphia: Temple University Press; Hagedorn, J. 1988. *People and Folks: Gangs, Crime and the Underclass in a Rustbelt City*. Chicago: Lakeview Press; Huff, C. 1990. Denial, Overreaction, and Misidentification: A Postscript on Public Policy. In C. Huff (ed.), *Gangs in America*, pp. 310–317. Newbury Park: Sage; Huff, C. 1993. Gangs in the United States. In A. Goldstein and C. Huff (eds.), *The Gang Intervention Handbook*. Champaign: Research Press; Katz, C., and Webb, V. 2003. *Police Response to Gangs: A Multi-site Study—Final Report*. Washington, DC: National Institute of Justice; Kennedy, D. 1998. Pulling Levers: Getting Deterrence Right. *National Institute of Justice Journal*, 236, 2–8; Kurki, L. 2000. Restorative and Community Justice in the United States. *Crime and Justice: A Review of Research*, 27, 235–303; Moore, M. 2003. Sizing up COMP-STAT: An Important Administrative Innovation in Policing. *Criminology and Public Policy*, 2 (3), 469–494; Umbreit, M., Vos, B., Coates, R., and Brown, K. 2003. *Facing Violence: The Path of Restorative Justice and Dialogue*. Monsey: Criminal Justice Press; Weisel, D., and Shelley, T. 2004. *Specialized Gang Units: Form and Function in Community Policing—Final Report*. Washington, DC: National Institute of Justice; Whitehead, J., and Lab, S. 2006. *Juvenile Justice* (5th ed). Cincinnati: Anderson Publications.

BILLY LONG

RUSSIAN GANGS. Street-based youth groups have come to public attention in Russia since the end of the 1980s. However they have a longer history. In the 1920s and 1930s, and again after World War II, millions of orphaned and neglected children roamed the streets of Russian cities. *Besprizorniki,* as these children were called, adopted a variety of survival strategies, including crime—such as theft of food or money—and were known to form cliques, sometimes with recognized leaders (Bosewitz, 1988; Stolee, 1988; Goldman, 1993; Ball, 1993). With the start of market reforms in the 1990s street children again became a feature of the Russian urban landscape. Research shows that while most such street children tend to join unstable peer groups and lead a hand-to-mouth existence, a minority form more durable groups and engage in street crime, combined with other day-to-day survival strategies (Stephenson, 2001).

Although territorial groups of young people were not a subject of social research in the Soviet Union from the second half of 1930s to the 1980s (with official criminology mainly classifying group violence as hooliganism), group delinquency was widespread in Soviet urban and rural areas. Juvenile peer groups protected their turf and attacked their peers and the passers-by in parks, dance halls, sports stadiums, and other local "arenas." The group members were predominantly new urban dwellers, who came to cities and towns during the rapid urbanization of Russia, and many of their practices can be traced to rural communities, with their traditions of violent feuds between rival villages and informal rules of masculine honor (Schepanskaya, 2001; Salagaev and Shashkin, 2005). Groups were organized around leisure activities, and conflict and control over territory served to foster their social bonding and integration.

The transformation of some of these peer groups into "entrepreneurs of violence" (Blok, 1974; Volkov, 2001), who used violence as an instrument of criminal business, began in the end of 1960s and beginning of 1970s, with the emergence of shadow "off-the books" production in Soviet enterprises. Shadow economic activities gave rise to new deviant and criminal networks. Needing to ensure safe transportation, storage, and sales of their products, illegal entrepreneurs employed young people from local neighborhoods. Some territorial peer groups became involved in protection and violent enforcement for this market. This new role speeded up the transformation of these groups into more structured, disciplined, and violent gangs. Simultaneously, criminal groups that attempted to extract their own share of the illegal profits from shadow production began to mobilize their own troops of local youth. One such network emerged around the Kazan-based criminal gang, Tiap Liap, which existed from the end of the 1960s until 1978. In response to the Tiap Liap growing dominance of the urban territory, other gangs emerged—often organized to defend their turf rather than engage specifically in criminal activity (Salagaev, 2005).

Street gangs became particularly visible in Kazan in the early 1980s, when young people started to wear group uniforms, organize mass fights, and engage in such street crimes as robbery and mugging. There were about 100 gangs in the city at the time (Salagaev, 2001). By the end of the 1980s, some forty cities of the former Soviet Union (Kazan, Tomsk, Ul'ianovsk, Ioshkar-Ola, Naberezhnie Chelni, and others) were reporting "gang problems." Most gangs were neighborhood groups with mixed social, ethnic, and class composition. A well-known exception was the youth scene in Liubertsy, a Moscow suburb. Here working-class young people formed gangs that saw their role as to fight against "degenerate" Moscow youth, for which purpose they made frequent trips to the capital (Ovchinskii, 1990). In the same period, in the more open climate of Gorbachev's *perestroika*, non-criminal youth subcultures such as football fans, bikers, or heavy metal music fans began to emerge in Russian cities. Some of these soon became involved in the protection of local turf (Sibiriakov, 1990; Pilkington, 1994).

With the end of state socialism and the start of market reforms at the beginning of the 1990s, the social organization and practices of street groups changed again. The collapse of the formal economy and weakening of the state, together with the opening up of new opportunities in the shadow economy, saw an epidemic spread of crime and violence. During the 1990s new Mafia-type structures emerged in the country, made up of hierarchically organized gangs, each with a grip on a specific bit of turf or having control over specific businesses (Varese, 2001). Some of these gangs were formed by territorial peer groups, while others were created by students, members of sports clubs, or ethnic minority groups (Volkov, 2002). They used violence mainly in order to extract profit from protection racket or extortion. If we look at the features of street gangs in Kazan and some of the other cities in the Volga region, we find that they tend to be stratified on the basis of age, with age cohorts forming their own mini-gangs. They often have well-defined hierarchical structures, with strict rules of admission and exit. Most gangs have a common fund (*obschak*) which is used to support the incarcerated members and to fund joint activities (e.g., leisure, expenses on criminal operations). These street gangs are predominantly male. Even when women are present in the gang, they tend to have a subordinate role (Pilkington, 1994; Omel'chenko, 1996; Salagaev, 2001). Youth gangs develop their own illegal enterprises, often independent from those of adult criminal groups. They engage in control and regulation of the street-level economy (illegal parking lots, drug trade, prostitution, violent enforcement and protection rackets), and commit offenses such as burglary and street crime (extortion, robbery, and mugging). They also protect their turf and fight with rival gangs. The gangs tend to be well integrated in the local community. The "business" objectives of territorial groups dictate that expressive violence is limited and unnecessary conflict with the adult members of the community (including teachers and the police) is avoided.

Some of the street groups form the lower divisions of the criminal society and act as enforcers for the mafia. This symbiosis between the street gangs and the world of **organized crime** is to a large extent a product of a regime of mass incarceration in Russia. Russia currently has the second highest rate of incarceration in the world, with 564 prisoners per 100,000 population. This makes the "prison culture" easily accessible for young people. Many of the norms and cultural practices of young gang members derive from this culture, and these are reinforced when gang members leave prison and return to their gangs (Omel'chenko, 1996; Stephenson, 2001; Oleinik, 2003). Those young people who prove to be resourceful and brave can be allowed to graduate into adult criminal groups. At the same time far from all street youth groups are associated with organized crime or aspire to "criminal careers." Some territorial groups of young people (such as *gopniki*) have been mainly involved in the protection of the local turf and fights with members of other youth subcultures, such as hippies or rappers (Pilkington and Omelchenko, 2002).

Since the 1990s in a number of cities, particularly those with a high influx of migrants, such as Moscow, St. Petersburg, Voronezh, and others, there has been proliferation of violent **skinhead** groups. These groups, which reportedly have links to organized crime, are involved in racist attacks on foreigners and non-Russian migrants (Tarasov, 2000). Skinhead groups are extremely violent and have been responsible for pogroms of ethnic markets, racially motivated assaults, and murder.

Youth work (and street work in particular) is still in its infancy in Russia. The law-enforcement bodies attempt to control gang members through registration, or prosecute them for offenses such as hooliganism, theft, or burglary. Over the recent years there have also been several well-publicized trials against gangs (one such trial took place in Kazan against the Khadi-Taktash gang), and a limited number of prosecutions for racially motivated offenses.

References/Suggested Readings: Blok, A. 1974. *The Mafia of a Sicilian Village*. Prospect Heights: Waveland Press; Bosewitz, R. 1988. *Waifdom in the Soviet Union*. Frankfurt: Verlagt Peter Lang; Juviler, P. 1985. Contradictions of Revolution: Juvenile Crime and Rehabilitation. Reprinted in A. Gleason and A.N. Oleinik (eds.), *Organized Crime, Prison and the Post-Soviet Society*. Aldershot: Ashgate (2003); Omelchenko, E. 1996. Young Women in Provincial Gang Culture. Case Study of Ul'anovsk'. In H. Pilkington (ed.), *Gender, Generation and Identity in Contemporary Russia*, pp. 216–235. London: Routledge; Ovchinskii, V.S. 1990. Gastrolnie Poezdki Antiobshestvennikh Gruppirovok Podrostkov i Molodezhi—Novii Fenomen' (The "Tours" of Anti-social Groups of Teenagers and Youth—A New Phenomenon). In *Kriminologi o Neformalnikh Molodezhnikh Ob'edineniiakh*, pp. 192–196. Moscow: Iuridicheskaia Literatura; Pilkington , H. 1994. *Russia's Youth and Its Culture*. London: Routledge; Pilkington, H., and Omelchenko, E. 2002. *Looking West? Cultural Globalization and Russian Youth Cultures*. University Park: Pennsylvania State University Press; Salagaev, A. 2001. Evolution of Delinquent Gangs in Russia. In M.W. Klein, H.Y. Kerner, C.L. Maxson, and E. Weitekamp (eds.), *The Eurogang Paradox: Street Gangs and Youth Groups in the U.S. and Europe*, pp. 195–202). Dordrecht: Kluwer; Salagaev, A.L. 2005. Issledivaniia Podrostkovo-molodyozhnykh Delinkventnykh Soobschestv (gruppirovok) v Rossii i v Byvshem SSSR (The Studies of Youth Delinquent Groups [gangs] in Russia and in the Former Soviet Union). In A.L. Salagaev and M.E. Pozdniakova (eds.), *Deviantnoe Povedenie v Sovremennoi Rossii v fokuse Sotsiologii*, pp. 184–195. Moscow: Institut Sotsiologii RAN; Salagaev, A., and Shashkin, A. 2005. After-Effects of the Transition: Youth Criminal Careers in Russia. In V. Puuronen, J. Soilevuo-Gronnerod, and J. Herranen (eds.), *Youth—Similarities, Differences, Inequalities: Reports of the Carelian Institute*, pp. 1:154–172. Joensuu: University of Joensuu; Sibiriakov, S.L. 1990. Ulichnie Gruppirovki Molodiozhi v Volgograde (Street Youth Groups in Volgograd). In *Kriminologi o Neformalnikh Molodiozhnikh Ob'iedineniiakh*, pp. 168–176. Moscow: Iuridicheskaia Literature; Stephenson, S. 2001. Street Children in Moscow: Using and Creating Social Capital. *Sociological Review*, 49 (4), 530–547; Tarasov, A. 2000. Porozhdenie reform: Britogolovie, oni zhe Skinkhedy (A result of the reforms: Shaved Heads aka Skinheads). *Svobodnaia Mysl*, 4, 5; Varese, F. 2001. *The Russian Mafia: Private Protection in a New Market Economy*. Oxford: Oxford University Press; Volkov, V. 2002. *Violent Entrepreneurs: The Use of Force in the Making of Russian Capitalism*. Ithaca: Cornell University Press.

SVETLANA STEPHENSON

S

SKINHEADS. The skinhead movement emerged from British youth culture beginning in the 1950s and 1960s and developed its more distinctive style in the associations of working-class youth and West Indian immigrants in the urban centers. While the skinhead movement began as a cultural movement, particularly in terms of music, its contemporary manifestations incorporate both cultural styles and political agendas. The economic and social problems of the 1970s and 1980s created anti-government and anti-immigrant attitudes among working-class youth who blamed their situation on a decline of white culture. Therefore, skinheads evolved into a more conservative political movement, with a particular concern about immigration and the loss of traditional British culture. By the 1970s skinheads in the United Kingdom had become linked with the right-wing National Front and the neo-Nazi movement (Wooden and Blazak, 2001). The British punk movement's entry into the American youth culture scene introduced American youth to skinheads thereby creating an indigenous American skinhead movement, generally situated in rural and suburban areas. The global skinhead movement splintered in the 1980s as some skinheads rejected racism and violence. The Anti-Defamation League of B'nai B'rith (1995) found skinhead groups in thirty-three countries in Europe, Japan, and North and South America, and estimates the worldwide number of skinheads in about 70,000. The skinhead movement is loosely organized and intra-group rivalries are common. Skinheads are typically viewed as uneducated, poor youth from dysfunctional families, but this is not necessarily true in all cases. Some skinhead groups are composed on middle-class youth who are not associated with the life situations usually seen as a risk factor in gang membership (Shafer and Navarro, 2003). The Hammerskin Nation is the largest neo-Nazi skinhead group in the United States, and its violence against minorities and others is well documented, sometimes against other skinhead organizations. The Hammerskin Nation is associated with White Aryan Resistance leader Richard Metzger. Metzger is the one major neo-Nazi leader who has embraced skinheads and was one of the first to organize the regional movements into a national movement. The Hammerskins Nation has about twenty chapters in the United States and a number in other countries. Recently the Hammerskin Nation has experienced a schism and is said to be in disarray. Other important skinhead groups include the Chicago Areas Skinheads (CASH), Detroit Area Skin Heads (DASH), the Eastern Hammer Skins (who operate from Maine to New Jersey in the United States), the Connecticut White Wolves, PEN1 in California, Volksfont, and WAR Skinheads.

Skinhead style includes shaved heads, and working-class dress including Doc Martens boots, suspenders, and military-style jackets. This style emerged as a rejection of the late 1960s hippies style and the "Rude Boy" style of West Indian Immigrants. Music is a central element of the skinhead movement and the lyrics suggest racism, violence, and militancy. Resistance Records is the largest producer of racist music CDs in the United States and was owned by National Alliance leader the late Dr. William Pierce. The National Alliance is considered the largest neo-Nazi organization in the United States and maintains an edgy relationship with skinheads generally. For example, the Hammerskins Nations sponsors concerts across the United States and views music as a key to recruiting alienated youth. So-called unity gatherings serve as the major cultural events for skinheads where skinhead bands are presented and working sessions are held. Hammerskins are also active in publishing and on the Internet. Ska music, the cultural foundation of the skinhead movement, has been supplanted by hard-core music, while ska has become the province of pop music and a relatively nonpolitical, eclectic middle-class ska scene. Most skinhead groups are short-lived and include younger males, some skinhead groups have members in their forties but this is rare. Female skinhead members comprise about 30 percent of members and refer to themselves as skinbyrds, skingirls, chelseas, or featherwoods.

References/Suggested Readings: Anti-Defamation League of B'nai B'rith United States. 1995. *Skinhead International: A Worldwide Survey of Neo-Nazi Skinheads*; Hicks, W.L. 2004. Skinheads: A Three Nation Comparison. *Journal of Gang Research*, 11 (2), 51–73; Schafer, J.R., and Navarro, J. 2003. The Seven-Stage Hate Model: The Psychopathology of Hate Groups. *FBI Law Enforcement Bulletin* (March); Skinhead Project. 2005. Available online at www.adl.org/racist_skinheads/skinhead_groups.asp. Hammerskin Nation; Wayne, S., Blazak, W., and Blazak, R. 2001. *Renegade Kids, Suburban Outlaws: From Youth Culture to Delinquency*. Wadsworth.

ALBERT DICHIARA

SOCIAL CONSTRUCTION OF GANGS. Social construction is a theory of knowledge developed by Peter Berger and Thomas Luckmann in their book *The Social Construction of Reality* (1966). The social constructionist perspective seeks to discover the ways that individuals and groups perceive, interpret, and create "social reality." From this perspective, people interact with the understanding that their perceptions of reality are shared and reinforced by interacting with each other. Over time these interpretations come to be seen as part of a larger, "objective" reality, as being natural and inevitable to the people who accept it. From a social constructionist prospective, the perception of reality is often more important that the objective reality.

The definition of gangs is often dependent upon our perceptions of the broader gang problem in American society, a social construction. As McCorkle and Miethe

(2002, p. 11) put it, "Social problems are not what people think are social problems; if they don't see a problem, for all intents and purposes, the problem doesn't exist. . . . What is thus important is not the actual nature of the condition, but rather what individuals say about that condition."

Construction of the Gang Problem

The gang problem received little attention by the media and by politicians until the 1980s. McCorkle and Miethe (2002, p. 4) report that in the United States during the 1980s, police began to report a sharp rise in gang activity: "Media coverage of gangs exploded. Newspapers, television, and films were suddenly awash with images of gun-toting, drug-dealing, hat-to-back gangstas . . . as we approach the new millennium we are informed that the gang threat has yet to peak."

They go on to argue that gangs came to be defined as a major source of crime and violence in the United States at a time when the media seemed obsessed with stories of crime and violence. Do the images and rhetoric surrounding street gangs accurately reflect the nature and extent of the threat? Is the resultant public fear of gangs and the changes in criminal justice policy toward gangs commensurate with the actual threat posed by these gangs? It is possible that the gang problem has been exaggerated, distorted, and exploited by the media, by politicians, and by the criminal justice system? McCorkle and Miethe (2002, p. 6) argue that "the media's coverage of gangs . . . is typically inflammatory and sensationalized, equates gangs with violent crime, and portrays gangs as dominated illegal drug markets." This type of exaggeration and distortion often gives rise to stereotyping and **moral panics**.

Stereotypes

Joan Moore has compiled a list of the most common stereotypes of gang members in the United States (Moore, 1993, pp. 28–29):

1. They are composed of males (no females) who are violent, addicted to drugs and alcohol, sexually hyperactive, unpredictable, and confrontational.
2. They are either all African American or all Hispanic.
3. They thrive in inner-city neighborhoods where they dominate, intimidate, and prey upon innocent citizens.
4. They all deal heavily in drugs, especially crack cocaine.
5. "A gang is a gang is a gang"—in other words, they are all alike or "you see one and you see them all."
6. There is no good in gangs, it is all bad (a corollary to this is that anyone who would want to join a gang must be stupid or crazy).
7. Gangs are basically criminal enterprises and youths start gangs in order to collectively commit crimes; in other words, there is a tendency to confuse individual and group criminality.
8. The *West Side Story* image of aggressive, rebellious, but nice kids has been replaced in recent years by the "gangster" image of a very disciplined organization complete with soldiers.

According to Moore, our legal and criminal justice policies rely on these stereotypes. Consequently, it is not uncommon for white citizens to have a completely different response when they see a group of African American teenagers at the mall as opposed to a group of young white males, even if each group is wearing clothing and/or colors that are stereotypically associated with gang attire (Shelden, Tracy, and Brown, 2004, p. 25).

Moral Panics

The term "moral panic" was popularized by British criminologist Stanley Cohen when describing the reaction to various youth problems in Britain in the 1960s (called Mods and Rockers). Cohen gave the following definition (1980, p. 9):

> A condition, episode, person or group of persons emerges to become defined in a styl-ized and stereotypical fashion by the mass media; the barricades are manned by editors, bishops, politicians and other right thinking people; socially accredited experts pro-nounce their diagnoses and solutions; the ways of coping are evolved or . . . resorted to; the condition then disappears, submerges or deteriorates and becomes visible.

These panics are "far more likely to be perceived during times of widespread anxiety, moral malaise, and uncertainty about the future" (McCorkle and Miethe, 2001, p. 19). Youth gangs become visible symbols of the widespread perception that social order is deteriorating. Panics build on the social divisions already present, especially race and class. Moral panics usually focus on the behavior of the young because they represent the most serious challenge to conventional values held by adults. This, combined with the emergence of the "underclass" in the 1980s gave rise to the wide-spread concern with gang violence in the American inner city in the 1980s (Shelden, Tracy, and Brown, 2004, p. 25).

According to Cohen, moral panics emerge as a condition, event, or group (real or imagined) becomes defined as a threat to the values and interests of society. Groups (in this case gangs) are demonized, transformed into "folk devils" by the mass media, groups of experts, and "right thinking people" who take moral positions, make judg-ments, and suggest how the threat should be handled. Cohen notes that there emerges a gap between the concern over a condition and the objective threat that it poses. In the case of gangs, the objective threat is less than popularly perceived. The condition that produced the moral panic then either disappears or becomes more visible. The threat is generated by the media or by special interest groups. Concern over the threat reaches a peak, subsides, and perhaps reemerges (Cohen, 1980).

When moral panics arise, there is a tendency for politicians and others to react viscerally and harshly. The War on Drugs is an outgrowth of politicians acting quickly rather than following a reasoned and informed policy approach.

Conclusions

Gangs must be understood as both an objective and a subjective social problem. The social construction of the gang problem arose when the media and politicians began to focus on the gang problem in the 1980s. As a result, the public became conscious of the problem and the result was a moral panic that lingers to this day. The reaction to the construction of the gang problem is very real: spending on gang units, "punk prisons" for the young, and the war on drugs continues to increase. Public fear of crime also continues to increase.

References/Suggested Readings: Berger, P., and Luckmann, P. 1966. *The Social Construc-tion of Reality.* New York: Doubleday; Cohen, S. 1980. *Folk Devils and Moral Panics: The*

Creation of the Mods and Rockers. New York: St. Martin's Press; McCorkle, R., and Miethe, T. 2002. *Panic: The Social Construction of the Gang Problem.* New York: Prentice Hall; Moore, J.W. 1993. Gangs, Drugs and Violence. In Cummings and Monti (eds.), *Gangs: The Origins and Impact of Contemporary Youth Gangs in the United States.* Albany: SUNY Press; Shelden, R., Tracy, S., and Brown, W. 2004. *Youth Gangs in American Society* (3rd ed.). Belmont: Thomson.

WILLIAM J. FARRELL

SOCIAL DISORGANIZATION. Social disorganization theory emerged from the Chicago school which emphasized social ecology as the key factor is social order. It is assumed that industrialization and urbanization reduce internal and external social controls, which are the principal crime-producing effects of social disorganization. Typically, social disorganization is indicated by high levels of divorce, transience and residential stability, low SES, family disruption, and ethnic heterogeneity. In such conditions, conflict over values and norms and weakened primary relationships serve to produce models of behavior that support crime.

Social disorganization theory is influenced by the work of Robert Part and Ernest Burgess who studied the changing nature of neighborhoods in Chicago at the turn of the twentieth century. Park and Burgess applied the ideas of adaptation to a changing or new environment to understand Chicago's growth. Clifford Shaw and Henry McKay are considered the creators of social disorganization theory and were motivated by the increasing rates of crime and deviance that were the result of migration from rural areas and by immigration from Europe. Further, social disorganization emerged as a way of changing the debate about crime from an emphasis on defective individuals and toward sociological forces which influence behavior. Orderly communities and neighborhoods are able to control deviance more effectively than are those in which the major institutions of society are weakened. Using the ideas of Park and Burgess, Shaw and McKay established that the highest rates of crime were found in what is called the transitional zone, that part of the city characterized by older houses, a large number of rental units, and generally poor living conditions. Transitional zones, or interstitial areas in the words of **Frederic Thrasher**, are also characterized by large numbers of unsupervised youth who are at risk of delinquency and gang involvement.

Since the 1980s there has been growing interest in revitalizing social disorganization theory (Bursik, 1988; Sampson and Groves, 1989; Massey and Denton, 1993) and concepts from other theories have been used to clarify the ways in which social disorganization operated to produce crime. Bursik and Grasmick (1993) have shown that elements of opportunity theory are related to social disorganization theory and Meithe and McDowall (1993) have used routine activities theory to reshape social disorganization theory. Researchers have shown that "collective efficacy" (Sampson and Groves, 1989), the informal controls that result from stronger friendship and neighborhood networks are crucial in the operation of social disorganization as a cause of crime. Further, recent research has challenged the idea that ethnic heterogeneity, a principal indicator of social disorganization, is less important than is segregation (Massey and Denton, 1993; Warner and Pierce, 1993). Further, segregation is said to produce changes in the normative environment that also influence crime rates. Here for example, family disruption, a core indicator of social disorganization, may lose its criminogenic effect when family disruption in the form or single-parent families and divorce becomes normative in a neighborhood. The support for social disorganization theory in the new breed of empirical work has been only marginally supportive (Beaulieu, 2004).

References/Suggested Readings: Beaulieu, M. 2004. *Social Disorganization Revisited: A Longitudinal Analysis of Effects on Urban Residential Segregation on Crime.* Doctoral dissertation, State University of New York Albany; Bursik, R. 1988. Social Disorganization Theories of Crime and Delinquency: Problems and Prospects. *Criminology*, 26 (4), 519–551; Bursik, R., and Grasmick, H. 1995. *Neighborhoods and Crime: The Dimensions of Effective Community Control.* Lexington: Lexington Books; Massey, D., and Denton, N. 1993. *American Apartheid: Segregation and the Making of the Underclass.* Boston: Harvard University Press; Miethe, T.D., and McDowell, D. 1993. Contextual effects in models of criminal victimization. *Social Forces*, 71, 741–759; Park, R., and Burgess, E. 1925. *The City.* Chicago: University of Chicago Press; Sampson, R., and Groves, W.B. 1989. Community Structure and Crime: Testing Social Disorganization Theory. *American Journal of Sociology*, 94 (4), 774–802; Shaw C., and McKay, H. 1942. *Juvenile Delinquency and Urban Areas.* Chicago: University of Chicago Press; Warner, B., and Pierce, G. 1993. Reexamining Social Disorganization Theory Using Calls to the Police as a Measure of Crime. *Criminology*, 31 (4), 493–517.

ALBERT DICHIARA

SOUTH AFRICAN GANGS. Gangs are a pervasive presence in South Africa. They figure prominently in the public discourse about crime, and they are linked in direct and indirect ways to the daily insecurity experienced by many South Africans. Gangs in South Africa operating in urban and rural areas across the country are involved in a wide range of criminal and non-criminal activities that impact heavily on black African and colored communities in particular.

The gang phenomenon is a complex one, and an agreed-upon definition of gangs by criminologists remains elusive. As the scholarship suggests, the term "gang" can refer to quite a wide range of organizations engaged in a broad spectrum of activities, in some cases serving functions for members and the communities in which they operate which are not reducible to criminal activity and deviance.

As in most countries, different types of criminal organizations operate within South Africa. There are foreign criminal organizations inside the country, including Chinese, Russian, and Nigerian syndicates; there are local or regional **organized crime** groups that specialize in particular kinds of operations, from cash-in-transit heists to auto theft; and there are the more traditional street and prison gangs. The focus here is on the last of these groups, the street and prison gangs. It is these groups which are most intimately linked to township communities from which their members are drawn, and thus to the challenges of crime, insecurity, and development in the daily lives of many South Africans.

Origins

Gangs have taken, and continue to take, a variety of forms in South Africa. However, beneath the differences between street gangs and prison gangs, as well as between black African and colored gangs, are important commonalities. (I use the basic racial categories employed by the census—black African, colored, Asian, and white. However, in distinction from the census terminology, I use the term *black* standing alone as distinct from *African* to refer to all nonwhites.) Indeed, gang formation in South Africa can be linked to a set of very specific conditions that have persisted throughout decades of white minority rule and settler colonialism: racism, the destruction of established communities, poverty, marginalization, regulation of black labor, and urbanization.

In response to these conditions new social formations began to emerge as one survival mechanism for young men and migrants in particular, who found them-selves in the mining camps, prisons, and urban townships of late nineteenth- and early twentieth-century South Africa. In the context of structural violence and exclu-sion these formations often represented a means to achieve status and masculinity, a sense of belonging, and access to material resources when traditional avenues were crumbling and "legitimate" ones were blocked by racial discrimination.

In late nineteenth-century Durban, for example, as the historian Paul la Hausse has described, the destruction of the Zulu kingdom and the growth of white-con-trolled commercial agriculture pushed many single young men into urban areas in search of work. Once there, poverty, racism, isolation and other disorienting changes associated with the rapid shift from rural to city life fostered the emergence and growth of the amalita gangs at the turn of the century. Although formed more as part of a "struggle by migrant youth for control over urban space" than for criminal ac-tivity these groups of young African men existing at the margins of urban life invari-ably came into conflict with the law, particularly as white anxiety around the changes associated with black urbanization increased (La Hausse, 1990, p. 91). The resulting criminalization of African youth would become a recurring theme throughout the twentieth century.

Similar dynamics were repeated in other urban areas and in the county's gold and diamond mining compounds. Organizations of township and camp residents began to emerge in response to social marginalizaton and served to absorb the influx of young men from rural areas whose social structures were collapsing under the weight of colonialism. The structures, however, were often involved in a variety of activities that complicate the somewhat simplistic implications of the term "gang." In labor compounds, for example, gangs preyed on recently arrived migrants, but also pro-vided "loans, employment leads, access to housing, and physical protection for their members" (Kynoch, 1999, p. 10).

South African prison gangs emerged at approximately the same time and under pressure of the same forces, although they took a different form. South Africa's prison gangs are today divided into three separate organizations, the 26s, 27s, the 28s, and are commonly referred to as the Numbers. The Numbers evolved in late nineteenth-century Johannesburg out of outlaw bands such as the Ninevites, led by the famous Zulu migrant Nongoloza, which often preyed on African workers drawn from the same social strata as the bandits themselves. Although the Ninevites as a marauding gang were brought under control by 1910, the group had infiltrated the prisons and was actively recruiting among the growing inmate population, made up of black men criminalized by South Africa's racial laws, such that by the 1930s the precursors of today's Number gangs had spread to virtually every prison in the country (Steinberg, 2004).

Gangs under Apartheid

The implementation of apartheid by the National Party after 1948 both repro-duced existing conditions giving rise to gangs and set in motion new ones. The rise of the colored gangs which receive so much attention in South Africa today can be traced directly to removal policies implemented beginning in the 1950s. There were gangs in the colored communities of Cape Town, where the majority of the nation's colored population lives, prior to the forced removal, but these were generally marginal social formations, their growth checked by tight-knit communities in places like District Six.

The removal of entire communities from the inner city and surrounding suburbs of Cape Town to the distant and desolate Cape Flats tore the social fabric, generating unemployment, separating families, and provoking social instability, all of which provided ideal conditions for the gangs to flourish (Merten, 2002). The introduction of the addictive drug Mandrax to the Western Cape in the 1970s further entrenched the gangs in the local economy and in Cape Flats communities, generating income but also exacerbating social instability in the form of substance abuse and related problems, and leading to an increase in gang violence.

The demise of the Ninevites did not mean the end of African gangs. Rather, gangs persisted in townships, prisons, and labor compounds across the country as migration, urbanization, poverty, and marginalization continued to define social conditions for many young men. Combined with increasingly punitive measures aimed at urban blacks by the apartheid state these conditions ensured the expansion of the black criminalization. With the growth of political activity and political organization sparked by the Soweto uprisings of 1976, however, gang activity subsided for a about a decade, as political organizations provided alternatives for township youth and acted as counterweights to gang growth.

The state's relationship to gangs during apartheid took three general forms: corruption, collaboration, and disinterest. Each of these, in their own way, contributed to the gang problem as it exists today. Prior to the 1970s police either ignored gang activity in non-white areas, as it had little bearing on the safety and security of the white community, or police were paid to turn the other way. As the anti-apartheid struggle intensified, however, the state saw in gangs a potentially useful destabilising force in African and colored townships, as well as an important source of intelligence. In some areas gangs aligned themselves with either the state or with the liberation movements.

In general, however, as state repression escalated in the 1980s, gangs took advantage of the chaos and began to reorganize, becoming increasingly involved with planned murders, extortion, bribery, theft and robbery rackets, and drug and gun syndicates, their activities often overlapping with the state's counterinsurgency agenda. The decade stretching from 1983 to 1993, when state violence was at its most intense, proved to be a period of renewed gang activity (Haefele, 1998).

Gangs in South Africa Today

Gangs in South Africa today are in the process of transformation and growth. The traditional distinction between prison gangs and street gangs is in the process of dissolution and local gang structures are becoming linked to regional and international criminal networks. These changes mean new and expanded opportunities for gangs. Gangs from the Cape Flats, for example, are involved in, among other things, the alcohol and drug trades, prostitution, trafficking in stolen cars, gun smuggling, and large-scale theft. Gangs have also become more involved in legal businesses, putting money into hotels, night clubs, public transport, shops, and commercial fishing boats (Standing, 2003). Gang growth is also fueled by the expansion of the market in illicit drugs, facilitated by the opening of the country's borders.

This opening of South Africa after 1990 afforded local gangs access regional and international criminal networks that had been inaccessible prior to the transition, as indicated by the growth of foreign criminal organisations operating inside the country. While South Africa's insertion into the processes of globalization is undoubtedly an important factor in understanding the gang phenomenon in contemporary South Africa, important aspects of gangsterism in the post-apartheid era are domestic in nature. Indeed, in townships across the country conditions remain distressingly similar to those under which gangs initially emerged and grew. Poverty, inequality, the prevalence of violence, and the marginalization of youth remain features of the post-apartheid landscape.

For most South Africans today gangs are experienced at the level of the community and neighborhood. Cycles of gang violence, whether caused by disputes over territory, drug and liquor markets, girls, or shifting alliances, disrupt school, often for days at a time, interfere with travel to work and to places of worship, and contribute to high levels of anxiety, trauma, and feelings of daily insecurity. At the same time income from gang activity often provides money for rent, food, and electricity in communities where unemployment is often over 50 percent, and gangs fund sports and other activities for youth in areas with few, if any, alternatives. Consequently, gangs continue to draw young men and women into their orbit.

Their continued strength is not simply, as some argue, a reflection of an inefficient, under-resourced and lenient criminal justice system, or the opportunities afforded by globalization, but is the legacy of decades-long state negligence and underdevelopment in the majority of the country's communities. Over many years the gangs have come to occupy a prominent place in the local economy, as a source of income, and in local socio-cultural networks, as a source of masculine status. To date, efforts by government to address underdevelopment generally and youth marginalization in particular have proved inadequate. Gangs such the Americans or the Hard Livings on the Cape Flats, two of Cape Town's largest street gangs, have shown themselves perfectly capable of filling some of these gaps left by the state.

Responses to gangs in the post-apartheid period range from peaceful community initiatives to violent vigilante action by groups like PAGAD (People Against Gangsterism and Drugs), and aggressive "war on crime" approaches by the police. Although the government acknowledges the socio-economic roots of gangsterism it continues to rely heavily on law enforcement solutions, often borrowing ideology and practice from the West. Not only has this approach failed to stem the growth of gangs, but by sending thousands upon thousands of youth every year into the same prisons gangs have ruled virtually unchallenged for almost a century, anti-gang and anti-crime initiatives have in some ways become central to the reproduction of gangsterism, particularly as the links between prison gangs and street gangs strengthen.

The existence of and danger posed by organizations of young men in South Africa's urban areas has often been explained through reference to youth who thrive on or beyond the edges of normal society and adult control. Fear of young black men in urban areas throughout the twentieth century most often was articulated through the language of disorder and criminality, functioning to mobilize social control mechanisms which served to reinforce race and class boundaries. However, attempts to view these social formations strictly through the lens of criminality have been no more successful since 1994 than they were before. The failure of anti-gang strategies in fact shows that the term "gang" itself may hide more than it reveals about the complex phenomena of youth, development, crime, and urbanization in modern South Africa. Until solutions which acknowledge that these organizations can serve a variety of functions, some positive as well as the negative, gangs are likely to remain a significant presence in the country's townships.

References/Suggested Readings: Breckenridge, K. 1990. Migration, Crime and Faction Fighting: The Role of the Isitshozi in the Development of Ethnic Organisations in the Compounds. *Journal of Southern African Studies*, 16 (1), 55–78; Dissel, A. 1997. *Youth, Street Culture and Urban Violence in Africa*. Proceedings of the International Symposium held in Abidjan, Ivory Coast, May, pp. 405–411; Gastrow, P. 1998. *Organised Crime in South Africa: Monogram 28*. Institute for Security Studies. Pretoria: South Africa; Glaser, C. 1996. *We Must Infiltrate the Tsotsis: School Politics & Youth Gangs in Soweto, 1968–1976*. Africa Studies Centre, University of Cape Town; Haefele, B.W. 1998. Gangsterism in the Western Cape: Who Are the Role Players? *Crime & Conflict*, 14, 19–22; Harri, C.K. 1998. *Policing Gangsterism in the Next Millennium*. Cape Town; Kinnes, I. 1995. Reclaiming the Cape Flats: A Community Challenge to Crime and Gangsterism. *Crime & Conflict*, 2; Kynoch, G. 1999. *From the Ninevites to the Hard Livings Gang: Township Gangsters & Urban Violence in 20th Century South Africa*. Institute for Advanced Social Research, Wits University, Johannesburg; La Hausse, P. 1990. The Cows of Nongoloza: Youth, Crime & Amalaita Gangs in Durban, 1900–1936. *Journal of Southern African Studies*, 16 (1), 79–111; Merten, M. 2002. A Brotherhood Sealed in Blood. *Mail & Guardian* (August), 2–7; Penn, N. 1990. Droster Gangs of the Bokkeveld and the Roggeveld, 1770–1800. *South African Historical Journal*, 23, 15–40; Redpath, J. 2001 (March). The Bigger Picture: The Gang Landscape in the Western Cape. *Indicator South Africa*, 18 (1), 34–40; Salo, E. (2001). *Mans Is Ma Soe: Ideologies of Masculinity & Ganging Practices in Manenberg, South Africa*. Africa Studies Centre, University of Cape Town; Shaw, M. 1998. Organised Crime in Post Apartheid South Africa. Occasional Paper, 28. Institute for Security Studies, Pretoria; Simpson, G. 2001. Shock Troops & Bandits: Youth, Crime & Politics. In Contemporary Youth Culture: An International Encyclopedia. Shirley Steinberg (ed.), pp. 115–128. Greenwood; Standing, A. 2003. The Social Contradictions of Organised Crime on the Cape Flats. Occasional Paper, 74. Institute for Security Studies, Pretoria; Steinberg, J. 2004. *Nongoloza's Children: Western Cape Prison Gangs during and after Apartheid*. Centre for the Study of Violence and Reconciliation, Johannesburg; Vetten, L. 2000. Invisible Girls & Violent Boys: Gender & Gangs in South Africa. *Quarterly Journal of the South African National NGO Coalition & Interfund*, 3 (2), 39–49.

TONY ROSHAN SAMARA

SPANISH GANGS. In 1975, when General Franco died, the presence of youth subcultures was something "unnatural" in the Spanish political scenario, even if the street gangs of children and adolescents (*pandillas*) had been present since the beginning of the urbanization process. Only after 1960, with economic development and the "opening" of Spain, could the international youth lifestyles gain visibility. The tourist boom and the new media (both commercial and countercultural) introduced new youth movements (mostly hippies and rockers)—albeit with some particularities: they arrived some years after their European counterparts and they settled only in metropolitan areas. The normalization of the Spanish youth scene came about through the process of transition into democracy (1975–1981). All the youth styles that had been created in Europe and America during the post-war period mixed and burst upon the public scene at the same time and were christened by the media with a very popular local term—*tribus urbanas*: urban tribes (something similar happened in Russia in 1989, during the perestroika, with the so-called *neformalniye grupirovnik*—informal groups). Nevertheless, only after the integration into the

European Union (1986) were Spanish "urban tribes" definitively included in the global youth scene. Hovewer, at the beginning of the new milennium, the arrival of new international migrants caming from Latin America and other countries, reintroduced the "street gang issue" as one of the more visible faces of the presence of second (and more precisely 1.5) generations of transnational youth actors.

Golfos and Jipis

Los Golfos, one of the first films by Carlos Saura (1959) shows the adventures of a youth gang in a Spanish suburb still in the middle of the post-war period, though on the threshold of modernization under the auspices of the "plans for development," which were being drawn up that year. The film is a story about four young people in a Madrid suburb, progressively inclined toward a more engaged offensiveness. Inspired by Luis Buñuel's *Los Olvidados* (The Forgotten), Saura pictures with a reportage-like style (converging with the cinéma verité) the frustrations of youth in the beginning of this development. *La lenta agonía de los peces* (1974) [The Slow Agony of the Fish] portrays the doubts of a young Catalan man who falls in love with a Swedish girl in the Costa Brava, and discovers the countercultural movements. Each of these films shows totally opposed youth cultures (proletarian *golfos* and upper class *jipis*) that become the symbol of the process of accelerated cultural modernisation taking place in the country.

In 1970, Father José María López Riocerezo, author of many edifying works for young people, published a study titled *The worldwide problem of vandalism and its possible solutions,* in which he shows interest in a series of demonstrations of youth nonconformist, offensive trends: *gamberros, blousons noirs,* teddy boys, *vitelloni, raggare,* rockers, beatniks, *macarras,* hippies, *halbstakers, provos, ye-yes, rocanroleros, pavitos,* etc., were variants of the same species: the "rebel without a cause." Although he considers Spain safe from this dangerous trend ("maybe because of historical constants, the weight of centuries and family tradition"), he concludes by wondering whether these trends have something to do with the transformation of a rural or agricultural society into an industrial or post industrial society: "When this step is taken quickly, there is a cultural and sociological crisis, like an obstruction of the channels of the individual's integration into the regulations of society" (López, 1970, p. 244). The author, who used to be a professor in criminal law at the Royal College of Advanced Studies of El Escorial, considers *gamberrismo* (vandalism) one of the most pressing social problems of our civilization:

> We need to pay good attention to such an important issue; we are used to following the news from abroad and we hear about it all the time—and specially its most serious consequences. We hear about English teddy boys, Italian *teppisti,* the French *blousons-noirs,* the German *halbstarker,* Venezuelan *pavitos,* and we think the whole thing is alien to us, serious as it is. We should be able to distinguish wide different areas, beginning with the badly behaved and rude young people and ending in the criminal. If we understand that gamberro is the one that breaks basic social rules to seek his own satisfaction or his own comfort, without paying any attention to his neighbour's concerns, we cover a wide social area, really unsuspected and impressive. (López, 1970, p. 60)

For the author, a gamberro is nothing but the Spanish variant of the foreign model being imported. He discusses the etymology, as the word is not included in the dictionary of the Royal Academy of the Spanish Language. He searches in Basque-French (*gamburu*: joke, somersault, open air diversion) and into Greek (*gambrias*: with the same meaning as our own word). This second meaning not only justifies the declaration of dangerousness "against those who cynically and insolently attack the rules of social coexistence by attacking people or damaging things, without a cause or a reason," in the Ley de Vagos y Maleantes (Tramps and Malefactors Act) but also explains its origin or objective. He starts by drawing the international panorama, based on the available criminological literature (starting by biological determinists like Lombroso), to focus later on the Spanish case from press news, papers issued in church magazines or magazines from the regime (mixing up data about simply delinquent gangs with information about trends and student movements). He ends up wondering about the causes of this wave of youth rebelliousness:

> Where is the deep evil created by English and American teddy-boys, the French *blousons noirs*, the Swedish *raggare*, Italian *vitelloni* or Spanish *gameberros* to be found? The problem is not in their external features: their odd way of living, their extravagant hair style, their taste for trouble making, their liking of rock and roll or twist, their passion for exceeding the speed limit and their gathering in gangs. The real problem lies in their lack of discipline and self-control, and their parties reach the edge of anti-social behaviour, so they easily step into delinquency. (López, 1970, p. 17)

About the Spanish case, he insists that the phenomenon is still not too apparent. According to 1963 statistics, there were only 161 offenders per 100,000 inhabitants in Spain (the figures abroad were 852 in England, 455 in the United States, 378 in Germany, and 216 in Italy).

Punkis and Progres

Pepi, Luci, Bom y otras chicas del montón, the first of Almodovar's films (1980) shows the beginning of the *movida madrileña*, the more or less spontaneous youth movement that reflected in an anarchic way the effects of Spain's transition to democracy: the explosion of urban tribes. Three women of different ages and social circumstances (Alaska, well inside the punk wave, a postmodern Cecilia Roth who lives life madly, and Carmen Maura, the housewife in her forties married to a policeman) share the nights of a cool and exciting Madrid that is becoming a hub of modernity thanks to the mayor, Tierno Galvan. Almodovar would picture the subculture of la movida in a more elaborate way (but just as ascerbic) in his later work *Laberinto de pasiones* (1982).

By the end of the 1970s, along with the transition to democracy, a new social subject appeared in the Spanish scenario, labeled very significantly, Tribus Urbanas (Urban Tribes). The mainstream media would soon devote great attention to the phenomenon, inciting campaigns of **moral panic** in tandem with commercial appropriation (like the reports advertising where to buy each tribe's outfit). A teddy boy from Zaragoza wrote a letter to the director to remind him that "the only tribes in the world are the blacks of Africa." But a disabled punk ("el Cojo") became famous thanks to television for breaking a street light with his crutch during the huge student demonstrations in 1987, which prompted this comment from a columnist: "Sociologists should give an explanation for this African and underdeveloped phenomenon" (quoted in Feixa, 1998). The institutional context of the time was characterized by the democratization of the Youth Institute and the transfer of competence on youth to local councils and autonomous communities. In nearly all fields, one of the first initiatives of organizations was to promote youth studies, nearly always through opinion reviews, brilliantly analyzed and criticized by Cardús and Estruch (1984) for the Catalan case.

In 1982, Isaías Díez del Río, director of a college in Madrid, published an article in the *Revista de Estudios de Juventud* under the title "La contracultura" (The Counterculture) although it is really about a new type of youth movement, appearing in Spain immediately after the transition to democracy, which was commonly called *pasotismo*. In the 1980s, the most widespread vision of youth—nearly always analyzed as a homogeneous social sector, using a quantitative methodology, or described in opinion essays—pictured a generalized lack of interest in social problems and the loss of any form of revolutionary spirit which, according to analysts, had marked the preceding generations. The central thesis of the study is that pasotismo is one of the many youth movements appearing in the West as a product of and response to the breakdown of a society in crisis. Díez del Río takes the loss of interest in political militancy and social battles on the part of the majority of the youth culture at the time as contradictions embedded in society itself. Pasotismo is a lifestyle that symbolically protests through new means of fighting against the values that institutions and the dominant culture are trying to impose.

In 1985, sociologists Enrique Gil Calvo and Elena Menéndez published *Ocio y prácticas culturales de los jóvenes* (Youth Leisure and Cultural Practices of Young People), which is part of the Youth Report in Spain, promoted by the Youth Institute on the occasion of the International Year of Youth. The authors suggested the following definition of youth culture:

> The problem is not that young people are more closely related among themselves than with others: the problem is that their relationships are closed to the outside, sealed off, totally enclosed; and such a closure traps each young person into the group, not letting them out, establishing unsurpassable borders that separate the comfortable inside of the centripetal group from the outside chaos and darkness, where the young person is horrified to venture into. This could be called youth subculture or something like it: what's important however, is not the name, but the facts that we want to illustrate with data in the next chapter. (Gil Calvo and Menéndez, 1985, p. 238)

Something similar would appear in Madrid in 1978 and would last until 1983: *la Movida*. By analyzing the composition of the music bands that identified with la Movida, Gil Calvo and Menéndez tried to demonstrate their definition of a youth movement. For this purpose, they used an organization chart where they showed the relationship between the musicians of different groups, which was supposed to demonstrate that youth cultures were closed, impermeable groups.

Such a movement had an exclusively musical public expression (politics, "culture," and ideology were absent): it was started, composed, promoted, developed, and made to succeed by a bunch of young musicians and FM DJs. Twenty music groups composed this "modern" or "new-wave" movement during those five years. Something is curious about it: only thirty young people, under the age of twenty-five, composed the twenty different groups—simply the same people, friends among themselves flowed from one group to another. The world of the Madrid "modern" "new wave" in 1978–1983 were thirty people: totally closed to the outside, even declared enemies of other "musical/youth groups" as closed as themselves (and these other enemy worlds of the modern world, were also perfectly visible due to their own closedness: rockers, heavies, punks, hippies) (Gil Calvo and Menéndez, 1985, p. 238).

Pijos and Makineros

Historias del Kronen (Kronen Stories), the film by Montxo Armendáriz (1994) based on the novel by Alfredo Mañas (1989) shows the life of a group of upper-class young people (*pijos*), their night-time adventures, their fresh styles, and their uneasy feelings about life. Other films of the same time picture the birth of other forms of youth sociability: *El angel de la guarda* (1995) presents the life of a young mod, belonging to a family who sympathizes with Franco's regime, and who is in conflict with other young rockers. It is the time of the socialist government in Spain, when the generations that had led the fight against Franco are settling into power and view with suspicion the apathetic and apolitical young people, and see their aesthetics and ways of living as purely commercial and consumerist. From the point of view of youth cultures, this period is characterized by three different processes: the segmentation of youth cultures into many styles that appear like a shopping catalog; the revival of the pijo (a way to openly recover a higher class identity); spearheading the night life with the generation of a new style: the *makinero* (between the proliferation of new clubs, the explosion of electronic commercial music, and the results of synthetic drugs). A sociologist even suggested that the term "urban tribes" be replaced by "shopping tribes":

> Those rebel tribes, inorganically organized, who invented cries like songs, who knew how to make a great to-do to create social uniforms. They invented a way of drinking, a way of eating, a way of sitting down, a way of walking, a way of talking or cheering, and dressing. They don't have sense any more. . . . Hippies were buried long ago. . . . *Pijos*, on the contrary, are unconditional kings of big shopping areas, and they are certainly the hegemonic tribe in the 1990s. (Ruiz, 1994, pp. 192–196)

In 1989 the linguist Francisco Rodríguez edited *Comunicación y lenguaje juvenil* (Communication and Juvenile Language), an anthology that gathered together some of the main contributions on youth cultures by Spanish researchers. The aim of all the essays, each one from a different perspective and academic area, is to describe and analyze the pattern of young people's linguistic behavior as a means of understanding their cultural expressions in general. The authors include anthropologists, sociologists, linguists, experts in communications, etc. The theoretical, methodological, and thematic perspectives are diverse, although the red thread running through all the studies is the analysis of language as a system of symbols in relationship to significant and symbolic elements of youth cultures (music, clothes, cultural practice, etc.) and to other channels of communication such as fanzines, comics, graffiti, etc. Among all the articles, we want to highlight the analysis of fashion as a communication system amongst youth in the 1980s (Rivière, 1989). The article's author is a journalist who analyzes the transformation process that fashion followed from the beginning of the twentieth century and its appropriation by young people who would radically transform its significance. First, they broke the old pattern of fashion as a marker of social class; second, they de-sexualized it: boys' and girls' styles became much more similar. Another interesting element was the rejuvenating power that fashion had—and still has:

> In the 80s everyone wants to look (be) young to the point that social marginalisation occurs in all cases, to the those who, for their age, cannot look young any more. The outfit is the main . . . vehicle for eternal youth. Although a juvenile outfit does not hide certain effects of old age, the young people's trends (for our mass and communication culture's adults) are imperatively categorical in their most generic features, both formal and mental: the compulsory physical rejuvenation brings along a certain cultural infantility. (Rivière, 1989, p. 73)

Okupas and Pelaos

Taxi, one of the latest films by Carlos Saura (1999), depicts the life of a group of young *pelaos* who are manipulated by an extreme right-wing taxi driver. They attack immigrants and homosexuals, and they get as far as murder. Pelaos are the Spanish version of *naziskins,* neo-Nazi young people getting into the **skinhead** movement and carrying out some dramatic actions (somehow linked to the football hooligans) according to the Spanish press in the late 1980s (although the pelaos don't really become socially well known until the mid-1990s, because of the greater social concern about the arrival of new waves of immigrants). They coincide with the explosion of *okupas,* the Spanish version of the squatters who appeared after 1968, linked to the occupation of empty houses and to experimenting with new alternative and countercultural ways of living together. From the social point of view, certain structural problems such as the new immigration, limited access to housing for youth, and the nocturnization of youth leisure open spaces for renewed youth culture activities. From the media point of view this phenomenon is shown by newspapers and campaigns reflecting moral panic nearly always following the same pattern: news event—media amplification—creation of a social problem—feedback in youth cultures—new news event. As regards social control, the different police bodies (state, autonomous, and local) organize specific brigades, and sometimes issue reports that reach the press. In universities, "urban tribes" as a subject attains status and starts to be the subject of numerous publications (a decade after the advent of the actual phenomenon). Publications vary a good deal in quality and are based on studies done previously, often with an outdated theoretical methodological approach. In spite of this, they make up a corpus of publications, theories, and empirical data that will contribute to consolidate an "object." Thematically, these studies have three prominent features: a non-critical concept of urban tribes and a stereotyped catalog of different styles, a denial of political conflict (presented as a set of aesthetic conflicts), and a removal of differences (i.e., "all skins are the same").

In 1996 Costa, Pérez, and Tropea published *Tribus Urbanas* (Urban Tribes), a book that would become a best-seller. The text is the fruit of a piece of research, the results of which are not presented as such, but used to construct a narrative text addressed to a broader public, with the aim of spreading knowledge of the phenomenon called urban tribes. The three authors come from the Faculty of Communication Sciences of the Universitat Autònoma of Barcelona, where the theoretical perspective of this research stems from. Although the authors' main aim is said to be disseminating knowledge about the phenomenon of urban tribes, when they list the theoretical approaches from different disciplines used to examine youth cultures, the subject of the work is defined as urban violence and tribes as a phenomenon. This places them within the tendency to see youth styles from a stigmatizing perspective; for example, they quote relevant key concepts in neuro-psychiatry (syndromes, paranoids, and schizoids) and criminology (deviant behaviors). The main sources for the book are both internal and external. Internal sources include the testimony of the protagonists, and external sources include the communication media, and agents of public order and the prison system. All of these are considered key informants for the qualitative interpretation of youth cultures. The work's methodological orientation is therefore qualitative or, according to the authors, the data were gathered by means of observation techniques and in-depth interviews. In describing the theoretical framework and designating all youth movements as a "neotribal" phenomenon, and therefore, its members as "asphalt indigenous," the authors summarize the meaning of "urban tribes":

> a set of specific rules according to which young people model their image. The tribe's development is like a small mythology; their representative games are closed to "normal" individuals; their differences from and with other young people are made evident, and their identification with the group takes the form of the contradiction of a uniform dressing up. All "urban tribes" constitute a potential factor of social agitation and disorder and their aesthetics show a desire for aggressive self-expression. (1996, p. 91)

Fiesteros and Alternativos

With the change of millennium, Spanish youth cultures' characteristics may be generalized from three major tendencies. First, a certain activism in the public sphere is revived and reflected in the anti-globalization movement and its cultural effects (from the singer Manu Chao's hybrid music to a neo-hippie trend). Second, the dance culture becomes symbolized in the different expressions of the *fiestero* movement (the most intellectualized around festivals like Sonar, digital publications, and the techno style; the most ludic around new clubs and fashion style; and the most clandestine around rave parties). Third, the Internet opens a space to the generation of room cultures and virtual communities that express different styles (like cyberpunks and hackers), although the use of virtual space affects all groups. The impact of the various cultures' distinctive elements is projected into different age groups. But what is most representative of this period is the fading of boundaries between the different subcultures, and the processes of social and symbolic syncretism ("mixture and union," using the terms of the journalistic report).

In 2001, Romo published *Mujeres y drogas de síntesis. Género y riesgo en la cultura del baile* (Women and Synthetic Drugs. Gender and Culture in the Dance Culture). Romo is an anthropologist and this publication is part of a wide analytical and descriptive effort. The research is located in the second half of the 1990s, when the dance culture related to drugs and car accidents became an omnipresent paradigm in institutional and media speech. Her primary aim was to analyze the drug consumption in the *fiesta* and electronic music context for both men and women, later to focus on the interpretation of the women's specificity from a comparative perspective: in other words, find out whether there were any differences in drug consumption between boys and girls. Examining the state of the art reveals that there is no research about the female role within youth cultures in relation to electronic music and synthetic drugs. This research was done to contrast different hypothesis under the form of an open question to which the author tries to find an answer: what is the role of women within the youth culture associated to the consumption of ecstacy and other synthetic drugs; are there any gender differences in their perception or in the limiting strategies; what are the "style" features of the female consumers; what are the differences in the strategies of obtaining substances; and what is the role of women within the illegal synthetic drug market. The methodology was qualitative, although quantitative methods were used as well. The chief ethnographical locus was Costa del Sol, Andalucía, but also Madrid and Valencia. In order to deepen her knowledge of the phenomenon itself, Romo completed the fieldwork with visits to other European countries, including England and the Netherlands. This kind of observation technique allowed the researcher to introduce herself into the environment and become a group member. Her role within the youth culture was as an "active member," taking part in their main activities, until she reached the status of "complete member" like the rest, sharing their experiences with the same level of intensity and feeling (Romo, 2001, pp. 46–47). This closeness to her informants allowed her to collect data not only from party environments, but in other circumstances, sometimes intimately related to the girls' daily life (walking around, shopping, going to the cinema, meetings at home, etc.). The researcher stated how her age, similar to that of the subjects under study, made it easy for her to approach them and to be accepted into the group (Romo, 2001, p. 50).

Romo's most interesting contribution is her description of intersubjective relationships from inside the group. The author describes elements of cultural consumption (the body, music, focal activities) through the concept of style, emphasizing not only material and immaterial elements in themselves but in the ways they are used. The gender perspective must be evidenced too. The whole work is based on female specificities in relation to synthetic drugs and parties. The author claims that all the literature devoted to female drug consumption describes them as doubly deviant: "Their experience is usually analysed as a deviation from the rule, an altered version of what would be considered as a 'normal woman' or 'normal feminity'. Most of the specific research about women and use of drugs focuses on heroin or cocaine consumers" (Romo, 2001, p. 282). The stigmatization that both academia and mainstream media reserve for this sort of research is reflected in the female perception of risk and the resources used to make their "transgression" invisible. Such a strategy is totally opposed to men's behavior: girls usually take synthetic drugs in private, far from the gaze of other consumers, and avoiding public places like dancing venues, where male consumption increases. Finally, the anthropologist defines the phenomenon of the "devirtuation" of the youth dance culture, which permits us to talk about two different stages in the identity expression of the movement:

> The popularisation and vulgarisation of the youth movement allows it to get to other sectors than the first "fiesteros." A series of elements get into youth culture that affect relationships between the sexes and the role of women in youth culture. The increase of violence or the change into a more sexual environment makes women refrain from participating in these festive elements and establish new strategies of control to minimise risk situations. (Romo, 2001, p. 283)

Latin Kings and Moro Kings

The last wave of youth gangs presence in Spain is related to a new kind of migratory processes, not yet national (like the golfos gangs in the 1960s) but international (teenagers coming from North Africa, Asia, Eastern Europe, and Latin America). Particularly, the presence of the so-called Latin gangs, composed by young people coming from Ecuador, Colombia, the Dominican Republic, and other Latin American countries, thanks in part to family reunion legislation. On the 2 October 28, 2003, a Colombian adolescent was murdered as he left his secondary school by a group of youngsters in Barcelona. According to a subsequent investigation, the murder was an act of revenge by members of another American-origin Latin gang—the Ñetas—who allegedly mistook the victim for a member of the **Latin Kings** with whom they had fought a few days before. This case "unveiled" the phenomenon of Latin street gangs to the Spanish media and awoke a wave of moral panic that has not stopped yet. In a perhaps ironic twist, it has motivated the creation of new Latin gangs in Barcelona and other European citites, like *Vatos Locos,* inspired by 1950s Mexican American Crazy Boys; *Panteras Negras,* inspired by 1960s Afro-American

Black Panthers; and *Maras Salvatruchas*, inspired by Central American post–civil war gangs. Even if these groups also attracted young boys and girls from other origins (Spanish, Russian, Moroccan), they also motivated the creation of other ethnic replicas, like Barcelona's Moro Kings (composed by youngsters of North African origins) and the Gypsy Kings (composed by young gypsies from poor neighborhoods). This also motivates some conflicts between migrant youths and working-class Spanish youngsters, like the January 2007 battles in Alcorcon (Madrid). Nevertheless, the presence of Latin gangs, and the investigations and social interventions that followed, also motivated the experience of transforming them into youth associations, which is described in another part of this encyclopedia.

References/Suggested Readings: Costa, Pere-Oriol, Pérez, José Maria, and Tropea, Fabio. 1996. *Tribus urbanas* (Urban tribes). Barcelona: Paidós; Díez del Río, Isaías. 1982. La contracultura (The counterculture). *Revista de Estudios de Juventud*, 6, 101–132; Feixa, Carles. 1998. *De jóvenes, bandas y tribus* (On youth, gangs and tribes). Barcelona: Ariel; Feixa, C., and Porzio, L. 2005. Golfos, pijos, fiesteros. Studies on Youth Cultures in Spain 1960–2004. *Nordic Journal of Youth Research*, 13 (1), 89–113; Gil Calvo, Enrique, and Menéndez, Elena. 1985. *Ocio y practicas culturales de los jóvenes* (Leisure and cultural practices of young people). Madrid: Instituto de la Juventud; López Riocerezo, J.M. 1970. *Problemática mundial del gamberrismo y sus posibles soluciones* (The world problem of gangs and its possible solutions). Madrid, Studium; Rivière, Margarita. 1989. Moda de los jóvenes: un lenguaje adulterado (The fashion of young people: The adulterated language). In Francisco Rodríguez (ed.), *Comunicación y lenguaje juvenil* (Communication and juvenile language). Madrid: Fundamentos; Rodríguez, Francisco (ed.) 1989. *Comunicación y lenguaje juvenil* (Communication and juvenile language). Madrid: Fundamentos; Romo, Nuria. 2001. *Mujeres y drogas de síntesis. Género y riesgo en la cultura del baile* (Women and synthetic drugs. Gender and risk in dance cultures). Donostia: Hirugarren Prentsa; Trías, Sebastián. 1967. Apuntes para una clasificación de grupos juveniles (Notes about the classification of youth groups). *Revista del Instituto de la Juventud*, 13, 61–95.

CARLES FEIXA AND LAURA PORZIO

STREET ORGANIZATIONS. In recent years the types of gangs that have emerged across the United States have changed in line with new structural conditions brought about by de-industrialization, globalization, the reconfiguration of urban space, the shift of lower class populations to the suburbs, the porosity of U.S. borders, and the merging of the informal with the formal economy. In a four-year study of the **Almighty Latin King and Queen Nation** in New York City during the late 1990s researchers found that the group had moved from its prototypical gang formation and was taking on the characteristics of a social movement. Brotherton and Barrios (2004) devised the term "street organization" to replace the heavily pejorative term "gang" to describe this transitional stage. Their new definition of a street organization read as follows:

> a street organization is a group formed largely by youth and adults of a marginalized social class which aims to provide its members with a resistant identity, an opportunity to be individually and collectively empowered, a voice to speak back to and challenge the dominant culture, a refuge from the stresses and strains of barrio or ghetto life and a spiritual enclave within which its own sacred rituals can be generated and practiced. (Brotherton and Barrios, 2004, p. 23)

Whether the gang was and is a street organization remains an empirical question, the notion of another type of street subculture that does not neatly fall into the discursive boundaries of gang studies raises a number of theoretical questions. In Table 1,

Table I   Comparative Approaches to Youth Subcultures

Domain	U.S. Model	British Model	Street Organizational Model
Methodology	Early humanistic-naturalist models of Chicago sociology giving way to criminal justice positivism, privileging notions of measurement, causality, rational action, and the research practices of empiricism	Strong emphasis on cultural criticism and neo-Marxist interpretive, heuristic paradigms where in situ studies are the exception	Plurality of methods, drawing from Chicago naturalist traditions, British neo-Marxist culturalism and contemporary trends in cultural criminology
Class Values	Lower class, proletarian and subproletarian (i.e., underclass)	Specific to the working-class and middle-class history of the subculture	Working-class and subproletarian strongly infused with specific racial and ethnic experiences
Agency	Rational action, compensating for lack of status, class strain, and making good on opportunity structures. Such action can also be highly pathological and is a form of underclass socialization	Heavily symbolic, aesthetic and stylistic. Linked to magical solutions and different forms of leisure in a class-bound capitalist society. Socially reproduces the working class	Performative, both rational and irrational, political and ideological in a global capitalist society. Linked to identity construction, space creation, and different modes of class construction
Historical Contingency (i.e., does the analysis take pains to dialectically and historically situate the phenomena?)	Mostly transhistorical or ahistorical, however there are exceptions, such as the work of Hagedorn (the black underclass) and Moore and Vigil (the Latino underclass)	Rooted in specific historical conditions	Highly historical, shaped by discrete resistances from below and social control processes from above
Representational Forms	Socially organized, displays of turf allegiance, some later attention to attire and both body and verbal language	Wide range of symbolism involving music, attire, and language	Wide range of performativity and symbolism involving music, graffiti, physical and verbal language, attire, and written texts

the essential characteristics (domains) of two primary approaches to gangs are compared in two major homes of criminology: the United States and Britain. In the first column are a range of gang properties that are commonly found in the U.S. gang literature, in the second column are characteristics drawn from the youth subcultural literature heavily influenced by the Birmingham School in Britain, and in the third column are listed the putative characteristics of a street organization based on the aforementioned study.

From the above, we see that the street organizational model not only is in contrast to most U.S. mainstream gang paradigms but also differs from the more critical perspectives of the Birmingham School. Each of the comparative domains above are briefly discussed below.

Methodology

Orthodox criminological approaches to gangs generally privilege the methods of positivism. Long-standing epistemological debates on the ideological nature of social scientific truth claims, the asymmetrical relationships between the observer and the observed, or the politics of grant-financed research rarely enter the discourse. Much of the data are drawn from law enforcement data, selective self-report surveys, and structured interviews (Hughes, 2004). Criminologists working within this discourse are still unsure whether the diversity in the findings of gang research reflects different characteristics of gangs and gang members in different places or is an artifact of research methods. In contrast, the Birmingham School literature is mostly theoretical but where data collection takes place it is highly interpretive (see Willis, 1979). A big criticism of the Birmingham School is that its adherents ventured too infrequently into the field to test out their claims regarding youth culture and subcultures. The street organization model calls for both qualitative and quantitative approaches but tends to privilege the former. This model embodies a critical approach to scientific objectivity, to the influence of funding agencies, and argues for a developed practice of sociological reflexivity.

Class Values

In the orthodox literature the class of gang members is generally referred to as "lower class" and in the last decade it is more assumed that such groups are part of the "underclass." This notion of class is primarily understood in stratificational terms and sees gang members as positioned in a social hierarchy with limited options for education, work, and legitimate income generation. The most critical concept in this approach is that of "multiple marginality," which views gang members at the intersection of urban, race, and class vectors. The consciousness of members from this "lower class" or "underclass" extends along a continuum. Some argue that it has its own distinct traditions, others who see it consisting of mainly oppositional values to those of the middle class, or still others who see it as accommodating the values of the middle class. The Birmingham School, in contrast, puts more attention on the specificity of working class consciousness and the ways in which this consciousness is penetrated by a hegemonic ruling-class ideology and the everyday rites and rituals of living in a working-class, bounded culture. The consciousness of street subcultural members is contradictory, but it does not lead to successful transformative practices that go beyond the cultural domain. The street organization model contends that gang members come from both working class and sub-proletarian origins. There is substantial agreement with the Birmingham School approach although there is disagreement on the degree of consciousness that might be called transcendental leading to the possibility of transformative practices of resistance.

Agency

Agency or the propensity for human action despite structural constraints is highly utilitarian in the orthodox framework. Much of the work is influenced by Mertonian notions of accommodation and innovation in strain theory. While it is true that the Birmingham School celebrates the notion of subcultural agency through style, it saw little transformative potential in such behavior. Much of the explanation for subcultural development is located in the tensions between adults and youth and that many youth subcultures express the contradictory need to both rebel against parental cultures at the same time as maintaining many of the class traditions which parents themselves embody. Hall et al. (1975) state that the subcultural, while it is stylistically oppositional, should not be mistaken for the agency of counter-cultures which are more consciously political, ideological, and organized. In contrast, adherents of the street organization model argue for a greater appreciation of transformative agency based on three considerations. First, that the subcultural in late modernity has become more autonomous as youth, in particular, chafe against the global corporatization of culture, time, space, production and social relations. Second, many contemporary youth subcultures emerge from the hyrbridization of street and prison cultures, especially in a period of mass incarceration for people of color, the working class, and the poor. Thus, the structuration of these groups can be expected to be more radical as politicized ex-inmates encounter and rejoin their civilian counterparts.

History

In the orthodox treatment of gangs, gang members are mostly seen as transhistorical with little recognition of the epoch (i.e., modern, late modern, or postmodern) in which such groups emerge or any grounded reference to the political economic structures in which these social actors are embedded (i.e., capitalistic, late capitalistic, or post-industrial). While cultural conflicts and social disorganization are often claimed to be major impulses behind gang growth, the discourse rarely includes more than a passing reference to the global economic pushes and pulls or the transnational contradictions that are ultimately behind the experience of these populations. On the other hand, the Birmingham School approach is highly historical and owes much of its approach to a Marxist and neo-Marxist conception of the relationship between individual and group practices, their culture(s), and the material and ideological forces of production. Thus, historical eras and periodizations such as Fordism, late capitalism, and postmodernity are strongly represented in their analyses. However, it is the intersection of individual biography and history (much like C. Wright Mills) and the ways in which the ideologies of a historically situated capitalism are mediated that are at the crux of this methodology. For the street organizational model, history is present at the macro level and at the micro level. This is particularly true of empirical gang studies on violence and drug use (particularly females) where such subcultures have long-standing local street traditions alongside community struggles of the past and/or present. Without history there is little presence of politics in the mentalities of these subjects at the social, cultural, symbolic, or organizational levels.

Representational Forms

The orthodox approach documents the representational forms of gangs, ascribing to them mainly rational and transparent purposes, e.g., graffiti is used to demarcate territory, send conflict-based messages to other gangs, and can have debilitating effects on communities through promoting a culture of social disorganization. In contrast, the Birmingham School analyzes such forms within a political economy of signs (semiotics), viewing such products as efforts of subordinate groups to break their cultural silences, stereotypical representations, and symbolic devaluations. This approach puts an emphasis on the reading and reinterpretation of cultural products and texts through a process of bricollage, i.e., the eclectic appropriation of symbols and their reconfiguration in a new representational form. The street organizational model draws strongly on the Birmingham School but extends its analysis through an engagement with performance and resistance studies. In this model contemporary gangs are seen as energetic producers and milieus of myriad cultural and communicative forms that are highly generative. Such forms include written texts, oral codes, music, dance, corporal gestures, and graffiti which combine to produce a cosmology of the marginalized.

References/Suggested Readings: Brotherton, David C., and Luis Barrios. 2004. *The Almighty Latin King and Queen Nation.* New York: Columbia University Press; Hall, Stuart, and Jefferson, Tony (eds.). 1975. *Resistance through Rituals.* London: Routledge; Hughes, Lorraine. 2004. Studying Gangs: Alternative Methods and Conclusions. *Journal of Contemporary Criminal Justice*, 21 (2), 98–119; Willis, Paul. 1977. *Learning to Labor.* Westmead, U.K.: Saxon House.

DAVID C. BROTHERTON

SUBCULTURAL THEORIES OF GANGS. The first sociological attempt to understand the world of gangs as comprised of distinct subcultures appears in **Frederic Thrasher**'s *The Gang*. Its emphasis is twofold: on the ways in which gangs provide for some of the needs of young people in "urban areas" where social institutions are overburdened or dysfunctional, and ways in which they organize their environment and infuse it with meaning. In Thrasher's (1927) view, the symbolism and linguistic innovation—a "universe of discourse"—associated with gangs not only strengthen solidarity but also provide a sense of context for collective behavior and group dynamics—"participation in common interests, more especially in corporate action, in hunting, capture, conflict, and escape" (p. 37). In contrast, subculturalists of the 1950s and 1960s—who are mostly theorists whose work draws heavily on secondary sources and whose "observations" are mostly impressionistic—do not treat gang culture as a dimension of social action but instead as a substratum of meaning and motivation; which is to say, an underlying, hidden cause. For instance, Cohen (1955) tells us that gang members are lower class kids who secretly desire to be middle class, that they harbor resentment over standards of judgment associated with specifically middle class institutions, such as the school system, and that they react to those standards in precarious ways that produce "inadvertent" outcomes. Cohen also imagines that gang members spend much of their time seeking excitement, but not in the manner Thrasher describes—where the "gang boy" appears filled with the spirit of adventure. Rather, what counts as excitement in the gang, for Cohen, is a range of perverse activities, including "stealing things that are then discarded," such as "clothes they cannot wear and toys they will not use" (p. 26). Miller (1958) argues practically the opposite, in that gangs are assumed to share lower class values which translate into various "focal concerns" (autonomy, fate, excitement, smartness, toughness, and trouble) that are in conflict with middle-class society but not anything else. In this account, too, gangs are seen as impulsive and preoccupied with finding excitement at every turn, perversely, but not in reaction to anything in particular.

These accounts are tautological in a way that is common to all modes of analysis that draw on "middle range" theories of deviance, in that they begin with a discrete set of theoretical assumptions that are borne out through selective observations. Moreover, they resurrect a traditional, essentialist logic under the guise of "theoretical" analysis—variations on the kind of functionalism that dominated sociology in the 1950s, where deviation from the norms of society appears as the result of improper or inadequate value socialization. These arguments are not then "merely" theoretical but also reactionary in the extent to which they render "values"' a basis for invidious distinction among a range of groups without any real basis for comparison. Instead, "mainstream" and "middle-class" groups are idealized as free of pathologies, and not ordinarily perverse, reactive, impulsive, etc. Thus, gangs appear qualitatively different from other types of groups not because of what any of them are doing, but because their actions appear motivated by deviant values or simply for the thrill of being deviant. The relation between deviance and social order is thereby made unambiguous; such that "disorder" may be associated with the very existence of particular groups, especially gangs, and not with the massive disruptions and dislocations of political economy, or class antagonisms, state policies, etc.

The movement in the theoretical literature on "deviance" away from explanations involving values had already been initiated in the work of Sutherland, which draws attention to the cultural contexts of deviant behavior, that is, the ways in which groups become cultures that embody expectations and judgments, provide vocabularies of motive, etc. Sutherland's concept of "differential association" may also be distinguished from the logical positivism that characterized the "decade of theorizing" and much of contemporary sociological discourse on the topic of gangs, through its emphasis on complexity and contingency: "a complex of many things" that must be brought into view wherever causal statements are made, even the most general. For instance, Sutherland tells us that

> in an area where the delinquency rate is high a boy who is sociable, gregarious, active, and athletic is very likely to come in contact with the other boys in the neighborhood, learn delinquent behavior from them, and become a gangster; in the same neighborhood the psychopathic boy who is isolate, introvert, and inert may remain at home, not become acquainted with the other boys in the neighborhood, and not become delinquent. In another situation, the sociable, athletic, aggressive boy may become a member of a scout troop and not become involved in delinquent behavior. (1947, p. 9)

The "other" (any) situation is never simply a reflection of social facts or indices (segregation, urban decay, etc.), but also includes such things as the history of groups in a particular area, the presence or absence of gang rivalries, policies and tactics of the police, etc. This is what Sutherland means when he says "the person's associations are determined in a general context of social organization" (1947, p. 9). In later adoptions of this theory, however, the idea of *contingency* is lost and the idea of complexity is made synonymous with objective circumstances and ideal-typical responses to them that are always already known in advance (by sociologists, criminologists, and their readers), and, moreover, the concept of values is usually reintroduced in roundabout ways.

Such is the case, for instance, in the influential work of Cloward and Ohlin (1960), which advances an explicitly political argument centered on the lack of legitimate opportunities in urban areas. We are here told that "gang subcultures" develop around forms of "specialization," like fighting or stealing, as natural responses to the presence or absence of legitimate and illegitimate structures of opportunity—hence, the problem is assumed to be that gang members share the values of mainstream groups but not the opportunities. For instance, a criminal subculture is deemed a natural response to a lack of legitimate opportunities but only in areas where there are sufficient opportunities for illicit commerce. This typology also joins Sutherland's notion that deviance is "learned" in a group setting with Merton's functionalist theory of deviance, where instances of stereotypical deviance are deemed motivated by the frustration (or "anomie") supposedly felt by those who fail to achieve conventional goals—money, status, power. The problem in this respect is that it tells us nothing about either the form or content of any gang subculture, i.e., what is actually learned beyond stereotypical deviance. Moreover, there is nothing in the work of Cloward and Ohlin or any of the literature developed around the Mertonian framework to indicate that members of any type of group are *more* frustrated than members of any other type; nor that fighting, stealing, drug use, and the rest are natural responses to anomie (as opposed, say, to suicide, as Durkheim argued). Further, it is not clear, in this account, what disparate groups labeled "gangs" have in common; for instance, what corner groups have in common with gang "organizations" and "nations"; thereby what is gained by saying that they are both conflict-oriented as opposed to retreatist or whatever else. Contemporary sociological and criminological discourse on gangs effectively brackets such issues as complexity, contingency, and differentiation through an endless proliferation of typologies in which the logic of "specialization" and the assumption that subcultures form in predictable ways in response to objective circumstances and situations remain intact (e.g., Hagedorn, 1998).

References/Suggested Readings: Cohen, Albert, K. 1955. *Delinquent Boys: The Culture of the Gang.* Glencoe, IL: Free Press; Cloward, Richard, A. and Ohlin, Lloyd, E. 1960. *Delinquency and Opportunity: A Theory of Delinquent Gangs.* Glencoe, IL: Free Press; Hagedorn, John. 1988. *People and Folks; Gangs, Crime and the Underclass in a Rustbelt City.* Chicago: Lakeview Press; Merton, Robert. 1957. *Social Theory and Social Structure.* Glencoe, IL: Free Press; Miller, Walter B. 1958. Lower Class Culture as a Generating Milieu of Gang Delinquency. *Journal of Social Issues*, 14, 5–19; Sutherland, Edwin H. 1947. *Criminology* (4th ed.). New York: Lippincott; Thrasher, Frederic. 1963 [1927]. *The Gang: A Study of 1,313 Gangs in Chicago.* Chicago: University of Chicago Press.

LOUIS KONTOS

SUBCULTURE OF GANGS. From the end of World War II, as economies returned to domestic from war production, employment opportunites for skilled and unskilled workers expanded in many countries. Such was the shortage of labor in regions within the United States and across Europe that the international recruitment of workers extended across continents. In many cities, this resulted in a concentration of attention on young people as the major supply of labor. Introduced into these calculations were new groups of young people, the children of migrant workers. This focus created "youth." Migrations increased the focus on "culture," especially relations between cultures. Merging these two concepts together gives the notion of "youth culture" as a source for sociological resarchers confronted with problems like "gangs of youth" and "delinquency." These became the prevailing social issues of the 1950s and into the 1960s.

Deviance and Culture

Sociological theories of gangs and subcultures have their source in the work of the French sociologist Émile Durkheim (1893). This gives us the first argument in the theory:

1. That no society can exist without a level of deviance. That if we eradicated all forms of crime and deviance in a society, then that society would define other types of activity as crime.

2. A definition of the normal is not in itself possible except by defining that which is abnormal or unacceptable, deviance or the deviant. Kai Erikson (1966) demonstrates this argument using the example of the exiled English Protestants to New England in the United States. A firmly honest, law-abiding community could not exist without defining the deviance within it—and so defined the most direct contrast to its main beliefs—against religious belief (heresy), then devil worship. The deviant was the witch. Incidentally, the witch had other qualities which made her the ideal target—a single woman, often the midwife, who owned but did not work her land, whose knowledge and skills with herbs and natural medicines threatened the male religious hierarchy. The Puritans reinforced their own sense of normality only by contrast to the defined deviant.

In *La Suicide* (1897), Durkheim gave the theory a third proposition:

3. That a state of anomie (normlessness) will cause the ultimate form of deviance, suicide. That the loss of direction, of the possibility of achievement, of a sense of purpose in life, breaks the bond between the individual and society. The individual cannot survive in this state and will take his/her own life.

Working from these three propositions, the American sociologist Robert K. Merton (1938) refined these ideas by arguing:

4. That a state of anomie can occur at different places, times and levels within a social structure (society) giving rise to different modes of adaptation by the individual to the dysfunctional situation.

Merton's (1968) *typology of modes of adaptation* argues that any role/status in society can be identified as a conjunction of cultural goals and legitimate institutionalized means for their achievement. To be a doctor is to have a cultural goal—to cure sick people—and to have fulfilled the legitimate means to achieve that goal, to have undertaken a prolonged general and specific education in medical science. Such a role is given status, prestige, and honor in society and is offered to young people as a respected profession to aim for. But not all young people, Merton argued, have equal access to legitimate means nor have they, then, the opportunity to achieve the goals offered. This situation applied particularly to poor, urban, working-class young people who were the perpetrators of much crime in American society. Merton suggested that this state of dissociation between cultural goals and legitimate means (a state of anomie) would produce different responses or modes of adaptation, depending on individual characteristics and social circumstances:

Modes of Adaptation

	Cultural Goals	Institutionalized Means
1. Conformity	+	+
2. Innovation	+	–
3. Ritualism	–	+
4. Reatreatism	–	–
5. Rebellion	+/–	+/–

Notes: + = acceptance; – = rejection; +/– = neither accept nor reject but replace.

Conformity is the normal response of the young person with access to means for the achievement of goals—s/he regularly attends school, works hard, is polite to adults, obeys the law, is the ideal young person. Confronted with neither means nor opportunity, the Innovator accepts cultural goals, the status symbols of a modern society—the motor car, fashionable clothing, money to spend, the images of a successful young person portayed in TV, films, and advertisements. The problem for them is how to achieve the goals and acquire the symbols of such achievement. Their solution is any means, criminal or non-criminal, that are available. If you need a motor car, then take one. If you need money, then steal it or steal something that you can exchange for money—the street criminal. The response of the Ritualist is to disregard the goals and the loss of the opportunity to achieve them and to continue to follow the institutionalized means knowing that goals can never be achieved. This urban, working-class youth will continue to work hard at school, will be the ideal child, will be disappointed when they fail to be accepted for university or medical school, will take a job as a clerk and will lead an ordinary mundane life hoping that some time in the future they may fulfill their goal. It never happens and the realization that it will never happen (the mid-life crisis) can lead to psychiatric illness or random extreme acts. Some forms of phobia or fixation may be explained as ritualistic responses. The Retreatist is sometimes referred to as the double failure. Usually aware that they cannot succeed in "normal" life, they have tried innovation and failed. Their situation becomes one of apathy or retreat from the challenge where neither the means nor the goals are acceptable and they find comfort in altered states through alcohol, drugs, or narcotics. The Rebel is perhaps the anti-hero of the 1950s movie (the James Dean or Marlon Brando characters) who rejects both the means for goal achievement and the goals and finds alternative goals and different means. Why have a job, work, and buy a house or apartment when an unused apartment can be occupied? Why adapt the status symbols of "their"' society when we can define a style more appropriate to our life style and living conditions? "I want to be everything that my parents disapprove of."

The Juvenile Delinquent

The 1950s and 1960s introduced a new phenomenon on the world scene, youth culture, and with it a new folk devil, the "juvenile delinquent." Sociological interest was in juvenile gangs, which had a long history in American sociology, especially the intense period of qualitative research by the Chicago School of Social Research in the 1920s and 1930s. In England, the approach was more individual, dominated by the work of psychologists like Cyril Burt (1937) and later Hans Eysenck (1965) whose explanations rest on on notions of weak and ineffective operant-conditioning and the consequent lack of self-discipline, conscience formation, and the need for negative reinforcement or corrective punishment. Russian criminological research followed similar lines presenting the criminal mind as a defective, cybernetic (information processing) system (Kudryavtsev, 1968). With recent advances in biological science, some attempts were made to identify genetic causes for crime and delinquency—relating violent behavior in psychiatric patients to abnormal chromosomes mosaics (the XYY man with an extra sex-determining chromosome or Klinefelter's syndrome).

Yet every country was affected by this new phenomenon—the Jacquet-noire in Paris, the street gangs of New York, the Mods and Rockers and football hooligans in England, street gangs and football hooligans in Moscow and St. Petersburg, **Skinheads** in Germany, the painted faces of football gangs in Holland and Italy—a phenomenon of groups of youths aged between fourteen and twenty-one years, mostly male, with some female "groupies," mostly urban, often racially, ethnically, or nationalistically identified and always drawn from the lower socio-economic groups in their society.

What was new about these gangs was their age and their activities. They were generally five to ten years younger than the adult gangs of pre-war America and Europe. Their violence or criminal activities were more intense and exaggerated than their predecessors. Their activities were more public and more notorious because of the spread of the international mass media which often produced copy-cat incidents in other countries. An incident in Berlin, Germany—a sexual assault with excessive brutality and murder by throwing the victim from an apartment balcony—was nearly an exact copy of a prior incident in Manchester, England, where a group of youths imprisoned a woman, raped and sexually assaulted her, and made a number of attempts to kill her before pouring petrol over her and lighting it. She died subsequently of her burns. Although beginning in the 1950s, and transforming in different directions, the juvenile delinquent and his (and later her) gang were still prevalent across the world in the 1990s and remain a phenomenon into the twenty-first century.

The Delinquent Subculture: An Explanation

Albert K. Cohen (1955) offered an explanation of the "new" phenomenon with his concept of the "delinquent subculture." His version of the anomie of Durkheim and Merton was "status frustration" (that working-class boys were subjected to middle-class aspirations or goals that they could never fulfill). This led to a "reaction formation," the creation of an alternative social form, the subculture, a negative version, a reaction to the dominant values of middle-class culture: orderliness, cleanliness, responsibility, the virtues of ambition and purpose, the postponement of immediate gratification and self-indulgence in favor of the planned achievement of longer term goals. The delinquent's conduct is right, by the standards of his subculture precisely because it is wrong by the norms of the larger culture (Cohen, 1955, pp. 25–32).

This subculture is based on short-run hedonism, the immediate gratification of those needs of the individual or the group which only they can achieve. The failure of their parents, their family, their community, for them is that these social institutions cannot meet their needs as adolescents for status and self-esteem for adulthood. These are achieved by seizing autonomy; not autonomy for the individual but the autonomy of the gang or group. The youth must commit and subordinate himself to the interests and demands of a new alternative culture (and, as a mirror image, it is not a new culture but a subculture) to achieve status and self esteem. The delinquency of Cohen's subculture lies in its negativity, the reaction formation. It must be by definition deviant or criminal in that it seeks to offend the dominant middle-class values it rejects.

So, the problem is not a psychologically abnormal young individual. It is not a deviant or criminal individual. It is a normal reaction formation of working-class young people in a post-war, materialist world in their search for status and self-esteem where aspirations had outstripped the possibility of their achievement.

Walter B. Miller (1968) wanted to extend this argument onto more general political ground by suggesting that Cohen's delinquent subculture was no more than a reflection of its lower class milieu and was a counterculture or oppositional subculture—an emerging class consciousness or awareness of a new urban proletariat. He argued that what Cohen was describing was not a parent-youth conflict but simply working-class culture.

The delinquent subculture theory offered a basis for understanding young delinquents. It was a social form, a definable social grouping of young people usually aged between fourteen and twenty-one years. Normally the group is all male although the group may be attended by one or more androgynous females who are with, rather than in the group. The group has admission rules. There might be joining rituals or oaths of allegiance. There are qualifications for joining based on age, race, ethnicitiy, and area of residence. It is geographically defined—its has its own turf, or area, its sources of gratification which it is prepared to defend against intruders. It is likely to have an argot or language specific to group members. Normally this will be the general language of the parent culture using the same language rules but with vocabulary specific to the group and its activities. Argot is a specialized vocabulary, sometimes with specific grammatical or lexical forms, which must be applied in the right context and with the correct reference points. A parent cannot have access to appropriate use of argot forms because whichever way they choose to use the word or grammatical constructions will inevitably be incorrect. Similarly, dress codes may use the same items of clothing and obey dressing rules (like dress in warm clothes when it is cold) but the combinations (expensive training shoes, one or more sizes too big, combined with several layers of relatively cheap T-shirts and jeans, with the hair long in parts but shaved close in others) are specific to young people. Individual groups may select argot and dress combinations from the specialized subculture and create or adapt their own specific versions. The culture may extend to ways of walking, forms of physical contact between members (high-five, hand-slap greetings), ways of sitting in or on a chair, diet and diet content (burgers and diet cola), correct ways of eating, places to eat, times to eat, and so on.

Some youth cultures (London, Paris, Milan, California) were and are particularly creative and communicate their new trends through popular music and the media. It is an interesting point to note that one of the main weaknesses of communist and religious control systems during the postwar period was their inability to prevent the spread of Western youth culture. Others (Japan, Germany, Holland, Canada, Australia) were more likely to copy their interpretations of youth forms of rock music, the international currency of youth culture, which is sung mostly in English and can translate or integrate into itself elements of African, Bangladeshi, Greek or Turkish culture, words, sounds, and rhythms but were rarely successfully translated into French, German, or the Scandanvian languages. Some aspects of these cultures have grown progressively more and more bizarre—ear, nose, and body piercing and tattooing—in the search to be different. Some have grown into alternative art forms—paint spraying, fashion design, motor car and motorbike style and decoration. Notably, many attempts to commercialize and normalize youth culture have failed, or their apparent success has produced an immediate rejection and replacement. Other commercial activities have had to follow diligently changes and developments—pop newspapers, music programs, pop videos, and TV commercial advertising—or have faded into the history of popular culture. The short-run hedonism means that change (constant cultural revolution) is a necessity. It is also worth noting that every ten years or so, today's oldest youth can become the parent to a member of an emerging subculture.

Delinquency and Opportunity

The integration of prior theoretical precepts like Merton's Modes of Adaptation with Cohen's Delinquent Subculture provides a theoretical account for the style of delinquent subculture that emerges in one place or at one time rather than another. Why are some youth groups (neo-Nazis and football hooligans) excessively violent when others seem to eschew violence and concentrate on technically sophisticated car or computer crime? What of the role of drugs?

Richard Cloward and Lloyd Ohlin (1960) offer three forms of adaptation not of individuals but of the subculture. Their improvement on delinquent subculture theory is based on the concept of differential opportunity—that the type of subculture that will emerge will reflect the availability of supporting elements available in the surrounding environment. A continuum of local social organization and integration was identified which direct the development of three types of subculture.

First, the criminal subculture will emerge in a closely integrated working-class urban community following organizing patterns laid down by the adult or mature criminal culture. The subculture is a training ground for progression into the adult criminal culture. The membership rules, argot, and dress code will still apply but the permitted activities of the gang will be carefully defined and may be policed by the adult criminal brotherhood. An example is the amusement arcade where the quick thinking, reaction speed, and manual dexterity shown on the machines (from pinball machines in the 1950s to the latest arcade computer games) are useful skills for some criminal activities (picking pockets, breaking into and entering houses). The arcades are usually owned and run to provide recruiting grounds for the adult criminal groups or their associates. In London's East End, there were reports that notorious gangsters actively supported boxing clubs for boys as a source of future muscle. In Berlin, children are frequently used in organized begging in tourist centers. Charles Dickens's Fagin in *Oliver Twist* survives in some form in every urban center in the world. Any activities of the subculture which might cause problems (from the police) for the adults (excessive stealing, assaults on elderly people) will be quickly stopped and may be severely punished. In Northern Ireland, for example, the IRA policed the Catholic areas of conurbations and severely punished sex or drug crimes by young people while actively recruiting them to their terrorist organization. Ironically, in these situations, the police and the criminal organizations are actively recruiting from the same social groups.

Where the surrounding environment is not structured and organized, a Conflict Subculture will emerge. The group will act randomly, engaging in any activity which appeals to them on the day or at the moment. It will inevitably conflict with any representatives of the adult world who try to contain or control it. Its activities cannot be predicted and it is here perhaps that the current debate about the influence of TV and violent video-films should be focused. These films are one source of ideas for the conflict subculture, among others, and can be argued to be the source internationally of many copy-cat crimes or deviant activities.

The Retreatist Subculture, Cloward and Ohlin's third type, is made up of those who are excluded from or who have failed in the other two types. These are the drug subcultures, the solvent abusers or glue sniffers—group who gather around some mind-altering activtiy which is a withdrawal from the day-to-day life struggle for identity and self-esteem. It is in these subculture where argot and dress codes can be most important because they are constantly in danger of arrest and suppression by the police. The argot and dress are means to identify members clearly so that outsiders cannot penetrate and expose the group. There major purpose seems to be as a focus for the supply of drugs and substances and as a training ground in the techniques of use and in understanding and interpreting the drug experiences (Becker, 1963). The squat (Alternativ-haus) is the home for the Retreatist Subculture, but it is always temporary and easily moved in it attracts too much police attention.

References/Suggested Readings: Becker, H.S. 1963. *Becoming a Marijuana User.* Glencoe: Free Press; Burt, C. 1937. *The Young Delinquent.* University of London Press; Cloward, R., and Ohlin, L. 1960. *Delinquency and Opportunity.* Glencoe: Free Press; Cohen, A.K. 1955. *Delinquent Boys.* Glencoe: Free Press; Cohen, S. 1972. *Folk Devils and Moral Panics: The Creation of Mods and Rockers.* London: McGibbon & Kee; Durkheim, Emile. 1893. *The Division of Labor in Society,* translated by George Simpson. New York: Free Press (1947); Durkheim, Emile. 1897. *Suicide.* The Free Press (reprint 1997); Erikson, K. 1966. *Wayward Puritans.* New York: Wiley; Eysenck, H. 1965. *Crime and Personality.* London: Routledge and Kegan Paul; Kudryavtsev, V. 1968. *Prestupnosti.* Moscow: State Publishing; Merton, R.K. 1938. Social Structure and Anomie. *American Sociological Review,* 3, 672; Merton, R.K. 1968. *Social Theory and Social Structure.* New York: Free Press; Miller, W.B. 1958. Delinquency and Lower Class Culture. *Journal of Social Sciences.* Excerpted and reprinted in Wolfgang, M.E., Savitz, L., and Johnston, N. 1968. *The Sociology of Crime and Delinquency.* New York: Holt; Yablonsky, L. 1967. *The Violent Gang.* Harmondsworth: Pelican.

RUSSELL KELLY

SUBURBAN GANGS. Gangs are no longer a problem limited to major city centers; their influence has contaminated the surrounding suburban areas and spread to rural communities (National Alliance of Gang Investigators Associations, 2005, p. 14).

Gangs in the suburbs? Irrevocably, yes. As American society is becoming more diverse and heterogeneous, as more people are moving into the suburbs, gangs are not just an inner-city problem. While the first scholarly work on suburban gangs acknowledged this (Monti, 1994), that mid-1990s book is still the only one of its kind solely devoted to suburban gang issues.

Findings from the 2002 National Youth Gang Survey found all cities with a population of 250,000 or more reporting gang activity in 2002, as did 38 percent of responding suburban counties, 27 percent of responding smaller cities, and 12 percent of responding rural counties (Egley and Major, 2004). As shown, gangs are emerging in suburbs and small towns. Using Spergel and Curry's (1990) model of identifying two major types of areas based on the extent of the gang problem, many suburbs would fall under emerging gang problem cities. While chronic gang problem cities are those which have had a history of gang problems for numerous years, emerging gang cities are those which have experienced problems recently.

It could be argued that concern over gang migration is most pertinent to emerging gang cities and suburbs. This migration perspective would suggest that people move and are mobile and as such, bring or import their gang to this new area. However, it also may be the increased accessibility of guns, the lack of social control institutions to effectively deal with the increased number of youth and children, apathy and indifference, and living in homes where both parents work full-time, the latter of which is a common factor for high-risk youth outside the inner cities.

Interestingly enough, there may be more of a sense of community in urban and inner-city areas which acts as an extension of their community and neighborhood, something that suburbs do not enjoy. The extent to which suburbs have a "real" sense of community is suspect but then again, this would depend largely on what type of suburb they reside. Moreover, just as gangs are not monolithic, neither are suburbs. Suburbs can be quite diverse in many ways but one theme that appears to be widespread is the suburbanization of poverty.

According to the U.S. Bureau of the Census, 13.8 million poor Americans now live in the suburbs, almost as many as the 14.6 million living in central cities. The suburban poor represent 38.5 percent of the nation's poor, compared with 40.6 percent of the total who live in central cities. While not independent of itself, poverty represents a significant risk factor for a number of social ills including crime, violence, and gangs. Contemporary American suburbs are becoming less affluent and more diverse and heterogeneous, accompanied by continued changes in ethnic and social composition.

To illustrate, located in the northwest Atlanta, Georgia, metropolitan area, suburban Cobb County has 607,751 people (U.S. Bureau of the Census) living in six cities and unincorporated areas. The county's continuous growth is evident with a population of 654,005 just four years later, according to the 2004 U.S. Census Estimate. Moreover, Cobb grew 35.7 percent from 1990–2000 alone (with a population of 447,745 in 1990).

Similar to many suburbs, Cobb County has experienced rapid growth and racial and ethnic change. Much of the suburban growth has been due to working-class, often Hispanic, immigration rather than by upscale whites (Katz and Lang, 2003). According to the 2000 Census in Cobb County, 72.4 percent of the residents were white, 18.8 percent black, and 7.7 Hispanic (with the Hispanic population increasing by nearly 6 percent since 1990) with Hispanics accounting for approximately 47,000 residents and with a transient undocumented population that may exceed 160,000 (U.S. Department of Labor). As a result of tremendous growth, the county's adjacent proximity to urban Atlanta, and the increase in minorities, especially Hispanics, many newcomers are gang members who have been forced to move but bring (import) their gang affiliation with them to suburban Cobb County.

To help confront gang issues, in 2002 the Cobb County Police Department created the Cobb Anti-Gang Enforcement (CAGE) Unit. Currently, the unit is formed of ten full-time officers assigned to tackle gang issues in the suburbs. Most of the gangs in Cobb County are of Hispanic origin. Good paying jobs are difficult to find, especially for those entering the United States illegally. Many Hispanics do not attend school or attend only for a short time before dropping out. New Hispanic residents are forced into lower income areas of the county due to lack of resources, money, and being illegal aliens. Culture and language barriers prevent traditional mechanisms of intervention in schools and police from working. Some gang members in

Cobb County are fifth- and sixth-generation members having moved from California, Arizona, and Texas.

Since its inception, the CAGE Unit has identified more than twenty-five different gangs and more than 1,000 gang members with 90 percent Hispanic, 5 percent black, and the remaining 5 percent of other groups (CAGE, 2006). Due to the continued growth and changing demographics, one would expect the gang numbers to increase. This is why it is critical to have gang units within police departments and to create awareness that gangs, too, are in the suburbs.

References/Suggested Readings: CAGE. 2006. *The Changing Face of Suburbia: Is it a Melting Pot?* Presented by Cobb County anti-gang enforcement unit at Kennesaw State University, 4th annual conference on suburbs, Kennesaw, GA; Egley, A., and Major, A.K. 2004. *Highlights of the 2002 National Youth Gang Survey (Fact Sheet).* Washington, DC: Office of Juvenile Justice and Delinquency Prevention; Katz, B., and Lang, R.E. (eds.). 2003. *Redefining Urban and Suburban America: Evidence from Census 2000.* Washington, DC: Brookings Institution Press; Monti, D.J. 1994. *Wannabe: Gangs in Suburbs and Schools.* Cambridge: Blackwell; National Alliance of Gang Investigators Associations. 2005. *National Gang Threat Assessment.* Retrieved January 2006 from www.ojp.usdoj.gov; Spergel, I.A., and Curry, C.D. 1990. Strategies and Perceived Agency Effectiveness in Dealing with the Youth Gang Problem. In C.R. Huff (ed.), *Gangs in America,* pp. 288–309. Newbury Park: Sage; U.S. Bureau of the Census. Retrieved January 2006 from www.census.gov; U.S. Department of Labor. Retrieved January 2006 from www.dol.gov.

REBECCA D. PETERSEN

T

TERRORISM AND GANGS. This entry takes a close look at the degree to which the "line" has been blurred between traditional street gangs and terrorist groups. This is achieved by examining the general trend in policies aimed at gangs and terrorism both before and after September 11, 2001. The change in the perception of gangs by the public, law enforcement, and policy makers is also briefly discussed.

To what degree has the "line" been blurred between **street gangs** and terrorist groups? It is important to note that "much American crime prevention is incident driven," due to the fact that "the United States does not have a specific agency responsible for crime prevention" (Schuck, 2005). What impact has post-9/11 policies had on this development? Are these policies appropriate to both gang members and terrorists? In analyzing the shifting policies as a test of social control and labeling theory, does the "War on Gangs" and the shift in focus to the "War on Terror" "control" members of gangs in the same way? And has this shift incorporated gang members to the point where they are adopting Islamic fundamentalism and support terrorism?

The definitional "line" between the street-level gang and terrorist organizations has been blurred on several fronts. To a lesser degree, they have been equated to each other theoretically (Turnley and Smrcka, 2002), but have long been defined politically as similar. Today, 70 percent of states have specific legislation aimed at street-level gangs, many of it adopted in the 1980s and 1990s (Institute for Intergovernmental Research, 2000). Much of this state legislation is called "Street Terrorism Enforcement and Prevention," which not only functionally includes specific punishments for those as identified as gang members, but reinforces the image of gang members as terrorists. Thus, even pre-9/11, gangs were being redefined and labeled as "domestic terrorists" by policy makers.

Post-9/11, with the passing of the USA PATRIOT Act, the Domestic Security Enhancement Act of 2003, Intelligence Reform and Terrorism Prevention Act of 2004, and thirty-six state-level terrorism laws, there is an undoubtable impact on gang members. Highlights include the indictment of nineteen members of the Saint James' Boys gang under New York Terrorism Law (Garcia, 2005), and the ongoing arrest of MS-13 members by Immigration and Customs Enforcement in Operation Community Shield, whose alleged ties to terrorist organizations have since been rejected (Immigrations and Customs Enforcement [ICE], 2005). Recently, ICE has expanded its Operation Community Shield to other street gangs, arresting 1,502 members total as of October 2005 (including 746 MS-13s). These other targeted gangs, which include Sureños, 18th Street gang, **Latin Kings**, Vatos Locos, Mexican Mafia, La Raza gang, Border Brothers, Brown Pride, Norteno, Florencia 13, Tiny Rascal, Asian Boyz, and Jamaican Posse, do not have ties to traditional international terrorist organizations.

Yet others contend that the "War on Terror" is actually drawing attention away from the older "War on Gangs" and the "War on Drugs" (Campo-Flores, 2004). What is actually happening? Do gang members have increased or decreased scrutiny since 9/11? According to the 2005 National Gang Threat Assessment, only 5.7 percent of police forces polled claimed that gangs were connected with terrorist organizations in their area (Bureau of Justice Assistance, 2005). Thus, the connection between gangs and terrorism does not appear to be widespread, despite reports of relationships between gang members and terrorist networks (Hagedorn, 2005). Furthermore, most of these terrorist groups identified as having local gang connections are not international Islamic extremists, but rather white supremacist "domestic terrorist" groups (Bureau of Justice Assistance, 2005).

Though the "War on Gangs" and the "War on Terrorism" may be, at face value, separate wars, there is enormous potential for members of disparate street organizations to be also swept up under the latter. It is possible that this is because the "war on gangs" is an old battlefront and is now getting a cosmetic makeover in order to increase the fear and win back support. Either way, it is important to see if there is a distinction between "terrorists" and "gangs," and furthermore, see how the shifting policies are (or are not) effective in "controlling" gang-related crime.

Major Policies of the "War on Gangs"

The "war on gangs," like the "war on drugs" and the "war on crime," developed during the early 1980s as a result of the perceived increase of gangs, and the accompanying political pressure for police agencies to respond (Weisel and Shelley, 2004). Specialized police "gang" units such as California's Community Resources Against Street Hoodlums (CRASH) were utilized to monitor gang crime specifically. This monitoring of gang members by using proactive intelligence makes assumptions about their sophistication, and predisposed involvement in crime. It assumes that certain individuals, because they are gang members, are cohesive enough to commit strategic crimes that require the police to use intelligence—just like the military would in a regular war. Because of the "war-like" setup of the units, it resulted in corruption: "The success of CRASH, however, came at a price. Officers developed an independent subculture that embodied a war on gangs mentality in which the ends justified the means. They resisted supervision and control and ignored department procedures and policies" (Los Angeles Police Department, 2000). After peaking in 1993, many CRASH units were disabled, likely due to the same political forces that formed them in the first place. Thus, functionally, the "War on Gangs" at least appears to be slowing.

On the legal end, a parallel effect developed: in one 1995 study, 30 percent of prosecutors in large jurisdictions formed "gang units using vertical prosecution to focus on gang members" (Johnson, Webster, and Connors, 1995). These policies of prosecuting gang members were supported by numerous state and local laws (Garcia, 2005).

Even more important, the application of the term "terrorists" to members of **street organizations** occurred a decade before 9/11 redefined America's perception of "terrorism." In 1988, the California Street Terrorism Enforcement and Prevention Act (STEP) was enacted, shortly followed by STEP Acts in Florida, Illinois, Georgia, Louisiana, and Montana (Johnson, Webster, and Connors, 1995; Montana Street Terrorism Enforcement and Prevention Act). The application of the title thus "inscribed in the language of law the image of gang members as terrorists" (Conquergood, 1996).

Perhaps even more telling is the trend of federal legislation being used against gang members. Federal legislation is "much more stringent . . . the legal reach is broader than the power of local and state authorities" (Evering, 2005). The image of a highly organized militias has fueled the utilization of the Racketeering Influenced and Corrupt Organization Act (RICO) against gang members. RICO, traditionally used for organized crime syndicates, also stretches the image of the gang to fit a similar image. RICO not only applies to an entire organization, but also is used to "remove the leadership and the most dangerous members of violent street gangs and seize their assets." Inherent in the application of RICO is the idea that gangs are a cohesive unit similar to organized crime.

Nor does this increasing image of "terror" appear to be slowing post-9/11, where the image of the "home-grown terrorist" has been solidified with the proposed Gang Deterrence and Community Protection Act of 2005 (the Gangbusters Bill). One of the co-sponsors, Representative Frank Wolf, has commented that the Gangbusters Bill is a remedy to terror: "no one should have to live in fear" (Evering, 2005). Thus, "living in fear" proposes that living with gangs equates living with terrorists, who, by definition, are "spreaders of terror."

Major Policies of the "War on Terror"

In the 1990s, terrorism was introduced to the American consciousness through a number of attacks, including the following (Close Up Foundation, 1997):

- 1993 World Trade Center bombing
- 1995 Oklahoma City bombing
- 1996 arrest of Ted Kaczynski (the Unabomber)
- 1996 Olympics bombing in Atlanta
- 1998 bombing of the U.S. embassies in Kenya and Tanzania

As a response to the increase in attacks, the 1996 Anti-Terrorism and Effective Death Penalty Act was signed into law by President Clinton. The act allotted $1 billion toward curbing terrorism, increased penalties for terrorist offences, tightened immigration, and expanded federal agencies' power to conduct surveillance. In conjunction with the Immigration and Naturalization Services (INS), illegal immigrants, some of them members of street organizations, were deported by the agency with little judicial oversight.

The Federal Bureau of Investigation was already one step ahead, launching Violent Gang and Terrorist Organizations File (VGTOF) a year previous to the act (Episcopo and Moor, 1996). The VGTOF is a subsection of the National Crime Information Center (NCIC), a national law enforcement database. Its title suggests an equation between violent gangs and terrorist organizations. Furthermore, the database not only tracks those individuals identified with a particular organization, but also "pronounces an individual guilty by mere association with a gang or terrorist group." Thus, for many individuals, an entry into the database is inevitable. Categories are wide-reaching as well; as of 2002 it contained categories such as "anarchists," "militia," "white supremacist," "black extremist," "animal rights extremist," "environmental extremist," "radical Islamic extremist," and "European origin extremist" (Davis, 2003).

Though the concept of terrorism did not suddenly materialize post-9/11, no terrorism-related activity has had as much impact on public policy. The policy reaction to 9/11 was not only radical, but swift: by December 2001, twenty-nine state-level terrorism laws had been passed or were in consideration (National Conference of State Legislatures, 2001). Since then, a total of thirty-six states added "terrorism-related laws to their criminal codes" (Garcia, 2005). The new terrorism laws appear to be split into two main categories: increased security and increased punishment for terrorist acts, with the majority of legislation on the security side.

Not to be outdone, the federal government's Uniting and Strengthening America by Providing Appropriate Tools Required to Intercept and Obstruct Terrorism (the USA PATRIOT) Act passed the legislature almost unanimously shortly following 9/11 (Department of Justice, n.d.). Included in the bill is the "shift [of] the primary mission of the FBI from solving crimes to gathering domestic intelligence" (McGee, 2001). Similar to the anti-gang legislation, there is a resulting shift in the traditional "reactive" nature of policing to *proactive* domestic intelligence gathering (Haberfeld, 2002). This shift in orientation is problematic, because "proactive intelligence gathering," by definition, is based on investigating individuals who have not yet committed a visible crime. This means that there will be some "mistakes" made—not everyone that is investigated is guilty of terrorist activities. About two years after the passage of the USA PATRIOT Act, nearly half of the cases designated by the Department of Justice as terrorism-related were misclassified (Subcommittee on Immigration, Border Security, and Claims, 2003).

Since the passage of the USA PATRIOT Act, other legislation along the same vein has also been passed. Most relevant is the Domestic Security Enhancement Act of 2003, which "grants sweeping powers to the government, eliminating or weakening many of the checks and balances that remained on government surveillance, wiretapping, detention and criminal prosecution" (Edgar, 2003). The act, also referred to as the PATRIOT Act II, is so radical as to leave some to speculate that its intention was to be used as a bargaining chit for later, scaled-down versions. Leaked to the public before its release, parts of the PATRIOT Act II have since been included in other legislation and passed. Though this act has not been incorporated in its entirety, it certainly illustrates the "change in the nation's thinking about domestic security and civil liberties" (McGee, 2001).

Redefining "Domestic Terrorism"

Many contend that "domestic terrorism" has been "overshadowed by 9/11 and the hunt for terrorists abroad" (Copeland, 2004). However, one of the most notable features of the PATRIOT Act is establishing a definition of "domestic terrorism."

> Activities occurring primarily within the territorial jurisdiction of the United States involving acts dangerous to human life that . . . appear to be intended to intimidate or

coerce a civilian population, influence the policy of a government by intimidation or coercion, or affect the conduct of a government. (FBI, 2004)

One of the reasons to emphasize foreign terrorism over domestic terrorism is because "there's a tendency to want to externalize the threat and say the people who want to hurt us don't look like us, they don't worship the same god and don't have the same skin color" (Copeland, 2004). However, this same "ease" of externalizing the threat happens as well within the United States to many black and brown people. Individuals identified as gang members fit within this scope. Although they are increasingly labeled "domestic terrorists," they often have nonwhite skin, and they oftentimes do not speak English as their first language or worship a Christian god. This shift in perspective is radical; most of the traditionally identified "domestic terrorists" are white supremacist groups such as the Aryan Resistance, Hammerskins, Ku Klux Klan, Neo-Nazi Party, and National Socialist Movement (Bureau of Justice Assistance, 2005).

The Public Perception

The post-9/11 media are instrumental in the re-labeling of gang members. Increasingly the perception of danger has increased, as the perception of gang members has turned from "kids hanging out on the street corner," to "gang-banging and selling drugs," to "monsters," to "domestic" or "urban" terrorists. This trend was happening even before 9/11: "Gangs are portrayed in the media and public discourse through the pattern of three dehumanizing metaphors: (1) gangs are a virulent disease, (2) gangs are vicious animals, (3) gangs are violent terrorists" (Conquergood, 1996). This latter label has persisted in the media: "if the terror network succeeds in turning our nation's street gangs into a 'weapon of mass insurrection,' urban warfare will become a horrifying reality" (Grigg, 2002). This tie has been apparent on two fronts: between gang members and international terrorists as well as labeling gang members as "domestic terrorists." There have been two highly publicized cases supporting the former: the arrest of Padilla, and reports of the Mara Salvatrucha (MS-13).

The arrest of Padilla, sensationalized in the news, planted firmly in the minds of the public that terrorists were not just lurking outside of the United States, but were also being home-grown: "the revelation that a Brooklyn-born citizen may have been a foot soldier in Al Qaeda challenges easy assumptions about who the adversaries of the US war on terrorism really are" (Scherer and Marks, 2002). Always mentioned alongside his arrest is the fact that Padilla is a former gang member, and the media emphasizes this connection between gangs and international terrorism: "America's tough urban streets have long had odd connections with Middle Eastern and Islamic terrorism" (Weisman, 2002). The publicity surrounding Padilla is misleading: not only does he become the "norm," not the exception, but there is little effort therein to distinguish between Islam and terrorism.

In 2004, a new crossover gang appeared: Mara Salvatrucha (MS-13). Described by many accounts as having an "international profile" and "causing terror," there were allegations of connections between the gang and Al Qaeda (Campo-Flores, 2004). Recognizing MS-13 as a "homeland security risk," ICE established Operation Community Shield, an aggressive measure to target the gang in February 2005 (Garcia, 2005). Since then, it has expanded to "target the proliferation of gang violence throughout the country," and thus is now a more general measure against street gangs. The publicity surrounding MS-13 was especially misleading; despite the allegations of a connection, the FBI established that "there is no basis in fact to support this allegation of al-Qaeda or even radical Islamic ties" (Harman, 2005).

The re-labeling of gang members as "domestic terrorists" has been less publicized, but is nevertheless misleading. It furthermore has an enormous opportunity for growth, since "language is plastic" (Garcia, 2005). At the forefront of this endeavor is Los Angeles Police Chief William Bratton, who commented that "street gangs have become so violent they are practicing what amounts to domestic terrorism" (Organized Crime Digest, 2003). Not only the media but policy has allowed for the reclassification of these individuals. Many of the terrorism laws contain "vague and open-ended language that allows the term to easily slip from its original meaning" (Garcia, 2005). In New York, the prosecution of Edgar Morales and the Saint James' Boys under the state's terrorism law is an example. In this case, the district attorney applies the label of "terrorist" to gangs: "the terror perpetuated by gangs . . . also fits squarely within the scope of this nature." The original intention of the law is redefined in this statement to fit the needs of law enforcement and "justice" agencies. Similar to the "cross-over" legislation of the earlier STEP acts under the rhetoric of the "War on Gangs" and the "War on Crime," gang members are placed into the category of "terrorists" by the law under the "War on Terror."

The rhetoric leading to the redefinition of "domestic terrorists" is not new. It is the same rhetoric used in the "War on Crime" in the 1980s and 1990s. For example, in 1988 LAPD's Operation Hammer, which was "aimed squarely at the stop and search of minorities" resulted in the arrest of over 1,400 minority youths in one month alone. Most of these youths were later released with no charges (Crank, 1998).

> The brutality witnessed for both the Los Angeles City and County police stemmed form its intense focus on law enforcement, an "us versus them" or siege mentality, fostered by management and the chilling rhetoric of a "war on crime." It's easier to justify an "us versus them" mentality when the "them" is a different skin color, or speaks a different language. (Crank 1998, p. 213)

History repeats itself. This is the same rhetoric that is being repeated today to make it easy for policy makers and the public to casually accept the fate of certain black and brown individuals as casualties of war.

What Is Going On?

There appears to be a considerable divergence between the public's perception of the link between gang members, Islam, and terrorism, and the reality of the situation—that the link is tenuous at best. Ties between Islam in the United States and terrorism appear to be truly exceptional: a historical examination indicates only a handful of connections. Pre-9/11, connections between individuals in this country and international terrorist organizations include the Nation of Islam (NOI) leader Louis Farrakhan, and former Black P Stone Nation Leader Jeff Fort. Post-9/11, Padilla (as aforementioned) is the singular link between gangs and international terrorism. These few connections, however, do not represent the majority of the Muslim population in the United States. They especially, by logic, cannot represent the majority of gang members.

Because there is an inferred connection between young black men, Islam, and terrorism, it is important to look at history. Historically, the connection has been fostered half a century before 9/11. Its earliest roots in the United States trace back to the 1930s, when Wallace Fard, an Arabian man, founded the Lost-Found Nation of Islam (Occhiogrosso, n.d.). He disappeared shortly thereafter, leaving Elijah Muhammad in charge of the Detroit-based organization. Soon its membership swelled to over one million. Elijah Muhammad employed a young man named Malcolm X as a representative, and the group preached a mixture of "unorthodox Islam and black separatism," claiming that blacks were the "original" race and that Caucasians were "white devils." It is important to note that the Lost-Found Nation of Islam's teachings are different from authentic Islam, and that after a trip to Mecca, Malcolm X split from Muhammad. After Elijah Muhammad's death in 1975, his son returned black Muslims to conventional Sunni Islam, later formally dissolving the movement.

Meanwhile, another group founded by Louis Farrakhan, the Nation of Islam (NOI), around Elijah Muhammad's teachings, has often been criticized for "separatism and anti-Semitism" (Occhiogrosso, n.d.). Additionally, there are Justice Department reports of the NOI receiving money from an official in the Libyan government (who has supported terrorist activities in the past), as well as having connections to the "terrorist dictator" Muammar Qaddafi (Grigg, 2002). Despite these allegations, the NOI officially condemned the 9/11 attacks and has refuted its anti-Semitic characterization (Nation of Islam, 2001). Even Farrakhan's questionable 1997 World Friendship Tour, when meeting with "radical Muslim regimes" in Iran, Nigeria, Sudan, Libya, Iraq, and Syria, was "well within a substantial 'legal' framework" according to the U.S. State Department (Muhammad, 1997). Thus far, there have not been any NOI arrests. Moreover, there is no legitimate comparison between NOI and any street gang, as inferred in several media articles (Grigg, 2002; Weisman, 2002).

The second connection between gangs, terrorist organizations, and political Islam is Jeff Fort, the leader of the Black P Stone Nation. During the late 1960s Fort took control of the Blackstone Rangers (former name of the Black P Stone Nation), and formed a "nation" of numerous street organizations (Grigg, 2002). This organization gained legitimacy when it received money from the Office of Economic Opportunity for a peace truce with another Chicago gang, the Eastside Disciples. However, some of the money was funneled into the drug trade, and Fort himself was arrested and served time for cocaine trafficking. During this period, he converted into the "Black Nationalist variant of Islam," and "tried to have the gang recognized under a religious order called the "Moorish Science Temple of America, El Rukn tribe." Around 1996 Fort reportedly developed plans for terrorist activities in exchange for $1 million per year from the Libyan government, and had members of the Black P Stone Nation meet with representatives from Libya twice.

Padilla represents the third connection between gangs, terrorist, and political Islam. This link, however, appears to be even weaker than the two aforementioned cases. The media has emphasized his role as a "troubled kid from the streets of Chicago" and a gang member. However, Padilla converted to Islam after his 1991 arrest on weapons charges, and after his release from prison, moved to south Florida (Weisman, 2002). He remained there until 1998, when he went to live in Egypt, Afghanistan, and Pakistan, supposedly "to make common cause with Al Qaeda" (Weisman, 2002; Karon, 2002). At the time of his move to the Middle East, he had been away from the Chicago area for over seven years. Arrested on "suspicion to detonate a radiological 'dirty bomb,'" there is little evidence that he was "integrated into the organization he was desperate to join" (Karon, 2002) and some evidence to the contrary including his 'dubious past'" (Bin Laden's men tend to be repressed puritans rather than penitent sinners).

Blurring Distinctions

The "blurring of the line" between gang members and terrorist organizations has been occurring in policy even before 9/11 with the introduction of the STEP Acts and proactive policing and intelligence gathering from specialized gang units. The few connections between gangs and international terrorist organizations in the Nation of Islam and the Black P Stone Nation support this approach. There is a faulty chain of logic represented by these cases: gang members do not equal Muslims, who do not equal terrorists.

Although the public perception and introduction of the idea of a "domestic terrorist" occurred before 9/11, the post-9/11 policy measures have accelerated this idea forward in both arenas. There is indication that this term is starting to be applied to gang members, both by the media and policy. This newest development in "blurring the line" between gang members and terrorism has potential to result in a more stringent hold on the former. If the trend of looking inward and gathering intelligence for domestic terrorism continues, it will result in (1) increased scrutiny of gang members, and (2) further application of terrorist policies to gang members. This may be tempting for policy makers, who could gain additional funding for anti-gang measures if they are redefined as "anti-terrorist." Though the door may be closing to the "War on Gangs," it is wide open to the "War on Terror," with gang members being redefined as "domestic terrorists."

References/Suggested Readings: Bureau of Justice Assistance. 2005. *2005 National Gang Threat Assessment*. National Alliance of Gang Investigators Associations; Campo-Flores, A. 2004. The Most Dangerous Gang in America: They're a Violent Force in 33 States and Counting. Inside the Battle to Police Mara Salvatrucha. *Newsweek*, March 28; Close Up Foundation. 1997. *Domestic Terrorism*. Retrieved October 13, 2005, from www.closeup.org/terror. htm#domestic; Conquergood, D. 1996. Stereotypes. *One City*. Retrieved on October 23, 2005, from www.uic.edu/orgs/kbc/Features/Power.htm; Copeland, L. 2004. Domestic Terrorism: New Trouble at Home. *USA Today*; Crank, John. 1998. *Understanding Police Culture*. Cincinnati, OH: Anderson Publishing; Davis, A. 2003. Use of Data Collection Systems Is up Sharply Following 9/11. *Wall Street Journal*, May 22; Edgar, T. 2003. Section-by-Section Analysis of Justice Department Draft "Domestic Security Enhancement Act of 2003," also known as "PATRIOT Act II." American Civil Liberties Union. Retrieved on September 21, 2005, from www.aclu.org//safefree/general/17203leg20030214.html; Episcopo, P., and Moor, D. 1996. The Violent Gang and Terrorist Organizations File. *FBI Law Enforcement Bulletin*, October; Evering, K. 2005. House Bill, FBI Target Gang Violence. *American Observer*, 10 (10); Federal Bureau of Investigation. 2004. Terrorism 2000/2001. U.S. Department of Justice, FBI Publication #0308; Garcia, M. 2005. *Immigration and the Alien Gang Epidemic: Problems and Solutions*. U.S. Immigration and Customs Enforcement, U.S. Department of Homeland Security; Garcia, M. 2005. N.Y. Using Terrorism Law To Prosecute Street Gang: Critics Say Post-9/11 Legislation Is Being Applied Too Broadly. *Washington Post*, January 31; Grigg, W.N. 2002. Weapons of Mass Insurrection. *New American*, 18 (24); Haberfeld, M. 2002. *Critical Issues in Policing Training*. Upper Saddle River, NJ: Pearson Education; Hagedorn, J. 2005. Gangs and Terrorism. Retrieved on December 11, 2005, from gangresearch.net/Globalization/ terrorism/terrorism.html; Harman, D. 2005. U.S. Steps up Battle against Salvadorian Gang MS-13. *USA Today*, February. Retrieved on September 23, 2005, from www.usatoday.com/ news/world/2005-02-23-gang-salvador_x.htm; Immigrations and Customs Enforcement. 2005. *Operation Community Shield*. Retrieved October 24, 2005, from www.ice.gov/graphics/ investigations/comshield/index.htm; Institute for Intergovernmental Research. 2000. *Analysis*

THRASHER, FREDERIC   257

of Gang-Related Legislation. Retrieved on October 20, 2005, from www.iir.com/nygc/gang-legis/analysis.htm; Johnson, C., Webster, B., and Connors, E. 1995. Prosecuting Gangs: A National Assessment. *NIJ Research in Brief,* February; Karon, T. 2002. Person of the Week: Jose Padilla. *Time Magazine* Online Edition. Retrieved October 4, 2005, from www.time.com/time/pow/article/0,8599,262269,00.html; Los Angeles Police Department. 2000. *Report of the Rampart Independent Review Panel.* Los Angeles Police Department; McGee, J. 2001. An Intelligence Giant in the Making: Anti-Terrorism Law Likely to Bring Domestic Apparatus of Unprecedented Scope. *Washington Post,* November 4; Montana Street Terrorism Enforcement and Prevention Act (1997). Retrieved on October 4, 2005, from data.opi.state.mt.us/bills/mca/45/8/45-8-401.htm; Muhammad, T. 1997. State Department Concedes World Tour Violates no U.S. Laws. Retrieved on December 11, 2005, from worldfriendshiptour.noi.org/state-dept12-9-97.html; Nation of Islam. 2001. Press Conference Transcript on 911 Attacks on World Trade Center and Pentagon. Retrieved on December 11, 2005, from www.noi.org/statements/transcript_010916.htm; National Conference of State Legislatures. 2001. *Protecting Democracy: State Legislation Addressing Terrorism.* Retrieved on October 21, 2005, from www.ncsl.org/programs/press/2001/freedom/terrorism01.htm; Occhiogrosso, P. The Black Muslims. Caroline Myss, Ph.D. Retrieved on December 11, 2005, from www.myss.com/worldreligions/Islam11.asp; *Organized Crime Digest.* 2003. *Los Angeles Gangs Are "Domestic Terrorists." Organized Crime Digest,* 24 (18), 5; Scherer, R,. and Marks, A. 2002. Gangs, Prison: Al Qaeda Breeding Grounds? *Christian Science Monitor;* Schuck, A. 2005. American Crime Prevention: Trends and New Frontiers. *Canadian Journal of Criminology and Criminal Justice,* 47 (2); Subcommittee on Immigration, Border Security, and Claims of the Committee on the Judiciary, House of Representatives. 2003. *War on Terrorism: Immigration Enforcement Since September 11, 2001*; Turnley, J., and Smrcka, J. 2002. Terrorist Organizations and Criminal Street Gangs: An Argument for Analogy. Advanced Concepts Group, Sandia National Laboratories; U.S. Department of Justice. n.d. The USA PATRIOT Act: Preserving Life and Liberty. Retrieved on September 19, 2005, from www.lifeandliberty.gov/highlights.htm; Weisel, D., and Shelley, T. 2004. Specialized Gang Units: Form and Function in Community Policing. National Institute of Justice. Retrieved on October 13, 2005, from www.ncjrs.org/pdffiles1/nij/grants/207204.pdf; Weisman, J. 2002. American Terror Suspect Is Not Unique. *USA Today,* June 11. Retrieved December 11, 2005, from www.usatoday.com/news/nation/2002/06/11/suspect-usat.htm.

MARISA OMORI

THRASHER, FREDERIC. Frederic Thrasher's *The Gang: A Study of 1,313 Gangs in Chicago* (1927) is widely considered the founding, classic text in the study of gang life. It is cited as such in nearly every major treatment of gangs to this day—even those critical of it. This includes books like *Islands in the Street* (Martin Jankowski), *In Search of Respect* (Philippe Bourgois), *The American Street Gang* (Malcolm Klein), *Gangs* (Scott Cummings and Daniel Monti), *People and Folks* (John Hagedorn), and *Gangsters* (Lewis Yablonsky). In particular, Daniel Monti (1993) highlights the ways that the questions posed by Thrasher are the questions researchers still wrestle with—What is a gang and who is in it? Where are gangs found? How are gangs organized? In what kind of activities do gangs engage? What is the gangs relation to the community? And, finally, What is to be done about gangs? Monti sums up much, when he writes, "Any assessment of what we know and do not know about gangs in this century must begin with Frederic Thrasher" (Monti, 1994, p. 135). He continues, noting that the "ghost" of Thrasher seemed to be "rattling around the room" when he conducted his own interviews with gang members (p. 135).

Like many cities, Chicago at the turn of the last century was marked by unprecedented expansion. The urban infrastructure grew quite rapidly during this period.

As Thrasher's mentor at the University of Chicago, sociologist Robert Park, noted, "the skyscraper, the subway, the department store, the daily newspaper," all rapidly peppered the emerging cityscape in new and exciting ways (Park, 1925, p. 47). Above all else, the city seemed a site of almost limitless potential and possibility. As Thrasher wrote, "we are still, for the most part, in an epoch of feverish mobility and expansion consequent upon the peopling of a new continent and the exploitation of virgin natural resources" (1927, p. 487). Indeed, the United States itself seemed at the very beginning of an unprecedented economic and cultural revolution—a new frontier.

This rapid expansion and growth was replete with both possibility and danger, a point underscored by Park time and again. City life meant the breakdown of the kinds of traditional social roles and responsibilities which often marked rural life. Urban life meant new divisions of labor as well as new modes of association, new kinds of human connections around a wide range of tastes, dispositions, and life-styles. Here, "divergent types" could reinvent themselves with like-minded others— "Association with others of their own ilk provides not merely a stimulus, but a moral support for the traits they have in common which they would not find in a less select society" (1925, p. 45). In fact, one could "map" the city's various regions as "moral areas" where particular such communities gelled together. (The Gang included a now rare foldout map of "Gangland." Other books of the period contained similar such maps, including Creesey's Taxi-Hall Dance and Shaw's The Jack-Roller.) People who inhabit these regions were "dominated, as people are not normally dominated, by a taste or by a passion or by some interest" (p. 45). For Park and his students Chicago was a laboratory where "human nature and social processes" could be studied in their most crystallized forms (p. 46).

According to Thrasher, youth gangs were a product of "in between" urban spaces. In an article published in 1926, "The Gang as a Symptom of Community Disorganization," Thrasher writes: "Three-fourths of the population are composed of foreign-born peoples and their immediate progeny. These diverse cultural elements have added greatly to the general confusion. Chicago is a mosaic of foreign colonies with conflicting social heritages." He continues, "There has not yet been a time for adjustment among these diverse elements and for the development of a consistent and self-controlled social order. The gang is one symptom of this 'cultural lag'" (p. 4).

The young children of immigrants, according to Thrasher, did not have access to the old world customs and mores that moored their parents—they were thrown headlong into the seemingly seediest aspects of American culture, "the more racy and the more vicious aspects," as Thrasher would write in 1927 (p. 490). There was, to Thrasher, a "blind groping for order, without much understanding of the nature of the problems involved or of their difficulties" (p. 488). This search for "order" lead to the organization of what would amount to these alternative, mini-societies in what he would famously term "interstitial" areas of Chicago. These areas, collectively, comprised what he would call Chicago's "gangland."

Thrasher would call the concept of "interstitial" sites the most important of the book. These are "spaces that intervene between one thing and another" (p. 22). He continues, "In nature foreign matter tends to collect and cake in every crack, crevice, and cranny—interstices. There are also fissures and breaks in the structure of social organization. The gang may be regarded as an interstitial element in the framework of society, and gangland as an interstitial region in the layout of the city" (p. 22). For Thrasher, these gangs did not grow up in the "better" parts of the city but were part and parcel of the kinds of social, cultural, and material dislocations which marked urbanization and immigration. According to Thrasher, "purely residential and well-organized suburbs of the better type such as Oak Park and Evanston, are practically gangless, for the activities of the children are well provided for in family, school, church, and other established institutions" (p. 20).

Though limited by his moment, it is worth pointing out that Thrasher does not locate the various problems of gang life in young people themselves. In fact, Thrasher explicitly argues against the idea that there is some "gang impulse" that controls boys, that it is the product of some biological impulse. According to Thrasher, this "traditional explanation" of gang behavior was lacking an understanding of the "plasticity" of boys as well as the pressures of social circumstance. He writes, "[Man's] nature is plastic and he excels in his capacity to adapt himself to a multiplicity of circumstances for which instinct could not fit him." Arguing against dominant logic of the time, Thrasher continues, "[The gang boy] is primarily a creature of habit, but the patterns of his habits may be infinitely varied in varied circumstances" (p. 43).

This concern for the social, for people's "varied circumstances," is important. Thrasher's "unit of analysis" for understanding young people's lives is what he calls "the situation complex," a notion deserving more acute attention than it has perhaps received. Thrasher uses the term in a few different ways throughout *The Gang*. Early in the volume, he notes that the various "conditioning factors within which the gang lives, moves, and has its being, may be regarded as the 'situation complex' within which the human nature elements interact to produce gang phenomena" (p. 144). Here, Thrasher stresses the kinds of spatial factors that both enable and constrain the kinds of activities boys can engage in. The layout of buildings, streets, alleys, bodies of water, etc., all interact to allow for certain kinds of activities and not others.

Later in the book, Thrasher moves beyond the geographical to talk about "the situation complex" in broader and more expansive ways. It is here that we see Thrasher at his most powerful and most problematic:

> Such underlying conditions as inadequate family life; poverty; deteriorating neighborhoods; and ineffective religion, education, and recreation must be considered together as a situation complex which forms the matrix of gang development. It seems impossible to control one factor without dealing with the others, so closely are they interwoven, and in most cases they are inseparable from the general problem of immigrant adjustment. (p. 491)

Of course, we see here an extension of the pathologizing discourses Thrasher deploys throughout the volume (e.g., "inadequate family life," etc.). Yet we also see a broader effort to situate these young people's lives within a web of influences that cannot be understood except in relation to each other. The point is important. While this book focuses on gangs, we see a constant effort to see these young boy's life in context. One can only understand the effect of any aspect of boy's lives in relation to others. Indeed, while this book is of course "about" gangs, it is more wide ranging in scope than much work in the delimited field of "criminology" (a point made, as well, by Venkatesh, 2003). It does not prefigure the role and importance of gangs in young people's lives, but situates these organizations in a broader institutional matrix. As noted, Thrasher argued that we cannot understand gangs unless we understand competing institutions, such as religion, family, school, and other social networks, including so-called play groups.

Indeed, Thrasher argues throughout *The Gang* that "the majority of gangs develop from the spontaneous play-group." These groups, he continues, become "gangs" through conflict and acquire structure through their activities. The play group "does not become a gang . . . until it begins to excite disapproval and opposition, and thus acquires a more definite group consciousness" (p. 30). He continues, "It discovers a rival or enemy in the gang in the next block; its baseball or football team is pitted against some other team; parents look upon it with suspicion or hostility" and so on (p. 30). These are the real beginnings of group consciousness, the real point at which the gang becomes a conflict group and solidifies its borders.

This has often been considered Thrasher's main finding. Others such as Daniel Monti and John Hagedorn have used the notion in their own work. According to Jankowski (1991), however, the implications of Thrasher's insights go further, to acknowledge all the ways in which gangs function as organizations. Thrasher notes that gangs are "elementary societies" which develop their "own organization and codes in independent or spontaneous fashion" (p. 277). Much of this has to do with the kinds of activities these boys engage in. In a sense, their shared history emerges from the sediment of these activities over time. These can range from playing pranks to athletic contests to raiding and robbing to charitable enterprises (p. 277).

Like many classic sociological texts, *The Gang* is both dated and timely. Clearly, the book is marked by normative assumptions that make it seem largely anachronous today—assumptions about assimilation, middle-class values, immigrant communities, and even research itself. Such assumptions would become common place for much of the gang work that followed. In addition, most gang researchers today do not wholly adopt the linear model of gang development that Thrasher posited throughout. In its most reductive iterations, such notions substitute a kind of organic, developmental logic for descriptions of the often unpredictable and context-specific ways such groups develop. Today, we have many more sophisticated and detailed studies that have challenged these logics.

But the book remains interesting for other reasons form. Most important was Thrasher's impulse to understand "the situation complex" of boys' lives, his insistence that one can only understand the gang in relation to other institutions including the family, church, school, etc. Looking at one in isolation is largely misleading. Thrasher remained committed to understanding particular lives and experiences in context. He argued from the beginning of his career until the end that nuanced case study work was most important.

References/Suggested Readings: Bourgois, P. 1995. *In Search of Respect: Selling Crack in el Barrio.* Cambridge: Cambridge University Press; Hagedorn, J. 1989. *People and Folks: Gangs, Crime and the Underclass in a Rustbelt City.* Chicago: Lakeview Press; Jankowski, M. 1991. *Islands in the Street: Gangs and American Urban Society.* Berkeley: University of California Press; Klein, M. 1995. *The American Street Gang: Its Nature, Prevalence, and Control.* Oxford: Oxford University Press; Monti, D. 1993. Origins and Problems of Gang Research in the United States. In S. Cummings and D. Monti (eds.), *Gangs: The Origins and Impact of Contemporary Youth Gangs in the United States,* pp. 3–25. Albany: SUNY Press; Monti, D. 1994. *Wannabe: Gangs in Suburbs and Schools.* New York: Blackwell Press; Park, R. 1925. The City: Suggestions for the Investigation of Human Behavior in the Urban Environment; The Growth of the City: An Introduction to a Research Project. In R. Park and E. Burgess (eds.), *The City: An Investigation of Human Behavior in the Urban Environment,* pp. 1–61. Chicago: University of Chicago Press; Thrasher, F. 1926. The Gang as a Symptom of Community Disorganization. *Journal of Applied Sociology,* 1 (1), 3–27; Thrasher, F. 1927. *The Gang: A*

Study of 1,313 Gangs in Chicago. Chicago: University of Chicago Press; Venkatesh, S. 2003. A Note on Social Theory and the American Street Gang. In L. Kontos, D. Brotherton, and L. Barrios (eds.), *Gangs and Society: Alternative Perspectives*, pp. 3–11. New York: Columbia University Press; Yablonsky, L. 1997. *Gangsters*. New York: NYU Press.

GREG DIMITRIADIS

TRANSNATIONAL GANGS. On July 31, 2006, the Generalitat—the autonomous government of Catalonia—recognized for the first time a youth gang as cultural association. The Organización Cultural de los Reyes y Reinas Latinos de Catalunya—the local version of one of the most popular and feared global gangs, the **Latin Kings**—was inscribed in the Register of Catalan Associations. The same month, a jury in Madrid started procedures to reclassify them as a "criminal organization." The news has been reproduced by a lot of Spanish and international newspapers (see the article in *El Pais*, "Los Latin Kings en Cataluña inician sus actividades como entidad cultural," August 27, 2006, available at www.elpais.es). What kind of cultural organization are the Latin Kings and Queens? How in the same country and in the same time the same group provokes such different reactions? Which models of post-nationalism are involved in those transnational groups?

The Latin Kings' presence in Spain is strongly linked to recent immigration—thousands of young men and women of Latin and South American origin who arrived in Barcelona and Madrid after the new millennium, thanks in part to family reunion legislation. They were effectively exiled from their original homes and social environments at one of the most critical times in their lives—the currently fragmented transition into adult life. Their cultural identities emerge in a border area where, on top of the hegemonic host culture and the traditional parent culture, various other subcultural traditions meet (Matza, 1973; Brotherton and Barrios, 2004) in both virtual and real time and space. In this kind of evolution, we can find four basic matrixes. The first matrix begins with the North American tradition, represented by the original gang model theory. Youth gangs were tightly tied to the process of urbanization in the United States, and to the process of "magical recovery" of ethnic identity by second and third generations of young people whose parents or grandparents were immigrants. This was translated into the model of a territorial gang, well-organized and basically composed of males—the classic object of urban ethnography (Thrasher, 1926; Whyte, 1943). However, in the last decade there has been an evolution of gangs toward more complex forms of socializing (Hagedorn, 2001; Vigil, 2002).

The Latin Kings—now considered one of the major North American gang networks—appeared in Chicago at the end of World War II when different Latin American petty gangs amalgamated. By the 1990s the Latin Kings had evolved from criminal to political organization, focused on the claiming of Latin identity and the condemnation of police brutality. The gang network—a complex confederation of local groups—was renamed the Almighty Latin King Nation, and a female version was added—the **Latin Queens**. A series of cultural productions was created—manifestos, magazines, Web sites. International expansion followed national diffusion—Latin America and then Europe. The original Latin Kings had become a sort of transnational franchise with multiple "global" connections (Kontos, 2003; Brotherton and Barrios, 2004). This example demonstrates the new forms of mediated youth sociability that cross geographical and time borders to reconstruct exclusive global identities, and how important postcolonial migration fluxes are in the phenomenon. In a moment of further global hybridity another gang has recently emerged—the Moro Kings—the North African reply to the Latin Kings. There is evidence that young Pakistanis and Filipinos are also attempting entry to some of these semi-clandestine groups, or trying to create their own globally oriented gangs. In all this there are some interesting implications for ethnographies of youth in habitually focusing on bounded sites of research. In the global gang phenomenon, contact with local leaders of global gangs can only take place after contact has been made with the leaders and mentors at their transnational headquarters. So research in Barcelona and Genoa is only possible after connections have been established with New York and Guayaquil. "Global" youth implies global multi-sited research.

The second matrix of global gang evolution is exemplified by the difference in scale between Latin American gang formations: *pandillas* and *naciones*. A pandilla is a social street group organized under neighborhoods with precise geographical boundaries. Pandillas produce two types of behavior on a regular basis: aggressive confrontation, and material and/or symbolic solutions. Even though their external appearance borrows some features of hip-hop culture, they create a distinctive and rich lifestyle that solves conflict through street music and dance defiance. Naciones represent a higher level of gang organization. In Ecuador they are a sort of brotherhood or tribe, mainly pacifist, devoted to music and graffiti. They are bigger organizational units than pandilla, with many hundreds of members—often involved in illicit activities. Naciones have evolved further toward the creation of empires, an even more elevated level of organization, which not only provides for widespread mobilization of youth, but may connect with organized transnational crime or mass social movements opposed to corporate globalization (Reguillo, 2001; Cerbino, 2004).

The third trope of youth transnationalism is represented by the subcultural lifestyles that young migrants meet when they arrive, for example, in Europe. Although these young people might have had access in their places of origin to some of these styles already internationally diffused (like punk or hip-hop), it is after arriving in Barcelona or Genoa or Manchester that they get in touch with the globally mediated youth scene. They meet the local tradition, represented by existing neighborhood gangs and more or less traditional youth associations. However, the European tradition is also present as a sounding board for styles born in certain cities of the old continent in the 1960s, such as **skinheads**. At the same time they can connect to subcultural lifestyles such as hip-hop and rastafari that, in spite of having appeared first in the Caribbean or America, have evolved as more or less underground trends in the big immigrant-receiving cities of Europe. As nomadic social actors immigrant youth are mediated by global networks to pass (metaphorically or actually) through local gangs to global tribes. Yet on the connections and disconnections between migrant youth cultures from different origins, so far we have news from conflict interactions only, not from creative exchanges (Queirolo and Torre, 2005).

As the fourth and last matrix we have the virtual tradition represented by youth identity models that circulate through the net. In this case, rather than subcultural (or cybercultural) traditions, they are new communication spaces. They are the means and the message at the same time. The Internet is a place for consumption and information that spreads and amplifies new rhetorics of identity. For example, Latin American immigrant youth in Spain can access the Internet through the local cybercafés which they share with adult immigrants and autochthonous young people.

Here they can access Web pages about the gangs, develop blogs about their complex lives, and get involved in forums. In the months following the death of Ronny Tapias in Barcelona, Latin Kings and Ñetas exchanged insults and defied each other freely in Internet discussion group forums. They provided links to pages where youthful supporters could find products related to the gang, like clothes, music, and—apparently—even weapons. Some of these forums showed very high rates of participation (over twenty daily interventions at peak times). Significantly, all sorts of people could participate: gang members from Barcelona and Madrid, young people in Latin American cities, Spanish youths sympathetic with gangs, xenophobes, and even members of the North American chapters of those gangs who, in their typical Spanglish, were wondering why the Latin Kings and Ñetas were still at war in Barcelona when they had made it up in New York. The Internet has effectively "globalized" the gangs. These new "global gangs" are not strictly territorial any more, nor do they have a compact structure. They're nomadic identity clusters that mix cultural elements from their respective countries of origin, from their host countries, and from many other transnational styles that circulate through the net (Feixa and Muñoz, 2004).

References/Suggested Readings: Brotherton, D. and Barrios, L. 2004. *The Almighty Latin King and Queen Nation*. New York: Columbia University Press; Hagedorn, J.M. 2001. Globalization, Gangs and Collaborative Research. In M.W. Klein, H.-J. Kerner, C.L. Maxson, and E. Weitekamp (eds.), *The Eurogang Paradox: Street Gangs and Youth Groups in the U.S. and Europe*. London: Kluwer; Kontos, L. 2003. Between Criminal and Political Deviance: A Sociological Analysis of the New York Chapter of the Almighty Latin King and Queen Nation. In D. Muggleton and R. Weinzierl (eds.), *The Post-Subcultures Reader*. London: Berg; Matza, D. 1973. Subterranean Traditions of Youth. In H. Silverstein (ed.), *The Sociology of Youth: Evolution and Revolution*. New York: Macmillan; Nilan, P., and Feixa, C. 2006. *Global Youth? Hybrid Identities, Plural Worlds*. London: Routledge; Queirolo, L., and Torre, A. (eds). 2005. *Il Fantasma delle Bande: Giovani dall'America Latina a Genova*. Genova: Fratelli Frilli Editore; Reguillo, R. 2001. *Emergencia de Culturas Juveniles*. Buenos Aires: Norma; Thrasher, F.M. 1926. *The Gang*. Chicago: University of Chicago Press; Vigil, J.D. 2002. *A Rainbow of Gangs*. Austin: University of Texas Press; Whyte, W. 1943. *Street Corner Society*. Chicago: University of Chicago Press.

CARLES FEIXA

TRENCHCOAT MAFIA. The Trenchcoat Mafia (TCM) was a loose collectivity of about fifteen mostly male Gothic students at Columbine High School, whose acknowledged leader was Joe Stair. Stair graduated in 1998, a year before the Columbine shootings. Members of the TCM, in the immediate days following the Columbine shootings on April 20, 1999, were accused of conspiracy in the shootings in local and national media reports. All members were interrogated by local authorities and the FBI. Neither Eric Harris nor Dylan Klebold, the shooters in the Columbine massacre, was considered a member of the TCM, although they had friends who were members. The confusion over the role of the TCM in the Columbine shootings derived from two sources. First, in the assault, Harris and Klebold wore dusters to hide their weaponry, which were the identifying characteristic of the TCM; second, Eric Harris designed the Trenchcoat Mafia Web site on his AOL account. Most of the members of the TCM were unaware of Eric Harris's Web site, which he used to advertise racist, anti-Semitic, and generally nihilistic views on the world. He also used that site to threaten people, reveal his plans about blowing up his school, post rock lyrics from his favorite band, and celebrate the vandalism that he perpetrated against the property of people he considered his enemies.

The TCM was originally formed for self-protection against predation of outcast students by the jocks. Its identity came about accidentally, when one of the boys' parents bought him a duster. Friends thought that wearing a duster looked "cool," and started buying them and wearing them to school. They discovered that this gave them a collective identity and that members of the football and wrestling team reduced their level of intimidation and harassment. Therefore, they took to wearing the dusters on a daily basis, even when the weather was warm.

Ironically, they received their name from one of the most vicious and predatory members of the football and wrestling teams when he apparently confronted them, saying, in reference to their clothing, something like, "what are you, some kind of 'Trenchcoat Mafia'?" The outcast students turned this appellation on its head by making it a positive identifier among themselves rather than a stigmatized label. They wore their trench coats proudly and saw themselves in opposition to the preppy-dressed majority of students.

The TCM was not a gang; it was just a group of outcast students trying to protect themselves from harassment by their higher status peers. In the wake of the shootings, they were vilified by the press and placed under suspicion by the authorities without any evidence of their involvement.

References/Suggested Readings: Larkin, Ralph W. 2007. *Comprehending Columbine*. Philadelphia, PA: Temple University Press.

RALPH LARKIN

V

VICE LORDS INC. "From 1965 to 1969 over 290 persons have been slain in gang-related crimes. In 1967, the worst year of gang violence, over 150 people were murdered by Chicago gangs." These statistics were announced in Mayor Richard Daley (Sr.)'s formal declaration of war on Chicago gangs in 1969 (Fry, 1973). On the city's west side, the Conservative Vice Lords simultaneously came to symbolize gang expansion, community transformation, and political repression in late 1960s Chicago.

In the 1960s, the Vice Lords were centered in a community on the western border of Chicago known as Lawndale. Street gangs were not new to Lawndale which in previous decades experienced gang wars between Polish and other Eastern European gangs (Thrasher, 1927). During the 1950s, Lawndale underwent a significant demographic shift which resulted in a predominantly African American population well below the poverty level (Hagedorn, n.d. b). For black people coming of age in Lawndale's bleak atmosphere, their reality stood in contrast to the feelings of hope and prosperity described in many depictions of the early 1960s.

It was in this environment that the Vice Lords flourished through violent expansion and intimidation. Fights with rival gangs occurred regularly and in a few instances bystanders were beaten or shot (Dawley, 1992). By the mid-1960s, the Vice Lords had established themselves as one of the largest, most sophisticated gang structures in Chicago. There were formal positions of leadership, large-scale recruitment efforts, as well as expansion into multiple west side neighborhoods (Keiser, 1979). Through these activities, the Vice Lords set standards in the gang world, establishing their longevity and eventually outlasting most neighboring gangs (Chicago Crime Commission, 1995). Even during their reign of street control, the Vice Lords were still citizens of black America and aware of developing political responses to racial oppression and notions of black empowerment (Dawley, 1992). By 1967, realizing they had the power to influence more than a local park or pool hall, the Vice Lords of Lawndale set their sights on some larger issues confronting their community.

In an attempt to start a grassroots movement, the Vice Lords of Lawndale renamed themselves the Conservative Vice Lords and became incorporated (Dawley, 1992).

It has been speculated that the added title of "Conservative" symbolized the Vice Lords' desire to conserve or protect community resources while some others suggest the Vice Lords were now identifying with more conservative politics (Hagedorn, personal communication). Alternately, the use of the term may have been less literal; generally indicating a conservative move toward more organized structure and pro-social activities. Under the leadership of charismatic members such as Bobby Gore, gang violence and overall crime began to decline in Lawndale. In addition, the Conservative Vice Lords also held neighborhood clean-up initiatives and job training workshops (Dawley, 1992). Seeing what appeared to be a genuine positive effort by the Conservative Vice Lords, many eager, predominantly white, social workers and activists volunteered their assistance. The most notable activist and supporter of the Conservative Vice Lords was David Dawley. Dawley had come to Lawndale in 1967 working as a researcher with fundraising knowledge and a desire to help (Dawley, 1992). With help from Dawley and other supporters, the Conservative Vice Lords were able to obtain both federal and private grants to develop community-based initiatives (Dawley, 1992; Hagedorn, n.d. b).

With the funding received, the Vice Lords opened neighborhood businesses such as an ice cream parlor known as Teen Town, "Afro-American" art and clothing stores, a pool hall, as well as a recreation center/headquarters known as the House of Lords. The House of Lords operated as a place for meetings as well as an after school setting which held employment training, academic tutoring, and nutrition programs (Dawley, 1992). At this point the Conservative Vice Lords were receiving praises throughout the city of Chicago and beyond. The once notorious street gang was now covered in a favorable light by local newspapers such as the *Daily Defender*, the *Sun Times*, and *Chicago Tribune* and west side politicians sought Conservative Vice Lord support in coming elections (Dawley, 1992). The Conservative Vice Lords formed youth coalitions in conjunction with community activist organizations from New Orleans to California (Hagedorn, n.d. b). Celebrities like Sammy Davis Jr. and the Staple Singers gave public and financial support to the Conservative Vice Lords. Probably the most notable alliance the Conservative Vice Lords built was with Dr. Martin Luther King Jr. (Hagedorn, n.d. b).

During 1967, King moved into an apartment in Lawndale in an effort to address poor housing conditions in Chicago's black communities. The Conservative Vice Lords immediately offered their support and King accepted. Conservative Vice Lord leaders joined King in his controversial march through Gage Park amidst death threats, pelted rocks, and fireworks by local white residents. King and other marchers rated the antagonism at Gage Park to be worse than in many areas previously marched through in the south (Hagedorn, n.d. b).

Yet with all their civic achievements and support gained, the Conservative Vice Lords still had strong critics. Among their largest opponents was Chicago's Mayor Richard Daley. The Mayor's office along with law enforcement agencies intensified the "war on gangs" in 1968. The targets of this war included the Conservative Vice Lords along with some of their former rivals such as the **Gangster Disciples** and the Black Stone Rangers who now often worked alongside the Conservative Vice Lords in their community efforts (Fry, 1973). Regular surveillance and police raids were used on the House of Lords and other Vice Lord establishments as well as political speeches denouncing Chicago gangs in general. While the negative attention caused supporters to shy away from the Conservative Vice Lords, many were not deterred.

Some of the most significant financial support obtained by the Conservative Vice Lords came out of the private sector. Wealthy figures such as W. Clement Stone, an insurance executive and Charles Merrill Jr. of Merrill-Lynch provided funding and loans at low interest rates to the Conservative Vice Lords and other gangs (Hagedorn, n.d. c). In addition, the Conservative Vice Lords received funding from the Rockefeller Foundation as well as the Sears corporation. Most of these financial supporters were heavily censured by law enforcement and city hall officials for funding gangs. The criticism was reciprocated. For example, Charles Merrill publicly accused law enforcement of rampant harassment and slander toward gangs like the Conservative Vice Lords (Hagedorn, n.d. c). In some sense, the feud symbolized a larger conflict between Mayor Daley's Democratic machine and the private funders, many of whom were Republicans. Many conservatives admired the Vice Lords' bootstrap style of economic and political initiatives, as Clement Stone explained after his initial loans toward Conservative Vice Lord programs, "I know what a first break can do and what charity cannot" (Hagedorn, n.d. c, p. 3). The Conservative Vice Lords' work ethic and commitment challenged conservatives to live up to some of their political philosophies. In 1969, Jeff Fort, the leader of the Black Stone Rangers, was formally invited to Richard Nixon's presidential inauguration (CCC, 1995).

While the Conservative Vice Lords were generally appreciative of the opportunities afforded them through various benefactors, not all assistance appeared genuine to them. Early in the Vice Lords' transformation many with local business interests aided community initiatives with an implicit obligation for the Vice Lords to act as a bulwark for business owners' west side property (Dawley, 1992). Initially accepting this role, the Conservative Vice Lords deterred any and all rioters from touching west side property during the summer of 1967, ultimately leading to a confrontation with the Black Panthers and other militants. After their property was saved in the 1967 riots, some business owners did not come through on commitments made to the Conservative Vice Lords, sparking distrust and hostility on the part of the Conservative Vice Lords. During the next spring when Dr. King was assassinated and riots started throughout Chicago, many Conservative Vice Lords participated in the destruction of west side businesses while others simply stayed home, refusing to intervene (Dawley, 1992). The Conservative Vice Lords had long since had reservations about working with outside parties on either side as in previous years they had also been disappointed by unfulfilled promises made by black militant groups (Keiser, 1979). Ultimately, it is hard to determine precisely where the Conservative Vice Lords stood politically. While they stood in favor of the civil rights and black power movements and opposed black participation in the Vietnam War they also worked within the mainstream, embodying efforts of Lyndon Johnson's "great society" program with a belief that empowerment could be achieved through democracy and capitalist ventures, notions long since rejected by most militants.

It was during this period of rioting and controversy that Mayor Daley increased attacks on the Conservative Vice Lords and other gangs. Daley himself was no stranger to street gang structure, once a leader of an Irish gang known as the Hamburgs (Cohen and Taylor, 2000). In 1919 the Hamburgs were charged with inciting a race riot aimed at African Americans (Hagedorn, n.d. a). Over time the Hamburgs exerted some influence on local politics giving Daley his introduction to an extensive political career. Now as Chicago's mayor, Daley set up a team of politicians and law enforcement officials, headed by state's attorney Edward Hanrahan, to exact a zero-tolerance crusade against gangs. Many of Daley's critics argue that serious gang violence had continued for years without much attention from city hall until the community organizing efforts of gangs became apparent (Fry, 1973; Dawley, 1992).

Despite critiques of Daley's methods of law enforcement by numerous factions including members of his own Democratic party, the mayor used his influence and connections to wage war on his terms. With varied law enforcement agencies and many former FBI personnel, a conglomerate emerged known as the "red squad" (Rosoff, Pontell, and Tillman, 2002). Using tried methods from FBI counter-intelligence programs previously used on suspected communists, the red squad infiltrated and used questionably legal tactics to bring down political groups such as the Black Panthers, Young Lords, and the American Indian Movement, as well as street gangs who had attempted truces with other gangs to pursue common social goals. All targeted parties were loosely labeled as being under the influence of communists or "reds" (Churchill and Wall, 2001).

Throughout Daley's crusade, Conservative Vice Lords headquarters were often raided, its members harassed, and arrested on what many claimed were illegitimate charges (Dawley, 1992; Fry, 1973). Furthermore, not all Conservative Vice Lords' conduct was uniform. Some Conservative Vice Lords still fought with remaining rival gangs and committed crime for their financial and personal gain. However, the Conservative Vice Lords claimed this behavior was not condoned by the organization (Dawley, 1992). At the height of such turmoil came the symbolic arrest and murder conviction of praised leader Bobby Gore in late 1969. Gore had been perhaps the most notable member of the Conservative Vice Lords during this period, known as a chief spokesman for community empowerment and peace between the Conservative Vice Lords and other gangs (Dawley, 1992). Gore was convicted of a murder of which to this day he claims he is innocent, ultimately spending ten years in prison before being released on parole in 1979. As of this writing, Gore's case is being investigated by Northwestern University's center for wrongful convictions (Hagedorn, n.d. b).

As the 1970s brought Gore's criminal conviction and the loss of his inspiration, the Conservative Vice Lords saw their past achievements rapidly deteriorating. Police attacks and gang rivalries increased while both public and private funds diminished (Dawley, 1992). What many benefactors saw as a promising opportunity for self-help in the black ghetto a few years prior now appeared a lost cause. Some supporters continued to assist the Conservative Vice Lords (Hagedorn, n.d. c). However, by the mid-1970s, virtually every initiative developed by the Conservative Vice Lords had become a memory.

Modern-day Lawndale continues to experience high crime and poverty rates, and hope and self-esteem are rarely found among young residents. The Vice Lords have grown but also disbanded into different factions, often at conflict with each other (Dawley, 1992; CCC, 1995). Richard Daley Jr. has been Chicago's mayor for almost twenty years straight and the city's approach to gangs has remained virtually unchanged since 1968 (Dawley, 1992; Hagedorn, n.d.). The positive efforts of the Conservative Vice Lords and other gangs are all but forgotten among Lawndale residents, current Vice Lords, and the American public in general. If one looks into Vice Lord history, there is little documentation in books, journals, or other scholarly or official accounts of these community initiatives. Most public depiction of the Vice Lords is characterized solely by drug-dealing and gang-related brutality. However, assessments of such overlooked examples of positive transformations by the Conservative Vice Lords and other gangs may be necessary in providing a means to successfully address current gang problems.

References/Suggested Readings: Chicago Crime Commission. 1995. *Gangs: Public Enemy Number One*. Chicago: Chicago Crime Commission; Churchill, W., and Wall, J.V. 2001. *The COINTELPRO Papers: Documents from the FBI's Secret War against Dissent in the United States*. Boston: South End Press; Cohen, A., and Taylor, E. 2000. *American Pharaoh: Mayor Richard J. Daley*. New York: Little, Brown; Dawley, D. 1992. *A Nation of Lords: The Autobiography of the Vice Lords* (2nd ed.). Illinois: Waveland Press; Fry, J. 1973. *Locked Out Americans: A Memoir*. New York: Harper & Row; Hagedorn, J. n.d. a. *Gangs and the 1919 Riots*. Available online at gangresearch.net; Hagedorn, J. n.d. b. Shattered Dreams: CVL History. Available online at gangresearch.net; Hagedorn, J. n.d. c. When Millionaires Funded Gangs. Available online at gangresearch.net; Keiser, R.L 1979. The Vice Lords: Warriors of the Streets. In *Fieldwork*. New York: Holt, Rinehart, & Winston; Rosoff, S.M., Pontell, H.N., and Tillman, R.H. 2002. *Looting America: Greed, Corruption, Villains, and Victims*. New Jersey: Prentice Hall; Thrasher, F. 1927. *The Gang*. Chicago: University of Chicago Press.

CHANO LABOY

VIETNAMESE ORGANIZED CRIME AND GANGS. The Vietnamese people have dealt with over 2,000 years of conflict that goes back to the Chinese invasion of Vietnam around the time of Christ. It was approximately 800 years later that the Chinese were finally removed from power in Vietnam. Vietnam as a country remained fairly stable until the arrival of the French in the mid-1800s. The French invaded Vietnam and within a short period of time took over control of this Southeast Asian country.

The French controlled Vietnam from the mid-1800s until their defeat by the Vietnamese army at Dien Bien Phu in 1954. During their rule in Vietnam, the French attempted to change the whole lifestyle and culture of the Vietnamese. For example, the educational system was modeled on the French system without giving any consideration to the long established Vietnamese educational system, while the French administration replaced village leaders with people who had an allegiance to the French administration in either Saigon or Hanoi. Finally, the French attempted to change the various written dialects of Vietnam language, supplanting it by the French language.

These changes made by the French reflected their colonialist outlook that people who were racially or ethnically different from the French were on this planet to be exploited by European nations who were deemed superior. (This type of sentiment was not only a French perception it was a belief that extended throughout Europe and Great Britain.) The European opinion that the destruction of a nation's culture would also bring a society to its knees was found not to hold true in Vietnam's case because in 1954 the Vietnamese defeated the French at Dien Bien Phu and chased them out of Southeast Asia.

It was not long after the demise of the French that U.S. military advisors started appearing in Vietnam to support the Democratic government in Saigon against the communist regime in Hanoi. History tells us what the ultimate result of this U.S. intervention but along the way the American interference caused the uprooting of over 25 percent of the villagers in Vietnam. The village and the family are very important factors to the Vietnamese people because family loyalty is a very important factor to members of this society and a major portion of this family allegiance is inherited from the village philosophy. The Vietnamese family notions have been conveyed to the Vietnamese street gangs whose members work close together like a family. The demise of the Democratic government in Saigon and the retreat of the U.S. military out of Vietnam in 1975.

Once the U.S. troops withdrew from Vietnam there was a large influx Southeast Asian immigrants who were perceived as being Vietnamese while some of these refugees were actually Laotian, Cambodian, and ethnic Chinese from Vietnam. In this first group of Vietnamese emigrants were some important Vietnamese citizens who had left the country because of their relationship with the U.S. military and, due to this association, they feared retaliation by the Vietcong regime. A major portion of these people had a good educational background and would easily adapt to the lifestyle in the United States because of their relationships with the American military personnel in Vietnam. Many of these new arrivals considered themselves well-qualified personnel that were no actual threat to U.S. citizens. They felt because of their credentials they should be easily incorporated into the American community and become fruitful members our society. The members of this group who were participants in criminal activities fit right into the Vietnamese communities. They became active within their local communities and quickly got mixed up in fraudulent types of scams including money transfer schemes and welfare swindle. An example of the type of criminal operation that the Vietnamese person would participate in took place in 1984 when sixty Vietnamese pharmacists and physicians deceitfully billed the California Bureau of Medi-Cal for $25 million (FBI, 1993). In most cases these purported professional people used Vietnamese gang members as their couriers.

The first groups that arrived from Vietnam managed to quickly create a number of communities throughout the United States, a major portion of these neighborhoods were located on the West Coast. These communities would soon become home bases for a second group of arrivals from Vietnam that contained more of a criminal element than the first group (FBI, 1993).

The second group of individuals arriving from Vietnam were what had to be considered true refugees and not immigrants. These expatriates were, in most cases, both socially and educationally different than the people who arrived in the first group. Most of them were from rural regions or coastal communities who had fled Vietnam in boats that were packed with other fleeing emigrants who diligently suffered through the abuses forced on them by pirates from Thailand who constantly tormented the fleeing "boat people." Within this group of new arrivals were people who arrived with their families and friends and another portion disembarked alone. There were a large number of unescorted children and an abundant amount of older sons who arrived alone with a strategy that included finding a job and working as hard as possible in order to gather sufficient funding to bring the remaining members of the family to the United States. There are several reasons for classifying the newly arrived Vietnamese as refugees. First, the refugee is compelled to leave his or her homeland. Second, the circumstances surrounding this person's escape are life threatening, and third, the refugee is without any specific direction or destination. This whole episode totally traumatizes most of the refugees. Another problem facing the new refugees can be described as culture shock. The culture shock that is encountered by Vietnamese refugees is a shock that is shared by all the family members and not just one specific person. It creates a stress that affects the entire Vietnamese family. This stress is further complicated by the anxiety placed on the new Vietnamese immigrants to learn a new language within a different culture. Stress seems to especially affect the adolescent members of this society and it is therefore not unusual for an youthful member of a family to set up family members to ultimately become victims of home robberies. The situation for some adolescents is even worse if there is no family unit available for the youth who in many cases has already become a gang member. Once a gang member this teenager adopts the gang as his/her family and responds to any stressful in the same way using desperation and violence (FBI, 1993).

Over the past several years many of the Vietnamese street groups have progressed from undisciplined and out-of-control groups to the designation as street gangs. A major portion of these gangs have joined together to form tightly knit organizations that are coupled to Vietnamese groups throughout the United States. This type of union provides some basic needs to other members of the Vietnamese gangs who are basically linked together for the self-preservation of each member and for their participation in the profits from gang ventures. The protection of the members is of utmost importance to all of the membership because of the tight family relationships within Vietnamese society. Gang members in different areas of the United States must be capable of providing refuge to members of traveling gangs who may be in route to a location to commit a crime or those members who may be retreating from a location where they have just committed a crime.

Vietnamese Gangs

The description of a Vietnamese traveling gang must be preceded by the definitions of what can actually be considered a street gang. As a group they

1. collaborate to perpetrate, or commit, a transgression against a specific person or group for profit;
2. identify themselves through the use of a name, sign, symbol or have an distinguishable leader;
3. have membership that is involved in criminal activities which is unusual in comparison to other identifiable groups;
4. proclaim that a the group will be operating in a specific area;
5. have membership that is identifiable by their garments, tattoos, the way the act, appear or communicate with other members (FBI, 1993);
6. are usually adolescents who came to the United States without any other family member traveling with them or already having a residence in the United States. This youth is alone and adopts the gang as his one and only family;
7. have come from a paternal type of society where everything evolves around a very tight knit family. The family is totally controlled by the father whose authority is never challenged. This adolescent now enters a foreign society whose members have throughout time questioned authority. It is not long before conflict between the father and son develops. This will ultimately, in some cases, cause the son to become ostracized from the rest of the family and seek out the family affinity supplied by the gang members.

Almost every street gang referred to in this book fits into the first five categories. It has just taken a longer period of time for the Vietnamese gangs to adapt to these types of gang ideology because of categories six and seven. It must be understood that in most of the other cases the gang members did not come out of a war-ravaged and chaotic situation in their homeland. Many Vietnamese youths entered the United States bewildered and unstable. These adolescences came from a basically agrarian society that in most cases lacked any gang-like organizations or groups to emulate upon their arrival in the United States.

The Vietnamese gangs in the United States have carefully done their apprenticeship under the guidance of the Chinese street gangs. This experience has helped the Vietnamese gangs grow into what now can be considered an organized criminal gang that has been well trained during their indenture with the previously established Chinese street gangs. The gangs that have come to the forefront from the training they received from the Chinese gangs are the Born to Kill who learned under the guidance of the Flying Dragons gang and the Hung Pho who were taught by the Wo Hop To gang. Most of the members of the gangs that have associated with the Chinese gangs are ethnically Viet-Ching gangs that could be easily assimilated into either group because of their ability to speak both languages and understand both cultures.

References/Suggested Readings: Federal Bureau of Investigation. 1993. *Vietnamese Criminal Activity in the United States: A National Perspective.* Washington, DC: FBI.

SEAN GRENNAN

VIGILANTE GANGS. The notion of "vigilante gangs" involves the practice of criminal law through the adoption of extralegal violence. Classic vigilantism, according to William E. Burrows, must fit specific criteria such as membership in an organized committee, membership in a community, and commitment to vigilante justice involving definite goals for a finite amount of time. Further, vigilantes must commonly profess to resort to extralegal measures as a response to ineffectual juridical law, and as an attempt to improve justice (Hine, 1998, pp. 1223–1225). Burrows's set of criteria so narrowly defines vigilantism as to effectively exclude groups widely considered to be quintessential practitioners of vigilantism, such as the Ku Klux Klan and the Black Panthers.

Changes laying the foundations of contemporary criminal justice were influenced by the Enlightenment, an intellectual movement seeking to rebuild social structures on the basis of modernist, rational principles (White and Haines, 2001, p. 25). The imperatives of imperialism incorporated modernist discourses of evolution, with its attendant dichotomies of degeneration and progress, civilization and barbarism. The promise of an impartial and orderly juridical process became symbolic of modern sensibility and civilization, presumably humanizing society though its required self-control. Well into the twentieth century juridical law competed with vigilante justice, gradually superseding it at least formally, as something borne out of private passion and revengeful force (Ayers, 1985, pp. 246–247; Strange, 1996, p. 12). Vigilante mobs driven by vengeance and impassioned, ad hoc violence violated law, order, and civilization (Raper, 2003, p. 117). Antimodernist vigilantes involved in racist lynchings became popularly rejected as too closely associated with the "savagery" ostensibly embodied by the mythical "Black Rapist" (Bederman, 1992, pp. 26–27).

Vigilantes seek punishment (for real or imagined crimes) that is more swift and sure than the judicial process may provide. While vigilante gangs directly oppose the juridical process, in their simple opposition they fail to innovate beyond the status quo. While their methods for attaining goals may vary from juridical norms, the wider popular culture still deeply informs their goals and values, such that vigilante gangs use extralegal means to pursue conventional ambitions such as wealth and power. Vigilante gangs thereby may only reinscribe prevailing power structures related particularly to class, race, gender, and sexuality.

References/Suggested Readings: Anonymous. n.d. Vigilantism, Vigilante Justice, and Victim Self-Help. Available online at faculty.ncwc.edu/toconnor/300/300lect10.htm; Ayers, Edward L. 1985. *Vengeance and Justice: Crime and Punishment in the Nineteenth-Century American South.* New York: Oxford University Press; Bederman, Gail. 1992. "Civilisation," the Decline of Middle-Class Manliness, and Ida B. Wells' Antilynching Campaign (1892–94).

Radical History Review, 52, 5–30; Hine, Kelly D. 1998. Vigilantism Revisited: An Economic Analysis of the Law of Extra-Judicial Self-Help or Why Dick Can't Shoot Henry for Stealing Jane's Truck. *American University Law Review*, 47, 1221–1255; Raper, Arthur F. 2003. *The Tragedy of Lynching.* New York: Dover Publications; Strange, Carolyn (ed.). 1996. *Qualities of Mercy: Justice, Punishment, and Discretion.* Vancouver: UBC Press; White, Rob, and Haines, Fiona. 2001. *Crime and Criminology: An Introduction* (2nd ed.). Melbourne: Oxford University Press.

ANNETTE L. BICKFORD

W

WILLIAMS, STANLEY TOOKIE. The state execution of Stanley Tookie Williams on December 13, 2005, exemplified the rigid, vengeful nature of law enforcement's long war on gangs. The one-sided war, which since 1980 claimed over 10,000 young black and brown lives in Los Angeles alone, is based on the theory of a super-predator caste of incorrigibles who can only be punished into submission. Stanley Tookie Williams, which was his birth name rather than a nickname, was the founder of the **Crips** gang, which made him the symbolic enemy of police and prison guards over three decades. In 1979, at age twenty-six, he was convicted of four motel killings during the course of a robbery, crimes which he denied committing, and spent the rest of his days on San Quentin's Death Row.

Tookie looked the part of a street godfather, with twenty-two-inch biceps, a fifty-eight-inch chest, and huge tree-trunk legs. When I interviewed him in San Quentin in 2003, he explained that as a youngster he was a "megalomaniac" who wanted to "create the biggest gang in the world, smash everyone, make a rep, get respect and dignity." The Crips were born in 1967 as a kind of miscarriage in the vacuum left behind by the civil rights movement in Northern cities. Tookie asked me at one point if I knew the meaning of "anachronism." Having become literate through a dictionary, he described his generation of young black men as "a kind of anachronism [who were] meant to be born in a warrior era."

His megalomania seemed long behind. He blamed "an embedded sense of self-hate" as the root cause of black rage and violence. Long years in the San Quentin hole, perhaps analogous to Plato's cave, had led to his steady rehabilitation. The prosecutors and guards dismissed this "redemption" as contrived, arguing that Tookie hadn't expressed legal remorse for the 1979 killings nor revealed what he knew about the Crips or other inmates. Of course, it was impossible morally for Tookie to switch his claim from innocent to guilty, and a dangerous violation of the prison code to "snitch" on others. In his own trial, such snitches were the source of the only evidence against him, receiving deals from the prosecutors in return.

But it seemed evident to me that Tookie was rehabilitated, at the very least in the legal definition, and that an overwhelming case could be made for either a retrial or executive clemency. Since 1992, for example, Tookie had effectively advocated a gang truce between Crips and **Bloods**, a position that arose from his reflections of black self-hate. He followed with a decade of consistent peace advocacy, children's books, and a Web site, coordinated with his outside associate Barbara Becnel, a former journalist. He expressed deep regret for founding and leading the Crips down the road of destruction. He gained a worldwide following, even a Nobel Prize nomination from European parliamentarians.

Law enforcement tends to believe in the iron maxim of once a gang member, always a gang member, however. This was the heart of the neo-conservative "super-predator" thesis that emerged in the early 1990s just as Tookie was transitioning. As theory, the notion has since been discredited, because it assumes that a certain percentage of youth of color are predestined to become violent street criminals. But the theory resonated for politicians, cops, and voter constituencies are the war on gangs gained traction. Tookie's claim of rehabilitation was a living example of problems with the theory. So was the Crips-Bloods truce, and many similar gang truces around the state and country. They were a threat to the hegemony of police, prison guards, and prosecutors who asserted control over every aspect of the criminal justice system.

There was a deeper background factor. Rehabilitated inmates, especially in the 1960s and 1970s, were liable to become revolutionaries, rechanneling their self-destructive violence into confrontations with "the real enemy," starting with the brutal prison guards themselves. Uprisings, hostage-takings, riots, and strikes, even occasional killings had become a threat to a repressive institutional system controlled by state power. In 1998, Tookie dedicated one of his "life in prison" books to a list of these feared revolutionaries, including Nelson Mandela, Geronimo Pratt, Assatta Shakur, Leonard Peltier, George Jackson, and Mumia Abu-Jamal, who "have to endure the hellish oppression of life behind bars. . . . Prison is hazardous to your mind, body, and spirit. May none of you ever have to experience the madness of incarceration." Nothing in the 1998 book remotely endorsed violence (on the contrary), but Tookie's expressed feelings of solidarity with other revolutionaries reinforced the inflexible hostility of his captors.

The legal case against Tookie revealed the deep distortions in the criminal justice system when alleged gang members are in the dock. Without going into the exhaustive details, he had an incompetent counsel who failed to present an opening argument, only gave a forty-eight-minute closing argument, and failed to present mitigating evidence. The witnesses, as noted, were rewarded later for their circumstantial evidence. The prosecution described Tookie in the courtroom as a Bengal tiger in a zoo. The jury was all white, the prosecutor having removed the only three black people from the pool. (The same prosecutor had been admonished before by the California Supreme Court for "invidious racism.")

Throughout the long appeals process, the courts were sharply divided as to whether to execute Tookie. The Ninth Federal Circuit Court opined that "Williams' good works and accomplishments since incarceration make him a worthy candidate for the exercise of gubernatorial discretion," or clemency. In the final days, the California Supreme Court split 4-2 over whether to grant a new hearing. In addition, such respected mainstream organizations as the NAACP promised to create a street peace program with Tookie if the governor granted clemency. Numerous religious, civil rights, and civil liberties advocates, including rappers like Snoop Dogg and actors like Jamie Foxx, signed petitions for his life, arguing that with clemency Tookie could play a valuable social role while still confined to prison for life. It appeared that the case was perfectly framed, so that the Governor could choose clemency between the alternatives of execution and release.

I briefly allowed myself to be hopeful. Gov. Arnold Schwarzenegger's legal secretary wrote on November 7, 2005, to express the governor's appreciation for my "thoughtful" clemency letter. "Clemency decisions are never easy, and certainly the case of Mr. Williams will be no exception. Only after serious consideration and careful deliberation of this matter will the governor make his decision."

This was a lie. Shortly before Tookie's execution, the Governor issued a terse letter denying clemency. There was not even a response to the arguments raised by the NAACP and hundreds of letters favoring clemency. The governor's letter dismissed Tookie's years of peace efforts, condemned his refusal to express remorse, and focused instead on Tookie's 1998 references to prison revolutionaries. The letter could have been, and probably was, written by the very prosecutors and prison guards who had pursued Tookie's death for twenty-five years. I personally know Arnold Schwarzenegger quite well, and believe that he knew that Tookie fit the definition of rehabilitation. But the governor was facing drooping poll numbers, was tangled in budget battles with the powerful prison guards union, and was advised to execute law enforcement's number one symbolic enemy. There simply was no "careful deliberation," as promised, unless it was careful deliberation of the politics.

It appears that Tookie died a horrific death by lethal injection. Perhaps it was only accidental, but the prison official in charge could not find a vein, despite his massive arms. Finally, the strapped-down prisoner was forced to exclaim, "Can't we just do this?" Those were his last words. Medical records concerning the delay and possibly impermissible pain remain classified as of this writing. Immediately following his execution, however, lawyers for Death Row prisoners nationally succeeded in raising the issues of whether lethal injections, as administered, violate the constitutional prohibitions on cruel and unusual punishment. A few months after his execution, the ashes of Tookie Williams were spread across the Blue Nile in South Africa.

The significance of Tookie's execution for the contemporary crisis of gang violence is its utter rejection of the concept of redemption. Ever since **Frederic Thrasher**'s interviews with Chicago street gangs in the 1920s, thoughtful sociologists have endorsed the concept of reformed gang members playing a key role in preventing violence. As Thrasher himself wrote in 1927, "were I to think only of the boys and their welfare, I would spend a large part of the money expended in institutions in hiring 'Boy Men' to cover the city and spend their entire time with the gangs."

But as Luis Rodriguez, the former addict and gang member turned counselor and poet, frequently points out, bringing gang members to the table is the option never explored. Those who started the madness may have the experience, insights, and communications skills to help end it, but they are rarely if ever consulted. Former gang-bangers are America's untouchables.

The Crips-Bloods truce of 1992 (and others like it) is derided as ineffective by law enforcement and even some academic experts, but the criticism is unjustified. If there can be diplomatic efforts at peace in Northern Ireland, why not south central Los Angeles? When the 1992 truce unexpectedly broke out, there were joyful parties everywhere in the projects of LA. There were promises of private-sector rebuilding of the inner city—responsible officials promised $6 billion in private investment to create 74,000 new jobs in five years in the riot zone. This too was a lie, or at least a false promise. The rebuilding agency closed its doors one year after the violence had subsided, with neither fanfare nor an explanation. Ten years later, officials acknowledged that a net 55,000 new jobs had been lost in the inner city.

As a community norm, however, the Crips-Bloods truce lasted among young people for several years despite the lack of a peace dividend. Five years after the 1992 riots, the *LA Times* reported that "police and residents of Watts confirm that gang-on-gang slayings over emotional issues of turf boundaries or gang clothing have virtually disappeared."

Today, however, all thought of economic development has been replaced by gentrification ambitions combined with the worst forms of repressive policing in the Watts projects, as confirmed by the most recent blue-ribbon report on the legacy of the LAPD's Rampart Division scandal (the fifth blue-ribbon report in as many years).

The 2006 LA city budget reveals that the priority is to suppress and incarcerate. Fifty-five million in tax dollars goes to gang suppression units, a token $12 million is directed to preventing kids from joining gangs, and only $2 million is spent on intervention programs aimed at working to prevent gang violence. Most of that funding is for consultants to study how to design a city department for gang violence prevention.

In the meantime, by city estimates, there are 93,000 Los Angeles young people out of school and out of work. There are some 150,000 inmates in the California prison system, two-thirds of them designated as gang members. Nearly all of them will be returned to the streets, school dropouts, unemployable, substance abusers. The recidivism rate in California is the nation's highest.

To their credit, California voters favor spending more tax dollars on prevention and jobs for young people than incarceration, but the politicians are incapable of listening. Instead the super-predator thesis provides a comforting scapegoat, $1 million in campaign contributions from prison guards, and ubiquitous police endorsements are controlling factors in politics—until yet another crisis erupts, and court orders follow.

Even behind bars, Tookie Williams might have been the "O.G." of community peace efforts. He even wrote a protocol to be followed by gangs trying to end violence in their communities. He was beginning to reach the status as a wise elder when he was executed. He is not likely to be replaced, leaving young people on their own.

So what is to be done? To step off the treadmill of violence to the path of peace, we all need to explore the following alternatives.

First, understand as Tookie did that gang members are traumatized victims of countless street wars, veterans who have no legitimacy, resources, or counseling. Since violent street gangs hardly existed as recently as the 1960s, there is no reason that their suicidal violence cannot decline. There must be massive rehabilitation programs on every level, including role models like Tookie Williams in their design.

Second, there must be deeper reform of the punitive police and prison practices represented in the remorseless treatment of Tookie Williams for three decades. In the same week he was executed, for example, it was reported that the same LA County prosecutor who led the charge for execution never brought a single criminal charge in 442 police shooting cases since 2001. This racist and elitist pattern cannot help but make young people completely cynical toward the so-called criminal justice system.

Third, recognize the crisis of exclusion and structural unemployment that renders so many young people hopeless, powerless, helpless, rootless, and meaningless, in the analysis of Luis Rodriguez. California taxpayers spend $9 billion annually on the prison system but virtually nothing on jobs programs for the inner city.

Revenge executions like that administered against Tookie Williams serve to divert some popular attention from their own government's negligence and law-breaking. It is easier to scapegoat the super-predator than the superpower. But unlike the white ethnic gang culture of yesterday, for which there is widespread nostalgia in the entertainment media, the only doors that are wide open for the new generations of street gangs are those of the prison system.

A country that fails to provide living wages to so many of its young is more committed to its present privileges than its future potential. To avoid the message, it thinks it can kill the messenger. But Tookie Williams has eluded his tormenters. His legend and message remain, paradoxically, as the alternative to violence. Sooner or later, as Arthur Miller wrote long ago, attention must be paid.

References/Suggested Readings: Stanley Williams (author), Barbara Cottman (author), D. Stevens (photographer). 2001. *Life in Prison.* Chronicle Books; Stanley Tookie Williams. 2005. *Blue Rage, Black Redemption: A Memoir.* Damamli Publishing Company.

TOM HAYDEN

Y

YABLONSKY AND *THE VIOLENT GANG*. In *The Violent Gang* (1962), Lewis Yablonsky offered a new and radical view of the "gang" compared with the traditional view of the pre-1940s Chicago School or the contemporary Subcultural Theorists. His study was part of a response to a series of violent incidents occurring in New York City and other U.S. cities but mirrored throughout the urban centers across the world. Yablonsky's radical view was that the new street gangs of the 1950s engaged in random violence in ways not seen in the gangs of the 1920s and 1930s or before. Prior to World War II (1939–1945), youth gangs offered organization, support and leisure and sporting activities to occupy bored, unemployed, isolated, and dissociated city youths. The post-1945 street gangs that he describes were more territorial, aggressive, and increasingly violent, enjoying the violence for itself rather than as a means to an end. The language or argot of the gang was changing with more focus on "protecting turf" or reinforcing status and reputation, "rep." Individual rep within the gang had to be established, reinforced, and maintained by demonstrable acts of violence. The gang became a ring-side where reputation was constantly challenged and threatened as if there was a limited amount of reputation to divide between gang members. Incidents, "japs," rumbles, wars were testing grounds for violent acts that built rep but also where a failure to perform could sacrifice rep and threaten status or membership.

   Yablonsky's view is that the violent gang or subculture is less permanent and structured than other forms of contemporary gang or delinquency group. The existence of the gang varies from the fantasy armies of divisions of soldiers led by Presidents, War Lords, and Lieutenants to the group who perpetrate homicidal and violent attacks reported so avidly in the media. Yablonsky's view developed from working directly with New York street gangs and especially from an incident which resulted in the death of Michael Farmer, beaten and stabbed as the "enemy" in a gang incident. A similar racist stabbing in London in 1993 resulted in the death of Stephen Lawrence in remarkably similar circumstances. Provoked into action by a small core of sociopaths the "gang" emerges in these incidents to brutally attack a lesser or weaker opponent—often only one or two boys—resulting in at least one homicide. His question relates to the role played in the incident by various categories of gang members and their consequent liability in prosecutions. Yablonsky has devoted much of his life appearing as an expert witness to testify as to the centrality of one or more defendants in a gang incident and whether their membership warrants treating the "gang" as an aggravating circumstance in the prosecution. He has an extensive reputation for helping courts to distinguish appropriate levels of participation and the concomitant level of liability in sentencing.

Six categories of membership are delineated (Yablonsky, 1997):

1. Veterans are members at the core of their gang. They have earned their place and their rep by "putting in the work" in the violent or illegal activities of the gang.

2. Gangsters or the everyday soldiers. Probably between ten and twenty are at the core of the violent gang.

3. Wannabes—aspiring members, usually juniors, who are "putting in the work"—committing acts or crimes—necessary to be noticed and recognized for promotion or inclusion in the higher group—in other words, "building rep."

4. Groupies—individuals who appeared on the periphery of the group and who gravitated toward the group and imitated members clothes or tastes. These individuals were often netted in police raids after some major crime or incident.

5. Local residents—youths in the same age group as gang members, often relatives or friends. These young men were counted in the total gang when leaders were claiming armies and were often forcibly "recruited"—declared their membership—when approached by warlords demanding shows of membership or loyalty. Sometimes unlucky to be in the wrong place at the wrong time, when arrested, they could be treated as gang members—"guilt by association"—but then released by the courts or not charged.

6. Former gang members who have matured out of participation. Many gang turfs are populated by ex-members who are now married, employed, or in education, and while they might occasionally visit with their old friends and could also be caught up in police raids, are no longer participants in any of the violent gang's core activities.

Yablonsky noted in the original research a tendency for the leaders of the Balkans or the Egyptian Kings to make grandiose claims about the size, scale, internal organization, and formal alliances of their gangs. Individual leaders often used their position as intermediary or peace-maker to lay claim to alliances with other gangs whose membership claims were equally inflated. Individuals who were not members could be double- and triple-counted in the divisions, with gangs and alliances summoning them to fight the war or to rumble. When Yablonsky and his co-workers began to challenge, and to persuade less committed gang-members to challenge some of these claims, the actual "army" would dissolve down to fewer than twenty who actually were ready to rumble. Most of the actual violence consisted of rapid, violent assaults by small groups on one or two supposed gang members who were usually junior, less experienced or more vulnerable members. Many of these incidents, which were much talked about, mythologized, and numerically inflated, could not be verified in many of their details. It is this "Near Group" that is Yablonsky's core concept in his account of the *Violent Gang*. It is the incident that creates the gang out of the Near-Group by the arrest and charging patterns of local police and courts and not the gang which coalesces out of the Near Group.

Collective Structures

(Features: Purpose, Focus, Organization, Clarity of Individual Roles, and Degree of Cohesion)

Loosely Defined   Clearly Defined
Features   Features

|--|--|

Mob   Near Group   Gang

Yablonsky was attempting to clarify distinctions in the way different sorts of groups or collectivities operated. The amorphous "Mob" has little central focus, little organization or structure. There were no clear roles for leaders, mediators, or representatives. These groups are commonly found in urban and race riots or in post catastrophe looting. It is a free-for-all. Europeans would experience this in soccer hooliganism or extreme kinds of pop concert audiences. In other places, the mob surfaces as a vigilante group pursuing pedophiles or before a lynching.

At the other extreme, various forms of "gang" have been identified. The social gang and sports club which might be very territorial are identified by their core activity. The sports club might frequent a particular park, play area, or sports field and hang out in a clubhouse, café, or bar. Some "gangs" might be cultural or artistic like punk-rockers or goths pursuing some cultural, artistic, or musical theme, reading and discussing newspapers, magazines, or watching particular TV programs. But these groups have fairly clear structures, with elected or appointed officers, regular meetings, and focused content, like sports practice, team selection, competitions, or debates and discussions. Similarly, the delinquent gang, characteristic of periods earlier than the 1950s, has leadership, focus, and organization often with skills practice and training whether the activity be shoplifting, car theft, burglary, or robbery. From the pickpockets of Charles Dickens's *Oliver Twist* to the ram-raiders or joy-riders of modern cities, these gangs have fairly tight membership, if only to maintain secrecy and confidentiality and to specialize in activities which require skills-learning, training, and organized levels of competence and participation. The key difference to the "social gang" is that the core of their activities is criminal or delinquent rather than involving degrees of social conformity. The latest version are probably the e-pirates who organize and set up file sharing systems on the Internet to deprive musicians and artists of royalty payments and provide free music, video, and film downloads.

The catalyst for the *Violent Gang* incidents was Yablonsky's "sociopathic personalities." Yablonsky interviewed both victims and perpetrators in various incidents to record the accounts of those involved. In 2000, we would describe this as an ethnography of street gangs. What is particularly striking about these accounts is the total lack of remorse or guilt felt by some gang members and a selfish concern about immediate personal standing in the gang. Predominant at the time was the **Differential Association Theory,** which argued that delinquency occurred when the definitions favorable to committing delinquent acts outweighed the definitions unfavorable (Sutherland and Cressey, 1960). According to this theory, the youth hanging out with friends in a deprived, urban neighborhood because of poverty, unemployment, prejudice, or racism had more reasons (definitions favorable) to engage in delinquent acts than their better-off, suburban, high school peers. Some might argue that, faced with the living conditions in the dilapidated and disintegrating projects or post-war housing, it might be hard to find reasons not to be delinquent. While this might account for stealing, robbery, pick-pocketing, and shoplifting, it did little to explain the recourse to violence. Part of this account was based on the personal history and characteristics of the individuals whom Yablonsky invited to hang out in his office. The gang leaders were characterized by histories of inconsistent or incomplete socialization in incomplete and dysfunctional families. Divorce, desertion, and abandonment by one or both parents were common. Any systematic discipline or learning of moral rules and proper behavior were learned from grandparents, single mothers, or, more often, by trial and error on the streets. The consequent youth was asocial and unable to develop or sustain stable social relationships with others. The inability to empathize, relate, or identify was consistent with the lack of conscience and the undue focus on the self and his needs. Responses to frustration or lack of satisfaction were immediate, aggressive, often physical, and designed to inflate a diminished self-esteem. In particular, rep or the sense of self-esteem was reinforced for the self by challenging that of others—the sounding process. The Near Group fit the needs of the sociopathic personality by its very malleability and the tendencies of members to fantasize compared with the demands and constraints of the more organized gang forms. Individual leaders could expand their rep by exaggerating the size of the gang, the number of divisions, and the number of alliances as they generated more and more anticipation of an upcoming rumble. Others might challenge and be put down or even be physically and verbally abused while rep is restored to the leader. The more emotional and bizarre the response, the more violent or aggressive the claims and undertakings, the more rep was restored or generated. It is exactly this individual outburst or response which other gang forms would suppress or curtail as it threatens the coherence of the group. On the other hand, this is why this gang form attracts the sociopathic personality, and why these outbursts or surges convert from fantasy into action that violent homicides result.

Yablonsky and his colleagues began to realize that the only way to diffuse the energy generated was to provoke other members to challenge the sociopaths expanding fantasy. He demonstrates what occurs and how easily the process of generating the *Violent Gang* out of a Near Group can be put into reverse. The status and rep of a leader can fade and disperse as rapidly as realistic estimates of gang membership are demanded. The fantasy army fades to reveal the risks in confronting the equally fantastic enemy that awaits. The gang session breaks up and leaders disperse after repeated challenges, sometimes to leave the area to pursue rep in more delinquent and destructive ways in drugs and drug dealing or individual violence and alcoholism.

References/Suggested Readings: Sutherland, E.H., and Cressey, D.R. 1960. *Principles of Criminology*. Chicago: Academic Press; Yablonsky, L. 1962. *The Violent Gang*. New York: Macmillan; Yablonsky, L. 1970. *Crime and Delinquency*. New York: Rand-McNally; Yablonsky, L. 1990. *Criminology* (4th ed.). New York: Harper Collins; Yablonsky, L. 1997. *Gangsters: 50 Years of Madness, Drugs, and Death on the Streets of America*. New York: New York University Press; Yablonsky, L. 2000. *Juvenile Delinquency: Into the 21st Century*. Wadsworth; Yablonsky, L. 2005. *Gangs in Court*. Tucson: Lawyers and Judges Publishing.

RUSSELL KELLY

Index

Page numbers in **bold** type refer to main entries in the encyclopedia.

About the Editors

LOUIS KONTOS is Associate Professor of Sociology at Long Island University and is the co-editor (with David C. Brotherton and Luis Barrios) of *Gangs and Society: Alternative Perspectives* (2003).

DAVID C. BROTHERTON is Associate Professor at John Jay College of Criminal Justice and is co-editor (with Louis Kontos and Luis Barrios) of *Gangs and Society: Alternative Perspectives* (2003).